D1716173

# The Development and Practical Application of Music Learning Theory

# The Development and Practical Application of Music Learning Theory

Edited by

## Maria Runfola
State University of New York at Buffalo

## Cynthia Crump Taggart
Michigan State University

GIA Publications, Inc.
Chicago

G-6656

Book layout: Paul Burrucker

Copyright © 2005 GIA Publications, Inc.
7404 S. Mason Ave., Chicago, IL 60638
All Rights Reserved
www.giamusic.com

ISBN: 1-57999-533-0

# Contents

# PREFACE

For nearly fifty years, Edwin Gordon has been unraveling answers to the question, "How do children learn when they learn music?" His answers to that question have inspired many thousands of teachers to improve their practice and challenge themselves to provide music instruction that meets the needs of the individuals in their classrooms.

In 1989, *Readings in Music Learning Theory* was published by GIA. This book represented the work of twenty-six authors at the forefront of applying Music Learning Theory to teaching children in a variety of settings. The authors reflected on what they had learned and provided meaningful steps toward improving and informing the practical application of Music Learning Theory. The editors wrote, "In his [Gordon's] mind, proponents of Music Learning Theory, whether now or fifty years from now, should never view Music Learning Theory as static. Simply put, teachers who base their teaching upon evidence of how learning takes place should never close their eyes and ears to new evidence if that new evidence is well-founded" (p. v). There is no question that Music Learning Theory looks very different today than it did in 1989. Back then, improvisation was barely mentioned, and although a discussion of early childhood music guidance was included, the theories upon which we now base our practice had yet to be fully developed. Today, improvisation is seen as central to music learning, and the stages of preparatory audiation have been articulated and serve as the foundation for practice.

As we neared completion of this book, we struggled to settle upon an appropriate title that fully reflected the book's contents. Obviously, the practical application of Music Learning Theory was a thread that tied the writings to one another. However, we did not feel that practical application alone captured the spirit of the book. Then, Maria suggested the word "development." In his chapter, Edwin Gordon shares the genesis of his ideas about music learning and teaching, and how those ideas have developed over time through his research and work with children. Clearly, the word "development" was central to his chapter. However, in thinking about it, we decided that "development" also is central to the entire book.

Music Learning Theory will always be a work in progress, developing through the learning that takes place as excellent practitioners use its principles in their teaching. This book represents best practices in teaching using Music Learning Theory at this point in time. However, what is best practice today must, by nature, continue to change and unfold as we learn more through practice.

Coordinating a project like this is a major undertaking, and this project was no exception. The editors would like to thank all of the authors who gave so generously of their time and energy in preparing their chapters for this book. We are especially appreciative of their patience, as preparing this book took much longer than we had originally anticipated. We are confident that their insightful writings and reflections on their practice will inform the next generation of music teachers who are exploring the applications of Music Learning Theory. We also are grateful for the assistance of Erin Hemond and Elisabeth Etopio, both of whom were tremendously helpful in preparing the manuscript for publication. We hope that this book provides you inspiration and enables you to approach your teaching and learning with new energy and ideas.

– The Editors

# FOREWORD

My memory takes me back to the late 1950s, soon after I received my PhD from the University of Iowa and became an assistant professor at that institution. In addition to directing research and teaching graduate courses, I was invited to assist in the education of prospective elementary classroom teachers who elected to take a music methods course. Soon I was responsible for several sections of classes, and I must say that as a result I met some of the most charming and intelligent students, their musicianship notwithstanding, who were attending the university. I pontificated on how to teach music until the students asked me why I was championing one teaching technique over another. That led naturally to the more important question of how teaching related to learning. I was unable to answer the students' questions with any degree of satisfaction for them or for me. It was then that I begun to realize how little I knew. My embarrassment became even more acute because I was teaching one class each semester in the university laboratory schools. The fact could not be escaped that I was teaching the way I had been taught to teach, not the way I should teach. Responsibility, if not integrity, quickly made it clear that research in the music learning process was long overdue. The initial research resulted in a paperbound book, which I had printed and made available to students. The title was *How We Learn When We Learn Music.*

As the research progressed and new findings were gathered as a result of observing preschool children's day-by-day spontaneous musical play at the university early childhood center and teaching children in the elementary laboratory school, a second edition of the book was an obvious necessity. Moreover, I, in association with graduate students, was involved in extensive research about the nature, description, measurement, and evaluation of music aptitudes. At the time I was unaware of the symbiotic relationship between Music Learning Theory and music aptitude. Perhaps it was sheer intuition that guided me in that direction, but in time there was no doubt that knowing about one and not the other was not sufficient for understanding the music teaching/learning process. Thus, my research in designing music aptitude tests and in investigating music learning processes became intertwined.

I was conducting research and publishing results for almost ten years before the music education profession became aware of Music Learning Theory. I really cannot take the credit for that awakening, because it was the educational psychologists who brought attention to the importance of distinguishing between teaching and learning, how the two interact with each other, and, particularly, the nature of learning in terms of the so-called academic subjects. It was I, though I may stand corrected, who first objectively adapted learning theory in an extensive, systematic way specifically to music education. That information is contained in part two of *The Psychology of Music Teaching*, published by Prentice-Hall in 1971.

Much has happened in the last thirty years or so, much more than I ever could have imagined or hoped for. For one thing, the sixth edition of *Learning Sequences in Music: Skill, Content, and Patterns* has been published, and it contains the most up-to-date information about Music Learning Theory, music aptitude, audiation, and curriculum development. An expansion of the theory of rhythm and the importance of very early childhood music education are given prominence in the book.

Though there are music educators who are not acquainted with Music Learning Theory as well as those who do not find it compelling, there are those intelligent musicians who have a courageous, inquisitive spirit who have bonded with the concepts that research in music aptitude and audiation have brought forth. Of course, the reasons are numerous, but primary among them is that teaching from a Music Learning Theory point of view has not only helped students to understand what they are being taught, but the teachers themselves have become better musicians. These teachers know that, regardless of a complete education in audiation, those who teach learn most, and they are most able to teach to the individual musical needs of students. Being sensitive to the individual musical differences among students being taught in a heterogeneous general music class or performance ensemble is a hallmark of Music Learning Theory.

It goes without saying that I am proud that the contributors to this book felt that their time would be well-spent in writing the chapters, and that their enthusiasm about teaching music should be broadcast in a scholarly manner. The variety of their topics offers indirect validity to Music Learning Theory. Moreover, as you might know or would have expected, I have experienced many lonely moments throughout the years in my attempt to design and carry out relevant research. Thus, I have learned to develop a sense of purpose and confidence as I encountered many obstacles in the presentation of the research findings to the profession at large. Nonetheless, I have enjoyed the company of many respected friends along the way, and that in itself makes it all worth it. But there is more; I am proud that my colleagues and I have made a contribution to music education. Perhaps we will leave more than we have taken. I hope so.

And so I say to you, read and enjoy the following pages. Though no one expects you to agree with everything, approach the ideas with an open mind. You will be rewarded in untold ways. Think of the difference between painting and sculpting. The former might be thought of as being more akin to creativity, and the latter to improvisation. In painting, the artist is constantly adding to the medium; in sculpting, the artist is constantly taking away from the medium. To follow the direction of Music Learning Theory is to do away with constraining thoughts, thoughts that limit a teacher. Understanding Music Learning Theory assists the teacher in discovering what is inside students, what is the essence of their musical being. To take possession of that information will naturally make learning your primary consideration. After all, we cannot with integrity teach students if we are unsure of how they learn. So, become a student again, learn, and re-learn, analyze the processes, and enjoy the journey.

Edwin E. Gordon
Columbia, South Carolina

*Theme:*

# Reflections on the Development
# of Music Learning Theory

*Edwin E. Gordon*

● ● ● ● ● ● ● ● ● ● ● ● ● ● ●

UNIVERSITY OF SOUTH CAROLINA

# Vectors in My Research

I have often observed that music education is a profession in search of a discipline. One of the significant contributors to this dilemma is the lack of a research base that could offer substance to the profession. Why this is the case I am not sure. Perhaps the word research at once invokes suspicion, respect, and/or confusion, even among music educators themselves. Suspicion comes about primarily as a result of ignorance of the need or of the process of research. The basis of respect and confusion, on the other hand, can be attributed perhaps to either not enough or to too much formal theoretical education that seems to have no relevance to the solution of immediate practical problems. The original word *re-search* meant simply to go back to the sources and reexamine them in the hope of discovering new and compelling information that might have been overlooked in the original documentation or in the previous search. Historians and compilers of bibliographies have engaged in that pursuit since the beginning of scholarship, and there is no evidence that the practice is on the wane. With the advent of the natural sciences, however, re-search became research, and, for scientists, the laboratory became predominant over the academicians' library. With the establishment of physical scientific research and the respect accorded it by the general public, social scientists believed that, in order to gain or maintain esteem in the eyes of the public, and primarily to gain favor from their colleagues in other disciplines in the academy, it would be most advantageous for them to conduct research modeled on the designs initiated by the physical scientists.

But the most important issues in the psychology of music cannot be studied through complex, or even relatively simple experimental research, because, for many reasons and known to only those who have attempted it, it is impossible to design relevant objective experimental studies that are

3

realistic and meet the assumptions of tests of statistical significance. There are only theoretical designs that are replete in text books and explained by university professors who do not engage in such research. Therefore, as will become obvious, I have engaged in various types of research, always deferring to the reality of the situation. Yes, I have engaged in traditionally designed experimental research, but in the past I also undertook what was then described as descriptive and investigative research, which is currently packaged as qualitative research. And more recently, I have necessarily devoted a great deal of attention to and confidence in empirical research as I work with very young children.

Neophytes who are not cognizant of the problems I have alluded to discover soon after collecting and analyzing "experimental" data that they cannot draw conclusions; at best they can only summarize their results and offer a discussion section. Therein lies the heart of the problem with research, perhaps in all of the social sciences, if even studies pertaining to the nature of living things and their manifestations can be considered scientific. That is to say that even the results of the so-called more objective scientific research do not enjoy stability, particularly over time. "Truth" is not forever, and, in fact, it is likely that it is not always uniform and constant even in the present moment.

For almost fifty years I have been engaging in research, and conditions permitting, I intend to continue to pursue that activity as it relates to my educational interests for years to come. As has been my custom, I continue to publish the results of many of the comprehensive traditional studies that I have undertaken. I use the word *traditional* in a special sense. By traditional, I mean that the studies were designed, conducted, and reported in a rigorous manner and were understood and approved of by the majority of my peers and editors of journals. The value of those studies put aside for the moment, it has come to my attention that I have been roundly criticized for drawing conclusions that are not based on the results of those published studies. That is, I write books and monographs explaining how we learn when we learn music without citing specific studies that support the ideas I advance, and yet I declare that the substance of the writings is based on research findings. That, in a word, is what upsets so many music educators and music psychologists, and they seem determined to obviate others from paying attention to what I say or to vitiate it all together. It is unfortunate that so few pundits are unaware that the words *experiment* and *experience* share the same etymology. It is these very issues that have precipitated the writing of this chapter, and I hope it will bring some closure, if not reality and finality, to the matter.

At the risk of it seeming to represent a solipsistic encomium, I feel the need to explain, not so much for my contemporaries but for persons in generations to come who may raise similar concerns, that much of what I have written and lectured on is indeed based on research findings. The primary reason there is a lack of familiarity and comprehension of the research I refer to is that some is not of the traditional type. What I mean to say is that many of the conclusions that have influenced my writings are based on indirect rather than direct findings. That is, perhaps many of the important ideas that I have garnered over the years have come from research that was designed to investigate issues not specifically related to the serendipitous results yielded, and, perhaps more important, studies that are designed to produce needed information to assist teachers in the classroom do not always fit into the conventional mold established by the academicians in positions of authority. Because of their unorthodox nature in the eyes of elitist journal editors—in terms of number of participants, experimental design, and/or because of their brevity, for example—written reports of many of the studies were not at the time considered suitable for publication and, therefore, rather than taking valuable time to compile papers of explanations and the rationale leading to the conclusions that were drawn, I opted for spending my time doing the research I considered important. Ironically, in today's milieu, such "participant-observation" studies are acknowledged as vital contributions to the canon of knowledge, because they better tell the "story" as a whole rather than in many discrete parts. Editors are currently soliciting reports of this type as legitimate scholarly research that must be published, and these documents are embraced with enthusiasm and praised as shedding light on the publications of stuffy "number-crunchers" who rule the academy.

It should be understood, however, that more than a few of my traditional research studies do include oblique findings, and those findings are often referred to as ancillary in the publications. And, of course, it should not be overlooked that the extensive manuals that accompany every one of my tests are rich with such information, if not in the discussion section of the rationale and development of the test, then as part of the technical considerations that are particularly associated with supporting statistics. Nevertheless, not by my choosing that time has come, and I must say it has come sooner than I would have wished, for me to speak out and explain the less common approaches I have found to be most advantageous for undertaking and interpreting some of my research.

I shall begin at the beginning, realizing full well that it is nigh on to impossible for me to remember my line of reasoning related to the interpretation of every study I engaged in over the past fifty years, Moreover, it

5

would be unrealistic for me to expect to recall every detail associated with each of the studies. Further, I have to acknowledge that occasionally I might have generalized conclusions that the data did not specifically support, but that were, in my opinion, logical extensions of their implications. Most important, however, the reader must forgive the occasional anachronistic timeline in the use of words that I have coined over the years. Although words and terms—such as *audiation, Music Learning Theory, discrimination learning, inference learning, macrobeats,* and *microbeats*—were reified at different times, the fact is that they must have always been lingering somewhere in my unconscious. My tendency will be to use current words and terms rather than the less precise terminology that precipitated them. To do otherwise might prove to be confusing to those who are not aware of my earlier writings. Nonetheless, when I consider it relevant and necessary, I will attempt to make reference to the corresponding old and new usages.

## Stabilized Music Aptitude

While I was working toward my PhD at the University of Iowa in the mid 1950s, it became readily apparent to me that I was destined to study music aptitude in all of its ramifications as a scholarly career. Strange as it seems as I now take stock of my varied interests over the years, at the time I was doggedly focused solely on the nature and description of music aptitude, being highly attracted to the pioneering work of Carl Emil Seashore. The truth is that I have never lost my zeal for music aptitude, but, nonetheless, my research in music aptitude was the catalyst that forced me to engage in tangential research. The first digression came about as a result of the eight-year development process and the eventual publication of the *Musical Aptitude Profile* (MAP) under the aegis of Albert N. Hieronymous. It was during the developmental research period of the music aptitude test battery and later in the national standardization program that included a stratified random sample of more than 10,000 students, that so much unexpected information was revealed. By unexpected, I mean that although my primary concern was with the subjective aspects of MAP—such as its content, construct, and process validity—I was inundated with unanticipated fascinating facts, facts relating to issues that had not crossed my mind and, thus, that I had no clue that might be uncovered. Those indirect findings were so compelling that they were instrumental in my eventual interest in two very important subjects that permeate my writings: audiation and Music Learning Theory. Before I become specific to the topic at hand, you might find it interesting to know that I discovered from an analyses of the data derived from the MAP standardization program, among many other compelling facts, that almost 50% of students in grades four through twelve across the country whose MAP composite scores were above the 80th percentile in the standardization program had not and were not receiving any special instruction in school music. And the situation has worsened over the years. The figure now for elementary school students who participated in the *Primary Measures of Music Audiation* (PMMA) and the *Intermediate Measures of Music Audiation* (IMMA) standardization programs is currently above 50%. This information is alluded to in the respective test manuals, and it is more patently direct in separate research undertakings that pertain to the validity of the tests. Perhaps the most striking example is found in the experimental study *Fifth-Year and Final Results of a Five Year Longitudinal Study of the Musical Achievement of Culturally Disadvantaged Students* and in the investigation *The Manifestation of Developmental Music Aptitude in the Audiation of 'Same' and 'Different' as Sound in Music.*

As you might suspect, a valid test of any sort does not just happen. The developmental research in terms of item analyses, central tendencies, variabilities, reliabilities, and preliminary validities of the subtests that arc intended to constitute a test battery, not to mention the intercorrelations among the subtests, takes time and patience. I was well acquainted with the *Seashore Measures of Musical Talents*, both the 1919 and 1939 editions, and the majority of the research of Seashore's advocates and adversaries in America and abroad. I also studied the work of Herbert D. Wing that culminated in England in the *Standardized Tests of Musical Intelligence*. The disagreements were enormous and, of course, I had opinions of my own. Fundamental among scholars—such as James Mursell and the majority of his American and European adherents who did not publish tests but nonetheless were ardent critics of Seashore's work—was the discussion of what should be included in a music aptitude test (content validity), how it should be measured (construct validity), and how test results are best inter-preted (process validity). Seashore was referred to as an "atomist" and Wing as a "Gestalist."

Brash as it may seem, I was not convinced that either the Seashore or Wing test included satisfactory music content, nor that the content used was being measured properly. For the record, both men were psychologists with an interest in music, and I am a musician interested in psychometrics. Seashore included a subtest of *Pitch* in his battery. Wing did not. Rather, Wing included three parts (not subtests) in his test that he considered analogous to and improvements over Seashore's *Pitch* subtest: *Chord Analysis*, *Pitch Change*, and *Memory*. In the Seashore pitch discrimination subtest, the listener hears pairs of pure (sine wave) pitches and is asked to indicate whether the second pitch in each pair is higher or lower than the first. In Wing's *Chord Analysis* measure, a single pitch or chord is heard and the listener indicates the number of pitches heard. For the *Pitch Change* measure, the listener hears two chords and indicates whether they are the same or different, and if they are different, whether the one altered pitch in the second chord moves up or down. The *Memory* measure includes a short melody of from three to ten pitches, and the listener indicates by number on the second hearing which one of the pitches was changed.

My concern was that I believed Seashore's subtest was one of auditory acuity, and that it had little to do with music itself. Certainly if one cannot discriminate pitch differences, it is doubtful that he or she will be a successful performer. But if one can discriminate pitch differences, that does not necessarily indicate that one has the potential to become a successful performer. I reason that an unsighted person does not have the potential to become a graphic artist, but that does not mean that simply because a person is sighted, he or she has the potential to become an artist. With regard to the Wing *Chord Analysis* and *Pitch Change* measures, knowing the function of a chord horizontally in a harmonic progression has to do with matters of music, and knowing how many pitches there are in a vertical arrangement or knowing whether two chords outside of a musical context are the same or how they are different has little relevance to the practice of music. The *Memory* measure is the only one of the three that might have some association with music.

For all intents and purposes, interest in music aptitude had waned after World War II. As a graduate student, however, I believed strongly in the idea that, among other things, a well-constructed music aptitude test battery could provide teachers with the necessary information for improving music instruction by allowing them to teach to students' individual musical differences in terms of their musical strengths and weaknesses. I was convinced there was little interest in music aptitude because music educators realized, as I had, that the existing tests lacked substantial validity. Therefore, I set out to rekindle attention to and discussion about music aptitude by developing my own test.

In the initial developmental period, decisions had to be made about the content of the test battery, how many subtests might be included in the battery to cover the broad spectrum of music aptitude, what the content of the subtests might be, and how the content might be best measured. My approach was to examine and determine the subjective and objective validities of the better known existing tests, to develop different types of new tests in accordance with new knowledge and techniques, to compare the new tests to one another, and then to compare the new tests that proved viable with existing tests.

I will begin with the tonal tests that were initially designed for fourth-grade (nine-year-old) students and older. My findings coupled with assistance from knowledgeable colleagues and my own intuition suggested that what extant tonal tests were measuring, regardless of their titles, left much to be desired. Trying out various types of new tonal tests, it became apparent over a period of years that the fundamental aspect required for a tonal test to demonstrate substantial validity was that test content had to be embedded in a tonal syntax. There were other discoveries, too, and they are discussed in the MAP Manual under the extensive section dealing with the eight-year development of the battery.

1.  Simply establishing a tonality before pitches are heard or, even better, performing pitches in a musical context, raises validity coefficients significantly.

2.  The more tonalities included in a test, such as Dorian, Phrygian, Lydian, Mixolydian, and Locrian, in addition to Major and Minor tonalities and contemporary configurations, the greater the validity associated with the test. Particularly in this regard, it is important to understand that analyses of the data indicated no relationship between test scores and musical background and experience.

3.  The ability to discriminate between a pair of pitches heard in isolation of a tonality (for example, Major or Minor) might, at best, have borderline reliability, but only minimal concurrent (or criterion-related) validity when resultant scores are correlated with outside validity criteria associated with different types of music achievement.

4.  Students who score highest on tonal aptitude tests are able to sing with a singing voice quality.

5.  Formal instruction in music, knowledge of music theory, and the ability to read music notation are not necessary for scoring high on a tonal music aptitude test, although such knowledge and ability may be so indoctrinated in students that they may prevent a student who might have high music aptitude from scoring high. In fact, these were some of the variables that attracted students to depend on their musical knowledge rather than trusting their musical intuition. That, of course, depreciated the initial validity of the tests.

6.  Validity increases when short melodies of original music include three or more pitches compared to when only two pitches are used as content for test questions.

7. Without especially composed music, tests function primarily as music achievement tests and not as music aptitude tests.

8. Melodies performed on musical instruments, excluding the piano, are mandatory for obtaining acceptable validity and maintaining the interest of school-age students. (Over the years, however, this has not been found to be the case for very young children, and with the advent of the synthesizer, construct validity pertaining to media has become relatively complex.)

9. The need for at least two types of tonal subtests—such as melody and harmony—was obvious. The subtests demonstrated a low intercorrelation with each other but relatively high correlations with outside validity criteria, and combined subtest scores enhanced the validity of the total test scores. In most cases, scores on tests of harmony predicted success in school music better than scores on tests of melody.

10. Tonal tests that are in a rhythmic context offer greater validity with older students than when tonal decisions are made without interaction with rhythmic structure. However, students must be asked to concentrate on and answer questions about only tonal issues, ignoring specific aspects of rhythmic implications.

11. Music aptitude is multidimensional. That is, approximately two dozen music aptitudes were identified, with seven (two tonal) being fundamental. Although all had from low to moderate intercorrelations with one another, each of the seven contributed substantially to the validity of the composite test score.

12. Option responses, such as same or different, for responding to questions are not always the best choices. Asking whether an answer is like or different from a musical statement is often better if it is or is not intended to be a melodic variation of the musical statement. The latter options coincide better with the workings of the musical mind in terms of what later came to be defined as audiation.

## Tonal Implications

The above results acquired from research designed to establish guidelines for developing tonal aptitude tests have great value as indirect findings for understanding how we learn when we learn music. In other words, the discoveries pointed the way for creating a music learning theory, particularly one that has led to the derivation of the concept of audiation. I shall explain what I generalized from the facts.

There is both content and context in music. Context, analogous to syntax in language, is represented by tonality (and as we shall see, it is also represented by meter), whereas content is represented by tonal patterns (and rhythm patterns). Thus, it is obvious that, in the teaching and learning of music, students must acquire a sense of tonality (and of meter) as a readiness for learning content, in this case, tonal patterns. How does this happen? Just as young children acquire a syntactic listening vocabulary as readiness for developing a speaking vocabulary in language, they acquire a syntactic listening vocabulary as readiness for developing a singing (and chanting) vocabulary in music. The performing vocabularies (the speaking vocabularies in music) do not consist of isolated pitches or durations any more than the speaking vocabulary is dependent upon knowing the alphabet. We learn to speak words, not letters, and we learn to perform patterns, not individual pitches and durations.

A crucial aspect of all this is that, just as thought is basis of the listening vocabulary in language, a word was eventually coined to explain the nature of the listening vocabulary in music. That word is *audiation*, the ability to hear **and to give meaning to** music when the sound is not physically present or may never have been physically present. Without the audiation of context to serve as the readiness for the audiation of content, sound remains simply as sound and it is not translated into musical sound by the musical mind. It was clear to me that the acquisition of a sense of tonality and the recall of a vocabulary of patterns is fundamental to the music learning process. That is, context and then content, in that sequence, must be learned before all else in terms of formal instruction in music. Without the two being solidified in audiation, teachers can only build a faulty academic structure, because there is not a sequentially conceived foundation to support it.

The data offer even more specific insight into the nature of musical content and context that bears indirectly on Music Learning Theory and audiation. I have been alluding to context as if it is of a singular nature. It is not. Students who are most sensitive to the art of music and demonstrate high tonal aptitude are those who are informally familiar and comfortable with an array of contexts. It follows that music learning is enhanced when students hear two, and preferably more, contexts and are guided in comparing them to one another. Beneficial learning takes place when students are exposed to differences in context, not when they hear only one context, such as Major (or Duple) over and over again. It is difference, not sameness, that sparks and motivates learning.

## Rhythm Implications

For whatever the reason or reasons in terms of content and construct validity, the Wing test does not include a specific objective rhythm part.

The *Melody* part of his test does not ask students to consider rhythm at all. On the other hand, the Seashore battery includes both a *Time* subtest and a *Rhythm* subtest. In the *Time* subtest, the student is asked to indicate whether the second of a pair of sounds, outside of a musical context, is longer or shorter than the first. In the *Rhythm* subtest, which was included in the 1939 revision of the battery, the student listens to pairs of conjoined rhythm patterns, all in Duple meter, and decides whether they sound the same or different.

In contrast, interesting but not altogether similar facts emerged from evaluating the MAP tonal subtests and rhythm subtests. I will emphasize the important ones that apply specifically to rhythm and make only some reference to the irrelevance of formal instruction and knowledge of notation and music theory to rhythm aptitude. That is not to suggest that the tonal aspects of music aptitude are more important than rhythmic aspects. If anything, the opposite is true. Notice that I make a distinction between the words *note* and *duration*. A note is seen in notation, whereas a duration is heard in audiation.

1. Simply by establishing a meter before durations are heard or, even better, performing durations in a musical context, validity coefficients are raised significantly.

2. The more meters included in a test, such as Usual Combined, Unusual Paired, Unusual Unpaired, Unusual Paired Intact, and Unusual Unpaired Intact, in addition to Usual Duple and Usual Triple meters, the greater the validity associated with the test.

3. Although analyses of the data indicated no relationship between rhythm test scores and musical background and experience, successive versions of all rhythm tests had to be made increasingly easier in order to derive acceptable reliability estimates. Moreover, perhaps because of their impoverished musical backgrounds, it was not possible to explain to students in test directions the nature of a rhythmic variation within the same meter in words comparable to those used in the tonal tests. Thus, the option responses of like or different could not be used. Only same or different were functional.

4. Without the performers on the recording accenting each macrobeat (the words *macrobeat* and *microbeat* were actually coined later), the reliabilities of the rhythm subtests were low. That is, the majority of students were unable functionally to place underlying macrobeats, and thus, they were also unable to identify microbeats and the meter of the music to which they were listening.

5. Regardless of fast or slow tempo, accented microbeats (quarter notes in 3/4, for example) confused many students to such an extent that they would not even attempt to answer a question, but the issue was clarified when only macrobeats were accented (dotted-half notes in 3/4, for example).

6. The ability to discriminate between a pair of durations heard in isolation of a meter (for example, Usual Duple or Usual Triple) might, at best, have borderline reliability, but only minimal concurrent (or criterion-related) validity when resultant scores are correlated with outside validity criteria associated with different types of music achievement.

7. Students who score highest on rhythm aptitude tests are able to chant and to move comfortably in free continuous movement.

8. Formal instruction in music, knowledge of music theory, and the ability to read music notation may be so indoctrinated in students that any one or all of them may prevent a student with lofty potential from scoring high. In fact, they were some of the variables that attracted students to depend on their musical knowledge rather than trusting their musical intuition. That, of course, depreciated the initial validity of the tests.

9. Rhythm tests that are in a tonal context offer greater validity with older students than when rhythm decisions have to be made without tonal interaction. However, students must be asked to concentrate on and answer questions about only rhythmic issues, ignoring specific aspects of tonal implications.

10. Two rhythm aptitude tests, meter and tempo, were identified as being fundamental to music aptitude. They had from low to moderate inter-correlations with each other but each contributed substantially to the validity of the composite test score.

11. Meter and tempo aptitude together are more potent than melody and harmony together for predicting success in school music, and of the two, aptitude for meter has higher predictive validity than aptitude for tempo. Thus, it would seem that rhythm aptitude is basic when compared to tonal aptitude.

As I have said, the foregoing results for the rhythm subtests, like those for the tonal aptitude subtests, establish indirect evidence and offer implications for developing a music learning theory as well as for better understanding the process of audiation. What I generalized from the facts follows.

There are at least two important aspects of rhythm: meter and tempo. Both represent a context. There are various meters and, of course, a multitude of tempos. With regard to content, again it is patterns, specifically rhythm patterns and not individual written notes or durations that form one's rhythm vocabulary. The rhythm alphabet is bereft of context. It seems imperative that students develop a sense of meter, that they audiate differences among meters, and that they are able to perform essential patterns in many meters.

It was evident that, without a feeling for the placement of macrobeats, the ability to maintain a steady tempo, the wherewithal to discriminate meter, and the ability to comprehend rhythmic precision in rhythm patterns, an overall understanding of rhythm cannot be attained. That corroborated the belief that rhythm has three dimensions—macrobeats, microbeats, and rhythm patterns—and that they are hierarchical and must be learned in a sequential manner as they are coordinated with movement. (At that time, I referred to macrobeats as tempo beats, microbeats as meter beats, and rhythm patterns as melodic rhythm.)

With regard to information gleaned from the performance of different types of accents, it was clear that music written with the measure signature 3/4 is audiated with one macrobeat in a measure (the dotted-half note) and quarter notes are audiated as microbeats. Further, two measures of 3/4 and one measure of 6/8 are enrhythmic; that is, regardless of notation, they are audiated in the same manner.

Perhaps most important is that an understanding of rhythm is crucial for understanding the tonal dimension of music. In that rhythm is fundamental, students should be given informal guidance and formal instruction in rhythm at least concurrently with, if not preceding, such guidance and instruction in melody and harmony.

## Implications for Preference in Musical Expression

In the 1919 edition of the *Seashore Measures of Musical Talent*, Seashore included a test of consonance. It was a preference subtest in which students indicated which of two dyads sounded better. Probably because of its low reliability and questionable subjective validity, it was replaced by a *Timbre* subtest in the 1939 edition of the battery. Seashore evidently changed his mind and decided preference does not impact music aptitude. Wing, to the contrary, recognized preference as an important component of music aptitude. Four parts of his test were preference tests: *Rhythmic Accent*, *Harmony*, *Intensity*, and *Phrasing*. In the *Rhythmic Accent* part, two tunes are performed on the piano, and the student indicates whether they sound the same or different. If different, the student decides which is better on the basis of dynamic accents. In the *Harmony* part, two tunes are performed on the piano, and the student indicates whether they sound the same or different. If different, the student decides which is better on the basis of harmonic functions. In the *Intensity* part, two tunes are performed on the piano, and the student indicates whether they sound the same or different. If different, the student decides which is better on the basis of dynamic level. In the *Phrasing* part, two tunes are performed on the piano, and the student indicates whether they sound the same or different. If different, the student decides which is better on the basis of staccato or legato interpretation.

The content of all four parts includes primarily familiar music composed by established composers. None of the music is original, and that simplified, for Wing, the determination of "correct" answers. He decided that the preferred answers should be based on whether the music that constitutes the questions is performed as the composer intended. That puts the validity of the parts into question, because it is assumed that first, a composer always knows best and second, the performer always plays the original version better than the "mutilated" version. Regardless, because the music is extracted from well-known compositions, students who are familiar with the compositions should score higher. That places the measures predominantly in the realm of music achievement, not music aptitude.

After several years of experimentation, three of the seven subtests of what was to become the *Musical Aptitude Profile* were designed as preference measures: *Phrasing*, *Balance*, and *Style*. For the *Phrasing* subtest, students decide which of two renditions of the same melody is played with better (not the best) expression. For the *Balance* subtest, students decide which of two endings better fits the same beginning of a melody. For the *Style* subtest, students decide which tempo is more suitable for the same melody. All of the music was specially composed and performed on string instruments by professional musicians.

The content and construct validity of the three subtests were established by asking ten professional musicians at a time (more than twenty agreed to participate on an intermittent basis) who were associated with classical and popular music to listen to recordings of ten pairs of melodies. Unless at least nine of the ten musicians agreed with one another, the question was revised or eliminated from the subtest. It is interesting that I, the composer of the music, and some of the performers still disagree with the keyed correct answers to some of the questions.

In addition to what has already been put forth as indirect findings that can be generalized to the music learning process, the following additional findings associated with the preference subtests are unique.

1. Students who are most successful in school music score high on the preference measures.
2. Students who score high on the preference measures render more interpretive performances in terms of expression and overall sensitivity.
3. Scores on the preference measures are highly correlated with students' potential to learn to create and improvise music.
4. Scores on the preference measures intercorrelate exceptionally high with only one of the non-preference subtests. It is *Meter*.
5. Scores on the three preference measures correlate more highly with students' recall and ability to make musical inferences, whereas scores on the four non-preference measures correlate more highly with students' ability to memorize music and to learn to perform music by imitation.

What I generalized from these findings for Music Learning Theory was that what was eventually described in detail as audiation is essential for musical preference (which comprises creativity and improvisation). Thus, audiation is fundamental to both music aptitude and, necessarily, to music achievement. To create and improvise, however, is to be able to audiate in unique ways. That is, to truly create and improvise, students have to hear what they are going to notate or perform **before** they notate or perform it. Less than that constitutes, at best, mere exploration. It follows that a student cannot be **taught** to function at higher levels of music achievement. The best a teacher can do is to provide students with the readinesses to **learn** on their own to create and improvise. In order to create and improvise, students must have vocabularies of tonal patterns and rhythm patterns with which to create and improvise, and they must be able to distinguish among tonalities and meters. It is that concept that ultimately gave rise to the dichotomy of discrimination learning and inference learning, the former serving as a sequential readiness for the latter. I shall explain more about this in the next section.

With an overall analysis of the results derived from the tonal, rhythm, and preference subtests, it became evident that there are several levels of what was to be described later as discrimination learning and inference learning, each level serving as a sequential readiness for another, and all lower levels essentially becoming assimilated into the next higher levels. The individual levels of skill and content/context learning were observed in terms of discrete aspects of music aptitude that emerged from the research. Most compelling was the revelation gathered from questionnaires and interviews with students, parents, and teachers, that it is prudent to introduce students to improvisation as soon as possible, long before they are burdened with the formal learning of music notation and music theory. It is precisely that which later made clear the need for bridging (which I initially referred to as spiraling) within stepwise movement in the Music Learning Theory I was to develop a few years hence. Succinctly, music aptitudes and learning do not manifest themselves or are not acquired linearly; both take place in circular motion.

## Classroom Instruction, Instrumental Music, Music Learning Theory, and Audiation

Concurrent with my working in music aptitude at the University of Iowa, I chose to use a portion of my graduate fellowship time to teach in the University Laboratory Schools. I had had some public school teaching experience in Toledo, Ohio, prior to my arrival at Iowa, but I knew there was much more to know than was apparent to me at the time. Thus, I opted to teach various sections of general, vocal, and instrumental music, from kindergarten through grade twelve. That practice continued periodically throughout my graduate years and until I resigned as a professor some fifteen years later. It was during that time that it became clear to me that students were not ready to learn what most music teachers were trying to teach them, nor were many music teachers teaching substantial material.

I became upset with the necessity of so many general music teachers having to teach music appreciation, which ordinarily was an amalgamation of history and theory, because their students did not have the necessary informal musical experience and background to deal with music as a core subject. Moreover, instrumental and choral teachers were preoccupied with having students memorize music for the purposes of performing at concerts, contests, and festivals, and the majority of their students were not taught to understand what they were performing. I was aghast to discover that, when stopped before they were able to complete a composition, so few students could sing or play the tonic or tell whether the music was in Major or Minor tonality, let alone deduce that a tonal modulation had taken place. They were neither aware of where macrobeats were placed, nor of the meter of the music. I considered all of this to be dreadful, and set out to discover the source of the problem and how it might be rectified. I directed all the information I had acquired from my work with MAP to the birth of a practical music learning theory.

I was so convinced by the value of my discoveries that I wrote a practical explanation of the research findings for undergraduate and graduate music education students. The book is titled *How We Learn When We Learn Music*. Because I published the manuscript myself, I was able to revise it as often as I pleased in accordance with new research findings as they were uncovered. The third edition came to the attention of Charles Leonhard of the University of Illinois, who invited me to write a book on music learning theory to be included in a series he was editing. That book, *The Psychology of Music Teaching*, was my first, and it was published just a few years after the *Musical Aptitude Profile*.

The type of research I engaged in is what some referred to then as action research and now, as I have already suggested, might be categorized as qualitative research. Actually, it was observational research based upon different types of instruction with the same and/or different groups of students. That is not to say that quantitative analyses were not involved. That notwithstanding, I think it is safe to assume that all good research is both qualitative and quantitative. I shall give some background and examples of the research I undertook.

Initially, I followed Gagné's eight steps of a general learning theory, subsumed under the generic types of perception and conception, and I attempted to apply them to music. I soon discovered that was not possible, and I shall explain why soon with particular regard to verbal association. As I have already alluded to, it was not until later, when I was teaching at the State University of New York/Buffalo, that I posited the following two generic types of music learning: discrimination and inference, the former being the readiness for the latter. Discrimination learning has five levels and inference learning has three levels. It is important that I emphasize that all levels are sequential, each serving as the readiness for and becoming combined with the next higher level. Specific explanations of the parts will begin with the most elementary level of discrimination learning: aural/oral.

As you know, there has always been great debate, and it continues to this day among philosophers of music education, about whether the main focus of music education should be on listening (aural) or on performance (oral). I decided to investigate the question of whether one was actually more important than the other or whether both were necessary in a functional music curriculum. I randomly divided a third or fourth grade class (I cannot remember which) into three groups with equal numbers (approximately eight) of students. I taught each group separately for one academic year. One group only listened to music, another only sang, and the third both listened and sang. Specifically, the first two groups were concerned with recorded or published literature, whereas the third group listened to recordings, sang, and, in addition, they heard me sing and chant tonal patterns and rhythm patterns in various tonalities and meters, more than only Major and Minor and Duple and Triple. After they had established a sense of tonality (could identify a resting tone) and established a sense of meter (could identify macrobeats and microbeats), they learned to perform patterns in imitation and in improvisation. At the end of both semesters, students were asked individually to sing songs they had been exposed to for some weeks beforehand. The performances were tape recorded and rated by independent judges. The group that participated in listening, singing, and pattern imitation and improvisation performed significantly better than either of the other two groups. In my mind, those results justified the aural/oral level of learning not only as an integral aspect of musical under-standing, but more important, as fundamental. Both listening and performing are necessary for a well-rounded education in music. To argue about which is more important engenders misdirected energy, and the answer to the question may not be evident even when more sophisticated neurological technology becomes available. Suffice it to say that performance without listening is a limiting factor in musical development, and listening without performance produces acculturated sophisticates.

As stated, I read much in learning theory related to general education, being influenced most by Gagné. As a result, I specifically became intrigued with whether and how verbal association applied to music learning. When we learn words, we associate them with objects, but in music, we do not. So I taught patterns without and with tonal verbal association using a DO-based Major, LA-based Minor, RE-based Dorian, SO-based Mixolydian, and so on, and with rhythm verbal association using syllables based on beat functions. I found that elementary school children confused patterns with one another after they had learned to sing and chant about ten or twelve using a neutral syllable, but there was almost no confusion when tonal syllables and rhythm syllables were used. That is why, in contrast to Gagné's work, I include verbal association as the next higher level of learning above aural/oral.

I should add that I compared the tonal solfege system described above with the DO-based Minor system being taught in university music theory courses and with the perennial number system, and I compared the rhythm solfege system described above with the system that associates rhythm syllables with note values. I have only opinions about why, but the LA-based Minor system and the beat function system proved superior to all other systems in terms of contributing to the sizes of pattern vocabularies, to the abilities to sing in tune and to exhibit good rhythm in proper meter, and to ease in acquiring knowledge of and comfort with audiating and performing more than two tonalities and two meters. In short, without the LA-based Minor system and the beat function system, my research and teaching in Music Learning Theory could have never been brought to fruition.

19

Next, I became concerned with reading music notation. Instrumental music was compulsory in the elementary division of the University Laboratory Schools for one year: either string instruments in grade three, or brass, woodwind, and percussion instruments in grade four. I was receiving criticism from the orchestra and band directors who claimed that instruction based on my research findings was not preparing students to learn to play instruments. That is, students were entering their classes without the ability to name the lines and spaces of the staff and without knowledge of note values. That the students were well versed in tonal and rhythm syllables and could use them to read music notation fluently was ignored. As I look back on the situation, it should have been obvious to me that the teachers were threatened and felt intimidated because they were only partially familiar with tonal solfege and totally ignorant of rhythm solfege. The issue became so acute that even school administrators became involved in the problem.

As the discussions went forward, I was able to demonstrate that the students I had taught were readily able to learn to read music notation by associating tonal and rhythm syllables with notation, and they did it much quicker than students who the instrumental teachers had taught previously using letter names and time values in common-practice music theory fashion. The teachers were particularly pleased when it became evident that the intonation and rhythmic precision of students taught according to the tenets of even an inchoate music learning theory were superior to that of students they had taught previously. In my mind, the idea of teaching context (a sense of tonality and a sense of meter) before or along with content (tonal patterns and rhythm patterns) seemed to be the main reason why the students learned to read notation with such comfort and ease. That realization later formed the basis for including partial synthesis (the ability to recognize and understand the underlying syntax of the patterns being performed) in the finalized Music Learning Theory sequence, necessarily preceding the introduction of symbolic association (associating tonal syllables and rhythm syllables with notation). As a result, students are able to bring meaning to notation by associating what they are silently hearing with notation rather than by attempting to take meaning from notation by using theoretical knowledge. In time, that discovery gave rise to the word *audiation* and to the term *notational audiation*.

There were a number of students enrolled in the University Laboratory School who were taking private instrumental lessons from university professors and freelance music teachers in Iowa City and Cedar Rapids, Iowa. They were exempted from studying an instrument in the compulsory instrumental music school program, but nonetheless, many participated in school performance activities in junior and senior high school. It was clear to all that the students who learned to play an instrument in group instruction, although somewhat deficient in technique when compared to that of the private students, were more alert to adjusting intonation and tempo in ensemble, and their performances were far less mechanical. Because of the musicality exhibited by those who learned in groups, common sense indicated that group instruction in beginning instrumental music is superior to initial private instruction, although private instruction for advanced students was more advantageous for developing technique after they were able to audiate. In a word, in lieu of specifically designed experimental research, "the world" adequately served as a control group.

What followed was especially fascinating. The students who knew LA based Minor tonal syllables were able to recognize and identify the tonality of the music they were performing with very little guidance from the teacher. Similar findings in terms of meter were revealed with students who were taught rhythm syllables based on beat functions, and, of course, they performed with a more consistent tempo, functional meter, and more accurate rhythm. It was obvious to me that what I later called *composite synthesis* had to follow symbolic association in the Music Learning Theory sequence. Partial synthesis and composite synthesis differ in that the former involves an awareness of tonality and meter when only listening, whereas the latter presupposes an awareness of tonality and meter when reading music notation.

I realized at this point that students become overly dependent on a teacher because most of what they know was taught by rote. I had no choice but to consider the role of inference learning, which delighted me because it naturally incorporated improvisation. Before guiding students in learning how to use what they were taught in discrimination learning in order to improvise, I decided that a) it was best to begin with the voice, and b) students should learn to generalize before they improvise. I did not exper- iment with either of those suppositions. I just took a quantum leap and figured that if it did not work, I would at that time explore other possibil- ities. My notion was viable but, of course, that does not mean that there are not better ways of preparing students for engaging in improvisation. Nonetheless, when my ideas of Music Learning Theory were completed, I called the most elementary level of inference learning *generalization* and the next level *creativity and improvisation*.

For my doctoral research, I was able to work with two groups of junior high school students over a period of one semester. The purpose of my dissertation was to determine if either practice or training in answering questions similar to those found on extant music aptitude tests affects scores on the corresponding tests. During the extra time I had with the students, I taught improvisation in one group but not in the other. What was confirmed through the research was the importance of improvisation and its fundamental role in other types of music learning. The sooner students learn to improvise, the better they ultimately read notation and perform. It was at that time that I began to think about the necessity of bridging from discrimination to inference levels, particularly creativity and improvisation, in Music Learning Theory as an alternative to constant stepwise movement. I further determined that creativity and improvisation are on a continuum, and it is simply a matter of emphasis that determines which is being undertaken at a given time. But in another short study in which I worked with one group of students that learned to create before learning to improvise with singing and chanting patterns and another group that was exposed directly to improvisation by singing and chanting patterns, I realized that creativity was the necessary readiness for improvisation. Finally, without further research, I placed theoretical understanding (common-practice music theory) as the last level of learning. In fact, I am not convinced that it needs to be taught at all for understanding music, although it is necessary for communicating with musicians who were taught in a traditional manner.

## Developmental Music Aptitude, MAP Adaptation, and Pattern Research

I left Iowa to become the Director of Music Education at the State University of New York/Buffalo in 1972. During my seven years at that institution, with the assistance and deft interrogation of colleague Maria Runfola, I was able to bring precision to Music Learning Theory in its present form. It was then that I dealt with tonal content and rhythm content learning sequences and how they combined with skill learning sequence to establish a music curriculum. I was becoming increasingly convinced that, for a music curriculum to be feasible, simple statements of goals and standards, shrouded in techniques and literature, were inadequate. A viable music curriculum had to emanate from an analysis of what we audiate when we seriously listen to music, and then the curriculum should be designed around those essences. Although there were no experimental investigations completed theretofore pertaining to music curriculum development, there was a spate of research directed toward the identification of tonal patterns and rhythm patterns, their difficulty and growth levels, and how they might impact the development of a music curriculum based on Music Learning

Theory. That information led to the idea of developmental music aptitudes and to the intensive, detailed research that took place during most of my stay at Buffalo. It also offered direction for studying equally important issues, such as the later construction of practical and realistic bellwethers for formal music instruction in elementary and middle schools, manifested in *Jump Right In: The Music Curriculum*, and for informal music guidance in preschool outlined in *Music Play: The Early Childhood Curriculum*.

Before I delve into the specifics, a little history is necessary. Seashore developed norms for his test battery for students in grades four and higher. To the best of my knowledge, I do not know whether he tried or whether he simply decided not to establish norms for younger students. I can only assume that even his more robust subtests demonstrated rather low reliabilities when administered to young children. On the other hand, Wing did offer norms for children eight years old, but he admitted that the reliabilities were low. Arnold Bentley, another Englishman, who used the content of Wing's test as a paradigm, attempted to simplify test questions and directions and published norms for younger children. Neither Wing nor Bentley, however, investigated the validity of their measures for use with young children.

While at Iowa, I attempted to write a simpler version of MAP for use with children as young as five years of age. For example, using the same content, I limited the number of subtests to three, provided less complicated directions, designed color-coded answer sheets with larger spaces for children to mark their answers, and extended the time between questions on the recording for children to mark their answers. It worked well with kindergarten and first grade children selected by their district music supervisor in Ottumwa, Iowa, as being especially "musical," but the reliabilities were low for young children in general. A doctoral student, Charles Harrington, followed up on my research for his dissertation using a shortened version of MAP with young children who were attending the laboratory school at the University of Chicago. His results were not encouraging. It seemed at that time that it might not be possible to measure the music aptitudes of young children. At least that opinion accompanied me to Buffalo.

Now on to the *Iowa Tests of Music Literacy* (ITML) and pattern research, which actually began before I left Iowa. In fact, ITML, a multi-level music achievement battery, was recorded, standardized, and published in 1971, the year before I took up residence in New York State. The content of the six levels of ITML consists of tonal patterns and rhythm patterns that were developed over a seven-year period of research. The three subtests of the tonal section require students to listen to patterns and to identify the tonality of each, to identify the patterns in notation, and to actually notate the patterns. The three rhythm subtests paralleled in terms of meters and patterns the three tonal subtests. The test battery was initially developed to serve as validity criteria in *A Three-Year Longitudinal Predictive Validity Study of the Musical Aptitude Profile*, which was published in 1967, two years after the publication of MAP. ITML itself was subjected to a five-year longitudinal predictive validity study in which hundreds of students participated. The results boded well for the test battery, but, more important, the study also offered many indirect findings that corroborated what were to become the specific levels of Music Learning Theory and their proper sequential relationships.

I had investigated the musical characteristics of the patterns in ITML, but I was only superficially aware of their difficulty and discrimination levels. I wanted more precise information, so I specifically designed three sequential studies to investigate pattern difficulty levels and growth rates. (Growth rates relate to how the difficulty of patterns do and do not change as students get older.) All of the studies are published, with the final two incorporating so much information that they had to be reported in monograph form. The titles are (1) *Toward the Development of a Taxonomy of Tonal Patterns and Rhythm Patterns: Evidence of Difficulty Level and Growth Rate*, (2) *Tonal Patterns and Rhythm Patterns: An Objective Analysis*, and (3) *A Factor Analytic Description of Tonal and Rhythm Patterns and Evidence of Pattern Difficulty and Growth Rate*.

In the first study, I extracted all of the tonal patterns and rhythm patterns from ITML, re-recorded them, and asked students to listen to them and indicate whether the two tonal patterns or rhythm patterns in a pair sounded the same or different. I reasoned that by not presenting the patterns in a musical context—for example, Major, Minor, Dorian, or Mixolydian tonality or Duple or Triple meter—as was done in ITML, all of the patterns could still be used but changed to serve as content in a quasi music aptitude test rather than as they were in the music achievement test. The responses of various students in grades four and higher across the country were used to establish comparative pattern difficulty levels. My analysis was simple. If most students knew that both patterns in a pair were the same, I labeled the pattern easy. If the majority, no more than approximately 60%, of students knew that both patterns in a pair were the same, I labeled the pattern moderately difficult. If only a few, no more than approximately 20%, of students knew that both patterns in a pair were the same, I labeled the pattern difficult. I was astonished to discover a normal distribution of difficulty levels for the entire hierarchy of tonal patterns and the entire hierarchy of rhythm patterns for students in each grade (and, of course, all grades combined). However, the results for only the easy patterns, by themselves, yielded a wide range of difficulty levels for young elementary school students of the same age who had had no formal instruction in music. The process was obviously tapping into something other than music achievement. As a result of those findings, the concept of developmental music aptitude became clear. I made no attempt to analyze the patterns in a pair that were different because, of course, I had no way to determine objectively how the characteristics of one pattern in the pair uniquely affected the characteristics of the other.

The second and third pattern studies were designed to be cross-validations of the first and of each other. The second was like the first but included additional patterns, and the third included all of the patterns that were in the second but incorporated unique statistical methods for measuring the growth rates of the patterns in association with their difficulty levels. Ultimately, over an eight-year span, thousands of students listened to approximately one thousand tonal patterns and five hundred rhythm patterns in eight tonalities and seven meters. In all three studies, the pattern difficulty levels were normally distributed, the difficulty levels of the patterns remained relatively stable from grade to grade, and thus, there was little evidence of pattern growth rates in terms of comparative standard deviations. That is, the patterns that were easy at one school level were also easy at the other school levels, likewise for the moderately difficult and difficult patterns.

Now, back to developmental music aptitudes. Given the data from the pattern studies, I concluded that the reason it seemed impossible to achieve satisfactory reliability for extant music aptitude tests with students younger than nine years of age was that the test content was inappropriate; that is, the test questions were too difficult. Thus, I extracted all of the easy patterns from the tonal pattern and rhythm pattern taxonomies and compiled them into a tonal subtest and a rhythm subtest. I received advice from reading specialists about how to design answer sheets and what were common words that young children would easily understand in the directions for taking the tests. Moreover, I discovered through trial and error, coupled with continuous analyses of the reliability and validity coefficients associated with each attempt, that a developmental music aptitude test requires a different design in terms of construct and process validities as well as content validity. For example, unlike for a test of stabilized music aptitude, tonal content and rhythm content must be kept separate in a developmental music aptitude test. Young children cannot attend to two or more dimensions of music at the same time. What I put together constituted the first version of the *Primary Measures of Music Audiation* (PMMA). After engaging in typical test development, such as securing acceptable item analysis characteristics and test reliabilities for several revisions of the subtests, I undertook a longitudinal validity study. Shortly after I arrived at Temple University, I published the extensive results in a monograph titled *The Manifestation of Developmental Music Aptitude in the Audiation of "Same" and "Different" as Sound in Music.*

Perhaps the most compelling finding in the aforementioned study was that with appropriate informal guidance (such as being exposed to short excerpts of various styles of music in various tonalities and meters and being sung and chanted to on a one-to-one basis by a musical adult) and formal instruction in music, scores on PMMA increased as children moved from grade to grade, and without such guidance and instruction, their scores could decline as well as remain constant. In the case of MAP, research in the validity of the test battery substantiated the fact that scores do not increase with practice and/or training in music. It was obvious to me at that point that young children progress through a developmental music aptitude stage, and when they get older they enter the stabilized music aptitude stage. Although a specific point cannot be identified as the changeover time due to individual differences among children, it seems, as stated, that developmental music aptitude becomes stabilized at about age nine, coincidental with the approximate time that some neurologists report that physical changes take place in the myelination of the great cerebral commissures located in the frontal lobes of the brain. It follows that MAP, a test of stabilized music aptitude, is an appropriate test for elementary school students who have entered the stabilized music aptitude stage, whereas PMMA, a developmental music aptitude test, is an appropriate test for elementary school children who have not as yet left the developmental music aptitude stage.

At last some hard evidence had been shed on the "nature/nurture debate," which raged throughout the first half of the 20th century, with regard to whether innate potential or environmental influences were responsible for music aptitude. The answer is both. Music aptitude is a product of innate potential and early environmental influences from birth (or prenatally) until about age nine, and after that time, when music aptitude becomes stabilized, practice and/or training cannot alter a student's relative standing in music aptitude. Realistically, the purpose of music instruction after age nine is to assist students in achieving in music to the extent their musical potential will allow, whereas the purpose of music instruction before that time is to provide environmental influences for stimulating music aptitude.

Sooner than I might have expected, the critics took me to task, and some are still unhappy with the concepts of developmental and stabilized music aptitudes. Because a student's position on a valid music aptitude test must be impervious to practice and training, the argument is that if scores on a developmental music aptitude test fluctuate in accordance with exposure to and informal guidance and formal instruction in music, the test must be one of music achievement. The same faultfinding was directed toward MAP, because what escaped the reviewers was that, while raw scores (the number of questions answered correctly) on MAP increase with chronological age as is typically expected with tests, percentile ranks (relative standings) do not. What is of crucial importance to understand here is that, whereas scores on both developmental and stabilized music aptitude tests increase with chronological age, students in the stabilized music aptitude stage maintain their same relative positions in the score distributions, but children in the developmental music aptitude stage do not. The median correlation of scores on the same stabilized music aptitude subtests administered years apart approximate .80, but the median correlation of scores on the same developmental music aptitude test administered years apart approximate .30. The lower longitudinal coefficients on a developmental music aptitude test are a product more of the magnitude rather than of the direction of score changes from year to year, unlike the characteristics observed for raw scores on a stabilized music aptitude test.

Further, among other things not comprehended with specific regard to developmental music aptitude tests are the following issues. In the pattern studies, tonality or meter was established on the recording before students responded to pattern questions. On PMMA, that is not the case. The student must infer in audiation a subjective or objective tonality and/or a keyality or a meter and/or a tempo for each tonal pattern or rhythm pattern as it is being heard. Allotted time on the recording does not allow for the option of memorizing the first pattern in the pair for the purpose of comparing it with the second, memorization being a fundamental mainstay of music achievement. The patterns are presented on the recording in a musically atypical manner; it is not as one might hear music in a familiar milieu. Being adept at generalizing musical sound exemplifies audiation, and thus, is one of the primary aspects of music aptitude. Also, what is asked of the student and the nature of the option responses the student are to use are not taught in formal music instruction, let alone in informal guidance in music. Finally, and perhaps most important, is that even kindergarten children can attain perfect scores on one or both subtests without ever having any informal guidance or formal instruction in music. From follow-up studies it was discovered that, with very few exceptions, none of the high-scoring kindergarten children was exposed to music in or outside the home. Adversarial comments notwithstanding, suffice it to say that the objective longitudinal validity of the tests has been established in a variety of ways and in a variety of situations over a period of years. My research in developmental music aptitudes has been as substantial as that in stabilized music aptitude.

Within a year or two after the publication of PMMA, it came to my attention that the test battery was not complex enough to sustain the interest of students who were receiving superior instruction in music. I would not have been surprised to learn that those students were also exposed to a stimulating musical environment at a younger age. Although scores on the subtests approximated a normal distribution, it was skewed to the left, and thus, reliabilities decreased. In the cases that I was aware of, approximately 80% of children, even in the first grade, scored above the 50th percentile according to the norms published in the test manual. While on the one hand I was happy that test results indicated that students who received sequential instruction in terms of Music Learning Theory could and were effectively raising their music potential back toward their birth levels (their innate musical potential unaffected by early environmental influences), on the other hand I was displeased that the scores of children who were receiving the traditional five-fold general music instruction on a limited basis, or who were not attending any music classes at all, remained stagnant or even declined. That in itself was positive indirect evidence of the merit and importance of sequential learning in music and of exposure to various tonalities and meters through singing and chanting. It was obvious that a more advanced test battery was needed for the more fortunate students whose music achievement was being overseen by thoughtful and informed teachers.

I once again analyzed the data that were derived from the pattern studies and extracted only the difficult tonal patterns and rhythm patterns. They became the nucleus for the *Intermediate Measures of Music Audiation* (IMMA), and after the appropriate test development took place, it was published three years after PMMA. The design of the two test batteries is identical, the only difference being in the increased difficulty of the tonal patterns and rhythm patterns. As might be expected, both PMMA and IMMA were labeled music achievement tests with more vigor by erstwhile critics simply because, in their minds, the need for complex content meant achievement. The concept of fluctuating music aptitude and its ramifications still escaped them.

As you know, coming to terms with audiation has played an enormously important role in my personal as well as in my professional life. Thus, before I move on to the next section, though it is somewhat out of context, I feel it obligatory to report that, before I left Buffalo in 1979, I, with the assistance of Claire Ives, my editor, coined the word *audiation*. It appeared as a footnote in an early edition of *Learning Sequences in Music: Skill, Content, and Patterns*. It was not until the next decade when I was at Temple University that the concept of audiation came to full fruition, including eight types and six stages. Of course, there is no way to confirm directly the types and stages of audiation through experimental research any more than it is possible to explain objectively how and what we think when we think. Nonetheless, there is empirical evidence that the value of the theory of audiation has been embraced and sustained by professionals. It permeates Music Learning Theory and provides substantially for its structure; it serves as a defining feature of music aptitude as well as for music achievement. The word is being used more and more in scholarly journals and papers and in professional magazines, and music teachers find the philosophy surrounding audiation to be extremely helpful in organizing their thinking in terms of music curriculum development. As I reflect on events, it is apparent to me that audiation was the superstructure of Music Learning Theory from its very inception, but it took considerable time to find the language to know what to call it or how to explain it. At the time MAP was developed, the only option that seemed available to me, following Seashore's lead, was the word *imagery*. I did not realize until much later that confusion abounded as a result of so many persons thinking of imagery in only a visual sense, ignoring the aural sense, and thus, associating music imagery solely with notation. Many of my colleagues in music education as well as professional performers have told me that they were aware of the process of audiation but never had the words to describe it.

**Early Childhood Music**

For some time before leaving Buffalo and arriving in Philadelphia, I had realized that if I wanted to know more about the music learning process, I would have to begin by subjectively observing the indirect musical activities and analyzing the direct musical responses of very young children. I began my objective research many years before in Iowa with college and university students in association with test-development research, but I soon learned that much vital information was escaping me. I went on to work with high school students and then with elementary school children, including those in kindergarten. Nonetheless, it was clear that even elementary school children are too far into achievement, and thus, too sophisticated, to reveal the basics of music learning. Therefore, after a few years at Temple University, I became focused on early childhood music. I attempted to observe and analyze children's behavior as others taught in the established early childhood music program, but I was not able to secure the appropriate teaching conditions I believed necessary to garner the information I sought. To provide the necessary ambient factors for observing differences in growth between individual children and groups of children, it was necessary, among other things, for the teacher to sing both familiar and unfamiliar songs in various tonalities and meters, to engage children in chanting and continuous-flowing movement, and not to use recordings and instruments excessively. Moreover, the youngest children were three years of age, and that, I knew, was too old for my needs. Given the situation, I decided that in order to be successful in my endeavors, I, myself, had to teach children and that I had to begin with babies no more than a few weeks old. With that apparent, my new career in the early childhood music development program within the Temple University Music Preparatory Department was launched.

I started as the lone teacher, but it was not long before graduate students asked to teach with me. I found that having two teachers in the room offered many benefits, not only for teaching but also for conducting research. Soon there were various sections that other teachers and assistant teachers taught under my guidance, following the curriculum I was developing. Curriculum development was a living, continuous process based on observations gathered day by day. Before undertaking what I learned, a digression is necessary to explain the type of research I engaged in and why.

As I have already acknowledged, classically designed experiments that are taught in theoretical research courses are just that: theoretical. It should not take long for an experienced researcher with above average intelligence and common sense to grasp an understanding of the unrealistic demands of such designs, especially when they are applied to work with preschool-age children. Correlation studies, particularly those undertaken to investigate validity and related matters concerning tests, however, have much to recommend them. They are not dependent on levels of confidence and probability estimates. I have written a journal article about much of this (*Contemplating Objective Research in Music Education*), and I shall review a few of the more important issues here.

It would take an assemblage of many hundreds of students in order to select and equate randomly stratified samples of students to serve as parallel experimental groups, control groups notwithstanding. Even if that could be accomplished, the negative factor of the continuing participation of all children and attendance habits of parents over a period of at least one semester would interdict the study. And, even if by waving a magical wand those two problems could be ameliorated, consider the difficulty in finding pairs of equally competent teachers capable of teaching equally well using different methodological approaches. If that is not enough to dissuade a neophyte, consider the statistical implications. The assumptions for applying tests of statistical significance to resultant data would not be met, nor would it be possible to determine the degrees of freedom in an appropriate or trustworthy manner. For those reasons, among others, I chose to observe the reactions of children on a one-to-one basis, to maintain copious records in terms of rating scales that were constructed in such a way as to allow for estimating the reliability and validity of the teachers' markings, and to analyze the data subjectively, that is, without the use of tests of probability. Practical significance replaced statistical significance in the interpretation of the children's responses. I did not resort to tests of probability to determine whether what I was discovering was or was not a matter of chance, but rather, I relied on replications and the comparisons of different methodologies with different groups of children on different occasions that were taught by different teachers. If my findings were consistent even though so many divergent personalities and idiosyncratic teaching techniques were involved, I felt secure in generalizing the results.

On rare occasions for specific research purposes, I randomly divided perhaps twelve children, birth to eighteen months old, in one class into two groups of six and acculturated each group in different ways over a period of one semester or one academic year. (The personal needs and obligations of most parents prevented them from enrolling a child in a class on a coterminous basis. Thus, the possibility of conducting longitudinal group studies was precluded.) For example, in one group I would sing songs in only Major tonalities and in the other, songs in both Major and Harmonic Minor tonalities. When the children were able to sing tonal patterns in imitation as they got older, typically around two years old, the group of children that heard songs in both Major and Harmonic Minor tonalities sang Major patterns better in tune than did the group of children who heard songs in only Major tonality. I followed that with a similar study. One group heard songs in Major tonality, whereas the other group heard songs in Major, Harmonic Minor, Dorian, and Mixolydian tonalities. Again, the more tonalities the children were familiar with, the better in tune they sang tonal patterns in Major tonality. Further, the group that heard the four tonalities sang better than the group that heard two tonalities. I interpreted that result to corroborate the findings derived from doctoral dissertations I directed while still at the University of Iowa as well as to extant writings in other academic disciplines that profess that we learn best by attending to difference rather than to sameness. Repetition, other than necessary early imitation, has relatively little, if any, bearing on learning that goes beyond perfunctory training. From that point on, children in all of the groups were exposed to as many different tonalities as time permitted in a regular half-hour class period.

I did the same with meters, and this I find particularly important considering that most popular music children are exposed to is in Duple meter. Hearing songs and chants in only Duple meter was inferior to hearing songs and chants in both Duple and Triple meters. Better yet, the sooner children heard me sing and chant in Unusual Paired and Unusual Unpaired meters along with usual meters, the better they could eventually chant rhythm patterns in all meters. Not only could they sustain a steady tempo more appropriately, they maintained meter and performed rhythm patterns more confidently and with improved precision.

Although I did not study comparative achievement among groups by working with individual children—using words with some and a neutral syllable with others and then comparing the musical progress of one child to another—the measure was that, in all cases, singing and chanting without words was far superior to using a lyric. By that I mean groups performed better and were continually aware of a resting tone and the placement of microbeats (and for some, even macrobeats) as they were singing and chanting. Thinking about words distracted them from attending to the music itself through audiation. It seems that because children normally listen to conversation more than to music and are typically spoken to on a one-to-one basis, they naturally are attracted to words rather than to the tonality and meter of a song that they are hearing, let alone the tonal patterns and rhythm patterns that constitute the song. Children, in their instinctive need to learn, gravitate to what is familiar. Thus, now I always present songs and chants to children using neutral syllables until they are able at least to audiate a resting tone and macrobeats in music they are hearing or performing. I also discovered that if children learn to sing songs with words, they are inadvertently granted permission to continue to use a speaking voice quality when singing rather than learning to acquire a singing voice quality to balance their speaking voices. That is one of the reasons there are so many poor singers in our society. Watch and listen to young persons "sing." Most simply mouth all the words on the same pitch. Without hearing words, they might not even recognize a song that they have heard many times.

I dabbled a bit using a piano, rhythm instruments, and recordings in my teaching. With regard to the piano, autoharp, guitar, and ukulele, used either for melody or accompaniment (even if they are well tuned), I do not recommend their use. It is my opinion that, when played, children stop audiating and expect the instrument to do their musical thinking for them. Rhythm instruments signal fun-time, and musical learning ceases, except possibly for the opportunity to "explore." Personally, I would rather guide children in being creative and improvising rather than in exploring without purpose or simply to make noise. It is also my notion that playing recorded music during class is a "filler" and wastes valuable guidance and instructional time. Children need to be sung to and chanted to on a one to one basis as much as time will allow. Let me put it this way. If you think children can learn about music by listening to recordings, why not stop speaking to them and just play for them recordings of persons speaking English? If that sounds ridiculous, why then would one want to apply such inanity to learning to understand music?

There was ample opportunity in cross-sectional analyses (observing the action of different children of different ages) to document tonal patterns that children sang. First they preferred diatonic patterns. However, before they sang arpeggiated patterns, the typical child sang a resting tone or the dominant of the tonality. When given a tonal aptitude test when they were older, those who earlier sang the resting tone generally scored higher than those who started with the dominant, but children who initially sang a perfect fifth or fourth that included both the tonic and dominant of the tonality, scored highest. Most children sang two-tone arpeggiated tonal patterns before three-tone arpeggiated tonic and dominant patterns in Major and Harmonic Minor tonalities.

With regard to rhythm, most children were uncoordinated, and therefore they could not move with continuous-flowing movement in place or in space. It was soon obvious that free-flowing movement was a requisite for learning to chant microbeats in a consistent tempo and rhythm patterns with some degree of precision. Children knew intuitively that there can be space without musical time but there cannot be musical time without space. Rather than being concerned in the same way adults are with time, space, weight, and flow in that order, it was the exact opposite for children. Their primary considerations were flow and weight, with space and time being almost an imposition. I found that the physical audiation of flow and weight is the readiness for appropriately engaging in space and musical time, and the readiness for performing musical time accurately is the physical audiation of space. Think of it: one can count correctly, but unless the number is verbalized at the correct time, tempo becomes inconsistent, which in turn adversely affects meter and rhythm. It would seem impossible to perform an extremely slow, consistent tempo musically without imagining the feeling of the free-flowing movement of the body that indicates the amount of space that intervenes between the beats.

Children responded to microbeats and practically never to macrobeats before chanting rhythm patterns of the length of two underlying macrobeats in Duple meter and Usual Triple meter. Practically all children were capable of chanting rhythm patterns in which a division pattern was superimposed on the first underlying macrobeat but not on the second. The chanting of rhythm patterns four macrobeats in length came much, much later, but what came very early on was children's ability and preference to move in Unusual Paired meter (for example, 5/8) and Unpaired meter (for example, 7/8). As a matter of fact, children seemed more adept in comprehending Unusual Paired meter than Usual Combined (for example, duplets and triplets in 2/4). Children who displayed a slower personal tempo at an early age tended to score higher on a rhythm aptitude test when they were old enough to have one administered to them.

What was most compelling was what I learned through observation about the relationships among (1) singing tonal patterns or chanting rhythm patterns, (2) body movement, and (3) breathing. Though it was something that only young children could teach me, I believe that it applies to musicians of all ages. To begin, ultimately to sing and chant appropriately, each must be assimilated with movement and breathing. That is what I observed in children who sang and chanted naturally well, with little effort and with a great deal of confidence. What was easily perceived, and the opposite of what one might expect, is the following: When singing tonal patterns, body movement in the form of tension must precede inhaling by a fraction of a second, and then the voice becomes involved. When chanting rhythm patterns, inhalation precedes muscular tension by a fraction of a second and then the voice becomes involved. Notice that body movement occurs **before** breathing with tonal patterns, and breathing occurs **before** body movement with rhythm patterns.

After several years of intensive teaching and research in the early childhood music program, I felt confident in describing the music learning process of young children, children not yet old enough to attend a regular school. There is an obvious difference between the necessity for informal and formal guidance on the one hand that leads to formal instruction on the other. In addition to creating a practical curriculum, I developed a music learning theory for newborn and young children, which culminated in my book bearing that title. The theory includes three hierarchical types of learning—acculturation, imitation, and assimilation—with the assimilation of singing or chanting with breathing and movement being the ultimate goal for children to attain before they enter public school. It is no secret that the majority of children enter kindergarten or first grade without the readiness to learn what the traditional music teacher is attempting to teach them.

With regard to acculturation, imitation, and assimilation, which follow the same natural path of learning as the acquisition of language, I observed seven hierarchical stages within the three hierarchical types of learning. I refer to the process as preparatory audiation, which is the necessary requisite for engaging in audiation itself. In brief, the theory, which by this time may be a fact, posits the realization that, as in communication in which children must hear language spoken around them for a substantial amount of time before they are ready to speak, so it is with music. Children must hear music sung or chanted to them in a variety of tonalities and meters. I am not suggesting extended compositions, but rather, short songs and chants that are highly repetitious and sequential. Next, without the ability to imitate, a child will not have the necessary material to draw on when learning how to audiate. Finally, once a child can imitate tonal patterns and rhythm patterns, not complete songs or chants with or without text, the assimilation of singing or chanting with breathing and movement becomes a possibility. Ideally, with that accomplished, children are ready for school music that embraces a curriculum of education that takes precedence over entertainment.

There was no doubt that I was handicapped in my research with young children because I could not obtain any objective evidence of their music aptitudes until they were older. I felt I needed that crucial information as early as possible to teach adequately to their individual musical differences. My best approach for educing such information was to begin documenting their physical movements as babies when I sang and chanted to them in a variety of ways. Then I administered PMMA to those few who remained in the program on and off until they were four years old. I correlated the behaviors I subjectively observed with their objective test scores. The median correlation was approximately .50, and that relatively low coefficient could be due to a number of reasons. Primary among them are that the children were actually too young to take PMMA, the battery was administered to them individually over a period of weeks (perhaps ten to twenty questions at a time for the *Tonal* and *Rhythm* subtests), different persons administered the subtests, and the data were gathered over a span of years and then combined for the purpose of overall analysis. Nonetheless, when all the information was collated and alternative interpretations of the data were studied and compared, I came to the inevitable conclusion that the level of music aptitude a child is born with cannot be raised by music achievement. Regardless of quality and quantity of guidance and instruction in music, a child will probably not achieve in music at a level higher than his or her birth level of aptitude (potential) will allow. About all we can do realistically as teachers of early childhood music is to assist children in raising their music achievement back to their birth level of music aptitude, but to expect music achievement to go beyond their potential is wishful thinking. Think, however, if parents and teachers would accomplish even what seems to be possible, what wonderful advancements in musical under-standing and preferences will have taken place in our culture.

During the time I was teaching and engaging in research on a regular basis in the music preparatory department at Temple, I began conducting research at Immaculata College (located in a suburb of Philadelphia) with three- and four-year-old children who were enrolled in the regular preschool program that the college administered. My purpose was one: I was determined to design a valid music aptitude test for three- and four-year-old children to be used for the enhancement of music curricular research and for the teaching of young children. I taught some, but my main activity was to gain the trust of the children by becoming familiar to them. I asked many questions, administered sample test questions that incorporated the two-option response of same or different, and then asked more questions. After periodic visits for two years, one child in particular explained to me why I was having a problem developing a test. The reason was that children would answer same to most questions because they heard the same voice singing the two "songs" in a pair. It was the voice, not the music, that attracted their foci. The child also told me in an inimitable way that she did not understand the word *different*. She suggested the alternative option responses of *same* and *not same*, because, in paraphrase, she said that an unfamiliar woman "was not different," she "was not her mom." Unfortunately, it would not be until years later that I realized the value of her analysis and then began using her idea in future tests even with older students.

With further research, I discovered that a developmental music aptitude test for preschool children required different constructs than those required for a developmental music aptitude test for school-age children.

For whatever reason or reasons, preschool children need to hear both pitch and rhythm together in a test question, but they are only able to answer a question about either the tonal aspects or the rhythm aspects of the question. They cannot attend to both tonal and rhythmic elements at the same time. In 1989, the developmental music aptitude test, *Audie*, was completed and published. It is curious that the design of MAP (a test of stabilized music aptitude for school-age students) and *Audie* (a test of developmental music aptitude for preschool children) are similar in terms of that aspect of construct validity but, of course, not in content validity. I still cannot grasp why the design of tests of developmental music aptitude for school-age children, such as PMMA and IMMA, need to be different from *Audie* and MAP, given that PMMA and IMMA are transitional tests in terms of chronological age.

## Stabilized Music Aptitude Revisited

In the late 1980s, I was invited to speak at a convention of the National Association of Schools of Music. During my presentation, persons in the audience asked why neither I nor anyone else had ever developed a music aptitude test for adults. MAP is normed for only fourth through twelfth grade students. They did not want to use the test as a selection device for admitting prospective students to their schools, but rather, as an objective aid to supplement the many subjective criteria they were employing to assign students to different classes and teachers on the basis of each student's musical promise. The improvement of remedial instruction was of paramount importance to them.

Their interest in music aptitude was encouraging, so I set out to develop a music aptitude test for adults. Because they said there was only limited time for examining prospective students, I was asked to make the test no longer than twenty minutes and to have the test yield separate scores for the tonal and rhythm dimensions of aptitude. I derived unique ways of designing the test and, in particular, how it should be scored. All of that absorbing developmental research, particularly that of the comparison of various ways of scoring the tests to offer greatest validity, is reported in the test manual and in a monograph (*Predictive Validity Studies of AMMA*) that followed. The test, published in 1989, is called the *Advanced Measures of Music Audiation* (AMMA). Other objective studies were undertaken to investigate the predictive validity of the battery for high school students and undergraduate and graduate university and conservatory music students, and to examine the effects of practice and training on test scores. In addition, because some teachers objected to the length of MAP, they investigated the possibility of using AMMA with seventh and eighth grade students. They offered me their positive results, and thus, I included norms for twelve- and thirteen-year-old music and non-music students in the test manual along with corresponding musically selected and unselected norms for adults.

I should point out that the way acceptable reliability and validity coefficients were obtained for AMMA was to dwell on the constructs of the battery. Interestingly, the design of both the *Tonal* and *Rhythm* subtests was eclectic in terms of the dual characteristics of developmental and stabilized music aptitude tests. In a word, mature students must hear both tonal and rhythmic elements in every question, and they must listen simultaneously for possible changes in either tonal or rhythm components.

## Learning Sequence Activities

Music Learning Theory is theoretical, whereas Learning Sequence Activities are a part of the practical applications of the theory. I originally had no interest or desire to become involved in the systematic aspects of music curriculum development for older students, those attending elementary through high school. The reactions to my books, however, were such that readers could not fully understand the theory until they were given pragmatic applications of the implications of my research. Rather than simply writing more books that might guide them in the use of my ideas, I decided, with ample encouragement from my publisher, to actually create a model curriculum based on Music Learning Theory. To do that, it was my responsibility to be sure that the teaching techniques I needed to innovate actually worked in the classroom.

It was during that time in 1985 that I completed and published the first edition of the *Reference Handbook for Teaching Learning Sequence Activities* and the accompanying two *Tonal Register Books* and two *Rhythm Register Books*, forty-two tonal units and forty-two rhythm units in all. Suffice it to say that the practical research undertaken in the classroom with regard to the efficacy of teaching techniques, to combining Learning Sequence Activities with Classroom Activities, and for devising methods of measuring and evaluating students' progress was compelling in time, energy, and insights gained. In spite of all the benefits it may promise, I know I no longer have the wherewithal to repeat such a research program. There was time for only one scholarly paper, *The Effects of Instruction Based Upon Music Learning Theory on Developmental Music Aptitude*, to be written and published that pertains to a few of the research outcomes. The remainder of the findings are included in terms of practical teaching suggestions in the handbook and register books. Over the years, the content of the material has not changed much; it is the explanations of the teaching techniques that have commanded attention in the revisions. If I may be permitted to say and indeed without malevolence, negative reactions to the curriculum generally come from those who are bereft of the musicianship to employ the materials in a musically intelligent manner. They seem to be intimidated by what they do not know, and they recoil at the possibility of having to come to terms with gaps in their educational backgrounds. They are under the misapprehension that to understand Music Learning Theory and Learning Sequence Activities, they must deny their own education.

### Ancillary Tests – *Instrument Timbre Preference Test*

The longitudinal predictive validity coefficient derived from the three-year study of MAP was .75. Interpreted, that means that approximately 55% of the reason or reasons students are successful in school music is a result of their MAP scores. I never ceased being curious about the nature of the remaining 45% of the variance. That gave me cause to investigate, when I had extra time between other projects, the extent to which students' preference for instrumental timbre and range affected their success in instrumental music instruction. To study the matter, I authored the *Instrument Timbre Preference Test* (ITPT), which, after years of preliminary research, was published in 1984. The extensive pre-publication research on the development of the test and concomitant matters are reported in the test manual. Several post-publication studies on the predictive validity of the test are published in monograph form (for example, *Predictive Validity Studies of IMMA and ITPT*). The results of the studies suggest that when students are administered ITPT in conjunction with a developmental or stabilized test of music aptitude, longitudinal predictive validity can be raised to approximately .82, accounting for an understanding of 10% of the theretofore unknown variance.

The indirect findings in the development of the ITPT that bear on the music learning process were abundant, and they complemented much of what I had already learned from the indirect findings associated with previous test development. There is little doubt that music aptitude is a far more potent factor for learning music than is preference for instrumental timbre and range. However, preference for musical style, balance, and tempo, as measured in MAP, remained as important as ever. From a practical viewpoint, it is unconscionable that so few students learn to play an instrument for which they have a valid preference. And there are professional musicians who wish they had learned to play another instrument because they are not especially enamoured of the sound of the instrument on which they perform.

## Ancillary Tests – Harmonic and Rhythmic Improvisation Readiness

Coming from a professional background as a jazz bassist, it should not be surprising that I have always been fascinated with how musical improvisation is learned and by the specific mental processes, barring individual differences, that one engages in when improvising. Just as thought is required in order to participate in conversation, high levels of audiation are required to engage proficiently in improvisation. The performance of scales and of continually quoting oneself from moment to moment in a solo leaves much to be desired. Preliminary philosophical thought about improvisation had been a mainstay with me from the beginning of my research activities. In fact, I had difficulty in choosing between music aptitude and musical improvisation as the subject of my doctoral dissertation. It was not until late in my teaching career, in the mid 1980s, that I was able to turn considerable attention toward improvisation and its ramifications. As I comment on in the manual for the *Harmonic Improvisation Readiness Record* (HIRR) and the *Rhythm Improvisation Readiness Record* (RIRR), the most commanding type of contemporary improvisation is based on harmonic patterns that are combined into harmonic progressions.

Objective research in the development and use of HIRR, which was published in 1996, was sketchy compared to the enterprises associated with previous tests; but what I learned in a few short years was invaluable. In particular and perhaps most important, students who improvise well audiate chord changes—they are always prepared because they are able to anticipate, **in terms of time**, when new chords are to be sounded. Thus, they act rather than react in their improvisation. That was not the case with students whose improvisation is impoverished. Even if they are familiar with the chord changes in a piece of music, they are unsure when the actual chord changes are to take place. Therefore, they can only react to chord changes, and that impairs the quality of their improvisation. Readiness for harmonic improvisation, I discovered, is a product of the ability to identify chord changes and to accurately anticipate them. Thus, to further study readiness for improvisation and how to adapt instruction to students' individual musical differences, I designed RIRR, which was published in 1998.

The indirect findings that resulted from the objective published research pertaining to HIRR and RIRR were especially rich. The straightforward results and conclusions can be found in the test manuals and in the monograph *Studies in Harmonic and Rhythmic Improvisation Readiness*. I believe, however, the indirect findings, some of which I have already made passing reference to, are captivating.

1. Harmonic improvisation cannot be taught. All a teacher can do is provide students with the readiness to learn (teach themselves) how to improvise. That readiness is in the acquisition of a vocabulary of tonal patterns and rhythm patterns that resides in audiation to be linked into melodic patterns (combined tonal and rhythm patterns).
2. Further readiness consists of the ability to audiate harmonic patterns and time patterns that form the underlying structure of chord progressions.
3. It is not necessary for students to become familiar with the sound of a myriad of harmonic patterns—such as I–II–V–I and I–VI–II–V–I. What students need to audiate in order to begin participating in harmonic improvisation is the sound relationship of different chords to the tonic chord, in progression and retrogression. That understanding is the basis for practicable testing of harmonic improvisation readiness.
4. The teaching of the vertical structure of chords along with part writing skills is unnecessary for learning to improvise harmonically. What students need to audiate is the sonance of the horizontal relationship of one chord to another, irrespective of their inversions or melodic structures.
5. Initially, the teaching of complex chords, such as augmented elevenths with added thirteenths, should not be undertaken. They prove to be intimidating and confusing to the neophyte. In fact, patterns in Major, Harmonic Minor, and Dorian tonalities that include a IV chord are as basic as those that include a V7 chord, and both types of patterns should be taught as structures upon which the elaborate superstructures are based and serve as substitutes.
6. By physically engaging in time and space with appropriate body movement, students are able to transfer the "audiation of feeling" to the anticipation of and preparation for chord changes.

There is one objective result that, for me, defies interpretation. Time may reveal it to be one of the most important contributions I have made to psychometrics as well as to the psychology of music. It is this: regardless of chronological age, the average score (the mean) on HIRR remains at about 28 and the average score for RIRR remains at about 29. This is true for students in grade two through adults, both musicians and the musically uneducated, to whom the tests are administered. Is the finding simply an artifact, or have I unwittingly uncovered generic music aptitudes? I expect ongoing research to shed light on what I consider to be an enigma. Once I determine the longitudinal effects of instruction in harmonic improvisation on HIRR and RIRR scores on the one hand and the comparative predictive validities of the two measures on the other hand, I will have sufficient evidence to come to closure on the matter. Albeit, for the moment I must be content with joyfully struggling with the concept and the compelling possibility that music aptitude as measured by HIRR and RIRR reflect **outward flowing intuition**, whereas music aptitude as measured by MAP, PMMA, IMMA, and AMMA reflect **inward directed tuition**. (Etymologically, tuition is guidance and instruction, not the payment of fees.) If my speculations should prove to be grounded in fact, I anticipate that the indirect implications for audiation and Music Learning Theory will be enormous.

## Afterword

I think it appropriate, at the risk of sounding complacent and arrogant, that I mention that I have directed sixty or more doctoral dissertations and approximately ten masters honor-theses during my teaching career. Because students came to study with me largely because of my scholarly interests and wanted to learn how to conduct research in those academic disciplines, the subject matter of most of the dissertations and theses dealt with music aptitude, Music Learning Theory, rhythm, and/or audiation. Although not my own research, I could not but learn much from the students and their work, both directly and indirectly. That was my invigorating payoff for teaching.

Finally, I must acknowledge Philip Sklar and Gene Krupa. Phil was my bass teacher when I worked as a freelance musician in New York City after I graduated with a master's degree from the Eastman School of Music. He, at the time, held the principal chair in the NBC Symphony under Arturo Toscanini. What I learned from him was so vast that it would take a lifetime to relive the relationship. I am certain that most of what he inculcated in me resides somewhere in my unconsciousness, but I feel certain that it has and still contributes to the conclusions I draw from data as well as my interpretations of unexpected ancillary findings.

Gene was not a formally educated musician, but his understanding of rhythm was enormous. Much of my thinking about rhythm is derived from our conversations as well as from the experience accorded me as a result of nightly performances, during which I was ever next to him on the bandstand. He had different names for what I call macrobeats and microbeats, but the concepts coincide. He helped me become aware of the various components of rhythm, how they interact, and how one component simultaneously becomes the foundation for another. All it took was one viewing of him in performance to comprehend the value of continuous flowing movement in achieving rhythmic fluency. Although he and Phil were on different sides of the same extraordinary mountain, they agreed on so much when it came to musicianship. And it was my good fortune to be in the right place at the right time to learn in a unique way from both of these extraordinary musicians.

## Bibliography of Publications by Edwin E. Gordon

### Articles

Gordon, E. E. (1961). A study to determine the effects of practice and training on Drake Musical Aptitude Test scores. *Journal of Research in Music Education, 4,* 63-68.

——. (1967a). A comparison of the performance of culturally disadvantaged students with that of culturally heterogeneous students on the Musical Aptitude Profile. *Psychology in the Schools, 15,* 260-268.

——. (1967b). Implications of the use of the Musical Aptitude Profile with college and university freshman music students. *Journal of Research in Music Education, 15,* 32-40.

——. (1968a). The contribution of each Musical Aptitude Profile subtest to the overall validity of the battery. *Bulletin of the Council for Research in Music Education, 12,* 32-36.

——. (1968b). A study of the efficacy of general intelligence and music aptitude tests in predicting achievement in music. *Bulletin of the Council for Research in Music Education, 13,* 40-45.

——. (1968c). The use of the Musical Aptitude Profile with exceptional children. *Journal of Music Therapy, 5,* 37-40.

——. (1969). Intercorrelations among Musical Aptitude Profile and Seashore Measures of Music Talents subtests. *Journal of Research in Music Education, 17,* 263-271.

——. (1970a). Taking into account musical aptitude differences among beginning instrumental music students. *American Educational Research Journal, 7,* 41-53.

——. (1970b). First-year results of a five year longitudinal study of the musical achievement of culturally disadvantaged students. *Journal of Research in Music Education, 18,* 195-213.

——. (1970c). Taking into account musical aptitude differences among beginning instrumental students. *Experimental Research in the Psychology of Music: Studies in the Psychology of Music, VI,* 45-64.

——. (1971). Second-year results of a five year longitudinal study of the musical achievement of culturally disadvantaged students. *Experimental Research in the Psychology of Music: Studies in the Psychology of Music, VII*, 131-143.

——. (1972). Third-year results of a five year longitudinal study of the musical achievement of culturally disadvantaged students. *Experimental Research in the Psychology of Music: Studies in the Psychology of Music, VIII*, 42-60.

——. (1974). Fourth-year results of a five year longitudinal study of the musical achievement of culturally disadvantaged students. *Sciences de l'Art Scientific Aesthetics, 9*, 79-89.

——. (1974). Toward the development of a taxonomy of tonal patterns and rhythm patterns: Evidence of difficulty level and growth rate. *Experimental Research in the Psychology of Music: Studies in the Psychology of Music, IX*, 39-232.

——. (1975). Fifth-year and final results of a five year longitudinal study of the musical achievement of culturally disadvantaged students. *Experimental Research in the Psychology of Music: Studies in the Psychology of Music, X*, 24-52.

——. (1979). Developmental music aptitude as measured by the Primary Measures of Music Audiation. *Psychology of Music, 7*, 42-49.

——. (1980a). Developmental music aptitudes among inner-city primary grade children. *Bulletin of the Council for Research in Music Education, 63*, 25-30.

——. (1980b). The assessment of music aptitudes of very young children. *The Gifted Child Quarterly, 24*, 107-111.

——. (1981a). Music learning and learning theory. *Documentary Report of the Ann Arbor Symposium: Music Educators National Conference*, 62-68.

——. (1981b). Wie kinder klange als musik wahrnehmen - Eine Langschnittuntersuchung zur musikalischen begabung. *Musikpadagogische Forshung, 2*, 30-63.

——. (1984). A longitudinal predictive validity study of the Intermediate Measures of Music Audiation *Bulletin of the Council for Research in Music Education, 78*, 1-23.

——. (1985). Research studies in audiation: I. *Bulletin of the Council for Research in Music Education, 84*, 34-50.

——. (1986a). A factor analysis of the Musical Aptitude Profile, the Primary Measures of Music Audiation, and the Intermediate Measures of Music Audiation. *Bulletin of the Council for Research in Music Education, 87*, 17-25.

——. (1986b). Final results of a two-year longitudinal predictive validity study of the Instrument Timbre Preference Test and the Musical Aptitude Profile. *Bulletin of the Council for Research in Music Education, 89*, 8-17.

——. (1986c). The importance of being able to audiate 'same' and 'different' for learning music. *Music Education for the Handicapped Bulletin, 2*, 3-27.

——. (1988a). The effects of instruction based upon Music Learning Theory on developmental music aptitudes. *Research in Music Education, 2*, 53-57.

——. (1988b). Aptitude and audiation: A healthy duet. *Medical Problems of Performing Artists, 3*(1), 33-35.

——. (1988c). Music aptitudes and music achievement. *Ala Breve, 35*(3), pp. 9, 10, 30.

——. (1988d). Musical child abuse. *The American Music Teacher, 37*(5), 14-16.

——. (1989a). Audiation, imitation, and notation: Musical thought and thought about music. *The American Music Teacher, 38*(3), 15, 16, 17, 59.

——. (1989b). Foreword. *Readings in Music Learning Theory.* Chicago: GIA Publications, iii-iv.

——. (1989c). Tonal syllables: A comparison of purposes and systems. In D. Walters and C. C. Taggart (Eds.), *Readings in Music Learning Theory.* (pp. 66-71). Chicago: GIA Publications.

——. (1989d). Audiation, Music Learning Theory, music aptitude, and creativity. The Proceedings of *The Suncoast Music Education Forum on Creativity* Tampa, Florida, 75-89.

——. (1989e). Implications for music learning. *Music and Child Development: Proceedings of the 1987 Denver Conference.* St. Louis: MMB Music, 325-335.

——. (1989f). The nature and description of developmental and stabilized music aptitudes: Implications for music learning. *Music and Child Development: Proceedings of the 1987 Denver Conference.* St. Louis: MMB Music, 325-335.

——. (1990a). Two new tests of music aptitude: Advanced Measures of Music Audiation and Audie. *Measurement and Evaluation, 10,* 1-4.

——. (1990b). Nowe testy badania zdolnosci muzycznych. *The International Seminar of Researchers and Lectures in the Psychology of Music Akademia.* Muzyczna im. Fryderyka Chopina. Warszawa, Poland, 300-310.

——. (1991a). Gordon on Gordon. *The Quarterly, II*(1&2), 6-9.

——. (1991b). Sequencing music skills and content. *The American Music Teacher, 41*(2), 22, 23, 48-51.

——. (1991c). A study of the characteristics of the Instrument Timbre Preference Test. *Bulletin of the Council for Research in Music Education.* 110, 33-51.

——. (1991d). A response to Volume II, Numbers 1 & 2 of The Quarterly. *The Quarterly. II*(4), 62-72.

——. (1991e). Music Learning Theory in preparatory audiation. *Wahrnehmen, Lernen, and Verstehen.* Wilfried Gruhn, Ed. Gustav Bosse Verlag, Regensburg, Germany, 63-78.

——. (1992-93). Is it only in academics that Americans are lagging? *The American Music Teacher, 37*(5), 24, 25, 80-83.

——. (1993). Kodály and Gordon: Same and different. *Kodály Envoy, XX(1),* 22-28.

——. (1994a). Audiation, the door to musical creativity. *Pastoral Music, 18*(2), 39-41.

——. (1994b). Audiation: A theoretical and practical explanation. *Kodály Envoy, XX*(2), 12-14.

——. (1995a). Taking a look at Music Learning Theory: An introduction. *General Music Today, 8*(2), 2-8.

——. (1995b). The role of music aptitude in early childhood music. *Early Childhood Connections, 1*(1 & 2), 14-21.

——. (1995c). Testing musical aptitudes from preschool through college. *Psychology of Music Today.* Frederyk Chopin Academy of Music, Warsaw, Poland, 170-176.

——. (1996a). Early childhood music education: Life or death? No, a matter of birth and life. *Early Childhood Connections, 2*(4), 7-13.

——. (1996b). Music Learning Theory. *Contemporary Music Education*. Michael Mark (Ed.). New York: Schirmer Books, 169-180.

——. (1997a). Taking another look at the established procedure for scoring the Advanced Measures of Music Audiation. *GIML Monograph Series, 2*, 75-91.

——. (1997b). Music education: The forgotten past, troubled present, and unknown future [Special Edition]. *Audea*, 1-10.

——. (1997c). La clase colectiva de instrumento. *Eufonia: Diaactica de la Musica* Barcelona, Spain, 91-100.

——. (1997d). Early childhood music education: Preparing young children to improvise at a later time. *Early Childhood Connections, 3*(4), 6-12.

——. (1999a). All about audiation and music aptitudes. *Music Educators Journal, 86*(2), 41-44.

——. (1999b). The legacy of Carl E. Seashore [Abstract]. *Bulletin of the Council for Research in Music Education, 140*, 17.

——. (2000a). Contemplating objective research in music education. *Early Childhood Connections, 6*(1), 30-36.

——. (2001a). Contemplating objective research, *Audea, 7*(1), 4-8.

——. (2001b). The stakes are low but the consequences are high. *Bulletin of the Council for Research in Music Education, 151*, 1-10.

——. (2002). Audiation: The foundation for music improvisation *Człowiek-Muyka-Psychologia* Akademia Muzyczna im. Fredryka Chopina, Warsaw, Poland, 459-471.

——. (2003). All about audiation and music aptitudes. The Grandmaster Series. *Music Educators Journal*, 13-16.

——. (2004). Pattern preeminence in learning music. *Early Childhood Connections, 10*(2), 7-17.


**Books**

——. (1971). *The psychology of music teaching.* Englewood Cliffs: Prentice Hall. (Translated Japanese, Prentice Hall, Tokyo, 1973).

——. (1976). *Learning sequence and patterns in music.* Chicago: GIA Publications.

——. (1980, 1984, 1988, 1993, 1997). *Learning sequences in music: Skill, content, and patterns.* Chicago: GIA Publications.

——. (1984, 1997). *Study guide to Learning Sequences in Music: Skill, Content, and Patterns.* Chicago: GIA Publications.

——. (1986a). *Musikalischeb Begabung. Beschaffenheit, beschreibung, messung und bewertung.* Ubertragung aus dem Amerikanischen ins Deutsche von Michael Roske. Schott, Mainz.

——. (1986b). *Designing objective research in music education.* Chicago: GIA Publications.

——. (1986, 1999). *Jump right in: The music curriculum.* A Basic Music Series for Grades K-9. Co-authors Taggart, C., Bolton, B., Valerio, W., & Reynolds, A. Chicago: GIA Publications.

——. (1987a). *The nature, description, measurement, and evaluation of music aptitudes.* Chicago: GIA Publications.

——. (1987, 1997). *Jump right in: The instrumental curriculum.* A Beginning Book for Recorder. Co-authors Grunow, R. & Azzara, C. Chicago: GIA Publications.

——. (1989, 1997). *Jump right in: The instrumental curriculum.* A Beginning Instrumental Music Series for Standard Instrumentation. Co-authors Grunow, R., & Azzara, C. Chicago: GIA Publications.

——. (1990, 1997). *A music learning theory for newborn and young children.* Chicago: GIA Publications.

——. (1991). *Guiding your child's musical development.* Chicago: GIA Publications.

——. (1997a). *Creativity in improvisation.* Co-author C. Azzara. Chicago: GIA Publications.

——. (1997b). *Umuzykalnianie niemowlat i malych dzieci.* [A Music Learning Theory for Newborn and Young Children]. Kraków, Poland: Wydawnictwo Zamiast Korepetycji.

——. (1998a). *Introduction to research and the psychology of music.* Chicago: GIA Publications.

——. (1998b). *Jump right in: The early childhood music curriculum: Music play* Co-authors Valerio, W., Reynolds, A., Bolton, B., & Taggart C. Chicago: GIA Publications.

——. (1999a). *Sekwencje uczenia się w muzyce: Umiejé tności zawartość i motywy* [Learning Sequence in Music: Skill, Content, and Patterns]. Bydgoszcz, Poland: Teoria Uczenia Się Muzyki, Wydawnictwo Uczelniane Wyzszej Szkoly Pedagøgiczney.

——. (1999b). *Zanurz się w: program nauczania muzyki: dzialania w kolejności uczenia się w program nauczania: Podrecznik dla nauczycieli* [Reference Handbook for Using Learning Sequence Activities]. Bydgoszcz, Poland: Wyższa Szkola Pedagogiczna w Bydgoszczy.

——. (2000a). *Teoria de aprendizagem musical: Competências, conteúdos e padrões* [Learning Sequences in Music: Skill, Content, and Patterns]. Lisbon, Portugal: Fundação Calouste Gulbenkian.

——. (2000b). *Teoria de aprendizagem musical: Para recem-nascidos e crianas em idade pre-escolar* [A Music Learning Theory Newborn and Young Children]. Lisbon, Portugal: Fundação Calouste Gulbenkian.

——. (2000c). Podstawy teorii uczenia się muzyki według: Materialy z III Sympozjum *Gordonowskiego.* Bydgoszcz, Poland: Wydawnictwo Uczelniane Wyzszej Szkoly Pedagøgicznej.

——. (2000d). *More songs and chants without words.* Chicago: GIA Publications.

——. (2000e). *Rhythm: Contrasting the implications of audiation and notation.* Chicago: GIA Publications.

——. (2001). *Preparatory audiation, audiation, and Music Learning Theory: A handbook of a comprehensive music learning sequence.* Chicago: GIA Publications.

——. (2002). *Rating scales and their uses for measuring and evaluating achievement in music performance.* Chicago: GIA Publications.

——. (2003a). *Improvisation in the Music Classroom.* Chicago: GIA Publications.

——. (2003b). *L'apprendimento musicale del bambino.* Milano, Italy: GIA Publications.

——. (2003c). *Learning sequences in music: Skill, content, and Pattern* (Rev. ed.) Chicago: GIA Publications.

——. (2004a). *The aural/visual experience of music literacy: Reading and writing music notation.* Chicago: GIA Publications.

——. (2004b). *Canti melodici e ritmici senza parole.* Milano, Italy: Edizioni Curci.

——. (2005a). *Music education research: taking a panoptic measure of reality.* Chicago: GIA Publications.

——. (2005b). *Harmonic improvisation for adults.* Chicago: GIA Publications.


### Cassettes and CDs

——. (1981). *Tonal and rhythm pattern audiation cassettes.* Chicago: GIA Publications.

——. (1982, 1990, 1994, 1997). Lecture cassettes accompanying *Learning sequences in music: Skill, content, and patterns.* Chicago: GIA Publications.

——. (1987). *Tonal and rhythm pattern cassettes* from *Jump Right In: The Music Curriculum.* Chicago: GIA Publications.

——. (Speaker). (1989). Testing music aptitude. Audio Cassette from Series of *Voices of experience* (Cassette Recording No. 3019). Reston, Virginia: Music Educators National Conference.

——. (1991a). Cassettes accompanying *Guiding your child's musical development.* Chicago: GIA Publications.

——. (1991b). *Jump right in to listening.* Chicago: GIA Publications.

——. (1994). *The Reimer/Gordon Debate on music learning – Complementary or contradictory views?* (Cassette Recording No. 3004). Reston, Virginia: Music Educators National Conference.

——. (1997). Lecture cassettes acommpanying *Learning sequences in music: Skill, content, and patterns.* Sixth Edition. Chicago: GIA Publications.

——. (2001). *Preparatory audiation, and Music Learning Theory: A handbook of a comprehensive music learning sequence.* Chicago: GIA Publications.

——. (2002). *Rating scales and their uses for measuring and evaluating achievement in music performance.* Chicago: GIA Publications.

——. (2003a). *Improvisation in the Music Classroom.* Chicago: GIA Publications.

——. (2003b). *L'appredimento Misicale del Bambino.* Edizioni Curci, Milano, Italy.

——. (2004a). *The aural/visual experience of music literacy: reading and writing music notation.* Chicago: GIA Publications.

——. (2004b). *Canti Melodici e Ritmici Senza Parole.* Edizoni Curci, Milano, Italy.

——. (2005a). *Music education research: Taking a panoptic measure of reality.* Chicago: GIA Publications.

——. (2005b). *Harmonic improvisation for adult musicians.* Chicago: GIA Publications.

*Monographs*

——. (1965). *A three-year longitudinal predictive validity study of the Musical Aptitude Profile.* Iowa City: The University of Iowa Press.

——. (1967). *How children learn when they learn music.* Iowa City: University of Iowa.

——. (1970). *Experimental research in the psychology of music: Studies in the psychology of music.* (Vol. VI). Iowa City: The University of Iowa Press.

——. (1971). *Experimental research in the psychology of music: Studies in the psychology of music.* (Vol VII). Iowa City: The University of Iowa Press.

——. (1972). *Experimental research in the psychology of music: Studies in the psychology of music.* (Vol VIII). Iowa City: The University of Iowa Press.

——. (1974). *Experimental research in the psychology of music: Studies in the psychology of music.* (Vol IX). Iowa City: The University of Iowa Press.

——. (1975). *Experimental research in the psychology of music: Studies in the psychology of music.* (Vol X). Iowa City: The University of Iowa Press.

——. (1976). *Tonal and rhythm patterns: An objective analysis.* Albany, NY: The State University of New York Press.

——. (1978). *A factor analytic description of tonal and rhythm patterns and evidence of pattern difficulty level and growth rate.* Chicago: GIA Publications.

——. (1981). *The manifestation of developmental music aptitude in the audiation of "same" and "different" as sound in music.* Chicago: GIA Publications.

——. (1989). *Predictive validity studies of IMMA and ITPT.* Chicago: GIA Publications.

——. (1990). *Predictive validity studies of AMMA.* Chicago: GIA Publications.

——. (1991). *The Advanced Measures of Music Audiation and the Instrument Timbre Preference Test: Three research studies.* Chicago: GIA Publications.

——. (1994). *A Comparison of scores on the 1971 and 1993 editions of the Iowa Tests of Music Literacy: Implications for music education and selecting an appropriate string instrument for study using the Instrument Timbre Preference Test.* (No. 1). West Berne, NY: GIML Monograph Series.

——. (2000). *Studies in harmonic and rhythmic improvisation readiness: Four research studies.* Chicago: GIA Publications.

——. (2001a). *Test validity and curriculum development: Three longitudinal studies in music.* Chicago: GIA Publications.

——. (2001b). *Music aptitude and related tests: An introduction.* Chicago: GIA Publications.

——. (2002). *Developmental and stabilized music aptitudes: Further evidence of the duality.* Chicago: GIA Publications.

——. (2004a). *An investigation of the objective validity of music audiation games.* Chicago: GIA Publications.

——. (2004b). *Continuing studies in music aptitudes.* Chicago: GIA Publications.

### *Tests and Manuals*

——. (1965, 1988, 1995). *Musical aptitude profile.* Boston: Houghton Mifflin (1965) & Chicago: GIA Publications (1988, 1995).

——. (1970, 1991). *Iowa tests of music literacy.* Chicago: GIA Publications.

——. (1979). *Primary measures of music audiation.* Chicago: GIA Publications.

——. (1982). *Intermediate measures of music audiation.* Chicago: GIA Publications.

——. (1984). *Instrument timbre preference test.* Chicago: GIA Publications.

——. (1986). *Manual for the primary measures of music audiation and the intermediate measures of music audiation.* Chicago: GIA Publications.

——. (1989a). *Advanced measures of music audiation.* Chicago: GIA Publications.

——. (1989b). *Audie.* Chicago: GIA Publications.

——. (1996). *Harmonic improvisation readiness record.* Chicago: GIA Publications.

——. (1998). *Harmonic improvisation readiness record and rhythm improvisation readiness record.* Chicago: GIA Publications.

——. (2003). *Music audiation games.* Chicago: GIA Publications.

### *Videos*

——. (1990). *Video guide for Learning Sequence Activities.* Chicago: GIA Publications.

——. (1990, 1999). *Music play: Jump right in.* Columbia: South Carolina ETV.

——. (1991). *The importance of early childhood music.* Hartford: Connecticut Public Broadcasting, Television Division.

——. (1992). *Video guide to Learning Sequence Activities: Jump right in.* Chicago: GIA Publications.

# *Variation 1:*
# Early Childhood, Elementary General, and Choral Applications

*Elisabeth A. Etopio/Kilissa M. Cissoko*

••••••••••••••••••••••••••••

STATE UNIVERSITY OF NEW YORK AT BUFFALO/
MAKOWSKI EARLY CHILDHOOD CENTER, BUFFALO, NEW YORK

# The Hard Work of Music Play: Establishing an Appropriate Early Childhood Music Environment

## Introduction

Musical sounds surround a child from even before the moment of birth. Whether a child is listening to music, singing a song, or moving creatively to the sounds around him, music is a vital part of a child's life. Early childhood is a critical time during which to reinforce a child's natural music abilities. Children often create music as a part of their play experiences, thus sustaining imagination and creativity. Music enables children to express feelings and release energies and emotions in new ways.

In the past decade, early childhood music education has been the focus of a great deal of interest from parents and educators alike. Parenting magazines frequently publish articles promoting the non-musical benefits of music in early childhood. The governor of Georgia gave away free CDs to parents of newborns in a misguided response to the unsubstantiated claims that merely listening to Mozart makes children smarter. The amount of attention brought by the Mozart Effect has undermined the efforts of music educators who provide early music experiences for the sake of developing childrens' musical understandings. Franchise programs such as Musicgarten, Kindermusik, Mommy and Me, Music Together, and others are springing up in many cities to meet the demands of parents seeking opportunities for their children to be involved with music. While some programs benefit children by teaching music for music's sake, few early childhood music programs are based on a solid theoretical framework or recognize the ability of young children to audiate.

Music Learning Theory provides a theoretical foundation for under-standing the music development of children. As a result of considering the developmental characteristics of children, teachers more successfully can nurture their musical growth. Gordon (1997) describes the processes by which children acculturate, assimilate, and eventually gain fluency in their musical mother tongues. Although music is not a language but a literature, Gordon concludes that music is learned in much the same way that a language is learned. In general, both music and language begin with a period of exposure and absorption, move to a state of "babble," and emerge with a form of communication. The progression of development of the vocabularies of musical "language" and spoken language is hierarchical: listening, speaking, reading and writing. These vocabularies are developed within the context of audiation. Before children experience audiation, Gordon asserts that newborns and toddlers pass through developmental stages of preparatory audiation. Preparatory audiation deals with building an extensive listening vocabulary and initiating a speaking vocabulary[1].

Gordon maintains that every child is born with the capacity to under-stand and create music. Further, he stresses that unless a good music environment continually nourishes the level of music aptitude with which a child is born, the child's music aptitude will decrease, and, for all intents and purposes, may be lost. However, since most families do not regularly "speak" music to each other, and music exposure is often limited to mediated sources (recordings, television, video games, and movies), children's music development is typically stunted. There are then implica-tions for providing an appropriate music environment at the earliest possible age.

An appropriate music environment is geared toward each individual child's needs and promotes each student's music achievement. The *Music Play Early Childhood Music Curriculum* (Valerio, Reynolds, Bolton, Taggart & Gordon, 1998) was developed as an application of Gordon's Music Learning Theory. The curriculum reflects the philosophy that early music experiences are essential to cultivating young children's innate music potential or aptitude. The materials and techniques of *Music Play* were specifically developed to bring children through the stages of preparatory

---

[1] Within this book, see "A Music Acquisition Research Agenda for Music Learning Theory" for more information on how music development parallels language development.

audiation and build the critical skill of audiation—hearing and thinking music with understanding.

The co-creators of *Music Play* have successfully established programs at early childhood centers and music development centers at Michigan State University, University of South Carolina, and Temple University in Philadelphia. In 1999, faculty and students from the State University of New York at Buffalo began their own early childhood classes based on Music Learning Theory and the teaching practices described in *Music Play*. The process of establishing these classes has been both challenging and rewarding. Those of us involved in the process adopted a spirit of discovery as we negotiated this revolutionary way of teaching music. The purpose of this chapter is to provide a portrait of how Music Learning Theory and the *Music Play* curriculum were applied in an early childhood setting. It is our hope that sharing our struggles and experiences will help others as they engage in the hard work of *Music Play*.

## The "Ecology" of an Early Childhood Music Setting

While *Music Play* is playful, fun, interactive and spontaneous, it is difficult work to develop a smooth-running class and engaging music environment. Teachers must grapple with the intricacies of Music Learning Theory, detecting and responding to children's developmental levels within the stages of preparatory audiation, knowing well a large and varied body of songs inside, coordinating movement and use of props, planning appropriately paced lessons, improvising, working in a team, leading non-musicians, and striving to understand the developmental characteristics of young children. Thus, there are multiple levels in creating an appropriate music environment.

A child's development occurs within a complex system of relationships affected by multiple dimensions of the surrounding environment (Bronfenbrenner, 1979). So, too, does a child's music development. Bronfenbrenner (1979, 1989, 1993) is the originator of the ecological systems theory as illustrated in Figure 1. The child's biological dispositions join with environmental forces to mold development. In the "ecology" of teaching, different levels of influence have bidirectional and reciprocal effects on each other. In terms of Music Learning Theory, a child's aptitude combines with environmental forces to mold music development. Music achievement occurs within a "layered" environment or complex system in which children, teachers, and caregivers interact.

55

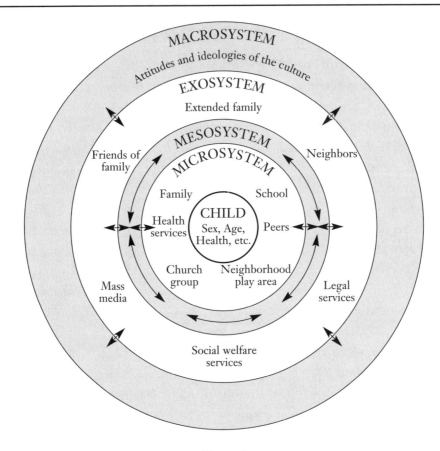

*Figure 1.*

From *The Child, Development in a Social Context* by C. B. Kopp and J. B. Krakow
Copyright © 1982 Addison-Wesley. Reprinted by permission of Pearson Education, Inc.

The macrosystem symbolizes the values, customs, and culture of a child. Aspects of the macrosystem have been referred to in the opening of this chapter. In general, Americans are beginning to recognize the value of music in early childhood. However, the focus often is on using music to teach other skills rather than being concerned with the aestehtic aspects of music development. As music specialists, we need to be aware of this and educate the parents and teachers we work with about music's intrinsic values as well as the value of fostering children's musical understandings and audiation skills.

The mesosystem reflects the exchange between levels of the microsystem (e.g., the relationship between music specialist and parents and the relationship between music specialist and preschool teachers). While these connections are vital to the health of our programs, the remainder of this chapter will be devoted to the child and the level closest to the child. The first and most important aspects to consider are the unique characteristics children bring to the music environment. The microsystem, or level closest to the child, represents the face-to-face interactions between the child and the immediate physical surroundings. The physical surroundings include characteristics of music specialists, preschool teachers, caregivers, class materials, and classroom settings. Special attention will be devoted to the interactions beween the music specialist and the children.

## The Child

The *Music Play* curriculum is geared toward each child's unique needs and strengths. Children bring many things to the music environment, including music aptitude and distinct personalities. While all children have the capacity to comprehend music, they display varying degrees of music aptitude (Gordon, 1997). Since music aptitude is not measurable until children reach three years of age, music specialists must be sensitive to infants' and toddlers' musical behaviors so as to provide appropriate guidance. In addition to their innate aptitude, children have their own temperament, personality, and preferences, all of which mediate how they respond in the music environment. It is important for teachers and parents to recognize how the characteristics of children influence musical behaviors.

### Children's Music Characteristics

In our program, we rely heavily on observation to assess the musical growth of the children and their progression through the stages of preparatory audiation. When observing the children, it is important to remember that they are at their own individual stage of development and that any response they give is "correct." Some children may prefer to sit, listen, and watch, while others will actively engage with the music. All of these behaviors are valid, valuable, and reflect music learning.

At the University of Buffalo, we use Gordon's stages of preparatory audiation as a framework to understanding our children's musical behaviors. Our observations of the children closely parallel the documentation of others (Gordon, 1997; Hicks, 1993; Reynolds, 1995; Valerio et al., 1998). Children in absorption tend to sit or stand very still and stare, often with a wide open mouth. Alternately, they may be playing nearby simply hearing the sounds. Children's random responses do not necessarily relate to the music. Toddlers may bounce their knees, wave their arms, laugh, shake rattles and scarves, and call out in verbal and music babble. Infants' random responses are typically more subtle (i.e., movement of a foot, wiggling fingers, and habituation to the sound source). Gradually, movement responses and music babble become more clearly related to the music. When the children reach the point of engaging determinedly with the music, they are giving a purposeful response. Movements may indicate that children are anticipating the endings of songs or are feeling some sense of beat. Music babble is still inaccurate but may include the utterance of fragmented rhythm or tonal patterns, repetition of the last word or beat of a song, and singing a series of tones or single tones—often the tonic or fifth.

After purposefully engaging with the music environment for some time, children realize that their responses differ from the adults. The audiation stare, usually shown by a sudden strange or quizzical facial expression, reveals a moment when children realize that their response is different than the adults'. We have also found that children in our program will go through a "silent phase" as they become more aware of these differences. As they emerge from the silence, children begin to emulate the adults' singing, chanting, and moving, but the responses are not coordinated. They eventually begin to control their responses, coordinate singing, chanting, breathing, and movement with the adult, and move freely and in synchrony. These behaviors evidence the beginnings of audiation, and from that moment on a child can move onto more formal instruction based on musical understandings.

### Children's Temperament

Gordon's developmental stages of preparatory audiation provide a solid foundation for evaluating young children's music development. Yet children's temperaments and personalities add another facet to understanding their musical behaviors. When we depict children as active, energetic, shy, or cautious, we are referring to temperament. Temperament has been defined as the stable individual differences in quality and intensity of emotional reaction, activity levels, attention, and self-regulation (Rothbart & Bates, 1998). In the longest and most comprehensive study of temperament to date, Thomas and Chess (1977) identified nine dimensions of children's temperament. They found that children vary in activity level, rhythmicity, distractibility, adaptability, attention span and persistence, intensity of reaction, quality of mood, threshold of responsiveness, and approachability. Variations of these nine dimensions grouped together create three general descriptions of children—the easy child, the difficult child, and slow-to-warm up child. The easy child quickly establishes regular routines, is generally cheerful and adapts easily to new experiences. Conversely, the difficult child has irregular daily routines, is slow to accept new experiences, and tends to react negatively and intensely. The slow-to-warm-up child is inactive, shows mild, low-key reactions to environmental stimuli, is negative in mood, and adjusts slowly to new experiences. Children's temperament directly impacts the way they will respond in an early childhood music environment.

How does the child's temperament relate to the music environment? In an early childhood music setting, we introduce children to novel music stimuli. An easy child will most likely respond positively, while a difficult child may respond with an intense negative reaction. More likely is the case of a slow-to-warm-up child. This child will prefer to sit in his mother's lap, absorb the sounds, and watch the other children for weeks at a time. About halfway through the semester, he will begin to participate with hesitation. Frequently, parents of slow-to-warm-up children report that children sing the songs readily at home where they are in a "safer" environment. There is a student in our program who is quiet in class and clings to her mother as a secure base. A few times during the summer, the class she was in only had three children in attendance due to illness and vacations. On these occasions the child came alive and gave perfect responses when imitating tonal patterns. This child seemingly jumped from absorption to imitation. In certain instances, prolonged amounts of time in absorption are more a reflection of temperament than music aptitude or understanding.

It is also important to gauge the other dimensions of a student's temperament. Children differ in the amount of attention they will give to an activity. Some children will remain captivated with the music for forty-five minutes to an hour. Other children will be ready to leave half an hour into class. If this is a consistent pattern for a child, the lack of persistence is most likely due to temperament rather than lack of interest in the music environment. Intensity of reaction is another aspect to examine. One of our students shouts "again, again, again!" after a favorite song. Other children will utter a quiet "more," and some will only grin. Teachers must be sensitive to these responses in order to meet the needs of the students.

The approachability of a child should also be considered. Children vary in their reactions to new people. Getting close to a child and buzzing them during *Bumblebee* (Valerio, et al., 1998) may not always be the best way to reach a child, as this approach may be too invasive. Some children will approach the teacher and ask for it. However, it is generally best for teachers to introduce themselves slowly to the children. Even after a ten-week session, there will be some children who will shy away if the teacher approaches them. Last, it is good to be aware of children's schedules (rhythmicity). Due to our limited number of classes, parents often have to work around children's naptimes/mealtimes to bring them to music class. This has the most effect on children who need a predictable routine and schedule.

The issues surrounding the temperament of a child are common sense to reflective practitioners. Good music teachers recognize the differences in students' temperaments and gear instruction accordingly. However, noting differences in temperament may enrich our ability to interpret behaviors children show during *Music Play* classes. *Music Play* teachers have to keep their eyes and ears open to catch all class activity. Meaningful learning may be reflected through other means of communication, and teachers can provide a musical link if they pick up on it.

## Developing Teachers' Musicianship and Skills

The early childhood music specialist is probably not the most important adult in a child's microsystem. They will, however, be the focus of our attention in this section, as they are the ones responsible for the ecology of the music class. The first "problem" the music specialist must address is that of an appropriate physical surrounding. We do not have our own space for music class at the university and have found it challenging to adapt occupied places to suit our needs. In addition to the setting, we found other areas that create a challenge for the teachers. These areas deal directly with teachers' musicianship. Our teachers found it difficult to learn the wide repertoire of music and incorporate the techniques described in *Music Play*. It also took time for us to become comfortable with moving freely as we sang. Once we began to feel at ease with our own musicianship, we were able to give attention to creating spontaneous and meaningful interactions with the children.

### *Preparing the Physical Surroundings*

The ideal classroom is one that offers open spaces for movement and is free from distraction. We do not have the luxury of our own space, so we continually struggle to provide an appropriate physical setting. When we began the program, we "pushed in" to the university's Early Childhood Research Center and provided music to children enrolled in the day care there. The children were readily distracted, because the classrooms had open floor plans with inviting play centers. Through trial and error, we worked out a combination of logistical and instructional ways to maximize our students' participation.

Because we were entering their "home turf," children did not feel compelled to stay in the music circle. Students joined the circle, left the circle at will, returned at will, or never joined at all. We were unfamiliar adults and did not have the time to develop relationships with the children. The music and activities were also unfamiliar to the children, and participation was low. The children were accustomed to hearing a constant stream of recorded music, which they largely ignored. The children were never taught to respond to the background music. Since they could ignore the other music, we should have expected them to ignore us, too.

The argument could be made that children who chose not to actively participate still "absorbed" the music and that music learning may have occurred. Preschool teachers may point out that learning is most meaningful when it is self-directed and that children should not be forced to participate. There are elements of truth to both arguments, but we didn't want to be treated like wallpaper, so we took steps to increase participation of the students.

We made the most strides when we realized that the children needed a special place for music. We had been meeting on a large rug that was used for circle time—a time and space that had certain connotations for the students. The first step we made was to roll up the rug every time we entered the Center. This became a routine, and children began anticipating the start of music time. We also encouraged the Center staff to join the circle and participate with the children. Students who had strong relationships with the staff were then more likely to involve themselves in music activity. We worked hard to increase our own appeal by making the activities more playful. We used more props and exaggerated our movements. As we gained confidence, we also learned to value the less-active absorption stage and recognized vicarious participation when children did stray from the circle. Children outside of the circle were still included as we used their names in songs, sought eye contact, and listened for and responded to their music babble.

Later, we began the more typical *Music Play* session to which parents bring their children. Finding space remained an issue for us. We currently use a community center that is affiliated with the university. Every week, we section off a corner of the room with sofas and chairs so that children associate a special place and time for music. We take care to cover the outlets and make the environment as safe as we can for the children. Even with our efforts to make the physical surrounding distraction free, children find things to get into. Establishing an appropriate physical environment is an important and necessary step, but we suspect that even the most perfect environment will not compensate for poor teacher musicianship or skill.

*Learning the Materials*

There was an initial feeling of awkwardness as we learned the *Music Play* curriculum, particularly in learning the songs. The music selected for our classes is rich in content and exposes children to a wide variety of tonalities, meters, and styles. *Music Play* emphasizes musical variety in order to promote both maximum auditory discrimination and music vocabulary building. Typical children's music is in Duple meter and Major tonality, but contrast is what helps children "break the code." When we expose children to yet other modes and meters (Dorian, Mixolydian, Phrygian, 5/8, 7/8, etc.), we widen their listening vocabulary, and allow them to assimilate more information into their cognitive map. The use of an extended music vocabulary that is rich in contrast promotes children's audiation as they begin to discriminate and comprehend the musical sounds that surround them.

In order to include songs in diverse modes and meters, the teachers involved in our program had to expand their own capacity for audiation. Many of us encountered challenges when studying the song materials, as we only had minimal exposure to other modes and meters. Most of this exposure occurred in undergraduate theory classes in which we learned that Dorian was the white keys on the piano from D to D. This theoretical knowledge was of little value to us, and we looked for ways to expand our own listening and speaking vocabularies.

Another challenge in learning the song repertoire is that many of the songs and chants do not have words. Interspersing songs and chants without lyrics helps children attend to the musical content without the distraction of words. In addition to the material in *Music Play*, Gordon and the other co-authors have collected and composed hundreds of compelling, varied songs to be used alongside the more familiar "standard" children's repertoire (Bolton, 1999, 2000a, 2002; Gordon, 2000; Gordon, Bolton, Valerio, & Taggart, 1993). The *Music Play* CD (Valerio, et al., 1998) and the CD recording *Pickles and Pie* (Bolton, 2000b) have also proved invaluable to us as we work to build our repertoire of songs. As teachers, we have come to realize that we learn new materials in the same way as children. We must first take the time to "absorb" and listen to the music before "speaking" it to the children.

At our program's inception, we struggled to remember the songs and chants without words. Some of our teachers found it useful to "audiate" words to songs without lyrics. Two examples are included in Figures 2 and 3. Those of us who have remained involved in the teaching have come full circle and now love the gorgeous melodies without lyrics. The struggle has become remembering the words when we choose to use them.

*Figure 2.*
Excerpt from "My Mommy Is a Pilot" (Valerio, et al., 1998, p. 50)

*Figure 3.*
Excerpt from "Winter Day" (Valerio, et al., 1998, p. 58)

## Learning to Move

*Music Play* incorporates research that has linked full body movement and music learning, particularly the work of dance educator Rudolf von Laban (1971). Laban believed that all movement and exertion spring from an interactive combination of four elements: time, weight, space, and flow. Laban has shown that the internal sense of rhythm evolves in young children through experience with free flowing movement, which is contrary to the way most music methods emphasize the concept of a "steady beat" to develop rhythm. Moog (1976) also observed that children coordinate their movements and music babble at an early age. He noted that the coordination between vocalizations and body movements was an outgrowth of coordinated breathing. Breathing and movement are inextricably linked with rhythmic development.

Early childhood music teachers are encouraged to model free flowing movement for children. This is often easier said than done. Adults' movements tend to be "bound" and serve as a poor example for children. We have found that it is easiest to free the arms in flowing movements, but that is not sufficient. Movements should involve the torso and lower body. Teachers find this more awkward, often because of our insecurities and our own lack of rhythm. One way of addressing this issue is by having teachers "do a dance for the right shoulder." Work down the torso doing a dance for each body part, but save the hips for last. Teachers will find it possible to isolate most body parts, but they will learn that moving the hips involves other parts of the body. If they can remember to engage the hips when modeling movement for children, it will be a good start. In addition, teachers must be reminded to breathe properly to ensure coordination of their movements. Props (such as scarves, balls, bean bags, stretchy bands, parachutes, and hoops) can be used to emphasize the elements of time, weight, space, and flow. However, teachers should first be encouraged to become more aware of their own body and how their movements relate to the music.

### Learning the Techniques

*Music Play* employs a "whole-part-whole" technique. Children first experience the "whole"; they are immersed in a vibrant music making situation in which adults model singing, chanting, and moving. Periodically, the adults examine the "parts" by isolating and highlighting tonal and rhythm patterns through improvised singing and chanting. This is similar to the way in which we call attention to language elements as we read a child a story and point to pictures, words, and letters. When the "whole" is reassembled—the complete song is repeated several times—the experience with the parts builds awareness and leads to musical growth.

A distinct feature of *Music Play* is to isolate tonal and rhythm patterns from the context of the song. Short "acculturation patterns" are performed by the teacher to aurally emphasize the tonal or metrical context. The acculturation tonal patterns consist of three-or-four-note stepwise melodies. For example, patterns to define a Major key could include: DO-RE-MI, SO-FA-MI, RE-MI-FA, DO-TI-DO. Tonal patterns are performed legato, slowly and evenly, with pauses in between to de-emphasize rhythm or two- to four-beat patterns. Rhythm patterns at the acculturation level are two macrobeats in length. The patterns are chanted on a neutral, non-pitched syllable in order to isolate rhythm information from tonal information. Imitation and assimilation patterns are introduced as children progress. Tonal patterns at this level feature arpeggiated triads, while rhythm patterns are increased to four macrobeats in length.[2]

Questions often arise about which patterns to use and when. We have found it useful to think of the acculturation patterns as listening patterns and the imitation/assimilation patterns as speaking patterns. The acculturation patterns highlight music syntax and are designed to introduce children to the order of music. Diatonic patterns are especially useful for helping children discriminate pitches. Young children may attempt to respond to the patterns but do so with little accuracy, as these patterns are

---

[2] For more information on the use of patterns in preparatory audiation, see *Music Play* (Valerio, et al., 1998)

actually more difficult for children to sing than the imitation/assimilation patterns (Gordon, 1997). Once attempts are made by a child to imitate, they should be encouraged to respond to the arpeggiated imitation/assimilation patterns. Arpeggiated patterns are best for teaching recognition and imitation, since the notes are farther apart and children are more inclined to hear the pitches before they sing them.

*Music Play's* technique of pattern isolation provides opportunities for satisfying interplay with even the youngest children. Singing a song in its entirety is an amazingly difficult feat consisting of rhythm information, tonal information, verbal information, and intricate motor-coordination. To have the expectation that children will enter music making at a full-blown level is almost certain to condemn them to failure. However, providing them the opportunity to engage meaningfully in music through utterances of patterns is much more aligned with their language acquisition, in which they babble randomly until sounds recognizable as words come out and provoke excited, reinforcing responses from adults. Most children succeed in learning language through pattern babble. Adults trained to interpret and respond to children's music babble can help them acquire music in bite-sized pieces.

### The Interaction between Teachers and Students

Perhaps the most salient feature of an appropriate music environment is the interaction between the children and teachers. A basic tenet of music play is interactive music making, a dialogue between student and teacher as they engage in musical language. This requires teachers to be comfortable with improvisation and spontaneity. Our teachers had varying degrees of experience with music creativity, which resulted in a slight awkwardness with knowing how to engage children in music dialogue. We made some attempts to be systematic—for example, we always inserted a pattern after the second repetition of the song. We have learned, however, that the flow is more natural and connections are more meaningful when we use patterns in response to children's actions.

In addition, class activities are orchestrated to create a playful environment in which music becomes the "toy." Children are encouraged to interact with the music in whatever way they feel most comfortable. Any vocal or physical response the child makes becomes part of the activity and facilitates music interaction. We closely observe the children and acknowledge their music responses by imitating and validating their expressiveness. When children have ideas, we try to incorporate them into the songs and activities we do. For example, as children experiment with different movements, we try to mirror what they do and gradually expand on the movement to scaffold learning. Children's musical sounds can also be incorporated into the material. After one repetition of *Snowflake* (Valerio, et al., 1998), a child said "uh – oh." On the next repetition we took the phrase "uh – oh" and incorporated those syllables as a nonsense text. The child responded with a mischievous grin. Additionally, children often express alternate words to a song. Instead of "touch your nose" in *The Wiggle Song* (Bolton, 1999), one child asked to "pat your belly" and "pet the doggy." Interacting with the children and integrating their ideas into the class activities makes learning more meaningful to the children and keeps the classes unique, unpredictable, spontaneous, and fun.

## The Hard Work Pays Off

Through learning, teaching, and studying *Music Play*, we have gained more awareness of the overt and covert qualities of students' musical behaviors. We have also come to appreciate that there is a symbiotic, mutually reinforcing relationship between teachers and students. When things went well, we felt a burst of energy go through the room; teachers were inspired when the students responded. This, in turn, brought forth more student involvement, creating a general sense of synergy. But if we experienced difficulties, the energy waned. If the teachers let the momentum slip, the students disengaged and then the teachers felt discouraged. But perhaps then a child would respond in an unexpected and delightful way, and a teacher would reply with a novel reaction of her own. These improvised elements might then become part of the way that song was done, creating a satisfying sense of ownership of the music class by all participants. Overall, establishing an appropriate music environment in which the beginnings of audiation can occur takes patience and creativity. In a short time, though, we have observed considerable growth in the children with whom we work. The long-term results of this method of teaching music to young children will be the ultimate litmus test of its effectiveness.

## References

Bolton, B. (1999). *The childsong collection, book one*. Philadelphia: Bestbael Music.

———. (2000a). *Autumnsong*. Philadelphia: Bestbael Music.

———. (2000b). *Pickles and pie*. Philadelphia: Bestbael Music.

——. (2002). *The childsong collection, book two*. Philadelphia: Bestbael Music.

Bronfenbrenner, U. (1979). *The ecology of human development: Experiments by nature and design*. Cambridge, MA: University Press.

——. (1989). Ecological systems theory. In R. Vasta (Ed.), *Annals of child development* (Vol. 6, pp. 187-251). Greenwich, CT: JAI Press.

——. (1993). The ecology of cognitive development: Research models and fugitive findings. In R. H. Wozniak & K. W. Fischer (Eds.), *Development in Context* (pp. 3-44). Hillsdale, NJ: Erlbaum.

Gordon, E. (1997). *A Music Learning theory for newborn and young children*. Chicago: GIA Publications.

——. (2000). *More songs and chants without words*. Chicago: GIA Publications.

Gordon, E., Bolton, B., Valerio, W., & Taggart, C. (1993). *The early childhood music curriculum: Experimental songs and chants, book one*. Chicago: GIA Publications.

Hicks, W. K. (1993). An investigation of the initial stages of preparatory audiation (Doctoral dissertation, Temple University, 1993). *Dissertation Abstracts International, 54*, 1277A.

Laban, R. (1971). *The mastery of movement*. London: MacDonald and Evans.

Moog, H. (1976). The development of musical experience in children of preschool age. *Psychology of Music, 4*, 38-45.

Reynolds, A. M. (1995). An investigation of the movement responses performed by children 18 months to three years of age and their caregivers to rhythm chant in duple and triple meters (Doctoral dissertation, Temple University, 1995). *Dissertation Abstracts International, 56*, 1283A.

Rothbart, M. K., & Bates, J. E. (1998). Temperament. In N. Eisenberg (Ed.), *Handbook of child psychology: Vol. 3. Social, emotional, and personality development* (5th ed., pp. 105-176). New York: Wiley.

Thomas, A., & Chess, S. (1977). *Temperament and development*. New York: Brunner/Mazel.

Valerio, W., Reynolds, A., Bolton, B., Taggart, C., & Gordon, E. (1998). *Music play*. Chicago: GIA Publications.

*Denise Guilbault*

• • • • • • • • • • • • •

Keystone Academy, Belleville, MI

# Music Learning Theory and Developmentally Appropriate Practice

Some who teach using Music Learning Theory techniques and ideas with young children do so within a public or private school environment, such as in child care centers, preschools, and/or early elementary classrooms. In most of these settings, the administrators, classroom teachers, and parents will require an explanation of Music Learning Theory, so the music specialist should be prepared to communicate effectively to them the strength of and the ideas behind Music Learning Theory. Most are unaware of the stages of music development and are unfamiliar with the importance of audiation, aptitude, tonality, and meter. Experience has shown that administrators, colleagues and parents are more than enthusiastic when they realize the richness and depth of the music program being offered.

However, music teachers also should know the overall educational philosophy, standards, and practices of the school. This information reveals a great deal about the school's view of how young children learn. It also helps Music Learning Theory teachers to establish a reciprocal relationship with the rest of the school community so that persons can learn from each other and work together to achieve shared goals for children. Most early childhood centers and elementary schools have adopted the standards and practices set forth by the National Association for the Education of Young Children (NAEYC). These standards are known as "developmentally appropriate practice" or DAP. Familiarity with DAP will help music specialists to speak in a language that early childhood administrators, educators, and parents understand.

The goal of this chapter is to present an overview of developmentally appropriate practice and to extend it in order to make connections to Music Learning Theory. Given the confines of this article, it is impossible to discuss every element found in the standards. Also, given the enormity of this task, Music Learning Theory comparisons will be limited to informal music guidance and not include formal instruction.

NAEYC believes that some of its most important functions as an organization are to improve the quality of early childhood programs, raise public awareness about what constitutes good quality, and build consensus about standards to guide early childhood professionals. NAEYC developed guidelines for high-quality early childhood programs, the results of which were published position statements on developmentally appropriate practice for children birth through age eight (Bredekamp, 1987). The guidelines are not intended as doctrine, but rather as a way to plan for providing supportive environments for young children. In the revised position statements (Bredekamp & Copple, 1997), developmentally appropriate practice is defined as the result of the process of professionals making decisions about the well-being and education of children based on a) what is known about child development and learning (knowledge about what activities, materials, interactions, and experiences will be safe, healthy, interesting, achievable, and challenging to children of various ages); b) what is known about the strengths, interests, and needs of individual children in a group so that professionals can adapt and be responsive to individual differences; and c) knowledge of the social and cultural contexts in which children live so that learning experiences are meaningful, relevant, and respectful of children and their families. Child development and learning, individual characteristics, and cultural/social contexts must be considered together in order to determine what is developmentally appropriate. Also, the three dimensions of knowledge are constantly changing as more and more information surfaces through observation and research.

Some of the primary issues addressed in DAP are curriculum and assessment, the role of the teacher, the importance of the individual, the role of culture in development, and relationships with families (Bredekamp & Copple, 1997). Because of this, making the connection between Music Learning Theory and developmentally appropriate practice is an easy task. Music Learning Theory is most certainly developmentally appropriate when it is looked at as the process of decision-making about the music education of young children based on what is known about music development, individual differences, and socio-cultural contexts. Gordon, through many years of extensive research, has provided the music profession with invaluable information about how young children develop an understanding of music (audiation). Music Learning Theory provides a framework for the preparatory stages of music development. It supplies teachers with the knowledge of how to guide young children from music babble into audiation. Guide is the key word. Children cannot be taught to understand music—they must teach themselves (Gordon, 1997). Teachers provide children with music experiences that do not impose information or skills on them. Instead, the teacher's guidance takes shape as individual children respond to musical sounds. In this way, children discover for themselves how to organize and give meaning to the songs and chants that they hear.

## Music Learning Theory and Developmentally Appropriate Curriculum

With the publication of *Music Play* (Valerio, Reynolds, Bolton, Taggart, & Gordon, 1998), early childhood music specialists have a curricular model that provides examples of activities that make music learning engaging, attainable, and challenging to children of various ages and stages of music development. Activities are presented to allow every child success. At the same time, the activities move just beyond the child's reach to provide the support system that encourages the child to take the next step. The activities in *Music Play* are playful in nature, as the title suggests. Play is a developmentally appropriate practice and an important vehicle for children's development (Bredekamp & Copple, 1997). Through play, children gain a sense of competence that allows them to practice newly acquired skills right away and to attempt new and challenging tasks that they may have not done otherwise.

The authors of *Music Play* successfully use play as an integrative force in learning. But what exactly is play? Definitions range from Montessori's "Play is a child's work" to Dewey's "Play is what we enjoy while we are doing it." Play is not the same as entertainment. Both play and entertainment are fun and enjoyable, but that is all the two have in common. The biggest difference can be seen in the educational outcome. Play is active and engages the learner. Entertainment is passive and can lure the learner into a cognitive slumber.

Play is something that requires and even compels the child's participation. And because play is active, it is an engine for learning. As participation grows, "ownership" grows, and that ownership opens the child to exploration, creativity, and further learning. The more active children are in determining and absorbing their own learning, the more they learn. In a passive, entertainment mode, children learn little. The active nature that distinguishes play from entertainment is central when considering the educational goals and objectives as described in DAP.

Early childhood music specialists must be aware of the difference between "educational play" and spontaneous, child-initiated play. Educational play is predetermined and controlled by the teacher, whereas child-initiated play is a natural outgrowth of the desires and ideas of children. Some believe that educational play is the only worthwhile kind of play and see child-initiated play as less desirable and not worthy of encouragement. Although there is certainly a place for teacher-controlled play in the curriculum, teachers must remember that guided play does not meet the DAP criteria of being child-initiated or freely chosen, because teachers tend to push children into following their ideas. An appropriate early childhood learning environment must provide many opportunities for children to play freely and spontaneously as their own ideas and feelings emerge. Skilled music specialists know that they can rely on children to bring a wealth of fresh and wonderfully fun ideas into the music classroom. Only when such opportunities for child-initiated play abound can children fully develop their ideas and musical skills. It is this kind of open, flexible play that provides the best opportunities for true learning and is the core of an appropriate early childhood music learning environment according to Music Learning Theory.

How can music specialists evaluate the playfulness of the curriculum they create? The following criteria might help:

1. Play is intrinsically motivating. Will children choose to become involved because they want to, because they are told to, or because they expect a reward for doing so? Music Learning Theory states that children should never be forced or coerced to participate in music activities but should be allowed and encouraged to explore and absorb all that they are capable of exploring or absorbing in the way that is most comfortable for them.

2. Play is freely chosen. Does this play allow children to freely choose what they wish to do for at least a portion of the class period? The skilled early childhood music specialist knows how to balance educational play and child-initiated play. Developmentally appropriate music activities always leave room for children to interject their ideas or to take teacher-developed activities through a variety of delightfully unexpected twists and turns.

3.  Play is process oriented. Will children find satisfaction while involved in this activity without the concern or pressure of a "finished product?" Product is never an issue when following Music Learning Theory's recommendations regarding informal music guidance. Informal music guidance does not demand or expect specific musical responses from children. Music Learning Theory does not expect the teacher to "teach" skills and information but rather to expose children to musical sounds so that they can "absorb" them and experiment with them as they choose.

4.  Play is pleasurable. Will children have fun while they are participating in this activity?

Music play is fun. Music play is satisfying. Music play surprises. Music play engages children actively. Music play creates a desire, presents a challenge, and results in accomplishment. Music play allows children to control their world and satisfy their curiosity, in addition to promoting musical understanding.

An early childhood music curriculum based on Gordon's ideas is much more than play. It is developmentally appropriate for many reasons. Bredekamp and Rosegrant (1992, 1995) outline twenty key points to consider when deciding the developmental appropriateness of a curriculum. Informal music guidance as described by Gordon (1997) and Valerio, Reynolds, Bolton, Taggart, and Gordon (1998) meets all of these guidelines.

1.  A DAP curriculum is theoretically based on and is consistent with research on how children learn. The Music Learning Theory curricular model developed by Valerio, Reynolds, Bolton, Taggart, and Gordon (1998) is an outgrowth of the most current and most extensive research available on how young children learn music.

2.  A DAP curriculum addresses the social, emotional, cognitive, creative, and physical domains of a child's development. The social atmosphere is important in Music Learning Theory, because it recognizes that children learn more when engaged in music play with other children and adults. The emotional needs of the child are of the utmost importance. Children are never forced or coerced to participate. Music Learning Theory addresses cognition through the idea that, with adult guidance, children will teach themselves to audiate in their own time and in their own way. Finally, creativity and movement are vital components of Music Learning Theory.

3. A DAP curriculum addresses the development of knowledge and understanding, processes and skills, dispositions and attitudes. Music Learning Theory guides children toward the understanding of music (audiation) in a way that allows children to associate positive feelings with music learning. If the curriculum were based on practice and drill of tonal and rhythm patterns, rather than on the interests and needs of the child, the children may choose not to engage musically because their music interactions might leave them feeling indifferent and with little ownership of the music learning environment.

4. A DAP curriculum addresses a broad range of content that is relevant, engaging, and meaningful to children. With a Music Learning Theory-based curriculum, music understanding and skills are developed within a meaningful context, not in isolation. This skill development does not involve knowing "about" music and learning specific definitions or musical names, because these are not relevant to children while they are still in music babble. In an appropriate early childhood music environment, children learn to audiate by listening and experimenting with singing, chanting, and moving in various ways to a wide variety of tonalities and meters. Children build a repertoire of patterns and movements through activities that appeal to their natural hunger to learn and are context laden.

5. A DAP curriculum has goals that are realistic and attainable. Developmentally appropriate music activities are not focused on formal music achievement. Specific music responses are not demanded or expected from children (Gordon, 1997). Teachers who use Music Learning Theory guide children through music babble into audiation by developing their listening vocabulary. There are no "right" or "wrong" music responses in informal music guidance. Music Learning Theory is flexible and dynamic in its goals rather than stiff and lethargic. Music Learning Theory suggests that teachers need to look to children's music and movement responses and use them as a springboard for the relationships that exist between music play, music development, and music guidance.

6. A DAP curriculum reflects and is generated by the needs and interests of individual children within the group. In Music Learning Theory, each song and chant can and should be adapted to different levels of learning so that the needs of individual children can be met. Appropriate music instruction also emphasizes the importance of respecting the interests of children by suggesting to teachers that they

rely on the children's music and movement responses to guide them, rather than depending on a teacher-centered plan.

7. A DAP curriculum respects and supports individual, cultural, and linguistic diversity and supports positive relationships with families. The individual child and his or her family are at the heart of Music Learning Theory. This will be discussed in depth later in this chapter.

8. A DAP curriculum builds upon what children already know and are able to do to foster their acquisition of new skills. A fundamental component of informal music guidance according to Music Learning Theory is that children cannot build a music vocabulary unless they have spent a great deal of time listening. All children, barring physical impairment, can listen. From the very beginning, Music Learning Theory teachers provide a musically rich listening environment. When children have a developed listening vocabulary as a base, they will naturally begin to respond. Once children exhibit musical behaviors, teachers can build from there.

9. A DAP curriculum provides a framework for children so that learning becomes more complex over time. A curriculum based on Music Learning Theory is sequenced in such a way that it leads children to conceptual knowledge by informally guiding them toward the construction of their own understanding of music. Children begin music learning by absorbing sounds in the environment. From there they begin imitating those sounds, becoming more accurate along the way. Eventually, they internalize the syntax of music, allowing them to coordinate their movements and breath with their singing and chanting.

10. A DAP curriculum allows for integration across subject matter by planning around experiences that provide opportunities for rich conceptual development. Although Music Learning Theory does not concern itself with curricular integration, it does reflect the natural way children learn. Early childhood professionals believe that the way children learn best is by making connections between all areas of their lives—bringing naturally-related subjects together. A child cannot develop audiation by relating their music vocabulary to math or science concepts. However, a curriculum based on Music Learning Theory encourages and supports the connections between what children musically experience in their lives and what they experience in music class.

11. A DAP curriculum has intellectual integrity; it meets the standards of the discipline. The ultimate goal in Music Learning Theory is to

develop children's audiation skills. A Music Learning Theory-based curriculum strictly adheres to the learning sequence and content that the theory provides. Music specialists can guide children toward audiation by providing them with opportunities to hear many tonalities and meters, move their bodies, and respond to tonal and rhythm patterns appropriate to their level of music development. This lays a solid foundation for all future music learning.

12. A DAP curriculum's content is worth knowing. In other words, is the content presented at a time when children can efficiently and effectively learn it, or is it better left for a later time? Music Learning Theory states that there is no better time to begin musical guidance than the day a child is born and that aptitude is positively affected when music is introduced as a significant part of the child's life from the very beginning. However, because the learning environment is child-driven, each child can take what they need musically when they need it.

13. A DAP curriculum actively engages children in the learning process. A foundational pillar of Music Learning Theory is that children cannot be taught music—children must teach themselves. The more active children are in determining and absorbing their own learning, the more they learn. Music specialists using Music Learning Theory recognize the value of activities that are playful in nature, because play necessitates the child's participation and opens the child to exploration, creativity, and learning.

14. A DAP curriculum views children's mistakes as an important learning experience and is not overly concerned with "correct" answers. According to Music Learning Theory, there are no "mistakes" in the music responses of young children. All responses are appropriate and used to help the music specialist guide the child toward the next step. Mistakes also facilitate learning by giving children the opportunity to discriminate between the child's performances and those of the adult.

15. A DAP curriculum promotes the development of cognitive abilities. A curriculum based on Music Learning Theory does this by stressing the process and sequence of music learning and by bringing understanding to music through tonal, rhythm, and movement experiences in the context of meaningful learning experiences. During informal guidance, children interact with music on an intuitive level. As they move through the process and sequence of music learning, children come to understand and respond to music on a cognitive level; they can demonstrate their comprehension of tonality and meter.

16. A DAP curriculum provides children opportunities to learn from peers. Children have many opportunities to learn from peers during music play. Children listen to and are encouraged to react to the responses of their peers. An important tenet of Music Learning Theory is that the ideal learning setting is the one in which there is a diversity of music aptitudes among children in the class. Low aptitude children learn from the responses of high aptitude children, and high aptitude children learn from helping low aptitude children.

17. A DAP curriculum is supportive of children's physiological needs. This relates to Music Learning Theory in the sense that appropriate play in music supports children's independence and guides them toward meeting their own needs, especially in relation to the need to move. Children are "wired" for movement—their bodies demand that they move. Music Learning Theory takes this into account and uses it to guide children through the process of music learning. Children are free to move at any time, and teachers should observe those movements and incorporate them into the flow of the class.

18. A DAP curriculum protects children's psychological safety. Children should feel comfortable and protected in the music environment. The activities in informal music guidance promote feelings of confidence and acceptance by creating a stress-free environment that does not have inappropriate expectations of children.

19. A DAP curriculum strengthens children's sense of competence and enjoyment of learning from their point of view. It is easy for a teacher to say that children are achieving and having fun, but it is more important for children to believe that themselves. Music specialists who use Music Learning Theory know this, because many parents report that their children freely choose to "replay" these activities at home.

20. A DAP curriculum is flexible, allowing teachers to adapt to individuals or groups. Children determine the content and flow of each class through their music responses; the teacher observes those responses and uses them to determine the next step in creating an appropriate music learning environment. A Music Learning Theory-based curriculum is extremely flexible. It provides activities for group instruction, individual instruction, and allows music specialists to use their creativity while remaining true to the theory.

## Music Learning Theory and Developmentally Appropriate Assessment

Bredekamp and Rosegrant (1992) define DAP assessment as the process of observing, recording, and documenting children's development and learning, evaluating it in light of the program goals and objectives, and incorporating it into educational decisions that benefit children. Assessment and curriculum go hand in hand. Behind much of the bad curriculum in the schools is bad assessment. Assessment is the tail that wags the curricular dog (Bredekamp & Rosegrant, 1992). DAP and Music Learning Theory strongly support the idea that assessment, curriculum, and practice must be united in order for optimal development and learning to transpire. Both DAP and Music Learning Theory view the functions of assessment as aiding teachers in developing instructional plans, communicating with parents, identifying children at the high and low ends of the learning spectrum, individualizing instruction, and evaluating the quality of the program and effectiveness of the teaching. A teacher's use of valid measurement tools coupled with skilled observation is a pivotal factor in the quality of the music learning environment. According to both Music Learning Theory and DAP, the best possible guidance occurs when teachers compare what a child is capable of to what the child does.

How do music specialists know what a child is capable of doing? Music specialists know that all children have some potential to learn music, which is called music aptitude. There are two types of music aptitude – developmental and stabilized. Developmental music aptitude occurs through approximately the first nine years of a child's life. During this time, the quality of the music environment can positively or negatively influence children's potential to achieve in music. The environment ceases to have an effect on aptitude at about the time children attain nine years of age. At this point, aptitude becomes stabilized and will remain so throughout the child's life.

Music specialists can begin to measure children's developmental music aptitude objectively at age three. *Audie* (Gordon, 1989) and the *Primary Measures of Music Audiation* (Gordon, 1979) are helpful tools in assessing young children's music development. Developmental music aptitude tests are extremely important, because without them we can only guess the capabilities of children based on their achievement (Gordon, 1998; Taggart, 1989). The problem with this is that what children do may not match their capabilities. When this is the case, children underachieve, and this underachievement goes undetected. Music specialists cannot possibly evaluate a child based solely on what is observed. Some children will have high developmental music aptitudes, and their musical behaviors will reflect that; however, sometimes they will not. It is through the use of music aptitude tests in conjunction with observation that music specialists can objectively identify the potential of the children they teach. Only after objective measurement has been made of a child's aptitude and achievement in music can a teacher expect to make a dependable subjective evaluation (Gordon, 1997).

Observation is a necessary component in assessing young children's music development. Observation is the most effective strategy for getting to know young children and is the most congruent with DAP, because it results in a low level of interference with the educational environment and little constraint placed on children. Informal methods such as observation should be the primary form of assessment in early childhood (Bredekamp & Rosegrant, 1992). Gordon (1997) has systematically planned for observation-based evaluation of young children by providing music specialists focus within the context of tonal and rhythm pattern guidance. The purpose of pattern guidance is to help children learn how to audiate, develop a syntax for tonality and meter, and build a music vocabulary (listening and speaking). Also, it gives music specialists opportunities to interact with individual children and to assess each child's music development through observation. Gordon gives focus to the observations by describing children's tonal and rhythm reactions to music that has been sung or chanted to them. By watching, listening, and making appropriate decisions quickly, music specialists can decide on the most appropriate interactions with children at that moment. By compiling running accounts of and reflecting upon children's tonal and rhythm responses, music specialists will remain informed concerning the stages of individual children's development and, in turn, what types of music experiences would be most beneficial to those children. Through observation, music specialists can successfully link theory to practice and make sound judgments about guiding children's musical growth. Assessment in terms of measurement and evaluation are essential elements in Music Learning Theory and all in line with, if not ahead of, DAP, as DAP relies heavily on evaluation and little on objective measurement.

Assessment not only has the potential to improve instruction, it also has the potential to serve teachers (Bredekamp & Rosegrant, 1992; Gordon, 1998). Appropriate assessment provides teachers with accountability by giving them information to communicate to parents. While assessing the musical growth of children, teachers in essence are assessing the quality of their teaching as well. A music specialist's effectiveness can be seen through the developmental music aptitude scores of children. When aptitudes rise or remain consistent over time, teachers can be fairly sure that they are providing the kind of environment that supports children's musical growth and development. If, on the other hand, the children's aptitude scores decrease over time, music specialists need to reevaluate whether their teaching is meeting the musical needs of their students.

## Music Learning Theory and the Individual

Each child is a distinct person with an individual pattern of development, as well as a unique personality, temperament, learning style, set of strengths and weaknesses, needs, interests, and experiential and family backgrounds (Bredekamp & Copple, 1997). NAEYC states that, for practices to be developmentally appropriate, they must be appropriate to each individual by placing importance on establishing a caring, inclusive community in which all children can develop and learn according to their potential. Developmentally appropriate teachers make it a priority to know each child well by establishing positive personal relationships, continual observation, knowing needs and potentials, and adapting responses to differing needs, interests, styles, and abilities.

The primary purpose of measuring children's aptitude is to provide music specialists with the necessary information needed to help them adapt instruction based on the needs of individual children (Gordon, 1997). Music Learning Theory is an interactive teaching paradigm in which music specialists vary their teaching depending on the goals of the activity and individuality of the children. Music Learning Theory is not a one-size-fits-all model for early childhood music education.

If we do not provide music experiences that are developmentally appropriate to the level of each child in the program, we inhibit meaningful music experiences for all children. A curriculum based on Music Learning Theory provides a diversity of activities and approaches so that each child is challenged and successful. All children benefit in this environment, because they are attuned to the responses of their peers and learn from them. Fitting activities to the skill and interest level of each child reinforces the success of individualized instruction (Bredekamp & Copple, 1997).

Developmentally appropriate activities consist of two major components: age appropriateness and individual appropriateness. An activity that is age appropriate means that the activity incorporates skills typical for use with children of that age. For example, it is not age appropriate for two-year-old children to move together in a circle dance. However, they can move with continuous fluid movement, alone and within a group. Age appropriate activities can be determined by finding out what types of activities are in line with expected abilities of children within the various age groups. A curriculum based on Music Learning Theory insures age appropriateness of activities.

Music Learning Theory also insures individual appropriateness. Individual appropriateness means that accommodations are made, when needed, to ensure that the developmental levels of every child are met with appropriate types of challenges. Music specialists must be aware not only of the differences among children in the class, but also of the strengths and weaknesses of individual children (Gordon, 1998). Music aptitude tests measure children's strengths and weaknesses in terms of tonal and rhythm aptitude. Music Learning Theory advocates for the individual by asking music specialists to modify and adjust their teaching in relation to the child's tonal and rhythm strengths and weaknesses. For example, knowing that a particular student has high tonal aptitude, the music specialist can challenge that student by giving him or her a more difficult task to perform. This same child may have a low rhythm aptitude and may need a task that is more easily accomplished. Furthermore, the music specialist should seek opportunities that aid the child in overcoming his or her weakness. A positive aspect of Music Learning Theory is that all children receive the same general content while working at the level that is appropriate to their stage of music development.

## Music Learning Theory and the Role of the Teacher

Individuals can realize their potential only within a community (Katz & McClellan, 1997). Social relationships have an impact on children's cognitive development. Young children who engage in gratifying exchanges and activities with adults and peers are more involved in the learning process and are better able to learn. Music specialists make many decisions about which specific teaching behaviors or forms of guidance are most suitable for a child in a particular circumstance and at a specific point in his or her music development. The teacher/child relationship can be helpful or harmful to a child's music development, and music specialists who follow the tenets of Musical Learning Theory understand which teaching behaviors and forms of guidance to embrace and which to avoid.

In Music Learning Theory, children must teach themselves, and the learning environment must be conducive to supporting children in this endeavor. This occurs through an appropriate balance between adult-initiated and child-initiated learning that shows respect for children by supporting their rights to their feelings, ideas, and opinions. In other words, Music Learning Theory teachers learn to use their authority selectively and refrain from using power unnecessarily. This gives children the opportunity to develop self-confidence, respect for self and others, and active, inquiring, creative minds. By reducing adult authority, one promotes children's self-regulation (DeVries & Zan, 1995).

If teachers have autonomy in mind for the children they teach, they will be careful to balance child-initiated and teacher-directed learning. Both are necessary elements of a high-quality learning environment. Although Music Learning Theory does not directly address teacher behavior in terms of "class management," it does imply that the teacher/child relationship is important. Music specialists must be prepared to be flexible and to know which teacher interaction is the best for individual children. DAP and Music Learning Theory foster a collaborative relationship between children and teachers, as the teacher becomes the facilitator of an environment that is safe, successful, personally satisfying, and skill-appropriate so activities are enjoyable for all students.

## Music Learning Theory and Culture

Understanding culture requires an understanding of the rules that influence behavior. NAEYC believes that too many teachers are unaware of the effects of culture on the development of children. Being knowledgeable about developmental stages is not enough. Teachers must also be knowledgeable about how social contexts can influence and shape a child's development. Risk of failure can be reduced for many children when teachers understand the influence of socio-cultural contexts on learning, and, in turn, accept that there are numerous ways for children to demonstrate achievement (Bredekamp & Copple, 1997).

Music Learning Theory is sensitive to the various socio-cultural experiences of all children. Because children are "guided" rather than "taught," information or skills are not imposed upon the children. Children can and should be exposed to their culture and given opportunities to claim that culture. Guidance is based on and operates in response to the natural sequential activities and responses of the child (Gordon, 1997). Children are not expected to conform to a set of required behaviors or respond with the "one" correct answer.

Insensitivity to cultural differences can be seen in test bias. Persons of certain cultures/backgrounds may be placed at a disadvantage because a test includes content that is unfamiliar to them (Boyle & Radocy, 1987). This may result in persons being denied access to various opportunities.

Gordon was sensitive to these cultural differences when he constructed his aptitude tests. A strength of Gordon's tests is that children can take them and achieve a high score without having had any formal music instruction. For that reason, a well-constructed music aptitude test is unbiased in terms of race, religion, and nationality and has no relationship with language literacy (Gordon, 1998).

## Music Learning Theories and Relationships with Families

The best and most appropriate environment for children is one in which parents and professionals establish relationships, maintain regular communication, learn from each other, and work together for the benefit of the child (Bredekamp & Copple, 1997). Early childhood music specialists using Music Learning Theory know that parents are vital to a child's music development. Home is the most important school that young children will ever know, and children's parents are the most important teachers they will ever have (Gordon, 1997). When parents are included in their child's learning, the child will be more successful. Parents must be intimately involved and understand their role in the education process (Henderson, 1988). Lack of explicit information about ways to enhance children's success at school discourages parents from becoming involved. Moreover, parents who have not developed a view of themselves as central to their child's learning often avoid involvement (Finders & Lewis, 1994).

Early childhood music specialists must spotlight the parental role in the music development process. There is no better time to capitalize on parents' initial willingness for involvement and to foster development toward participation than when children are young. There are several components to building a meaningful working relationship with parents. First, parents need to be provided with the tools they need to nurture and guide their child with confidence. Regardless of whether the parents attend class with the child, they need knowledge about how children develop an understanding of music. The process of music development, developmental music aptitude, types and stages of preparatory audiation, appropriate informal music guidance, appropriate music environments, and readiness for formal music should be part of the knowledge base for parents. Having this information will help parents form more appropriate expectations of the sequence of music development and the readiness required for formal music instruction. In addition, parents who attend music classes with their children should know that music class provides a learning environment for them as well. As the music specialist models music behaviors and responses during class, their understanding of how to interact with their children musically will deepen.

Music specialists will model what parents need to learn about how to observe their children's music behaviors and respond appropriately. For instance, with a one-year-old child who simply sits and listens, an informed parent will continue to make eye contact and sing, waiting for the moment that the child makes a response of some kind. An uninformed parent may try to force a response from the child, worried that "something may be wrong" with the child or the child is "behind." Knowledge of how children learn and sharpened observation skills will make possible more choices appropriate to different stages of music development and will help parents become attuned to making creative adjustments to a child's level of learning.

Many parents may have a fear of singing or moving in public because they think they do not possess any musical ability. A music specialist can alleviate these fears by reaching out to parents, finding ways to build connections, and dispelling feelings of being different or incompetent. Music specialists can work with these parents by focusing on their strengths and building from there. Parents must realize that, in order for children to be joyful and enthusiastic about music play, they must be joyful and enthusiastic as well.

Parents who feel valued as partners in their children's education are most likely to support and participate in the music program. Music specialists should make deliberate plans to be available before class to personally welcome each child and parent, demonstrating a genuine interest in the family. This type of relationship makes it more likely that the parent will share helpful information about the child. For example, Johnny may have been up very late waiting for his daddy to return from a trip, and he is a bit tired, or Melissa sang a song from last week's class at home and wants to sing that song in class today.

Parents should be informed of their child's progress. Taking the time to discuss a child's development is essential for successful parental involvement. At the beginning of each school year, music specialists should establish communication with parents, making clear the types of interaction they can expect. Consistent use of one or two selected communication strategies (meetings, developmental progress reports, newsletters, phone calls, personal notes) is most effective.

Finally, according to DAP, methods of working with parents should be "community-friendly" and shaped by the preferences and needs of families. To truly relate to families, the music specialist needs to speak the language of the families served and to show respect and understanding for the values and traditions represented among families in the music program. This helps teachers to anticipate differences in behavior and adjust to them. Knowing that parents from China, Japan, and Vietnam are likely to have different interaction styles allows music specialists to accommodate these differences. Knowing about culturally related learning styles might help music specialists increase children's success in music.

## Summary

In early childhood settings, music specialists may find it helpful to speak in terms of developmentally appropriate practice when explaining a music program based on Music Learning Theory. Following Music Learning Theory's recommendations, music specialists can communicate the developmental appropriateness of curricular models, as they are based on research, address the whole child, and promote cognitive development. Both Music Learning Theory and DAP tie assessment to curriculum, and both emphasize the value of attending to the strengths and weakness of each individual child. Finally, both Music Learning Theory and DAP recognize that the teacher, culture, and family play a significant role in the learning process. Making these connections will help school administrators, colleagues, parents, and caregivers understand high-quality music instruction and its place in early childhood education.

## References

Boyle, J. D., & Radocy, R. (1987). Contemporary issues in measurement and evaluation. In *Measurement and evaluation of musical experiences* (pp. 21-49). New York: Schirmer Books.

Bredekamp, S. (Ed.). (1987). *Developmentally appropriate practice in early childhood programs serving children from birth through age 8.* Washington, DC: National Association for the Education of Young Children.

Bredekamp, S., & Copple, C. (Eds.). (1997). *Developmentally appropriate practice in early childhood programs.* (Rev. ed.). Washington, DC: National Association for the Education of Young Children.

Bredekamp, S., & Rosegrant, T. (Eds.). (1992). *Reaching potentials: Appropriate curriculum and assessment for young children.* Washington, DC: National Association for the Education of Young Children.

———. (1995). Reaching potentials through transforming curriculum, assessment, and teaching. In S. Bredekamp & T. Rosegrant (Eds.), *Reaching potentials: Transforming early childhood curriculum and assessment* (pp. 15-22). Washington, DC: National Association for the Education of Young Children.

DeVries, R., & Zan, B. (1995). Creating a constructivist classroom atmosphere. *Young Children, 51*(1), 4-13.

Finders, M., & Lewis, C. (1994). Why some parents don't come to school. *Educational Leadership 51*(8): 50-54.

Gordon, E. (1979). *Primary measures of music audiation*. Chicago: GIA Publications.

——. (1989). *Audie*. Chicago: GIA Publications.

——. (1998). *Introduction to research and the psychology of music*. Chicago: GIA Publications.

——. (2003). *A music learning theory for newborns and young children*. (2nd. ed.). Chicago: GIA Publications.

Henderson, A. (1988). Parents are a school's best friend. *Phi Delta Kappan 70*(2): 148-53.

Katz, L., & McClellan, D. (1997). *Fostering children's social competence: The teacher's role*. Washington, DC: National Association for the Education of Young Children.

Taggart, C. (1989). The measurement and evaluation of music aptitudes and achievement. In D. Walters & C. Taggart (Eds.), *Readings in Music Learning Theory* (pp. 45-53). Chicago: GIA Publications.

Valerio, W., Reynolds, A., Bolton, B., Taggart, C., & Gordon, E. (1998). *Music play: The early childhood music curriculum*. Chicago: GIA Publications.

*Alison Reynolds*
• • • • • • • • • •
TEMPLE UNIVERSITY

# Guiding Preparatory Audiation: A Moving Experience

If you teach music, you move. Perhaps you sing or play an instrument, conduct, teach marching band drills, use choreography, or use movement to teach music objectives. Persons you teach move, too. Perhaps they sing or play instruments, march, perform choreography, or use movement to demonstrate competency with steady beats, rhythm patterns, phrases, forms, dynamics, textures, or pitch relationships. They also use movement to express their emotions to music that they hear or perform, or to participate in folk dances, singing games, or play parties.

Most music educators would agree that when students successfully participate in traditional movement activities, their kinesthetic involvement in a music objective is likely to assist with comprehending and retaining it, or with improving the accuracy with which they perform or identify it. However, if a child is not successful completing the movement task, chances are great that he or she will not be successful achieving the music objective. In the latter case, the music educator might not have considered that a child's lack of achievement is due to his or her lack of movement readiness to accomplish the movement and music objectives. In this chapter, I will summarize some of what we understand about movement as a readiness for formal movement and music activities, the ways we use movement to guide young children through the types and stages of preparatory audiation, and some observations of how movement assists young children's overall music development.

## What We Know About How Young Children Move to Music

Young children respond naturally and spontaneously to music. Moorhead and Pond (1978) were the first researchers to systematically observe music-related responses among young children in a classroom setting, and they found that children perform a limited variety of movement responses to music available in their classroom. Often children accompany their own babbling and creation of rhythmic and vocal music with coordinated movement. Moog (1976) investigated the spontaneous responses individual children performed in an environment created for research, rather than in an early childhood classroom, and found similar results. After observing that children between two and three years of age accompany themselves with movements coordinated with the rhythm of their own singing and babbling, he interpreted that

> Singing is produced by motor actions of the vocal apparatus and the breath. The rhythm of these songs depends on the rhythm of the breathing, and the vocal apparatus joins in at the same speed, so that the singing and the motor movements of the vocal apparatus are dependent on the organs of breathing and must therefore be synchronized. Since the vocal organs and those concerned with breathing are synchronized in any case, co-ordinated movement in another part of the body may be considered as an extension of a co-ordinated movement which, in the case of the child's own singing, has already occurred between the vocal and breathing organs. (Moog, 1976, p. 2)

Sims (1985) investigated the movement responses of children three and four years of age. Individual children were asked to move in the way that the recorded music made them feel like moving with no peers or adults present. She observed that, although the resulting list of all of the children's movements reflected a variety of movement responses, any one child typically performed only one or two types of movements. Sims concluded that young children either become fascinated with making one or two movements, or they have a limited creative movement repertoire that should be expanded with adult guidance.

Metz (1986) was interested in children's natural inclinations to perform music-related movements to recorded music, for example, to gallop to music in Triple. She compared music-related movement responses made by children two to four years of age performed first without and then with the presence of adult guidance and interaction. Metz concluded that when an adult interacts with children using a combination of modeling, describing, and suggesting movements, children increase the number of music-related movement responses they perform. She also encouraged the use of props to provide children with a visual representation of the adult's desired music-related movement response, such as providing children with a stick horse to encourage galloping.

Rainbow (1981) and Blesedell (1991) designed research in which they investigated the influence of consistent movement instruction upon rhythmic responses performed by young children. Rainbow, in a three-year longitudinal study, observed the influence of rhythmic movement upon the abilities of children three to five years of age to complete a series of rhythmic tasks. At the end of three intervals of instruction within each year, children performed a series of rhythmic tasks through either rhythmic speech or rhythmic movements, such as clapping, patting knees, or marching. All children were most successful completing rhythmic tasks in which they orally echoed patterns containing rhythmic speech. Some children successfully completed rhythmic tasks in which they clapped a pattern that previously had been performed with rhythmic speech. Few children successfully completed rhythmic tasks that require marching or marching and clapping simultaneously, thus tending to establish the type of rhythmic movement instruction that is least effective. Rainbow observed that children's achievement of each task generally improved with age.

Blesedell (1991) investigated the effects of Dalcroze- and Laban-based movement instruction upon the rhythmic achievement of two groups of children three and four years of age. She concluded that Laban-based movement instruction may be preferable for guiding the movement development of young children, whereas Dalcroze-based movement instruction may be preferable for guiding their rhythm achievement. In general, Blesedell believes that any type of movement instruction enhances the overall music development of young children.

With the exception of the Blesedell study, researchers have not investigated the effects of movement instruction on a child's overall music development. However, the combined information from these studies assists us with ways of thinking about how to be effective movement models and how to guide movement development in relation to a child's overall music development. Sims and Metz remind adults that children benefit from the adults' movement guidance. Rainbow discovered that movement activities previously emphasized in early childhood settings, such as clapping and marching, are not the most beneficial activities for children's rhythm achievement.

Moorhead, Pond, and Moog's observations about how children coordinate their movements with their own music babble are the catalysts for adopting new approaches to movement in early childhood music education. Because breathing is synchronized movement in itself, our task is to guide a child to synchronize his breathing with movement in another part of the body in order to coordinate himself with music from an external source. Traditionally, adults are eager for very young children to respond to the adult's music in coordinated ways by moving to and chanting steady beats in steady tempos, and by singing whole songs in tune. However, adults should be sensitive to the varying degrees to which young children coordinate themselves with their own music babble as observed by Moorhead and Pond and Moog. Adults can use movement readiness activities to gradually guide children to transfer their coordinated movement and babbling to coordinated breathing and moving while making the same music an adult is performing or that they have heard performed.

Gordon (2003a) seems to agree with Moog, observing that when a child successfully transfers the coordination of his breathing and moving to his coordinated music making from an outside source, he has emerged from music babble to music sense, or music syntax. Furthermore, Gordon states that a young child's success with that transition occurs because he or she is able to use movement first, to discover that his movement and music are not like the adult's and second, to teach him- or herself how to coordinate breathing and movement when making the adult's music. The implication is that such coordinated breathing and movement has the potential to affect a child's overall music development.

## Moving from Music Babble to Music Sense: Preparatory Audiation

Gordon (2003a) observes that young children progress through similar types and stages of music development that he has labeled preparatory audiation.[1] During three types and seven stages of preparatory audiation, children are "hearing and comprehending music while in the 'music babble' stage" (Gordon, 1997, p. 120). Informal comprehension of the sounds of music occurs as the child becomes aware of music syntax through his music and movement interactions with adults. Gordon maintains that a child adopts music syntax when he or she is able to move the whole body using continuous flowing movement while breathing freely

---

[1] For a complete description of preparatory audiation, consult *A Music Learning Theory for Newborn and Young Children* (2003a) by E. E. Gordon (Chicago: GIA Publications).

to sing tonal patterns and chant rhythm patterns. Until a child has achieved those skills, he or she is said to be in music babble. Music and movement-competent adults must guide young children from music babble to music syntax during the seven stages of preparatory audiation. Ideally this guidance occurs from birth to five years of age.

Gordon's three types of preparatory audiation are acculturation, imitation, and assimilation. During the first stage of the acculturation type of preparatory audiation, a child is actively absorbing music and movement stimuli, just as he is actively listening to the sounds of language. In the second stage of the acculturation type of preparatory audiation, a child makes random vocal and physical responses to music stimuli. It will be apparent that his sounds and movements result from the music and movements in the environment, but he will make no obvious attempt to imitate the adult. After continued music and movement interaction between the child and adults, the child eventually tries to relate his music babbling and movements to sounds of music in his environment. Such responses are purposeful responses performed in the third stage of the acculturation type of preparatory audiation.

A child ideally begins imitation, the second type of preparatory audiation, between two and four years of age. During the fourth stage of preparatory audiation, a child begins to shift his or her focus to the adults' music and movements. The child discovers that the purposeful vocal and physical responses he or she is making are not the same as those being presented in the environment. A child prepares to enter the adult's music and movement syntax in the fifth stage of preparatory audiation by imitating more precisely movement, tonal, and rhythm vocabulary he sees and hears in the environment.

From the ages of three to five, a child ideally continues to improve the precision with which he or she imitates tonal, rhythm, and movement responses. In the third type of preparatory audiation, assimilation, he progresses through two stages. During introspection, the sixth stage of preparatory audiation, the child becomes aware that when he sings tonal patterns he is not coordinating his body movement with breathing and that when he chants rhythm patterns he is not coordinating his muscular movement with his breathing. During the seventh stage of preparatory audiation, coordination, a child develops coordination between his performance and his muscular movement and breathing. Specifically, "in rhythm, movement is initiated by and is an outgrowth of breathing; in singing, breathing is initiated by and is an outgrowth of movement" (Gordon, 1997, p. 84). When a child progresses through the seventh stage of preparatory audiation, he or she has coordinated aspects of movement and music vocabularies necessary to develop music syntax during formal elementary general music instruction or private instruction on an instrument, such as the piano or violin.

## Guiding Preparatory Audiation: The Moving Experiences

Gordon's choices about how to move as a model for young children stem from his understanding of Laban's Effort Shape Analysis and interest in Weikart's approach to teaching music and dance. Laban (1971), a dance educator, analyzed movement in previously unequaled detail, describing it as an exertion of energy resulting from an interacting combination of four elements of effort: time, weight, space, and flow. Each effort element exists along a continuum for which the quality of a movement at each extremity is described. Time, therefore, exists as sustained or quick durations; weight as a strong or light sensation of body weight; space as direct or indirect in focus; and flow as free or bound bodily tension. Laban advocated that dancers become aware of their bodies through movements that emphasize time, weight, space, or flow in isolation prior to combining efforts in the use of rhythmic movement or specific dance steps. Later, Weikart (1982) developed a sequential approach to teaching movement and dance in which a child participates in creative movement experiences to organize his internal energy prior to his attempts to synchronize his movements to a steady beat from an external music source.

One can easily observe weight and flow as described by Laban in the movements an infant makes in his random and spontaneous responses to music in the environment. As an infant or toddler gains more control over his movement, his coordination matures and he learns to balance his head, lift up, roll over, pull up, sit up, crawl, and walk. Often during these developmental milestones, a child begins to make purposeful movements in response to the movements and music in the environment. The adult must insure that the developing child is given ample opportunities to observe and imitate the adult's continuous flowing movement model so a child maintains his or her use of weight and flow as he or she moves.

It seems that adults are not aware of their bodies in ways that enable them to model comfortably movements that emphasize weight and flow. Moreover, when adults are traditionally trained musicians, they often rely only on time and space movements to make rhythmic, metric, and temporal decisions. Therefore, adults must reacquaint themselves with the types of movements infants and very young children naturally perform. Gordon (2003a) recommends that adults model Laban-based movements that emphasize weight and flow with continuous, flexible, and free-flowing motion. Valerio, Reynolds, Bolton, Taggart, and Gordon (1998) recommend activities for adults to learn to model moving with flow, weight, space, and time. They also suggest movement activities that feature each effort element for guiding children's movement development.

Gordon encourages adults to patiently and expressively model flowing movements with a minimum of verbal or physical suggestions to a child. This way, a child is allowed to imitate the adult's movements and music as a result of his self-discovery that his movements are not the same as the adult's. A child's self-discovery through movement in part signals to the adult that the child is shedding his egocentric engagement with the music and movement in his environment. The adult relies on the premise that, as the child sheds egocentricity, he or she will apply the awareness of the body to attempts to imitate the adult's movements.

When a child is successful in moving with continuous flow with his whole body, he or she has developed general body awareness. The combination of body awareness and continuous flowing, whole-body movement seems to be the foundation for a child to positively control the energy while making music, an essential requisite for overall music development. He or she can use previous experiences in whole-body movement to positively control the energy as he or she breathes and uses a singing-voice quality, sings in tune and tonality, and sings with expression and sense of musical style. Eventually, that positive control of energy while singing can be transferred to performances on a music instrument. Obviously, the coordination will benefit children who learn to play instruments that require air flow to produce sounds, but it is crucial that adults assist children with that transfer even when their instruments do not require air flow to produce sounds, such as keyboard, mallet and percussion, bowed, and plucked or strummed instruments.

A child will apply the coordination he or she has learned by moving the whole body with continuous flow to his performance of discrete, or steady-beat, movements to tempo and meter in music. Flowing movement allows the child to experience the sensation of breathing while moving with weight and flow through space. Next, the adult guides the child to combine his ability to move with continuous flow with the elements of weight, space, and time and to use continuous pulsating flow. In order to audiate when in time and where in space to place a microbeat pulse, a child places energy in physical space using continuous flowing movement through the aural space and to fill the time between each beat. He or she uses weight to indicate the physical place in space that each microbeat occurs.

To assist a child with audiating time and space between the beats, the adult should begin to model flowing movements in conjunction with the pulsation of microbeats in music that is performed for the child. Pulsating with continuous flow requires movement initiated by various body parts simultaneously. The initiations coordinate continuous flow with changes of weight in different places in space. The amount of weight and space between pulsations is dependent upon the tempo and style of the music. Pulsating movements encourage a child's assimilation of the relationship of the performance to muscular movement and breathing. Specifically, a child can positively control his energy to avoid rushing or slowing the tempo. In assimilation, a child leaves behind the subjective nature of music babble and enters culture's music syntax. At this point, he or she is ready for formal audiation instruction.

Given the results of various researchers' studies and teachers' observations about how young children learn music, music educators interested in developing children's audiation skills should continue to use a dynamic movement approach. The fundamental relationship between movement experiences and music development is NOT a young child's ability to coordinate rhythmic movements with meter in music. Rather, the purpose of movement experiences during preparatory audiation is to guide a young child to rely on his body awareness and ability to move using continuous flow to teach himself to coordinate his breathing with his movement and his movement with his breathing as advocated by Gordon.

Gordon observes that, as a child makes random and then purposeful movement responses to music, he eventually will realize that his movements, although meaningful to himself at some level, are not as relaxed and free-flowing as the adults' movements are. The realization should occur after proper guidance from adults and as a result of the child's self-discovery that his or her singing of tonal patterns is not coordinated with his body movement and breathing, and that his chanting of rhythm patterns is not coordinated with his muscular movement and breathing. Finally, the conscious assimilation of the relationship of his performance to his muscular movement and breathing occurs.

## Observations of Young Children's Abilities to Move with Continuous Flow

Early childhood music educators observe that very young children absorb and imitate continuous flowing movements modeled by adults. For example, Hicks (1993) performed relaxed and free-flowing movements as she sang to children younger than eighteen months. Although the children were not asked or told verbally or shown through tactile modeling to respond to the music stimuli through movement, children performed continuous, free-flowing movements. She concludes that, when adults perform relaxed and free-flowing movements, very young children make random and purposeful movement responses that are developmental, dependent in part upon the physical and audiation maturation of each child. Hicks, like Gordon, says that children might perform purposeful movement responses before purposeful vocal (tonal and rhythm) responses.

In my dissertation study (1995), caregivers and I modeled a sequence of movements that contained continuous flowing, pulsating continuous flow, hopping, and discrete movements to a chant in Usual Duple and a chant in Usual Triple meter. Children eighteen months to three years of age first absorbed those stimuli. As they became familiar with the chants and movements, they performed continuous flowing movements.

## Music Stimuli That Elicit Continuous Flowing Responses from Children

Ideally, music and movement have a mutually beneficial relationship in an early childhood music environment. Movements elicit movement responses, and music stimuli elicit music responses. In addition, movements elicit music responses, and music stimuli elicit movement responses. Because of the dynamic nature of preparatory audiation classes, all adults who guide young children's music development observe how various characteristics of music stimuli elicit movement, tonal, and rhythm responses from the children. In turn, children's responses provide adults with valuable indications regarding the type and stage of preparatory audiation in which each child is functioning.

In general, adults who guide young children through types and stages of preparatory audiation create a music environment consisting of variety, repetition, and silence. Variety is achieved by singing and chanting without instrumental accompaniment in a variety of tonalities, meters, tempi, forms, and dynamics in conjunction with continuous flowing movements. The live music in that environment also includes chants accompanied with vocal rhythm ostinati and songs performed with vocal harmonies such as resting tone or chord root accompaniments, ostinati, descants, or other harmonizations. Adults reinforce the music babble of young children by echoing their babble. When adults improvise music by incorporating the babble that young children perform, children seem to increase the frequency of their movement responses.

Songs and chants in the preparatory audiation environment become familiar to children after repetition. There is no pre-determined number of consecutive repetitions that is most beneficial. Instead, the adult takes cues from the movements and music responses of the children and continues with a song or chant as long as the majority of the children seem to be absorbing the music. An adult can repeat a song or chant performed earlier in the same session at any time, but especially after observing a child moving or babbling in ways that possibly are related to the particular song or chant that was previously performed. Finally, repeating a familiar song or chant from one session to the next encourages different responses over time.

In my dissertation study (1995), I found that repeated presentations of chant stimuli containing only macrobeats and microbeats stimulate performances of flowing and pulsating movements by children eighteen months to three years of age at the onset. However, after about four weeks, children decrease the frequency with which they perform pulsating and free-flowing movements to such chants. Repeated presentations of chant stimuli with more intricate rhythm patterns such as divisions, elongations, and periods of silences (rests) result in a steady increase in continuous flowing movements over ten weeks of guidance. I recommend that teachers immediately introduce such chants in a variety of meters to young children with repeated performances over time.

When adults wait silently after they finish a repetition of a familiar song or chant, there usually is an awesome silence. Sometimes immediately with that silence is an awesome stillness. However, if adults can continue to refrain from talking or musicing, that silence provides an irresistible invitation for some children to let us know what they are thinking or audiating. When adults are silent after they have been singing or chanting in two or more parts or improvising as a group, it seems the typical silence is interrupted by an increase in the number of tonal, rhythm, and movement responses. Silences can also be created by silently audiating patterns or phrases within familiar chants or songs. Finally, one can create or improvise songs and chants that contain relatively prolonged rests.

When children make movement, tonal, and rhythm responses during the silences, they provide adults with information about what music development looks and sounds like. For example, Hicks (1993) found that adding silences during a song between repetitions of the same music and silences between different music performances encouraged movements. She observed that young children demonstrate through movement what they anticipate in their audiation will occur temporally in music. Given a familiar song without words in AB form, if the adult pauses before the B section, children will move showing the tempo at which they anticipate the B section to be performed. They also make tonal or rhythm responses related to the music in the B section.

## How Does an Adult Encourage Other Adults to Move?

When caregivers other than the teachers are present in the room, very young children do not watch their caregivers. Instead, they observe and imitate their peers and their teachers (Reynolds, 1995). This means that teachers should encourage caregiver-child music and movement interactions and provide caregivers with experiences leading singing, chanting, and movement activities. Such opportunities may help caregivers feel more comfortable with their movements, which might encourage them to engage in movement activities outside of the music class. Because caregivers in this study performed movements that are more often only related to rather than movements that are nearly the same as the teacher's movement model, teachers need to provide caregivers with specific verbal instructions and suggestions with regard to the use of their bodies to encourage their best models of free-flowing and pulsating movements and appropriate use of their voices while chanting. Also, caregivers benefit from being advised that children perform movements without being told by adults how to respond, and that an adult's physically moving the child does not encourage and, in fact, often inhibits the child's use of movement.

## What Types of Music Responses Do We Observe While Using Movement to Guide Young Children through Preparatory Audiation?

Infants and pre-toddlers who have not yet learned to talk demonstrate the benefits of movement in relation to their singing voices. Because their pre-verbal vocal responses are so much like singing, their tonal babble more often than not corresponds with the music adults are or have been singing. For example, very young children will respond to songs on the dominant, resting tone (tonic), or perhaps the median pitch of a song in Major or Minor tonality. What is thrilling about this is to observe that children who babble are indeed moving, as Moorhead, Pond, and Moog observed. In fact, I imitate their movements and incorporate their babbling and use those ideas as springboards for improvising tunes and chants in their keyalities, tonalities, and meters.

I observed during my dissertation study (1995) that the children eighteen months to three years of age who performed expressive, tonal, or rhythmic vocal babbling responses were the same children who previously had demonstrated continuous flowing movements. While they babbled music, they moved, but not necessarily with continuous flow. Most recently, in a musicianship class with children from three and one half to four and one half years of age who have been participating in preparatory audiation classes for two to six semesters, I observed informally that one child who achieved the most rhythmically and tonally was also the most confident and competent mover. She demonstrated body awareness by moving individual body parts and her whole body with continuous flow. She confidently moved through locomotor space and explored expansive space around her as she was stationary. She coordinated her jumping on the mini trampoline to microbeats and was able to jump with a full arm swing. When she did not echo a tonal pattern in tune, she acknowledged my continuous flowing model by imitating it and it seemed that her movement reminded her to breathe, which prompted her to sing in tune. She coordinated her four-macrobeat improvised rhythm patterns in Usual Duple with her rocking movement.

Meanwhile, one of her peers outshone her in spontaneous music-making. This peer was capable of the movements of the first girl I described, with the exception of moving her whole body with flow. She had not become aware of her body to the extent that she could positively control her energy and place it efficiently in the coordination of her breathing, movement, and music making. She was egocentric in all of her use of movement; she did not consistently attempt to imitate the stimuli in her environment. She was not aware of when she was the same as or different from that stimuli. This egocentricity kept her in the initial stages of imitation both rhythmically and tonally. No doubt, her understanding of imitation and improvisation will come. In the meantime, I encourage her music creativity and provide opportunities for her to experience continuous flowing movements for the express purpose of fostering her body awareness and to encourage her to shed her egocentricity.

## A New Movement Philosophy

Gordon departs from traditional music education by suggesting that adults cannot "teach" children to transfer the coordination they originally and naturally experienced in their babble to their music performances. Instead, a child must first discover that his or her movements are not like those that the adult is modeling and, second, that it is his or her lack of coordination that is different. Then, he or she has to teach him- or herself to coordinate his breathing, movement, and music making. Furthermore, adults cannot expect children to transfer the coordination they experienced in stages of music babble by participating in repetitious, steady-beat movement activities. Finally, while it is true that physical maturation improves children's movement abilities, it will not remedy the coordination transfer on its own.

What children need, therefore, is an underlying awareness of their bodies that will allow them to generalize more readily how to successfully coordinate their breathing, movement, and music making as they engage in music syntax. Adults need to insure that children have ample opportunities to decide how to apply their bodies and movement to a variety of moving and singing or chanting activities. Doing so appears to foster a child's coordination between breathing and movement and, in turn, the ability to sing in tune and to chant or move with a steady beat.

There is so much about movement in relation to music development we have not yet identified or learned. There are many uses of movement within the field of music education, and none of us has truly mastered all of those approaches. Outside of music education, the realm of possibilities for approaching movement is further expanded. There is also still much to be learned from the movements children make. I would like to encourage music educators to consider that body use is movement in itself. Because we use our bodies to make music, every music performance IS movement. Body use,[2] the extent to which we are positively aware of our bodies, and the necessity for coordinating our breathing with our movement and our music-making permeate everything we do physically when we make music. At this point in my education, I believe these are the readinesses for movement in music education and, indeed, for living life.

We are the movement models for children in ways we forget. They observe and imitate the most subtle of our movement habits. They imitate the way we use our bodies when we talk, sing, chant, sit or stand or "simply" move from sitting to standing. If our body use underlies everything we do, then the positive effects of our movement model (whether for formal movement or movement readiness activities) are surely limited by our ability to model good use. When one applies good use of self while modeling Laban-based movement activities, the potential results for all concerned are immeasurably positive. If a child naturally absorbs and imitates an adult's good use, his organized use of his body will permeate his preparation to audiate as well as all aspects of his daily life.

---

[2] Consult *The Use of the Self* (Rev. ed.) (1996) by F. M. Alexander. (Guernsey, Channel Isles: Guernsey Press Co. Ltd.) for a description of body use within the Alexander Technique.

# References

Alexander, F. M. (1996). *The use of the self* (Rev. ed.). Guernsey, Channel Isles: Guernsey Press Co.

Blesedell, D. S. (1991). A study of the effects of two types of movement instruction on the rhythm achievement and developmental rhythm aptitude of preschool children. *Dissertation Abstracts International, 52*(07), 2452A. (UMI No. AAT9134919)

Gordon, E. E. (1997). *Learning sequences in music: Skill, content, and patterns.* Chicago: GIA Publications.

——. (2003a). *A music learning theory for newborn and young children* (Rev. ed.). Chicago: GIA Publications.

——. (2003b). *Learning sequences in music: Skill, content, and patterns.* Chicago: GIA Publications.

Hicks, W. K. (1992). An investigation of the initial stages of preparatory audiation. *Dissertation Abstracts International, 54* (04), 1277A. (UMI No. AAT9316493)

Laban, R. V. (1971). *The mastery of movement.* London: MacDonald and Evans.

Metz, E. R. (1986). Movement as a musical response among preschool children. *Dissertation Abstracts International, 47* (10), 3691A. (UMI No. AAT8702942)

Moog, H. (1976). *The musical experience of the pre-school child* (C. Clarke, Trans.). London: Schott and Co.

Moorhead, G. E., & Pond, D. (1978). *Music of young children.* (5th ed.) Santa Barbara: Pillsbury Foundation for Advancement of Music Education.

Rainbow, E. L. (1981). A final report on a three year investigation of the rhythmic abilities of preschool aged children. *Bulletin of the Council for Research in Music Education, 66-7*, 69-73.

Reynolds, A. M. (1995). An investigation of the movement responses performed by children 18 months to three years of age and their caregivers to rhythm chants in duple and triple meters. *Dissertation Abstracts International, 56* (04), 1283A. (UMI No. AAT9527531)

Sims, W. L. (1985). Young children's creative movement to music: Categories of movement, rhythmic characteristics, and reactions to changes. *Contributions to Music Education, 12*, 42-50.

Weikart, P. S. (1982). *Teaching music and dance.* Ypsilanti: High/Scope Press.

*Wendy Hicks Valerio*
• • • • • • • • • • • • • •
UNIVERSITY OF SOUTH CAROLINA

# A Music Acquisition Research Agenda for Music Learning Theory

## Introduction

After extensively reviewing music education within popular early childhood education systems, Jordan-Decarbo and Nelson (2002) stated, "Overall, there is little literature to indicate that the majority of music curricula for young children are theoretically based or participate in any meaningful assessment" (p. 233). Unfortunately, those authors are correct because we have not yet convincingly documented young children's music development. Without that documentation, we have no basis for creating or developing meaningful early childhood music assessments. Yet many well-meaning parents and caregivers are eager for their young children to learn music, and many well-meaning early childhood music educators are eager to teach music to very young children. As long as children seem to enjoy music activities, those parents and caregivers may not care that most music curricula for young children are not Music Learning Theory-based. They also may not care that early childhood music development specialists do not know how to assess early childhood music development. But those of us who practice Music Learning Theory tenets with very young children must care, and we must begin to document early childhood music acquisition.

One music learning theory for young children (Gordon, 2003a) and several music curricula exist for young children between the ages of birth and age five (Valerio, Reynolds, Taggart, Bolton, & Gordon, 1998; Music Together, 1992; Kindermusik, 2002; Musikgarten, 1999). None of those curricula authors provides meaningful, standardized music assessment of young children's music skills. That music assessment will remain unachievable until music development researchers engage in the research necessary for documenting young children's music acquisition. We may begin the documentation process by developing a research paradigm that borrows from the rich history of English language[1] acquisition research.

Some music development research that resembles language acquisition research does exist (Hicks, 1993; Reynolds, 1995; Santucci, 2002). And, as determined by Chen-Haftek (1997), very early music development and language development may be closely related. But prior to designing new studies, we must define music acquisition and ponder commitment to music acquisition research. A brief analysis of language acquisition research and theory may be a helpful first step toward meeting those goals.

**Language Acquisition Research**

Language acquisition is difficult to define. Children display many pre-linguistic behaviors that generally are considered reflexes and not actual language acquisition behaviors. Most linguists and psycholinguists agree that initial language acquisition begins with the onset of single-word utterances. Following single-word utterances, children increase vocabulary, develop a sense of semantics, develop and increase lexicon, and develop and increase grammar. All the while, children's language production may not equal their language comprehension (Ingram, 1989).

Language acquisition research can be divided into four distinct stages. Those stages begin with 1) diary studies (1876–1926), 2) large sample studies (1926–1957), and 3) longitudinal language sampling (1957–1989) (Ingram, 1989). Those stages continue with the types of studies conducted and arguments posed by Moerk (1992, 2000).

More than one hundred years ago, Preyer (1889) and Roussey (1899–1900) used parental diaries to document, describe, and record their young children's language. Vinson (1915) used the same diary techniques to begin interpreting recorded children's language. Though considered biased and not useful for making generalizations, longitudinal diaries were used repeatedly as a means of language acquisition research. Moreover, by conducting those in-depth descriptive studies, researchers provided the baseline data necessary for large-sample studies.

Large-sample language acquisition studies became popular just after World War I with the scientific influences of behaviorists Skinner and Watson (Ingram, 1989; Woolfolk, 1998). Generally, children were viewed as passive language receptors, conditioned to utter inaccurate language

---

[1] Throughout this chapter the term language acquisition will be used to refer to English language acquisition.

sounds that were shaped into accurate language sounds through stimulus-response activities. Behaviorists assumed that children learned language without instigating interactions with language stimuli providers.

To document changes in specific language behaviors and to make generalizations about young children's language acquisition, behaviorists established language norms by studying large numbers of children cross-sectionally, rather than longitudinally, and by controlling language stimuli (Smith, 1926; McCarthy, 1930; Day, 1932; Fisher, 1934; Davis, 1937; Young, 1941; Templin, 1957). Those researchers provided extensive descriptions and means of one-word utterances, two-word utterances, and sentence-length percentages. They established norms that allowed children to be labeled as advanced or delayed with regard to language development. Their studies yielded, however, few results of practical significance for understanding how children learn to use language rules (Ingram, 1989).

During language acquisition, children learn to use language rules through imitation and inference. Researchers began to realize that studying utterances was insufficient for documenting and understanding those processes. To understand how children acquire language rules, children needed to be studied in-depth and over extended time periods. Longitudinal language sampling became the focus of the third period of language acquisition research.

Brown (1958, 1963, 1964, 1970), Bloom (1970), and Miller and Ervin (1964) studied individual children's language acquisition at regular intervals over a period of years. These researchers studied a minimum of three children in each systematic investigation for a minimum of six to eight weeks. Their results provided a rich baseline database of phonemes, morphemes, and grammar transformations, but those results were not all that was needed to begin understanding how children learn to use phonemes, morphemes, and grammar transformations to communicate with others.

Chomsky (1957, 1964, 1965, 1981), a nativist and constructivist, then motivated researchers to examine how young children acquire sentence formation rules with regard to syntax, rather than phonemics and morphology. Chomsky suggested that language acquisition occurs because humans are genetically predisposed with a language acquisition device (LAD) to communicate using language, and because of that, he purported that Universal grammar exists in all children. According to Chomsky, as children mature universal Grammar principals are activated mainly through parent/caregiver-conversation and child-directed speech (CDS). Those two techniques are used repeatedly so that children may acquire language rules and function linguistically in society. Most important, parent/caregiver conversations are creative and improvisatory. In essence, children learn many language skills by vocalizing many original utterances they have never imitated.

Another nativist and constructivist, Piaget (1971) proposed that children are genetically predisposed to develop language skills; however, children construct understanding by interacting with environmental language stimuli. With regard to language, children may be genetically stimulated to develop language skills, but they do so with encouragement and support from parents, caregivers, siblings, teachers, and media. Children construct and use language rules by developing them within a society of more knowledgeable language learners, not in a vacuum.

Interactionists Vygotsky (1962) and Bruner (1975) theorized that, though children may proceed through stages of language acquisition, children use language to talk to themselves and interact with others as they develop cognitively. Private speech is used to guide and monitor problem solving in a variety of symbol systems, including spatial reasoning, temporal reasoning, and spatial-temporal reasoning. Adults and more able peers use language to interact with children and support their learning by providing scaffolding experiences for them in the zone of proximal development. Children, in turn, acquire language rules as they develop thinking skills, in general. The majority of those interactions and scaffolding experiences occur naturally through play activities.

Recently, Moerk (1992, 2000) challenged the nativist notions begun by Chomsky. With regard to the LAD, Moerk argued that Chomsky and his followers, "committed a category mistake by confounding multiple social products, established over time and integrated from many geographic locations, with a genetic, and therefore individually-based knowledge structure" (p. 13). Moreover, Moerk claimed those theorists confused necessary causes with sufficient causes, because each individual's language process is highly dependent on the scaffolding supplied to each individual. "The task of the child has to be largely judged in relationship to the scaffolding provided: the better the scaffolding, the easier the task, the quicker the acquisition, and vice versa" (p. 14).

**Language Acquisition Research Summary**

In short, language acquisition researchers have proceeded through the following stages during the past 100 years. First, they provided diaries of children's utterances. Second, they conducted large-sample, cross-sectional studies of children's utterances. Third, they longitudinally studied how a few children acquired language rules during the first few years of life. None of the resulting types of research could have been possible without the type that preceded it. As a result, linguists and psycholinguists have developed many strategies for assessing young children's language acquisition (Genishi & Dyson, 1984; McDaniel, McKee, & Cairns, 1996). Some of today's language acquisition researchers question nativists' notions of innate language abilities, and they continue to refine the definitions of the terms language and language acquisition (Moerk, 2000).

### Music Acquisition and Music Acquisition Research

Each of the previously described language acquisition findings and theories may be useful for defining music acquisition and suggesting a music acquisition research paradigm that may be used for developing Music Learning Theory models, developing Music Learning Theory-based music curricula, and assessing music development. Research focusing on early childhood music development research is sparse, but by realizing how linguists and psycholinguists have documented and analyzed language acquisition, music acquisition researchers may prepare themselves to develop improved, theoretically-based early childhood music curricula and meaningful early childhood music assessments.

### Acquiring the Music Symbol System

Music is a symbol system parallel to, yet very different from, the English language symbol system. The primary difference, according to Gordon (2003b), is that music does not have a grammar; however, music does have a syntax. Syntax is order. Gordon defines music syntax as "the orderly arrangement of pitches and durations that establishes the tonality and meter of a piece of music" (p. 377). If music did not have order, we would not be inclined to listen to it, perform it, or compose it, as we understand music by thinking in and communicating ordered patterns of tones and durations.

A language is a human communication system that is understood by a people (Merriam-Webster, 2000). In the case of the English language, that communication system has been analyzed to comprise, at least, syntax, grammar, lexicon, and the many divisions of each catgegory (Ingram, 1989). Can music be a human communication system understood by a people? Music may be heard and used, but it is definitely not understood by the masses. The ways we currently use, teach, and investigate the music symbol system prevent music from being understood by limiting children to simple music imitation activities and by avoiding music inference activities. We use music for background noise, entertainment, ceremony enhancement, and stress relief. But, in general, we do not practice music as a symbol system with rules that may be acquired and used for interactive communication.

To acquire language, humans may come genetically equipped with a LAD, and they must participate in acquisition of that language through some imitation, and through much creativity and improvisation with guidance from more knowledgeable participants (Chomsky, 1981). To acquire music, humans may come equipped with music aptitude, the potential to learn music. Gordon claims that humans each are born with music aptitude that is normally distributed and is developed through types and stages of preparatory audiation and audiation from the earliest of human interactions (Gordon, 2003a). Only through audiation do humans acquire the rules of music. Just as children are guided through language acquisition by more knowledgeable learners and they operate within the zone of proximal development when in language acquisition with adults and more able peers (Vygotsky, 1978), children may be guided through types and stages of music acquisition.

To operate within a zone of proximal music development, children must not be left to develop musically on their own. Any music culture develops through generations and generations of transformation. Children of a culture must be guided through music acquisition by more musically knowledgeable caregivers and peers. Those caregivers and peers can provide music scaffolding through discrimination and inference music learning experiences. Those experiences will occur only when music is practiced as a viable, independent symbol system for communication.

**Music Acquisition Research: Unguided versus Guided**

Though no early childhood music development researchers have labeled their work as music acquisition research, some early childhood music development researchers have begun the task of documenting young children's music acquisition. Those researchers have not kept diaries of early childhood music behaviors or quantified music behaviors to the extent language acquisition researchers have with language, but they have begun documenting how infants and toddlers begin the process of acquiring music as an aural/oral symbol system.

The genre of music acquisition research may be divided into two categories: 1) studies of unguided music development and 2) studies of guided music development. Those two types of music acquisition research provide the baseline data necessary for designing what may yield results of practical significance. With that practical significance, we may begin to improve music curricula and develop an understanding of young children's music development.

Jersild and Bienstock (1934), perhaps the most behaviorist music acquisition researchers, studied young children's abilities to sing in controlled settings with experimental and control groups. In 1931, the researchers investigated forty-eight children between the ages of thirty-one months and forty-eight months. They found that children sing small intervals more accurately than they sing large intervals, and during sponta- neous vocalizations, young children sing descending intervals more frequently than ascending intervals. Jersild and Bienstock also found that vocal ranges of young children increase with maturity, and they confirmed the results of their first study.

Moog (1976) provided a type of large-scale music behavior diary when he unsystematically explored the responses made by 500 young children to live and recorded children's songs, rhythm chants with words, nonsense words, rhythms performed on unpitched percussion instruments, and recorded non-music sounds. Moog observed that a) infants actively respond to distinct qualities of sound by the time they reach the age of six months, b) infants often move rhythmically to music when they reach the age of twelve months, c) language babble and music babble become distinct after the age of twelve months, and d) music and play are related.

Moorhead and Pond (1941), Shelley (1981), and Miller (1986) conducted in-depth, longitudinal studies to determine music behavior development characteristics displayed by children without music guidance by a) observing children, b) recording, defining, and categorizing observed music behaviors, and c) examining music behavior development trends. Though they provided musical instruments, recordings, and, in one case, body and vocal exploration exercises, none of those researchers provided music guidance for their subjects.

For several years, Moorhead and Pond (1941) observed and documented the music behaviors of young children between the ages of one and eight. The children were not given music instruction but were supplied with a phonograph, recordings, and percussion instruments. The researchers observed that, when left to their own musical devices, children create primitive-sounding songs and chants.

Shelley (1981) systematically observed thirty, three-, four-, and five-year-old children in a childcare setting with a music center in each of two classrooms. Each music center was equipped with pitched and unpitched percussion instruments, and a music specialist led the children in voice and body sound exploration activities twice weekly. Shelley coded nineteen music behaviors. Though the children did sing with and without accompaniment, the two most frequently performed behaviors were going to the music center by choice and examining and manipulating instruments.

Miller (1986) systematically observed, recorded, and compared types and frequencies of music behaviors made by three-, four-, and five-year-old children in childcare classrooms equipped with music recordings and small pitched and unpitched percussion instruments. Throughout the data collection period, no music instruction was given by adult caregivers. Those caregivers did monitor child social interactions for safety. Miller found that some children sang along with recordings of songs with texts and that "chants and speech rhythms were performed alone and never repeated" (p. 10).

Gordon (1987) theorized that each child is born with music aptiude, the potential to learn music. Gordon (2003a) has theorized types and stages of preparatory audiation and recommended unstructured guidance and structured guidance techniques for adults who provide music instruction for very young children (Valerio, Reynolds, Taggart, Bolton, & Gordon, 1998). To verify those preparatory audiation types and stages, music acquisition researchers must observe infants and toddlers in the process of acquiring and using music independent from language acquisition. Few researchers have taken this path, and more must do so before music will be accepted as a symbol system that may be acquired during the first few years of life. By compiling such data, however, researchers may work toward developing meaningful music acquisition assessments.

When humans perceive and comprehend music that is or may never have been physically present, they are audiating (Gordon, 2003a, 2003b). In order to think music, humans must first perceive music. Young children's music perception has been well documented in laboratory studies (Krumhansl & Jusczak, 1990; Trainor, 1996; Trainor, Clark, Huntley, & Adams, 1997; Trainor & Trehub, 1992; Trehub, 1990; Trehub, 1993; Trehub, Bull, & Thorpe, 1984; Trehub, Thorpe, & Trainor, 1990; Trehub, Trainor, & Unyk, 1993; Trehub, Unyk, & Kamenetsky, 1997). Less prolifically, other researchers have documented the uses of music perception by young children in interactive, naturalistic settings (Hicks, 1993; Reynolds, 1995; Santucci, 2002). Those researchers documented how very young children respond to music presented to them by more knowledgeable music learners. Documentation of those responses and similar documentation from future research may form the basis for an understanding of music comprehension, which, in turn, might be used to develop meaningful music assessment tools for use with young children.

Hicks (1993) and Reynolds (1995) used complete participant-observer techniques (Spradley, 1980) to examine music acquisition in data collection situations that a) were void of music with text, i.e., language, b) used adults as music models for infants and toddlers, and c) encouraged infants and toddlers to use music. By recording, coding, and categorizing music behaviors performed in naturalistic music settings, the researchers found that infants and toddlers display relevant, yet often spontaneous, kinesthetic and vocal anticipatory responses to changes in familiar music and movement activities without language. In the first few months of life, infants and toddlers spontaneously respond to music, predict music patterns, and begin to demonstrate their music acquisition kinesthetically and even vocally. Through their exploratory studies, Hicks and Reynolds provided music acquisition evidence, but further exploration is needed to refine understanding of that acquisition.

Santucci (2002) investigated infant's responses to baritone and falsetto singing during face-to-face interactions. Santucci found that infants have no particular preference for baritone or falsetto singing by a male, and infants are highly engaged when sung to by a male. Moreover, in the Santucci study, infant males responded more vocally to adult male singing than did infant females.

## Music Acquisition Constructivists and Interactionists

Moog, Moorehead, and Pond (1941), Miller (1986), and Shelley (1981) observed young children acquire music in music environments without interfering or providing any sort of music guidance to the children. Perhaps those researchers could be labeled as *music constructivists*. They expected young children to construct music simply by being in the presence of music recordings and music instruments. The information provided by those researchers can be helpful if we expect each generation of young children to create a music symbol system for itself.

Valerio (1993), Reynolds (1995), and Santucci (2002) became participant observers in the music acquisition process. They provided music stimuli and music interaction for their subjects. Perhaps those researchers could be labeled as *music interactionists*. Though the information those researchers provided may be regarded as biased and not useful for making generalizations, their research designs resemble those of linguists and psycholinguists who studied small groups of children, in-depth and over time. With repeated efforts, the results of those types of studies will be useful for refining Music Learning Theory for young children, enhancing music curricula for young children, and developing meaningful music assessments for young children.

Through practical application of *A Music Learning Theory for Newborn and Young Children* (Gordon, 2003a), Valerio, et al. (1998) developed *Music Play*, an early childhood music development curriculum. Within that curriculum, the authors promote music development through the use of playful activities designed for children from birth through age nine. When encouraging music development among young children, the authors emphasize an abundant use of songs and rhythm chants without texts for the purpose of accentuating music development as opposed to other types of child development, i.e., social development, emotional development, or language development. That type of music environment must be created and used by other researchers who wish to document and to define music acquisition processes.

**Conclusion**

For research purposes, music acquisition must include how humans learn to use the rules of music to "think music" and participate in music activities void of language. Within music environments, language is a confounding variable. If researchers continue to gather data among very young children while creating music environments void of language, and with music acquisition guidance, those researchers may begin to refine the definition of *music acquisition*. Without such refinement, early childhood music educators are relegated to a lifetime of making music because music making is fun, music making is a diversion, or music making enhances other types of child development.

Unlike language acquisition researchers, music acquisition researchers do not have a rich database of music development diaries to use as baseline data. As a result, few music development researchers have conducted large-sample studies, and very few music acquisition researchers have studied longitudinally how small groups of children learn music or use music rules. Until we perform in-depth, longitudinal music acquisition studies, a) the majority of music curricula for young children will remain without a solid theoretical basis, b) no meaningful early childhood music acquisition assessment tools can be developed, and c) music will be taught because music instruction may enhance other types of learning.

**References**

Bloom, L. (1970). *Language development: Form and function in emerging grammars.* Cambridge: MIT Press.

Brown, R. (1958). *Words and things.* Glencoe, IL: Free Press.

——. (1970). *Psycholinguistics: Selected papers of Roger Brown.* New York: Free Press.

Brown, R., & Fraser, C. (1963). The acquisition of syntax. In C. Cofer & B. Musgrave (Eds.), *Verbal Behavior and Learning: Problems and Processes.* New York: McGraw-Hill, 158-201.

Brown, R., & Bellugi, U. (1964). Three processes in the child's acquisition of syntax. *Harvard Educational Review 34,* 133-5.

Bruner, J. (1975). The ontogenesis of speech acts. *Journal of Child Language, 2* 1-21.

Chen-Haftek, L. (1997). Music and language development in early childhood: Integrating past research in the two domains. *Early Child Development and Care, 130,* 85-97.

Chomsky, N. (1957). *Syntactic structures.* The Hague: Mouton.

——. (1964). Formal discussion. In R. Brown & U. Bellugi (Eds.),Three processes in the child's acquisition of syntax. (Vol. 34, pp. 35-39). *Harvard Educational Review.*

——. (1965). *Aspects of the theory of syntax.* Cambridge: MIT Press.

——. (1981). *Lectures on government and binding: The pisa lectures.* Dordecht: Foris.

Davis, E. (1937). The development of linguistic skills in twins, singletons with siblings, and only children from age 5 to 10 years. *University of Minnesota Institute of Child Welfare, Monograph Series* 14.

Day, E. (1932). The development of language in twins: 1. A comparison of twins and single children. 2. The development of twins: their resemblances and differences. *Child Development 3*: 179-99.

Fisher, M. (1934). Language patterns of preschool children. *Child Development Monographs* 15. New York: Teachers' College, Columbia University

Genishi, C., & Dyson, A. (1984). *Language assessment in the early years.* Norwood, NJ: Ablex.

Gordon E. (1987). *The nature, description, measurement, and evaluation of music aptitudes.* Chicago: GIA Publications.

——. (2003a). *A music learning theory for newborn and young children.* Chicago: GIA Publications.

——. (2003b). *Learning sequences in music: Skill, content, and patterns.* Chicago: GIA Publications.

Hicks, W. (1993). *An investigation of the initial stages of preparatory audiation.* Unpublished doctoral dissertation, Temple University, Philadelphia.

Ingram, D. (1989). *First language acquisition.* New York: Cambridge University Press.

Jersild, A., & Bienstock, S. (1934). A study of the development of children's ability to sing. *Journal of Educational Psychology 25,* 481-503.

Jordan-DeCarbo, J., & Nelson, J. (2002) Music and early childhood education. In R. Colwell & C. Richardson (Eds.), *The new handbook of research on music teaching and learning* (pp. 210-242). New York: Oxford University Press.

Kindermusik. (2002). Retrieved September 15, 2002 from
    http://www.kindermusic.org.

Krumhansl, C., & Jusczak, P. (1990). Infants' perception of phrase structure in
    music. *Psychological Science, 1*, 70-73.

McCarthy, D. (1930). The language development of the preschool child. *Institute of
    Child Welfare Monograph Series* 4. Minneapolis: University of Minnesota
    Press.

McDaniel, D., McKee, C., & Cairns, H., Eds. (1996). *Methods for assessing children's
    syntax.* Cambridge, MA: MIT.

*Merriam-Webster's collegiate dictionary* (10th ed.). (2000). Springfield, MA: Merriam-
    Webster.

Miller, L. (1986). A description of children's musical behaviors: Naturalistic.
    *Bulletin of the Council for Research in Music Education, 87*, 1-16.

Miller, W., & Ervin, S. (1964). *The development of grammar in child language.* In U.
    Bellugi & R. Brown, *The acquisition of language.* Monographs of the Society
    for Research in Child Development.

Moerk, E. (1992). *A first language taught and learned.* York, Pennsylvania: Paul H.
    Brooks.

——. (2000). The guided acquisition of first language skills. In I. Sigel (Ed.), (1985-
    2000) *Advances in Applied Developmental Psychology.*

Moog, H. (1976). *The musical experience of the pre-school child.* Trans. Claudia Clarke.
    London: Schott Music.

Moorehead, G., & Pond, D. (1941). *Music of young children.* Santa Barbara: Pillsbury
    Foundation for the advancement of music.

Music Together. (1992). Retrieved September 15, 2002, from
    http://www.musictogether.com.

Musikgarten, (1999). Retrieved September 15, 2002, from
    http://www.musikgarten.org.

Piaget, J. (2002). *The language and thought of the child.* (3rd ed.) New York: Routledge.

Preyer, W. (1889). *The mind of the child.* New York: Appleton. Original work
    published 1882.

Reynolds, A. (1995). *An investigation of the movement responses performed by children
    18 months to three years of age and their caregivers to rhythm chants in duple and
    triple meters.* Unpublished dissertation, Temple University, Philadelphia.

Roussey, C. (1899-1900). Notes sur l'apprentissage de la parole chez un enfant. *La
    Parole* 1: 790-880, 2: 23-40, 86-97.

Santucci, P. (2002). *Infant responses to baritone and falsetto singing during face-to-face
    interactions.* Unpublished master's thesis, University of South Carolina,
    Columbia.

Shelley, S. (1981). Investigating the musical capabilities of young children. *Bulletin
    of the Council for Research in Music Education, 68.*

Smith, M. (1926). An investigation of the development of the sentence and the
    extent of vocabulary in young children. *University of Iowa Studies in Child
    Welfare, 3*(5).

Spradley, J. (1980). *Participant observation*. New York: Harcourt Brace.

Templin, M. (1957). Certain language skills in children. *University of Minnesota Institute of Child Welfare Monograph Series* 26. Minneapolis: University of Minnesota Press.

Trainor, L. (1996). Infant preferences for infant-directed versus non-infant-directed play songs and lullabies. *Infant Behavior and Development, 19*, 83-92.

Trainor, L., Clark, E., Huntley, A., & Adams, B. (1997). The acoustic basis of infant preferences for infant-directed singing. *Infant Behavior and Development, 20*, 383-396.

Trehub, S. (1990). The perception of musical patterns by their parents. In W. Stebbins & M. Berkleyu (Eds.), *Comparative perception: Vol. 1. Discrimination* (pp. 429-59). New York: Wiley.

———. (1993). The music listening skills of infants and young children. In T. Tighe & W. Dowling (Eds.), *Psyschology and music: The understanding of melody and rhythm*, 161-176. Hillsdale, NJ: Erlbaum.

Trehub, S., Bull, D., & Thorpe, L. (1984). Infants' perception of melodies: The role of melodic contour. *Child Development, 55*, 821-830.

Trehub, S., Thorpe, L., & Trainor, L. (1990). Infants' perception of good and bad melodies. *Psychomusicology, 9*, 5-15.

Trehub, S., Trainor, L., & Unyk, A. (1993). Music and speech processing in the first year of life. In H. Reese (Ed.), *Advances in child development and behavior, 24*, 1-35. New York: Academic Press.

Trehub, S., Unyk, A., Kamenetsky, S. Hill, D. Trainor, L., Henderson, J., & Saraza, M. (1997). Mothers' and fathers' singing to infants. *Developmental Psychology, 33*, 500-507.

Valerio, W., Reynolds, A., Bolton, B., Taggart, C., & Gordon, E., (1998). *Music play: The early childhood music curriculum*. Chicago: GIA Publications.

Vinson, J. (1915). Observations sur le development du language chez il enfant. *Revve linguistic, 49*, 1-39.

Vygotsky, L. (1962). *Thought and language*. Cambridge: MIT Press. Translation of original Russian version of 1934.

———. (1978). *Mind in society: The development of higher psychological processes*. Cambridge: Harvard University Press. (Original works published 1930, 1933, and 1935).

Woolfolk, A. (1998), *Educational psychology*. Boston: Allyn & Bacon.

Young, F. (1941). An analysis of certain variables in a developmental study of language. *Genetic Psychology Monographs 23*, 3-141.

*Elaine Alba Mitchell*
• • • • • • • • • • • • • •
MusicTime Early Childhood Program, Vermillion, SD

# Using Music Learning Theory with the Preprimary Impaired Learner

All students can learn and succeed, but not all on the same day in the same way.

— William G. Spady (1992)

"Chugga-lugga choo choo, chugga-lugga choo" is often the first sound heard by the children in the preprimary impaired (PPI) class as they enter my music room. Some are holding on to a rope that guides them through the halls, while others may enter on wheels by way of a tricycle or wheelchair. The train of children is led by the teacher into a circle to mark the beginning of class. It is immediately apparent that this is not a typical class of young learners.

What can be learned by a child with special needs in music class? This question is often asked by people who are not familiar with the abilities of children with special needs. The answer is *much more than you may believe*.

Every child is entitled to a public education and to a music education. Children in the preprimary impaired class can learn music if the teacher understands the nature of the special learner. When music teachers are assigned a class of special learners, they often feel unprepared to face the challenge of teaching these students. Some resort to entertaining rather than educating this group of students, while others learn as they go. Perhaps this is because the teaching of children with special needs is often neglected in the college music education curriculum. In some college programs, music education students are required to take one class in this area, while some programs have no requirements. In addition, guidelines for special education programs in the public school systems vary greatly from district to district and from state to state.

## The Preprimary Impaired (PPI) Learner

In the PPI classroom, a child may be impaired in one or more areas of development compared to a child of the same chronological age in the "regular" classroom (MAASE, 1989). The ages of the children in this type of class range from two and a half to five years, with a range of disabilities represented. These disabilities might include cerebral palsy, autism, Down's Syndrome, or neurological disorders. Some children may exhibit language delay and lack of coordination. Other children may have social or emotional disorders but not language delay or lack of coordination. The special learner may have physical or neurological disorders; however, an impairment is not indicative of a child's music intelligence or readiness level.

Howard Gardner's theory of multiple intelligences (1993) suggests that we possess seven separate potentials or intelligences (linguistic, logical-mathematical, bodily-kinesthetic, musical, spatial, interpersonal, and intrapersonal). Although several other intelligences have been explored by Gardner since this time, the general issues and their relationships to music remain the same. The special learner may be impaired in the area of linguistics, kinesthetic, or mathematical intelligences, but not necessarily in the area of music. In a class of varying music intelligences, how does the teacher adapt music instruction for this class of special learners?

## Adapting Instruction for the PPI Learner

Edwin Gordon's *A Music Learning Theory for Newborns and Young Children* (2003) can be useful in planning a curriculum for use with the PPI learner. Gordon explains the types and stages of preparatory audiation and describes the musical behavior of children in these stages.[1] Due to the various developmental delays and the varying levels of music aptitude, Music Learning Theory works well with the PPI classroom if the teacher can identify each child's level of preparatory audiation.

### *Acculturation*

In the PPI classroom, acculturation is the main objective for most children. In this stage, the students' primary music activity is listening. The teacher may find him- or herself singing or chanting for the entire class

---

[1] Audiation is the ability to hear and comprehend music when the sound is not physically present. (Gordon, 1990, p. 18)

length with little or no vocal response from the students. This can be expected because the vocal control of some PPI children is comparable to that of newborn to eighteen-month-old children. However, with these children, musical responses such as swaying or rocking may still occur, and eye contact may be made between the students and the teacher. Music Learning Theory lends itself well to teaching children with language delay because their participation in music class is not dependent on whether they can sing or speak words.

In acculturation, exposure and exploration are the focus of instruction. Teachers should encourage any type of response, and correctness should not be expected from children at this stage. The Michigan Curriculum Guide (1989) for preprimary children in music, dance, and other means of aesthetic and creative expression states, "at this developmental level, exploration and expression are more important than accurate representation" (p. 17).

Teachers should create a musical environment in the classroom that consists of singing, chanting, and moving to many songs and chants in a variety of tonalities, keyalities, harmonies, meters, and tempos as recommended by Gordon (2003). An excellent reference for incorporating Music Learning Theory into the early childhood music curriculum is *Music Play* (Valerio, Reynolds, Bolton, Taggart, & Gordon, 1998).

In the beginning stages of acculturation, music teachers should make the following considerations in structuring the lesson. A class length of twenty to thirty minutes works well due to the short attention span of most PPI learners. The ideal schedule would allow for two or three short sessions per week. Each activity should be approximately two to three minutes in length. The sequence of activities is also important. Tempo, meter, tonality, and level of movement should be varied from one activity to another.

VOCAL EXPLORATION

Before a child can begin to sing, he or she must first be exposed to good singing models. Second, he or she should be given opportunities to experiment with vocal sounds. Through a process of trial and error, the child eventually teaches him- or herself to sing. Examples of this experimentation can range from a non-musical moan to a coo in the child's singing voice range. This experimentation assists children in finding the full range of their singing voices.

Because many special learners may have language delay or speech impairments, an additional benefit of vocal exploration is simply the opportunity to use the voice in a relaxed atmosphere. It is not unusual to have a student who may babble in speech but sing in tune and with clear pronunciation.

The following activities encourage vocal responses from the children. For the first activity, perform the chant in Figure 1 using a scarf to move with continuous flow and to pulsate to the beat. On the syllable "boo," throw the scarf up, and, as it falls, model a vocal sound like a siren or an owl. Allow silent time for responses. If responses do occur, then imitate the response.

Mitchell

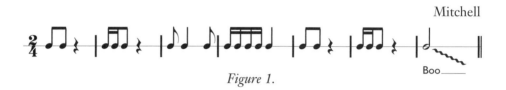

*Figure 1.*

In the next activity, sing the song "Clouds" (Figure 2) using a neutral syllable for the children. As you sing, move continuously with the arms and the hips. Periodically stop between phrases and sing the resting tone (tonic) while touching your nose, foot, or knee, etc. Repeat this activity, and touch each individual child's nose, foot, or knee while singing the resting tone. Allow quiet time for responses from the children. If responses do occur, then imitate the responses.

**Clouds**                                    Edwin E. Gordon

*Figure 2.* (Gordon, et al., 1993, #3)

MOVEMENT

Movement is an important component of the early childhood music curriculum recommended in *Music Play* (Valerio, et al., 1998). In *Music Play*, suggestions are given for developing a repertoire of movements to use in the classroom.

*Flow*. A sense of flow in music is essential to all musicians. Mature musicians internalize this sense of flow; children, however, need to learn to do this. By first experiencing flow in the body, a child can begin to perform movements with flow, to internalize that feeling and then apply that to their vocal or instrumental performance.

The following activity encourages continuous fluid movement as well as fast/slow movement. Sing "Merry Go Round" (see Figure 3) while moving arms in a continuous, fluid movement during the A section. Leave a few seconds of silence, and then move the hands rapidly as you perform the B section. After a few repetitions, add maracas to the song. With continuous fluid movement, stir, roll the arms, or make arches with the maracas during the A section; then shake the maracas rapidly during the B section. The children will begin to anticipate the B section.

*Figure 3.* (Gordon, et al., 1993, #20)

*Body awareness*. Another skill that mature musicians possess is full awareness of their whole bodies. To develop body awareness, children need to be able to identify their body parts as well as demonstrate how each body part works. Children in the PPI class may be physically impaired with limited motor skills. They may be able to identify their body parts; however, they may have difficulty demonstrating how those parts work. Gross motor skills as well as fine motor skills need to be developed. Most children find some of the gross motor skills easier to perform. This is also true in the PPI classroom. It is best to begin with activities with which the children feel most comfortable and then proceed to more challenging motor skills.

An activity such as "Move and Freeze" can be successful since the children in the PPI class most likely have more control over gross motor skills than fine motor skills. This activity allows students to move around the room and show control and body awareness by stopping their movements. Using a familiar song or recorded music, model the desired locomotor movement, such as stomp, hop, tip-toe, or gallop, for the students. Have them freeze when the singing or recorded music stops. Some children may only walk around the room; some may continuously run and not freeze. They probably will not be able to do all the different movements, but it is important to know what they can do and challenge them from there. This activity can be done throughout the year, and the students' progress should be noted and shared with the classroom teacher and parents.

When using recorded music, it is best to use high-quality recordings representing a variety of styles. Recordings should be selected according to the musical elements that the teacher wishes to reinforce. Instrumental music may be more beneficial than vocal music because it is difficult for children to focus on both the music and the text when listening to vocal music with familiar text. Since children spend most of their time in a language intensive environment, their music acculturation time should not be sacrificed by using music that distracts their attention from the elements of the music itself. Singing songs that they may hear at home or in the classroom will reinforce language development rather than music development.

*Adaptive techniques.* For children with limited mobility, there are a number of ways to encourage kinesthetic responses to the music. If a child is able to stand, hold hands with the child, and move the arms in a continuous flow. Both the child and the teacher must be relaxed for this to be successful. Also model bending or twisting for the child while holding his or her hands. Allow the child to move however he or she feels comfortable.

If children are unable to stand, place them on a mat or carpet and move their arms and legs in a continuous flow, again in a completely relaxed manner. This may also be done while a child is sitting in a wheelchair. Some children who find security in their wheelchairs may resist this type of movement at first. With repetition, they will become comfortable with the activity and respond more often to the music.

MUSICAL CONVERSATIONS

Just as children need to have verbal conversations to improve language skills, they need to have musical conversations to improve music skills. This can be accomplished by singing tonal patterns or chanting rhythm patterns on a neutral syllable and encouraging vocal response from the student. With any response, the student will then have entered random response, stage two of preparatory audiation. For example, if the teacher sings a diatonic Major pattern like the one in Figure 4 and the child utters a vocal sound, perhaps "bah" not on pitch, he or she is making a random response. Responses from children in the PPI class may range from a groan to an accurate imitation of the pattern. Any response should be encouraged, and the teacher can begin to converse musically with the student. Conversations should be very expressive, as if you are telling a story or having dialogue. Changes in vocal, facial, and body movements will keep the attention of the students and spark their imaginations. During the music conversations, an accurate imitation of patterns is not the goal.

*Figure 4.*

When a child begins to respond purposefully to the music, that is, when the child attempts to relate sounds or movement to the sounds of music in the environment, the child has entered stage three of acculturation/preparatory audiation (Gordon, 2003). For example, if a teacher sings a diatonic Major pattern and the child responds "bah" on D or A, then the child is making a purposeful response with some relation to what was just sung. It is not unusual to have a student in a preprimary class who is able to imitate your tonal or rhythm patterns or to sing along with you. Despite language delay, this child most likely has had a rich musical acculturation from birth. The teacher should continue to challenge this child musically by giving him or her more difficult patterns to sing or chant. When the child responds appropriately or with correct pitches, he or she is progressing to the second type of preparatory audiation, imitation.

*Imitation*

In the imitation type of preparatory audiation, children begin to respond to music more frequently. They also begin to realize the difference between a correct response and an incorrect response. Essentially, they are teaching themselves by trial and error to respond more correctly. More correct responses should be encouraged and expected by imitating the child's response, correct or incorrect, and then following this imitation with a correct response.

Teachers should remember that some children in the class may still be in the stages of acculturation, while others may be entering imitation. Therefore, instruction should continue to include activities appropriate for both types of preparatory audiation since acculturation is a basis for imitation.

MUSICAL CONVERSATIONS

As in acculturation, teachers should perform musical conversations with children in the stages of imitation. Conversations should continue to be performed with expression and vocal inflection. Children may have difficulty creating their own response and not imitating the teacher. Because children in this stage are more aware of their musical surroundings, their responses will begin to reflect this relationship. It may be challenging to explain to the students that you would like them to sing or chant something different from your patterns. If the students do not understand the concept, then continue to encourage imitation of tonal and rhythm patterns. You could also ask them to start the conversation so that they will not be able to imitate you.

MOVEMENT

*Flow with pulsations.* As stated above, the ability to perform with a sense of flow is important to all musicians. In addition, mature musicians are able to audiate the microbeat while performing with a sense of flow. Young children have difficulty doing this. Modeling flow with pulsations while singing or chanting will give students the opportunity to observe and then experiment with this advanced skill. Children in the PPI class may find this challenging; nevertheless, they should be given the opportunity to be challenged. The following activity incorporates moving with flow and pulsations.

Sing the song "Catch" (see Figure 5) while moving arms and pulsing wrists. After each repetition of the song, sing tonic or dominant patterns to the children. Allow silence for responses from the children. Add props, such as maracas or scarves, to this activity to provide visual and aural stimulation for the children.

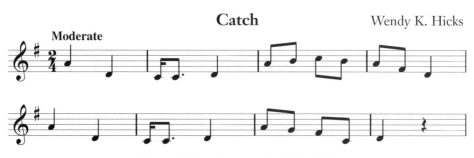

Figure 5. (Gordon, et al., 1993, #58)

*Steady beat.* The ability to maintain a steady beat is crucial to all musicians. Children generally acquire this skill between ages four and six if given an opportunity to explore beat. They need to be given many opportunities to perform steady beats with their bodies and voices before we can expect them to perform it on an instrument or with an ensemble. In time and with many experiences, children teach themselves to keep a steady beat. With students in the PPI class, this is still possible; it is just a matter of time, repetition, and patience.

The following activity reinforces beat and encourages audiation. Use a familiar chant (e.g., "Walking With My Mom," Figure 6) with the children while maintaining a steady beat with a hula hoop or a large rubberband as the children hold on to the prop.

### Walking with My Mom — Edwin E. Gordon

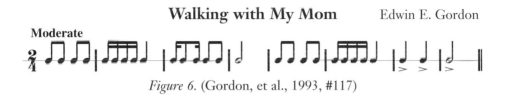

*Figure 6.* (Gordon, et al., 1993, #117)

With each repetition, vary the volume and style of your voice. Whisper the chant, then audiate the chant while maintaining a steady beat. It is during the silence when the students learn to audiate.

Resume chanting aloud. Intersperse four macrobeat patterns of the same meter between repetitions followed by the same length rests to allow for responses from the students.

### INSTRUMENT EXPLORATION

There are a number of benefits to using instruments in the PPI class. A child who is not as comfortable with using his or her voice may be more comfortable demonstrating his or her ability to keep a steady beat on an instrument such as a drum, tambourine, or resonator bell. Musical instruments also add some variety to the environment by exposing children to different timbres. When a child begins to wander around the room it can also act as a focal point to draw the child back to the group.

In the following activity, model the steady beat for the students on D and A resonator bells as you sing the song "Spinning" in Figure 7. Give each child a turn to play the set of bells while you sing and model the beat in front of them or on their shoulders or feet. Some children may have difficulty holding the mallets, while others may attempt to put them in their mouths. Playing resonator bells requires fine motor skill, so this may be difficult for many. This activity may also be done with a drum or tambourine. Children will have greater success with playing a drum or tambourine, as it is easier to strike with the hand, requiring less finely developed motor skill.

## Spinning
Edwin E. Gordon

*Figure* 7. (Gordon, et al., 1993, #11)

*Assimilation*

It is unusual to find young students from the PPI class in the assimilation type of preparatory audiation. In stage six students begin to coordinate their breath with singing or moving. This often occurs between the ages of four and six years in a regular classroom. Because coordination is key to progressing through to stage seven, children in the PPI class who lack coordination often move on to kindergarten before entering into the final stages of preparatory audiation.

**Instructing Your Support Staff**

In a PPI class, teacher aides often assist students throughout the day in all of their activities. It is important to inform the aides of their role in the music room. It is best to meet with the teacher aides before the school year begins so that they understand what is expected of them and the children during music class.

Teacher aides are accustomed to using verbal cues to assist or correct a student's behavior. However, this habit should be adapted for the music class, during which the music should be the only thing heard by the students. Because the music teacher is providing the musical environment solely with his or her voice, it is difficult for the students to listen to the music while someone else is speaking to them and correcting them. Suggest to the aides that they positively reinforce students' behavior using non-verbal cues, such as modeling by the aide or touching and smiling when a good behavior is elicited.

Teacher aides must understand that if a child wanders from the circle or appears to be distracted this does not mean that the child is not listening. Forcing the child back to the circle or into participating could create tension. This tension is more detrimental to listening and learning than off-task behavior. Ask the aide to move to where the student is and model the behavior while sitting next to the child. This may encourage the student to refocus and rejoin the circle.

The teacher and aide may need to develop an individual behavioral plan for each child and each class and continually assess and evaluate the plan. When the teacher aides understand what is expected of them, along with developing an understanding of Music Learning Theory, it will result in a pleasant and productive musical experience for all.

**The Classroom**

Teachers must also consider the physical environment since most music rooms are used for many grade levels. A room with few distractions is best. Equipment should be out of reach of the children. If possible, request time in the schedule to allow for "set-up" and "tear-down." In the Suggestions for Special Education Programs (MAASE, 1989), it is recommended that the classroom for preprimary-age children needs space for active children and for a variety of equipment and materials. Without an environment that is conducive to learning, a teacher with a strong philosophy, excellent techniques, and a well-planned lesson can still encounter difficulty.

**Conclusion**

When teachers have a clear understanding of the nature of a child with special needs and of how to teach to their individual music aptitude differences, music development will occur in the PPI classroom. However, it may take more time, adaptation of activities to accommodate students' special needs, and much patience. Children in the PPI class can make great strides in their music aptitude development and also find much enjoyment in music class. Also, music teachers of children with special needs often find satisfaction and pure joy in seeing (and hearing) the growth of each child.

## References

Gordon, E. E. (2003). *A music learning theory for newborn and young children.* Chicago: GIA Publications.

Gordon, E. E., Bolton, B. M., Hicks, W. H., & Taggart, C. C. (1993). *The early childhood music curriculum: Experimental songs and chants book one.* Chicago: GIA Publications.

Gardner, Howard (1993). *Frames of mind: The theory of multiple intelligences.* New York: Basic Books.

Michigan Association of Administrators in Special Education. (1989). *Suggestions for special education programs.* Oakland Schools, Oakland, MI.

Spady, W. G. (1992). *Master teacher posters* [Poster]. Manhattan, Kansas: MASTER Teacher, Inc.

Valerio, W. H., Reynolds, A. M., Bolton, B. M., Taggart, C. C., & Gordon, E. E. (1998). *Music play: The early childhood curriculum.* Chicago: GIA Publications.

*Cynthia Crump Taggart*
• • • • • • • • • • • • • •
MICHIGAN STATE UNIVERSITY

# Meeting the Musical Needs of All Students in Elementary General Music

## Introduction

Several years ago, I had the opportunity to observe in my son's first-grade classroom. All of the students were hard at work at math, and the teacher was quietly directing the activity from her desk. From a distance, I watched her work with individuals and was struck by the wide range of abilities of the children in her class. One student did not recognize the number thirteen; another was doing two-place multiplication. Neither of those students seemed bored or frustrated by the work, because both were engaged in appropriate tasks for their levels of mathematical skill. The teacher was individualizing instruction to meet the disparate needs of the two students, and, as a result, they were both challenged and learning. Imagine if those two students had been asked to perform the same mathematics task! Either the student who could not recognize the number thirteen would feel lost and frustrated, or the student who could multiply would be bored and might express this boredom through inappropriate classroom behavior. The teacher knew the mathematics potential of the students, their past performances in math, and the difficulty of the tasks that she was asking them to accomplish. As a result, she was able to meet their instructional needs.

As a rule, general music educators are much less aware of the needs of individuals in their classrooms than are other teachers. There are obvious reasons for this, beginning with the limited amount of contact time that most elementary general music teachers have with their students. Many see their students as seldom as once a week for approximately thirty minutes in groups as large as thirty. Diagnosing the needs of individual students and measuring the achievement of those individuals in such a setting may seem impossible. However, as evidenced above, in order to be effective in an educational setting, teachers must know their students well enough to teach to their individual needs; the lack of this in elementary general music has led directly to many of the challenging issues that are facing elementary general music today.

One of those challenging issues is that elementary general music often is not viewed as curricular. Rather, many educational communities see it as an entertaining and desirable "extra" that can be reduced or eliminated entirely in times of budget shortfalls without interfering with the learning that is fundamental in an elementary setting. Music is fundamental. If administrators, classroom teachers, and parents were aware of the curriculum in music, and if music teachers were able to address the achievement of every child in the classroom in terms of curricular expectations, music would be much less at risk (Taggart, 1991). There are children in every music classroom who have the potential to be better at music than at any other subject in school. To deprive these children of appropriate music instruction is to deprive them of their greatest opportunity for achievement. Moreover, every student has some potential to achieve in music. However, if music educators do not know the music potential and achievement of each child, they will never be able to facilitate optimal achievement from their students. In every curricular subject, the achievement of individual students is carefully monitored, and teachers are able to discuss and provide evidence of this achievement in a meaningful way.

Another challenge is the retention of students in school music programs. Typically in elementary school, students are captive audiences; they have no choice but to take music class. However, elementary general music programs often lay the foundation for the desire to participate in school music activities, many of which are optional, throughout their educational careers. If students find their first interactions with music in a school setting to be boring because they are not being appropriately challenged, or frustrating because they are being asked to do things that are too difficult, they will opt out of music participation when it is no longer required. If music teachers choose to teach all children in their classrooms in the same way by "teaching to the middle," boredom and frustration are guaranteed for a large number of students. In fact, nearly half of the children with high music aptitude have chosen not to participate in school music programs at the secondary level (Gordon, 2003). These same children may be engaging in music outside of school in a setting that is more sensitive to their musical needs and desires. By knowing the music potential (music aptitude) and commensurate achievement of every student, music teachers might be able to adapt instruction to meet their individual needs, keeping them engaged so that they see music in the schools as a positive learning experience.

## Music Aptitude

In order to individualize instruction, teachers benefit from knowing the potentials of their students. This is true both in the general academic classroom and in the music classroom. In general academic subjects, teachers have IQ scores, which can be used to determine whether a student is meeting his or her academic potential. If a student is not achieving to the extent that his or her test scores indicate should be possible, some kind of instructional intervention might be appropriate. Perhaps that student, who may have been identified by the teacher as a poor student as a result of poor past achievement, is disengaged. The school needs to help this student re-engage in the educational process through special programs, many of which are available in the schools, or through creative teaching in the regular classroom. The same is true in music. Many students who have high music aptitudes have not had the opportunity to achieve to the extent that their aptitudes would allow. This could be a result of a poor educational environment or lack of home support, and identification of those students might prevent their falling through the cracks of a less-than-ideal educational environment.

Concern that students are being labeled by their aptitude test scores is a hurdle that many teachers face. This is possible if test scores are misused. However, if they are used in an appropriate way, those scores can open the door to improved instruction for all students. A student never should be denied instruction on the basis of an aptitude test score, because test scores are only estimates, and estimates can be inaccurate. Perhaps the student had a bad day on the day of the test as a result of external factors, such as problems at home, poor testing conditions, lack of sleep or food, or any of a myriad of other factors than can affect test results. A bad test day may result in underestimating the potential of a student. Therefore, if a student is achieving more than one might expect on the basis of an aptitude score, it is probable that the aptitude score is inaccurate. In this case, instructional needs and decisions should be based upon past levels of achievement until the student can be re-tested. On the other hand, a high aptitude score does not occur by chance. If a student has a high music aptitude test score and is not achieving in music, something should be done to help that student achieve to the extent to which he or she is capable. Froseth (1971) found that students of all aptitude levels achieved to a greater extent when teachers had the music aptitude scores of their students and used them to adapt instruction to individual needs.

Music aptitude is either developmental or stabilized, depending upon the age of the child. Until a child is approximately nine years old, his or her music aptitudes are affected by the quality of his or her music environment. The better instruction that a child receives in music and the better the musical environment of the child when that child's music aptitude is in the developmental stage, the higher the level of music aptitude a child will have when his or her aptitude stabilizes. Because of this, meeting the educational needs of children in early elementary general music is especially important; the better the music environment for the children throughout elementary general music, the more lifelong potential those children will have for music learning.

Gordon has developed several music aptitude tests, some for developmental music aptitudes and some for stabilized music aptitudes, for preschool children, school-age children, and adults. Figure 1 lists the aptitude tests that have been designed by Gordon, along with the population for which each test was designed, general administration information, and the scores that they yield. All of these tests have been subject to extensive research and have been found to yield educationally valid results. They are available through GIA Publications.[1]

All of the tests shown in Figure 1 yield at least tonal and rhythm subtest scores, and MAP, which provides the most diagnostic information, yields seven subtest scores, three division scores, and a total test score. As rhythm and tonal aptitudes are not highly related, it is possible that a student may have high rhythm aptitude and low tonal aptitude, or vice versa. Few students will have both high tonal and high rhythm or both low tonal and low rhythm aptitudes. The same is true of tonal and rhythm music achievement. A student may have a high level of achievement tonally and be weak rhythmically, or the reverse. In other words, to teach to individual differences, teachers must take into consideration not only the differences in aptitudes and achievement between students but also the strengths and weaknesses within each student.

## Music Achievement

Whereas music aptitude is one's potential to achieve in music, music achievement is what one has actually accomplished. These accomplishments

---

[1] For more information about music aptitude and music aptitude tests, their administration, and their uses, see *Introduction to Research and the Psychology of Music* by E. E. Gordon (Chicago: GIA Publications, 1998).

| Test | Population | Administration Info. | Scores |
|------|-----------|---------------------|--------|
| *Audie* | Three- and four-year-old children | Administered on an individual basis by a familiar adult | Tonal subtest score<br>Rhythm subtest score |
| *Primary Measures of Music Audiation* (PMMA) | Kindergarten through third grade children | Administered in a group or on an individual basis | Tonal subtest score<br>Rhythm subtest score<br>Total test score |
| *Intermediate Measures of Music Audiation* (IMMA) | Children ages six to eleven who have scored high on PMMA | Administered in a group or on an individual basis | Tonal subtest score<br>Rhythm subtest score<br>Total test score |
| *Musical Aptitude Profile* (MAP) | Fourth- through twelfth-grade children | Administered in a group or on an individual basis | Melody subtest score<br>Harmony subtest score<br>Tonal score<br>Tempo subtest score<br>Meter subtest score<br>Rhythm Imagery score<br>Phrasing subtest score<br>Balance subtest score<br>Style subtest score<br>Music Sensitivity score<br>Total test score |
| *Advanced Measures of Music Audiation* (AMMA) | High school and college/university students | Administered in a group or on an individual basis | Tonal subtest score<br>Rhythm subtest score<br>Total test score |

*Figure 1.* Music aptitude tests

are a result of one's aptitude, the instruction that one receives, how hard one works, and many other factors. For a teacher, knowledge of each student's levels of music achievement is essential in order to individualize instruction.

In all subjects, appropriate instruction requires knowledge of readiness for specific learning tasks. A language teacher would never ask a student to diagram the parts of a written sentence if the student being asked was unable to speak, did not know the meaning of the words in the sentence, and was unable to read. That student simply would not have the readiness with which to approach the task successfully. A math teacher would never ask a student to solve for $16^2$ unless the student could add and could do easier, one-digit multiplication. Again, those are readiness for success with the task. Readiness exists in general music, too. For example, a student should not be asked to read music unless they have a large listening vocabulary and performance vocabulary. Yet general music teachers often are aware more of the general achievement level of a class than of the achievement levels (readiness levels) of individuals within the class. Some students in the class may find what is being taught to be too easy; these students need additional challenges. Others may be struggling with or not ready for certain curricular goals and have given up trying to achieve them.

When a teacher knows the achievement levels of the individuals in the classroom, that teacher will also know what the students, as individuals, need next in terms of instruction. However, the only way that music teachers will really know the achievement levels of their students is to measure those levels on an individual basis. Although this sounds daunting because of lack of instructional time and large numbers of students, it is possible to accomplish without disrupting instruction. Most measurement can occur in the context of regular activities within music classes with the use of rating scales and an appropriate record-keeping system. Following is an example of how that might be approached.

One curricular goal that an elementary general music teacher should measure is a student's ability to sing. In fact, MENC, in the National Standards for Music Education, has identified singing as Content Standard One of the nine content standards in elementary general music (MENC, 1994). Singing should be central to effective elementary general music instruction. However, by asking the class to sing as an ensemble, a teacher will never know the singing achievement of individuals in the classroom. Even by asking two students to sing in unison, a teacher can not be sure of the singing achievement of either, because one student may be split-second imitating the other rather than demonstrating the ability to audiate and perform the song independently. Only by asking students to perform alone can the teacher really know how well each student can sing.

Asking students to sing alone can be incorporated into a regular classroom game. For example, the traditional game song "Who's That Tapping at the Window?" can be used as a vehicle to measure singing achievement. Either the teacher or a student who is a confident singer could sing the first two phrases ("Who's that tapping at the window? Who's that tapping at the door?"). At the end of the first two phrases, that teacher or student could drop a bean bag in the lap of another student, who should then sing the last two phrases of the song ("Student's name's tapping at the window. Student's name's tapping at the door.") This game should be repeated as a part of several consecutive class periods until the teacher has heard every student sing alone. As the students sing individually, the teacher should be keeping a record of how well each student sings, using a continuous rating scale to guide what is recorded.

A continuous rating scale for singing would be a list of five descriptors of a student's singing behavior from the least to the most sophisticated, which could be used to identify a student's level of performance. For instance, such a rating scale for singing appears below.

1. The student performs in a speaking voice with lack of vocal contour.
2. The student maintains the contour of the song but performs inaccurate pitches.
3. The student sings part of the song on the correct pitches but is unable to maintain that for the entire song.
4. The student sings the correct pitches with minor flaws in intonation.
5. The student sings the entire song with correct pitches and accurate intonation.

The least advanced behavior would be that a student speaks with no contour rather than sings, and the most advanced would be that the student sings the entire song with correct pitches and accurate intonation. Whether a student uses an in-tune singing voice is not a yes or no question but rather a matter of degree. Students pass through a developmental process as they become confident, in-tune singers. That process is reflected in the rating scale, as it should be in all rating scales that help guide instruction. As the teacher listens to the students sing during the game, the teacher should rate each performance and mark the students' performance levels in a grade book or on a record-keeping sheet. As a result, the teacher will have information to use when planning future instruction. In the future, those students who sing well might be asked to sing in parts or might be given more difficult singing tasks to perform. Those students who have not found their singing voices will need to continue to become acculturated into singing.

Equivalent continuous rating scales can be developed for measuring other musical behaviors.[2] If a teacher commits a portion of each class period

---

[2] For more information about rating scales and their uses, see *Rating Scales and Their Uses for Measuring and Evaluating Achievement in Music Performance* by E. E. Gordon (Chicago: GIA Publications, 2002).

to measuring the music achievement of individual students in the context of regular Classroom Activities, that teacher will learn a tremendous amount about the individuals in his or her classroom. In addition to using this information for adapting instruction to the needs of individuals, it also can be communicated to parents, to other teachers, and to administrators, who, as a result, will be less likely to see music as a "frill" or "entertainment." Unfortunately, measuring the achievement of every curricular objective for every grade level may not be practical. However, measuring those achievements that will be most useful in informing the path of future instruction should be central to every general music classroom.

## Teaching Ideas That Allow for Individualized Instruction

### Learning Sequence Activities

Adapting instruction to meet the needs of individual students is built in to Gordon's Music Learning Theory through the inclusion of Learning Sequence Activities at the beginning of every class period. Learning Sequence Activities and Classroom Activities are the two primary components of Music Learning Theory, and together they constitute a whole-part-whole approach to music instruction. Typically, Learning Sequence Activities take place for no more than five to ten minutes at the beginning of a class period, and children participate in Classroom Activities for the remaining time. In Classroom Activities, students experience the "whole" of music; they sing, chant, move, play instruments, listen, and engage in the myriad of other activities that are a part of a typical elementary general music classroom. Through Classroom Activities, music is experienced in a holistic way, and children are introduced to tonalities and meters (the content of music) in a holistic setting. Without Classroom Activities, Learning Sequence Activities would have little value.

Learning Sequence Activities are the "part" of the whole-part-whole approach and are the vehicle for students to begin to learn formal music skills, such as associating solfege, labeling tonality and meter, reading music, and creating/improvising. During Learning Sequence Activities, children take the types of musical patterns that they have experienced in a holistic context during Classroom Activities and apply different skills to the musical content that they have already heard and performed. The audiation of tonal patterns and rhythm patterns is fundamental to Music Learning Theory, as the organization of tonal patterns within a tonality and rhythm patterns within a meter is what allows a person to give meaning to music. The patterns incorporated into Learning Sequence Activities are not drawn directly from the literature that is being experienced in Classroom Activities. Rather, the connection between Classroom Activities and Learning Sequence Activities is more general in nature. Students should not be learning Major or Minor patterns in Learning Sequence Activities unless they have developed a substantial repertoire of Major and Minor songs during Classroom Activities. Likewise, students should not be learning Duple or Triple patterns in Learning Sequence Activities unless they have developed a substantial repertoire of Duple and Triple songs during Classroom Activities. Once students have learned skills in Learning Sequence Activities, they can apply those skills, as well as their deepened knowledge of content, back to Classroom Activities. As a result, Classroom Activities can become more sophisticated and can be approached with greater understanding.

Teaching to individual differences occurs naturally in Learning Sequence Activities if they are taught according to Gordon's directions (Gordon, 2001). In Learning Sequence Activities, students are asked to perform tonal patterns or rhythm patterns, sometimes without and sometimes with syllables, sometimes from notation and sometimes from audiation, depending upon the level of the skill learning sequence in which the students are engaged. All students are learning the same skill. However, the more-advanced students engage in that skill with a larger vocabulary of patterns.

Each lesson in Learning Sequence Activities includes patterns of three difficulty levels. All students learn the easy pattern first. When a student successfully performs the easy pattern with the teacher and then alone, that student moves on to the moderately difficult pattern. When a student can successfully perform the moderately difficult pattern, he or she moves on to the difficult one. Some students with less developed skills may never progress past the easy pattern, and other more advanced students may learn all three. When approximately 80% of the students have accomplished the pattern at the difficulty level that is appropriate for their level of aptitude (low aptitude students performing the easy pattern, medium aptitude students performing the moderately difficult pattern, and high aptitude students performing the difficult pattern), the teacher should move on to the next lesson. However, teachers must always remember that aptitude scores are merely an approximation and could be wrong. Therefore, although aptitude scores are useful guides in most situations, if a student with a low aptitude score performs the easy pattern accurately, that student should be given the opportunity to progress to the moderate and even difficult patterns. A student should never be held back on the basis of an aptitude score, as it is possible that the aptitude score is not representative of the student's real potential. Because high-achieving students are developing a larger vocabulary than low-achieving students, they do not become bored, and because all students are learning the same skills, students who are not achieving at as high a level do not fall behind and become frustrated.

*Layering Lessons*

Individualizing instruction can also be accomplished with Classroom Activities that are designed so that they have multiple layers, each with different levels of difficulty. These types of activities have been used for years, for example in the form of multi-part tonebar instrument arrangements, but not always to best advantage. Often teachers have tried to teach all parts to all students, rather than asking specific students to learn the parts that are most appropriate for their levels of music development and achievement. With multi-part activities in which the parts are distributed according to the educational needs of individual students, all students benefit. All students can be given challenging but accessible parts, and students with less developed skills have the opportunity to observe the musical role models presented by the more developed students who are performing parts with high levels of difficulty.

In choosing parts to assign to specific students, several things should be taken into consideration. First, teachers must know the difficulty of each part, which is not always immediately evident. For example, beginning instrumental method books traditionally have had students begin by playing whole notes followed by a whole rest. Oddly, this is one of the most difficult tasks for a young musician to accomplish with accuracy. Although it is true that articulating and holding a single pitch may be less difficult from a technical or executive skills perspective, audiationally the task is extremely difficult. In order to perform a whole note with rhythmic accuracy, a student must have internalized macrobeats and microbeats and a consistent tempo. Audiationally, performing eighth-note microbeats is much less difficult. Consider a tonebar arrangement with a whole-note bordun, a quarter-note (macrobeat) parallel bordun, and an alternating eighth-note (microbeat) ostinato to accompany a melody. Although the microbeat ostinato is somewhat more difficult technically, as the students are being asked to alternate mallets rather than use parallel motion, that same ostinato is the least difficult to audiate, as the microbeats and macrobeats are outwardly evident as a part of the ostinato. The macrobeat bordun, although physically easy, requires the students to audiate microbeats to prevent rushing, and the whole note bordun is extremely difficult to audiate, as the students must audiate microbeats and macrobeats through space and time in order to know when to play the next pitch. In this case, students with the least developed rhythmic skills should be asked to perform the eighth-note ostinato, students with moderately developed skills should be asked to perform the quarter-note ostinato, and students with the highest level of skill development should be asked to perform whole notes. Audiational difficulty should take precedence over technical difficulty when assigning parts, because, even if a student has the physical coordination to perform a part, unless that student is able to audiate the part, he or she will be unable to attach the physical coordination to the audiation, which is requisite for an accurate performance.

Second, music teachers must know the music aptitude and achievement levels of their students when assigning parts. Often students' musical achievements will reflect their music aptitudes, but this is not always the case. As previously stated, sometimes students with high levels of aptitude have never had the opportunity to achieve or have chosen not to achieve in music. Because high levels of aptitude are not always reflected in high levels of achievement, knowledge of both is essential and should be considered. Even if a high-aptitude student has not demonstrated high levels of achievement in the past, that student should be given challenging opportunities. It is possible that the student is choosing not to participate or achieve as a result of boredom, which could be alleviated through an appropriate challenge.

Multi-part activities should be taught over several class periods, as they require extended instruction and time to develop. Consider again the tonebar instrument arrangement described above. In the first class period, the most basic elements of the lesson should be taught, such as the song and perhaps movement to macrobeats in parallel motion and microbeats in alternating motion to prepare the students for tonebar instrument performance. All students should be taught to move to macrobeats and microbeats, as this enables them to audiate meter. In the next class period, the microbeat ostinato could be transferred to the instruments, giving everyone a chance to perform. By assigning students who have higher levels of aptitude and achievement to the instruments first, the other students will have an opportunity to see the ostinato performed correctly, and the stronger students will be challenged to perform something that they have not seen demonstrated by others. Then other students can be moved to the instruments and can be shown how to perform the ostinatos by those who have already performed them successfully.

The macrobeat bordun might be introduced in the same class period or saved until the next, depending upon the flow of the class period. Only those students who have successfully performed the microbeat ostinato should be moved forward to perform the macrobeat bordun. Just as students worked their way through the easy pattern to the moderate pattern to the difficult pattern in Learning Sequence Activities, students can work their way through the parts in a multi-part arrangement. However, students who are still struggling with the microbeat bordun should continue to work on that before moving on to the more difficult tasks for which they have demonstrated that they do not have the readiness. Through the use of multi-part activities, students can be asked to perform those tasks that they have the readiness to learn and can be given the opportunity to observe those skills they will be ready to learn in the future.

*Creativity*

If children are to develop into fluent and independent musicians, they must be given opportunities to create and improvise. Through such activities, children solidify what they know musically by learning to manipulate it and apply it in new ways. Creative activities can also give the teacher a window into what individuals in their classrooms really "own" in terms of musical knowledge. What children incorporate into their musical creations will reflect directly their musical vocabularies and levels of musical understanding. In addition, children who are engaging in creative activities naturally gravitate toward the levels of difficulty that they need to facilitate their musical growth. Given a choice, they will do what is fun and interesting for them. The strongest students will usually try to challenge themselves to create something that is musically complex and reflects their capabilities, while the less accomplished students will work at the level at which they can be successful. The challenge for the teacher is to design creative activities that allow for some level of success on the part of all students.

Rhythm improvisation activities can be used to create an environment in which all students can work according to their levels of rhythmic development. Consider the following activity adapted from *Jump Right In: The Music Curriculum, Teacher's Guide Book 2* (Bolton, et al., 2001). Prior to engaging in this activity, the students should have had many opportunities to echo patterns performed by the teacher so that they have a vocabulary of rhythm patterns to use in their improvisations. They also should have heard and had the opportunity to perform a repertoire of songs and chants in Duple and Triple meters. The teacher performs the chant as follows:

138

"Hickety, Pickety Bumble Bee, can you chant a pattern for me?" The students respond either as a group or in solo by chanting a four-macrobeat pattern in response. Those students who have large rhythm vocabularies and a developed sense of meter and tempo will reflect them in their improvisations. Others with a less-developed vocabulary may simply perform macrobeats and microbeats in the appropriate meter and tempo. Still others may not have a sense of meter or tempo and may chant rhythms that do not represent the rhythmic context established by the teacher.

Having the students perform alone will provide the teacher with more information than having them create or improvise in a group. When students perform alone, the teacher can get clear insights into the achievement level of each student, which can, in turn, be used to improve instruction. If a student is able to create a complex four-macrobeat pattern in the "Hickety Pickety" activity, the next time the teacher might impose specific guidelines on the student in terms of the rhythm functions of the patterns to be used in improvisation. If the student had the readiness in place, he or she could even be asked to improvise using rhythm syllables rather than using a neutral syllable. Likewise, a student who was unable to improvise in the established meter needs different instructional techniques to help develop metric audiation. Rating scales can be used to keep records of the characteristics of the students' improvisations so that the teacher can remember the achievement levels of the students and can adapt instruction so that it better meets their needs over time.

*Solo performance*

The only way of truly knowing students' capabilities in music is to have them demonstrate those capabilities through solo performance. Consider instruction in an "academic" subject. Teachers would not measure the ability of students to read aloud by having the students read passages aloud as a group. Some students might not be able to read at all but may be skilled in imitating what is said by a student sitting nearby. Therefore, assuming that all students could read based upon their saying the words together would be misleading. Only by having students read alone is the teacher able to diagnose accurately the strengths and weaknesses of individual students in reading aloud. In math, teachers ask individual children to solve problems on a regular basis without the help of other students. Although group work is beneficial from a curricular standpoint because students learn from one another as they work together, measurement of what has been learned usually takes place on an individual basis. Yet in elementary general music children tend to sing, play, and move in groups and rarely perform alone. Because of this, it is not surprising that music teachers may not be fully aware of the abilities of the individuals in their classrooms.

Providing opportunities for children to perform alone during Classroom Activities may be time-consuming, but the time is well spent from an educational perspective. Several benefits follow naturally from solo performance. First, the teacher has an opportunity to hear what individuals are capable of performing, and, as a result, he or she will be able to diagnose the musical needs of the students to enhance future instruction. If a student struggles with an assigned task, the teacher knows that the student lacks the readiness to accomplish what is being asked. As a result, the teacher should determine what readinesses are missing and help to provide the student with opportunities to develop those readinesses. If a student finds the assigned task easy, the teacher knows that the student needs to be challenged with more difficult tasks in the future to prevent boredom and maximize achievement. This can be challenging for the teacher because he or she often must adapt instruction in the course of teaching, which requires a high degree of musicianship as well as teaching skill and flexibility. Second, asking children to perform alone allows teachers to give students of differing achievement levels tasks of differing difficulty levels according to their needs. No two students need to be given the same task. Those who need to be challenged can be challenged with difficult tasks, and those who need remedial help can be given easy tasks to provide a foundation upon which to build future music achievement. Third, students benefit from hearing themselves perform in solo. Often students are surprised by how they sound when performing alone because they have not paid especially careful attention to their personal performances as a member of a group. By performing alone, they are forced to accept responsibility for their musicianship, and, as a result, become more aware of their musical skills.

Many teachers are reluctant to ask children to perform alone; they are concerned that children will be nervous about performing in front of peers and will dislike music as a result. Teachers may also carry the additional baggage of having experienced performance anxiety themselves during their educational career and may project those feelings onto their students. Asking children to sing alone for the first time in mid- to upper-elementary school certainly will generate resistance from students. However, solo performance does not need to feel threatening if it is made a regular part of music instruction from the very beginning and if the teacher creates a welcoming environment in which all performances, including those of the teacher, represent an opportunity to learn. Most kindergarten and first grade students are excited about performing alone and will volunteer to do so with joy. If students get used to singing in solo as a part of every class period, singing alone will be part of the expected routine of music class in the same way that reading a passage out loud for the rest of the class is part of language arts and solving a problem at the board is part of math. Children expect to do these things and do not resist. If the environment in music class is primarily one of singing, rather than talking, the students will settle in and participate in that environment. In fact, the teacher should consider singing rather than speaking instructions to students. These can be sung on the resting tone of the song being learned at the time. This is helpful in several respects besides immersing children in singing; it reinforces the tonic for students, which facilitates tonal audiation, and promotes vocal health for the teacher. One of the most taxing things that a teacher can do vocally is alternate between speaking and singing. If a teacher is using his or her singing voice in a vocally healthy manner, singing all of the time rather than both singing and speaking will result in less vocal fatigue.

Even with solo singing being a regular part of every class, some children may be reluctant to sing alone. If this is the case, students should not be forced. Rather, they can be paired with another strong student so that they can perform in a duet rather than in solo. This may make the student feel more confident the next time. Also, at first students should not be asked to sing entire songs, but rather short patterns or portions of songs. Most will find this much less intimidating. Finally, rather than asking for volunteers to perform, who may be few and far between in the upper grades, the teacher can incorporate solo singing into a game-like format in which children get "chosen." This makes the whole experience more playful. For example, one might pass a bean bag around the circle, possibly to macrobeats, as students sing a song. The student who has the bean bag when the song ends should echo a pattern that is performed by the teacher. If the student chooses not to echo, the teacher should wait for the time that it would normally take to perform the pattern, so that the students who are audiating the echo can do so. Then the class should sing the song and pass the bean bag again without making an issue of the student's choice not to sing.

## Conclusions

Music teachers must engage children in instruction that is appropriate for them as individuals. Unless they do so, they are not meeting the educational needs of their students and, as a result, are not providing the best possible instruction. Fortunately, for most teachers, this is possible with only minor adjustments to the typical course of instruction. First, teachers must measure the music aptitudes of their students. This can be accomplished using a valid music aptitude test. Second, the teacher should make measuring the achievement of individual students a regular part of every class period in the context of regular Classroom Activities. Using rating scales and manageable record-keeping systems will facilitate this process. Once this is accomplished, teachers have most of the information needed to tailor instruction to specific students according to their musical needs. This can be approached using Learning Sequence Activities, layering difficulty levels within a lesson, incorporating creative activities, and encouraging solo performance.

Individualizing instruction is essential if music educators are going to be viewed as professionals. Even more important, though, music educators must individualize instruction if they want to maximize their students' learning in music and provide them with the best possible educational experience. Until this is the case, music programs will continue to be at risk, and probably with good reason.[3]

## References

Bolton, B. M., Taggart, C. C., Reynolds, A. M., Valerio, W. H., & Gordon, E. E. (2001). *Jump right in: The music curriculum, teacher's guide, Book 2*. Chicago: GIA Publications.

Froseth, J. (1971). Using MAP scores in the instruction of beginning students in instrumental music. *Journal of Research in Music Education, 19*, 98-105.

Gordon, E. E. (2001). *Jump right in: The music curriculum: Reference handbook for using Learning Sequence Activities* (Rev. ed.). Chicago: GIA Publications.

——. (2003). *Learning sequences in music: Skill, content, and patterns*. Chicago: GIA Publications.

Lehman, P. R., Hinckley, J., Hoffer, C., Lindeman, C., Reimer, B., Shuler, S., & Straub, D. (Eds). (1994). *The school music program: A new vision*. Reston, VA: MENC.

Taggart, C. (1991). Our role in educating the educational community. *General Music Today*, 14-17.

---

[3] Portions of this chapter first appeared in the *Michigan Music Educator*.

*Diane M. Lange*

UNIVERSITY OF TEXAS AT ARLINGTON

# Combining Music Learning Theory and Orff in the General Music Classroom

## Music Learning Theory and Orff Schulwerk Combined

Earlier in my career, I taught using an eclectic combination of music teaching approaches, mainly using Orff with a little Kodály and Dalcroze thrown in. A typical lesson plan included beginning with echo-singing, echo-playing, or echo-clapping, depending on the activity to follow. For example, if the students were to sing a song in Minor, I would echo-sing the phrases from the song using solfege and hand signs as a way of introducing it to the students. Then, the students would learn one instrument part for the song and all perform that part. Following the instrument portion of the class period, I would teach or reinforce a repertoire song, such as a patriotic song or play-party song. The lesson would conclude with a movement activity or a culmination activity for an earlier-learned song.

Although I believed that the children were learning music, as time went on, I felt uneasy about what I was doing. Something was missing from my curriculum, but I did not know what it was. Part of my uneasiness stemmed from my concerns that I was just teaching a bunch of songs, with no attention to the order in which skills were taught. I made sure that every concept for that grade level was introduced, but I introduced them in no particular order. For assessment, I kept track of performance abilities, such as who could keep a steady beat, echo a simple pattern, or sing in tune. I believed that I was accurately documenting learning and helping my

143

students to improve, and to some extent I was. Unfortunately, in retrospect, I have come to realize that I was not teaching my students to be independent musicians to the extent that I could have.

It was not until I encountered the writings of Edwin Gordon in textbooks and attended several workshops that I discovered Music Learning Theory. Still, I was skeptical about teaching patterns from a book that did not relate directly to the song repertoire I was teaching. I was also skeptical about giving aptitude tests. I thought that I could tell who my high and low aptitude students were without using a test. So, I decided to do my own mini-research experiment with my students to see if they improved as much as the workshop instructor had described. I divided my six second-grade classes into two groups. The only thing that I changed in my teaching was the beginning of each class period. Three of the classes received echo-clapping or echo-singing like I had taught before, and the other three received Learning Sequence Activity instruction. As a result of what I observed during this experiment, I was convinced of the value of Learning Sequence Activities. The lesson plans of those classes and the students' musicianship reflected the skills learned in Learning Sequence Activities, and the students responded well to the new type of instruction, both in terms of achievement and attitude.

After that experiment, which lasted six weeks, I began using Learning Sequence Activities with all of my classes instead of echo-clapping, echo-singing, or echo-playing. The amazing thing is that the rest of my classroom activities did not change; however, now my lessons followed a logical sequence as articulated by Gordon in his Music Learning Theory.

When I combined Music Learning Theory with my existing Orff approach, I found that it was a natural combination. The sequencing of Music Learning Theory and the teaching process of Orff worked logically together and helped me to organize my curriculum and sequentially teach skills and concepts. By incorporating Music Learning Theory, my classes had structure, and the musicianship of my students increased.

## Music Learning Theory

Music Learning Theory is a theory of how children learn music. Its application has two parts: Learning Sequence Activities and Classroom Activities. These parts are included in the whole-part-whole learning process that is described below:

Whole – Classroom Activities. Learning content (songs, chants, dances) in a natural setting and holistic way.

144

Part –    Learning Sequence Activities. Pattern instruction to develop skills and vocabulary outside of a "traditional" music context.

Whole – Classroom Activities. Application of what was learned in Learning Sequence Activities to musical repertoire and activities.

In Learning Sequence Activities, children learn new skills (i.e., solfege and reading music), and all new skills are introduced first in Learning Sequence Activities. In Classroom Activities, content, such as Major and Minor tonalities and Duple and Triple meters, is taught and reinforced through songs, chants, and other musical repertoire. Learning Sequence Activities should last for approximately five to seven minutes per class period. So, in a thirty minute class period, no less than twenty-three minutes will be devoted to Classroom Activities, the whole in the whole-part-whole learning process.

## Orff Schulwerk

Orff Schulwerk is a *learning by doing* approach to music education that introduces skills and music concepts to children while actively involving them in movement, speech, singing, playing instruments, and creating music (Ferguson, 1988). Orff called his music *elemental*, meaning that materials used to make music should be simple, basic, natural, and close to the child's world of thought and fantasy.

This learning by doing approach is a strength of Orff Schulwerk. Actively involving children in the process of music making is one of many things that Orff teachers do well. The process involves breaking down the whole into parts. These parts should be logically taught to everyone over a period of time and then be put back into the whole. This whole-part-whole learning process that Music Learning Theory has as a central part of its larger structure is used to teach individual pieces in the Orff approach to teaching music. Jos Wuytack (1990) advocates using the whole-part-whole learning process. He demonstrates teaching a song or poem as beginning with the totality and breaking the total into parts, then returning to the totality in a musical form. The following is an example of the process used to teach the song "Poor Old Crow" using the Orff process combined with Music Learning Theory (see Appendix A).

### Day One:

1. Introduce the song through movement. Have the students continuously move with scarves while the teacher sings the song without text. (The text of this song is difficult, so I chose not to use it.)

145

**Day Two:**

1. Sing the song without text.
2. Have the students mirror the teacher using body percussion to prepare them to play the instruments.
3. Reinforce body percussion using a paper xylophone. The teacher demonstrates the pattern with mallets on the paper xylophone while the students sing the instrument part and do the body percussion.
4. Model the part on the instrument.
5. Have the students work with partners sharing an instrument. This works well in terms of classroom management and compensates for a shortage of instruments.

**Day Three:**

1. Teacher sings the song again.
2. Teacher demonstrates unpitched instrument parts using beat-function rhythm syllables and body percussion.
3. Transfer body percussion to guiro and wood block or temple blocks.

**Day Four:**

1. Teacher sings the song again.
2. Teacher reviews all instrument parts with the students.
3. Sing the song with complete orchestration and have the those students who are not playing an instrument move continuously with scarves.

All of the students learn all of the instrument parts that they are capable of learning. At one of my choir concerts, my bass xylophone player was sick and unable to attend the performance. When the other students found out that he was not going to be at the concert, fifteen to twenty students begged to "fill in" for him. Everyone knew how to play his part, which was macrobeats on a C and G, and had previously performed it in rehearsal. The only fair way to solve the problem was to draw a name. However, if one is to truly individualize instruction, all students will not be able to play all of the parts. You might orchestrate the difficult instrument parts for the glockenspiel or soprano xylophone, as these parts add color and texture to an existing Orff ensemble and can be deleted if necessary. If the high aptitude students who play those difficult parts are absent from a performance, the Orff ensemble would sound fine without those students. It is comforting to have a performance that does not rely on a handful of students for its success. If the musical process is taught properly and instrumental instruction is individualized, many students can play most parts. However, at the same time you are providing challenges for those students who need them.

Lesson plans that combine the Orff process and Music Learning Theory are logical, easy to create, and sequential. Introducing music concepts and skills is simple when you follow the sequence laid out by Music Learning Theory. Once a skill has been introduced at the appropriate time in Learning Sequence Activities, the sequential teaching from simple to complex, called the Orff process, is used to reinforce that skill during Classroom Activities using traditional Orff repertoire. The following is an example of an aural/oral or first grade lesson plan combining both Orff and Music Learning Theory.

1.  "Hello, Everybody": Major/Duple
    Use a song such as this to begin each music class to provide a sense of routine.
2.  Learning Sequence Activities: Tonal Unit 1, Section A, Criterion C
    These tonal patterns in D Major should be sung using the neutral syllable "bum." Pattern instruction should last approximately five to seven minutes and include many students singing individually and the whole class singing in unison.
3.  "Old Joe Clark" (no text): Mixolydian/Triple
    Use rhythm sticks with this song to reinforce macrobeats and microbeats and as a readiness for mallet performance.
4.  "A-B-A" (American Orff Edition II, p. 46): Major/Duple
    This activity focuses on creativity. The objective is for students to create their own Duple patterns. Have students create and chant Duple patterns as a large group and individually between performances of the song.
5.  "Canoe Song": Minor/Duple
    The objective of this song is to have students accurately perform macrobeats or simple bordun on tonebar instruments. Prior to the students playing the instruments, have them pantomime paddling in a canoe to macrobeats.
6.  Rhythm Conversation in Triple with Puppets
    Many times younger students will be willing to sing to a puppet when they are reluctant to sing to an adult. Using the neutral syllable "bah," the teacher can have a triple conversation between two puppets and individual students and a puppet.

7. "Yonder Stands a Handsome Lady" (no text): Dorian/Duple
    This activity focuses on the resting tone and uses bean bags as a way to achieve student performance of resting tone. The teacher has one bean bag and stops singing at various spots during song performance. During the pause, the teacher tosses the bean bag to a student. That student sings the resting tone and tosses the bean bag back to the teacher.

8. "Sally Go Round the Sun": Major/Triple
    This song can be taught as a circle dance. Without giving verbal directions, the teacher performs the dance while everyone holds hands. For the first phrase, walk to the right; for the second phrase, walk to the left; for the third phrase, walk toward the center; and for the last phrase; walk back out to the original starting circle.

9. "Who Stole My Chickens and My Hens?": Major/Duple
    This a fun activity to use at the end of the music class. During the rests in the song, clap, snap, stomp, click, or perform any other appropriate movement created by the students.

10. "Goodbye, Everybody": Major/Duple
    This song uses the same melody as "Hello, Everybody." Have groups of students or individuals sing the resting tone before lining up at the door.

This lesson plan includes elements of both the Orff approach and Music Learning Theory. The differences from a typical Orff lesson are that a) the Learning Sequence Activity has replaced echo sing, b) a neutral syllable is used with both tonal patterns and Triple conversation rather than solfege, and c) an activity focuses on the audiation of resting tone. The similarities with a typical Orff lesson include a) students used rhythm sticks as a readiness for tonebar instrument performance, b) students were asked to engage in creative activity, c) students played a simple bordun on tonebar instruments, and d) students engaged in a singing game at the end of the lesson. The next music class would look similar because much of the lesson plan would remain intact. During each class period, the teacher would rotate concepts and skills in and out to thoroughly, logically, and sequentially teach the students music.

**Tonalities**

The pentatonic scale is used in Orff Schulwerk for a variety of reasons. First, there are no dissonances or tensions in pentatonic, so it is easier for children to improvise on the tonebar instruments in this context. Half steps and strong harmonic underpinnings create the tension in most tonalities, and these are not present in the pentatonic tonal system. Orff believed that a pentatonic scale created a feeling of openness that is stress-free and encourages student creativity. Second, Orff described the pentatonic scale as a universal language for children and believed that every culture in the world has folk music that is written in pentatonic. In the original five volumes of the Schulwerk, pentatonic is introduced in Book I before both Major and Minor.

Orff Schulwerk uses the pentatonic scale because it is useful for instrument performance, especially for playing bordun patterns and for risk-free improvisation. However, diatonic songs with underlying tonic function appearing on the strong beats of the measures work as well with borduns as do pentatonic songs. Plus, students need to experience both diatonic and pentatonic melodies. In fact, Gordon (2003) believes that pentatonic melodies should not be introduced until students have experienced diatonic music, because "the audiation of a tonality is typically imposed on pentatonic by listeners and performers as a result of their familiarity with Major and Harmonic Minor tonalities" (p. 157). Teachers of Orff Schulwerk teach their students six pentatonic scales, three Major and three Minor. But, without half steps, any of the five notes of these pentatonic scales could function as the resting tone. Further, teachers have heard many songs in Major and Minor; therefore, they can impose a tonality upon a pentatonic song and audiate one pitch as the resting tone. However, students have not had as much exposure to music and often cannot audiate the resting tone in pentatonic as a result of this more limited experience with Major and especially Minor tonalities. Therefore, students need to experience diatonic music and, when they do experience pentatonic songs, identification of the resting tone by the teacher is essential in order to help the students develop their tonal audiation skills rather than simply imitate.

Diatonic melodies are beautiful and can easily be orchestrated. For example, the folk song "Taking Gair in the Night" is a Dorian melody in Triple meter. The broken bordun works well with the triangle and glockenspiel, adding color and tension in the appropriate areas. Further, this song could be expanded into ABA form with the B section being Triple patterns or question and answer on unpitched instruments in Triple meter (see Appendix B).

The latest trend of American Orff teachers is to orchestrate diatonic melodies, primarily American folk music, and not all of this folk music is Major or Minor. Many songs are in Dorian, Mixolydian, Lydian, and some Phrygian. Use of these tonalities has been one of the central tenets of Music Learning Theory for many years.

## Improvisation and Creativity

Improvisation and creation are at the center of the Orff Schulwerk philosophy. Carl Orff and Gunild Keetman wrote five volumes, "Music for Children" (the original Schulwerk), as exercises for children. These volumes "provide us with exercises in speech, rhythm, melody, and harmony, all of which serve as guidelines to a sequential development of musical concepts" (Warner, 1991, p. 6). These exercises are a readiness for improvisation, because imitative experiences are the roots of improvisation (Steen, 1982). Steen further believes that a teacher who uses the Orff approach "can guide the child to more structured improvisation experiences which, through rediscovery and exploration, allow the child to build concepts and skills which lead to maturing musical choices" (p. 71).

Unfortunately, many Orff teachers believe that they are teaching creativity and improvisation when, in fact, they are teaching instrumental exploration and some improvisation. Kindergarten and first-grade students typically are exploring tonebar instruments, not improvising on them. On the other hand, fifth-grade students performing questions and answers with a sense of syntax are improvising. Improvisation involves audiation, comprehension of the musical progression, and an immediate reaction within specific restrictions. With creation and improvisation, students must hear their creations and improvisations in their heads a split second before they externally realize them. This is not the case with exploration. As an example, a teacher might ask students to create questions and answers for eight macrobeats in C Major. If a student is playing the question, that student might be told that he or she may not end on the resting tone, and if the student is playing the answer, that student might be told that he or she must end on the resting tone. When teachers place restrictions on children's creations, they become improvisations. When there are no restrictions placed on students, it is creativity. Therefore, Orff teachers need to understand that they are teaching exploration as a readiness for improvisation and should be aware of the differences between exploration and creativity and improvisation.

## Tonal Solfege

Most Orff teachers use tonal solfege with their students. Many use the syllables with the Curwen hand signs at an early age, usually during first grade. By doing this, a crucial step is missing in the learning process, that being singing using a neutral syllable before adding solfege. Gordon would say that Orff teachers are going straight to verbal association without providing the necessary aural/oral readiness. If Orff teachers would add

Learning Sequence Activities to their lessons, students would learn the sound before adding the syllables, and would know when students have the readiness to add the syllables. Additionally, using the Curwen hand signs is a crutch for students and allows them to imitate instead of audiate. Hand signs are a kind of iconic notation that Gordon believes is unnecessary.

## Rhythm

One fundamental difference between Music Learning Theory and Orff Schulwerk is the approach to teaching rhythm and meter. Orff uses a mnemonic approach, and Music Learning Theory uses a syllable system that is based upon beat function. The mnemonic approach uses words to teach durations or rhythm patterns. Notation of the words evolve out of speech and usually relate in some way to the words of the song. For instance, the mnemonic ostinato for the song "Are You Sleeping" could be "Wake Up Brother John." The words "wake," "up," and "John" are used to represent a quarter note and "brother" is used to represent two eighth notes. Usually, the mnemonic ostinato is taught by rote first through speech, then body percussion, and then transferred to instruments. If notation is used to teach the ostinato, the rhythm patterns would be associated with the mnemonic words rather than the meter or beat function. However, the mnemonic ostinato, "Wake Up Brother John," cannot be generalized to the song "Hot Cross Buns" because it does not relate to the text of the song. Further, this approach cannot be generalized to all rhythm patterns without creating new words or phrases because the mnemonic words are not always consistent with each note value. A quarter note can be any word that is one syllable.

Most Orff teachers use both mnemonics and the Kodály system for teaching rhythm and meter. However, the Kodály rhythm syllable system is based on note values rather than beat function. So when students chant eighth notes, saying Ti-Ti Ti-Ti, they may be unaware of where the macrobeats occur. Additionally, reading notation while teaching syllables is necessary because the syllables refer to specific note values and remain regardless of meter. For instance, the syllable for an eighth note is Ti in both Duple and Triple meters.

By using both mnemonics and Kodály rhythm syllables, the students could become confused by the inconsistency and therefore be less able to understand rhythm and meter. Students benefit when teachers use a consistent and logical system of rhythm syllables.

The beat-function syllable system as developed by Gordon (2003) is logical and differs from any other system because the syllable names are derived from meter and functions within that meter. Regardless of the meter, different syllables are used for macrobeats and microbeats. Likewise, "when rhythm syllables are based on beat functions and not on the time value of notes, they can easily and effectively be associated with patterns that become familiar to students at the aural/oral level of skill learning sequence, and so the ability to read music notation or to understand music theory is unnecessary" (Gordon, 2003, p. 79).

In the beat-function syllable system, every macrobeat in all meters uses the syllable Du. In Duple meter, the syllables used for all microbeats are Du De. In Triple meter, the syllables used for microbeats are Du Da Di. This system accommodates unusual meters by using the syllables Du Be when microbeats are grouped in twos and Du Ba Bi when grouped in threes.

The beat-function syllable system can be attached to movement meaningfully. It is based on how rhythm is felt, not on how rhythms are notated. How one feels meter should be how one defines it. The rhythm syllables then are attached based on audiation.

Both Orff Schulwerk and Music Learning Theory agree that movement is essential to the learning of rhythm. Body awareness activities are crucial as a readiness for movement. However, Orff Schulwerk's next step in the movement sequence involves beat competency, whereas Music Learning Theory emphasizes the Laban elements of flow, weight, space, and time in conjunction with coordination as readiness for beat competency. The core of movement for Music Learning Theory is continuous fluid movement because, regardless of musical style, rhythm audiation is dependent up a feeling of free, sustained movement in audiation. Once students can audiate flow, weight, space, time, and coordination, beat competency activities are appropriate.

**Evaluation**

Most teachers evaluate their students on participation and behavior. In addition, many teachers do not know what their individual students have achieved musically because tonal and rhythm responses are usually performed by the whole class rather than individually. Since all of the students in an Orff program perform all of the parts, teachers often evaluate students on participation and behavior rather than on achievement in terms of musical concepts and skills. A crucial step in evaluating students properly is to hear each one perform alone, and Orff teachers seldom require individual responses from their students. Adding Music Learning Theory and Learning Sequence Activities to an existing program allows for those individual responses.

Learning Sequence Activities are a means of continuous evaluation. While engaging in Learning Sequence Activities, teachers keep track of individual progress by making marks on a seating chart. This gives the teachers a concrete evaluation of each student and allows for individualized instruction. If a student has successfully performed the moderate tonal pattern in Learning Sequence Activities, he or she can be challenged by moving on to the difficult tonal pattern, which prevents boredom and facilitates learning.

In addition to measurement through Learning Sequence Activities, each student should be measured on his or her performance ability during Classroom Activities. One should use valid rating scales to measure students' music achievements, such as tone production on the soprano recorder, keeping a steady beat, and vocal accuracy.

## Conclusion

Music Learning Theory can easily be combined within an existing Orff program. In order to do this, the teacher would continue to use solfege, exploration, improvisation, and pentatonic in music lessons. However, the teacher would also make sure that these ideas are sequenced properly and would include elements of Music Learning Theory. First, the teacher would continue to use solfege with students but wait until after they have experienced tonal patterns with a neutral syllable to introduce the solfege. Also, the teacher would follow the sequencing inherent in Learning Sequence Activities to teach a tonal vocabulary logically.

Second, teachers should continue to have young students explore tonebar instruments and, as they get older, have them improvise. However, they must also include some activities focusing on creativity and clarify the difference between exploration, creativity, and improvisation in their own minds and the minds of their students. Finally, teachers should include diatonic melodies in all tonalities as well as pentatonic melodies in their repertoire and orchestrate them for students of all ages. By including these subtle but crucial ideas into an existing music classroom, the students will be more likely to sing in tune, understand tonal syntax, and be able to improvise and create with comprehension.

Teachers should continue to use rhythm syllables with students. However, they should be certain to use a logical system based on movement and beat function. Further, they must make sure to include Learning Sequences Activities and follow their sequencing so that rhythm syllables are taught after patterns have been experienced on a neutral syllable. Also, they must include movement activities with young children based on the

Laban elements of flow, weight, space, and time before focusing on beat competency with students.

Music Learning Theory is a theory for how one learns music. There are many possible curricula that could be generated from this theory. However, the sequence as defined within Music Learning Theory needs to be followed to teach audiation so that students can truly understand music and function as independent musicians.

Orff Schulwerk is an approach to and a process of teaching music. Therefore, Music Learning Theory and Orff Schulwerk can be combined. The Orff approach has outstanding, musically rich classroom activities but needs the sequencing of Music Learning Theory to move forward to musical understanding and independence. By combining the sequencing of Music Learning Theory and the teaching techniques and repertoire of Orff Schulwerk, students will learn to audiate and understand music.

## References

Ferguson, N. (July 1988). *Orff Schulwerk level I*. Lecture conducted at University of Arizona.

Gordon, E. E. (2003). *Learning sequences in music: Skill, content, and patterns*. Chicago: GIA Publications.

Steen, A. (1982). Improvisation and the young child. In Regner, H. (Ed.), *Music for children* (p. 71). England: Schott.

Warner, B. (1991). *Orff-Schulwerk: Applications for the classroom*. Englewood Cliffs: Prentice-Hall.

Wuytack, J. (July 1990). *Orff Schulwerk level III*. Lecture conducted at Memphis State University.

## Appendix A

# Poor Old Crow

Virginia Folk Song
Arr. Diane Lange

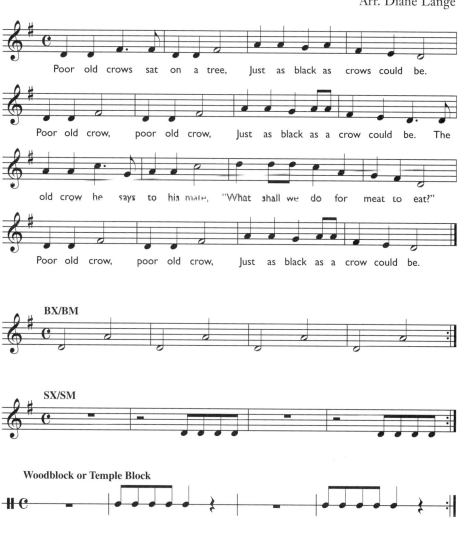

**Appendix B**

# Taking Gair in the Night

Newfoundland Song
Arr. Diane Lange

*Susan Wharton Conkling*
•••••••••••••••••
EASTMAN SCHOOL OF MUSIC

# Reframing the Choral Art

Although all students have some degree of musical potential, practical experience suggests that a wide range of readiness to comprehend, and therefore perform, choral music exists among the members of choral ensembles. In order to accommodate these individual differences, choral conductors may try to teach to the lowest achievers, having chorus members imitate phrase by phrase, part by part, work by work, until entire concerts are memorized. Alternatively, choral conductors may choose to teach only the highest achievers, forming select ensembles and thus eliminating many students from choral performance opportunities. According to the basic principles underlying Music Learning Theory, however, persons of all ages may achieve musically and find personal fulfillment through singing in a choral ensemble. In order to make the choral art accessible to all students, regardless of their age or prior experience, choral conductors must reconsider their role as teachers: teachers of voice, teachers of audiation, and teachers with an ultimate obligation to ensure each choir member's musical independence.

## The Conductor-Teacher and the Singing Voice

*Tasha is a thirteen-year-old who joined her school choir because her mother wanted her to stay out of trouble. She had almost no experience performing in school, church, or community choirs before seventh grade. When Tasha is asked to perform in solo, she performs all rhythm patterns accurately, but she is reluctant to perform tonal patterns. When she does try to perform tonal patterns, she uses speech-like tones with little inflection. Paradoxically, Tasha has a dramatic personality, and she imitates characters from movies and television with ease. I chose some song repertoire for Tasha with only a few pitches in an overall low range, trying to eliminate the temptation for her to use modal or low-register voice quality when she performs. I asked Tasha to imitate several characters that she knows well while*

157

*performing this repertoire. When she performed as "Cinderella," her voice was breathy, but finally in tune. I wondered if Tasha could sense this difference, so I took the accompaniment away and asked Tasha to sing again in her "Cinderella" voice. The singing remained tuneful and accurate.*

Choral conductor-teachers must commonly judge whether students' difficulties in singing arise from problems of audiation or from lack of experience in employing the voice for singing. The problems are not mutually exclusive, yet diagnoses can be complex. Unlike the instrumental conductor, who sees obvious indicators of sound production, such as fingerings, bowings, and embouchures, the choral conductor-teacher cannot see, and therefore cannot adjust, the workings of the larynx and vocal tract where sound is produced and shaped for singers. Choral conductor-teachers' confusion about how to work with voices is exacerbated further, since they usually receive little training to help them understand the vocal anatomy and patterns of growth and development. They may also have little access to resources that help them maintain an environment where vocal health may be fostered.

Confusion can be mitigated as conductor-teachers understand why many students have problems employing the voice for singing. For children, these problems may arise from insufficient vocal exploration. During childhood, the normal range of frequencies produced by the voice fall within about two and one half octaves, but children usually have the most experience engaging the frequencies of the modal register, that is the lower register where speech sounds are produced. Many children also report the greatest comfort singing in this register, although the comfort of singing in the register where voices are most frequently exercised may relate more to habitual use than to ease of vocal production (Langess, 1997). It should not be surprising, then, that some children may not hear and physically sense the differences between speaking tones and singing tones.

Adolescents go through such rapid physiological growth that the quality of the voice may seem to change daily. Both males and females experience major alterations in laryngeal anatomy during adolescence, with male vocal fold length increasing 63% from prepuberty to adulthood, and female vocal fold length increasing 34% during the same period (Kahane, 1982). The mean fundamental frequency of speech lowers for both males and females. Adolescents usually encounter breathiness and hoarseness, and during certain periods of development they may be temporarily unable to create any sound at all in a range of pitches (Cooksey, 1997). Many adolescents find estimation of a comfortable singing range to be difficult and frustrating.

Adults who choose to perform in a chorus for the first time or after many years' absence from singing often find while singing that their voices no longer sound as they remember them. As a result, their singing may be timid. Complaints such as, "I can't sing that high" are common. Although changes in quality may be primarily attributable to muscle disuse, adults may also hear and sense the effects of smoking, caffeine, alcohol, or prescription medications.

Children, adolescents, and adults all must be taught carefully and consistently in the choral rehearsal. The choral conductor may be the only voice teacher, or at least the first voice teacher, that the student will encounter, and her first obligation is to be keenly aware of the vocal anatomy and to be alert for signs of vocal misuse and potential dysfunction. Exercises designed to help students sense physical relaxation, proper body alignment, and consistent exhalation, as well as designed to help the students make use of the whole singing range, must be employed in every choral rehearsal. During these exercises, the wise choral conductor-teacher will frequently allow students to be heard in brief solos. Not only does this create an opportunity for assessment of an individual's vocal quality and progress in singing, it can also guide all students in discriminating among vocal sounds and in developing a vocabulary to describe vocal qualities. Even young children can become keen observers of vocal quality in this manner. The choral conductor-teacher must also reinforce the sensations of healthy singing during the rehearsal of the repertoire and must carefully monitor her own speaking and singing throughout the rehearsal.

**Cultivating Audiation**

A student may have developed the physical awareness necessary for singing, and he or she may be able to produce a healthy tone, but this does not guarantee that the student can perform with tonal and rhythmic accuracy. The second and perhaps most critical obligation of the choral conductor-teacher is to cultivate audiation. This process of audiation should ideally begin with a repertoire of songs that each student has listened to and can perform in solo. Not surprisingly, the same students who arrive in choral ensembles with limited experience employing the voice for singing also arrive with limited experience listening to and performing song reper-toire. It may be left to the choral conductor-teacher to search for appropriate song repertoire and to create opportunities for students to listen to and perform that song repertoire in solo.

Solo repertoire should consist of songs in many tonalities, meters, and styles. In the youngest choirs, the solo repertoire should consist of folk songs of limited range; in older choirs, the repertoire may extend to art songs and arias with expanded ranges. Students should be encouraged to learn both the melody and the harmonic progression, formed by the chord roots, for every song in the solo repertoire. If the harmonic progression is introduced simply as a "partner" song with the original melody, students are usually eager to perform duets with a peer or with the teacher. An example of a folk song and its harmonic progression, appropriate for an intermediate singer, is found in Figure 1.

*Figure 1.* Melody and harmonic progression

Listening to repertoire, which is as important as performing the repertoire in the development of audiation, can be accomplished in several ways. Primarily, students can and should perform for each other. Not only does this engender the collaborative ethic necessary for choral performance, it also assists students in making comparisons between tonalities, meters, styles, and types of vocal expression. Solo song instruction and solo song recitals can be incorporated at least once per week in most choral rehearsals. The conductor-teacher may also assign "buddy" practice, during which students are paired and evaluate the tonal and rhythmic accuracy as well as the vocal quality and expression of each other's performances using rating scales or rubrics.

Students should also hear performances by professional singers in order to make similar comparisons and to develop for themselves an ideal of tone quality. The conductor-teacher must take particular care to suggest live performances and recordings that exhibit healthy, expressive singing. One way to ensure that students regularly hear the performance of professionals is the maintenance of a recording library. Students should be encouraged to check out the recordings for overnight or weekend use, and they may learn new repertoire and develop ideals of stylistic performance through listening.

Whereas readiness for audiation may be achieved by listening to and performing songs in many different tonalities, meters, and styles, audiation itself may be more formally developed through Learning Sequence Activities. Learning Sequence Activities are most effective when students are first given a standardized music aptitude test and when tonal and rhythm patterns are performed in accordance with an individual's aptitude. Individual students should perform tonal and rhythm patterns in teaching mode (that is, with the teacher) and in evaluation mode (in solo). Ideally, pattern instruction should occupy no more than ten minutes at the beginning of a rehearsal, and tonal pattern instruction and rhythm pattern instruction should alternate weekly.

Used in this manner, tonal and rhythm patterns are generalizable across several styles and genres in the choral repertoire. Many choral conductor-teachers confine tonal and rhythm patterns to this use, although patterns may also be used effectively for other purposes. Consider that many choral rehearsals are carefully constructed so that the contrasts between works will maintain the attention of chorus members. For example, a work in a fast tempo is rehearsed following a work in a slow tempo, a work in Major tonality is rehearsed following a work in Minor tonality, a work in Triple meter is rehearsed following a work in Duple meter. This kind of rehearsal organization may well maintain the attention of the chorus members and may even provide an opportunity for the chorus members to make informal comparisons among choral works. Chorus members, however, may find it difficult to make the transition between contrasting works. The use of patterns to set the context for a choral work about to be rehearsed may ease the difficulty of that transition. In this kind of use, all patterns should be performed as class patterns, yet tonal patterns should remain free of rhythmic elements, and rhythm patterns should remain free of tonal elements. Patterns may be performed using a neutral syllable or with verbal association, depending on the students' level of learning. If a conductor-teacher anticipates that the work at hand will require substantial rehearsal on its rhythmic components, he or she may establish only a rhythmic context. Likewise, if the conductor-teacher anticipates that the work at hand will require substantial rehearsal of its tonal components, she may establish only a tonal context.

In an analysis and preparation of a choral work, the conductor-teacher will undoubtedly discover tonal and rhythm patterns characteristic to that work. These characteristic patterns can be useful for introducing students

161

to the work. The choral director should first extract the patterns from the work. As in Learning Sequence Activities, tonal patterns should be performed without rhythm, and rhythm patterns should be performed without melody. The patterns may be performed using a neutral syllable, with verbal association, or read from notation, depending on the students' level of learning. The characteristic patterns will usually be performed as class patterns, but they might also be valuable as individual patterns. Unlike the use of patterns in Learning Sequence Activities, these tonal and rhythm patterns are not intended to be generalizable; they should be unique to a particular choral work.

## The Conductor-Teacher and "Sight-Reading"

*Chad is a twelve-year-old who has been singing as long as he can remember. He performs in several church choirs with his mother and grandmother, and he performs in his school choir as well. In all of those choirs, the conductor-teachers primarily use rote teaching techniques. Some never use printed music at all. Chad and I once sat together at the piano as he played his tenor part from works that his choirs were performing. Then Chad played the bass part, the alto part, and the soprano part from those same works. Finally I inquired, "Do you take piano lessons?" "No," came his response. "Do you read music?" I asked. Of course, his answer was "no." I worked with Chad for a semester, helping him attach solfege syllables to familiar tonal patterns and rhythm syllables to familiar rhythm patterns, labeling tonalities and meters. The next semester, I notated familiar tonal patterns on the blackboard and showed Chad how to find DO. He read easily through those familiar patterns and has transferred that knowledge to unfamiliar choral music ever since.*

Perhaps no other aspect of a choral conductor-teacher's responsibilities is as controversial as developing the students' notational audiation. This type of audiation may be referred to as "sight-reading," and is often a critical component of the evaluation of choirs at contests and festivals. The music education research literature abounds with studies on sight reading in the choral rehearsal, and from that literature, one could conclude that the predictors of sight reading ability include daily drill (Cutietta, 1979), private piano study (Henry & Demorest, 1994), and school choral experience using a moveable-DO solfege system (Demorest & May, 1995). Such studies can be seriously misleading for the choral director. As Gordon points out, "To be able to sight read, one has to be able to read. If one can read, one can sight read because one is always reading at sight" (2003, p. 114). Reading music, that is, bringing meaning to what is seen in music notation, involves comparing notated patterns to music that has been previously heard and

162

performed and making sense of those patterns based on familiar music syntax. Eisner puts it this way:

> We normally believe that reading music, like reading a text is essentially a decoding process. The score is on the stand and the performer needs to follow it. Yet, to make sense of those notes just as it is necessary to make sense out of written text, one must construct the meaning of the score…It is a process not simply of decoding, but of encoding, of making sense of the music. (2000, p. 21)

An individual who has built large listening and performing vocabularies of familiar tonal patterns, rhythm patterns, and songs may reasonably be expected to make more accurate comparisons and predictions about unfamiliar notated music than an individual who has limited vocabularies. By extension, it can be reasoned that a choir will read at sight an unfamiliar musical work with more accuracy and expression when the conductor-teacher has emphasized the development of the listening and performing vocabularies of individual choir members.

Within the ensemble, readiness to make sense of what is seen in notation may differ vastly between students. It may be impractical, especially with older choirs, for the conductor-teacher to withhold notated music from the ensemble until all choir members, or even until the majority, can demonstrate readiness to comprehend notated patterns. In presenting a folder of printed music to every student, the conductor-teacher must be aware that those students who cannot make sense of music notation will only be able to use the printed music as an aid in learning and memorizing texts. These students may learn to identify some interpretive markings and some conventions of music notation, such as staves, barlines, and systems; they may even be able to differentiate between a half note and a quarter note, but they will not be able to read music with comprehension.

Imitation of more experienced singers or of the conductor will be the frequent mode of music learning for these students. The conductor-teacher, remembering that audiation begins in imitation, must exercise patience, and he or she must provide the means and encouragement for these students to continue building their listening and performing vocabularies, thus giving them the readiness to construct meaning from music notation. Additionally, the conductor-teacher should consider that not all musical practices require the use of notation. Works in gospel, jazz, and many folk idioms may be learned authentically through various rote teaching techniques. Including such works in the choir's repertoire and learning them in an authentic manner can help foster audiation for all ensemble members.

## Ensuring Musical Independence

The traditional emphasis on sight-reading in the choral rehearsal rightly points toward an even greater obligation on the part of the conductor-teacher to ensure that the students understand the choral works that they perform. Understanding, in turn, ensures musical independence. Though a student should come to understand a musical work more deeply in all of its dimensions each time he or she audiates it, in general a student can be said to understand a choral work when he or she can bring a unique interpretation to bear on its performance. Musical interpretation, while intensely personal, may only be achieved through an in-depth compre-hension of idiomatic standards and practices.

*Pamela is an African American soprano in my collegiate choir, and she is the soloist for a gospel work we are performing. In today's rehearsal, she is addressing the choir: "This piece is based on a spiritual, and it is rooted in slavery." She is so articulate that the choir is absolutely silent. "Slaves were usually forbidden to talk to each other when they worked, and so they sang. When they sang about a 'holy city' they were surely singing about their final deliverance from this world, but they might also be referring to a specific place where a slave could find the Underground Railroad and be delivered to the North." She continues, "When you sing, you have to find a way to feel and show the same kind of intense yearning that a slave must have felt. It's all about emotion, people. If you can't perform with emotion, then you shouldn't perform at all."*

*Then the choir begins their final run-through, obviously heeding Pamela's words. Their sound is full and earnest, even in the softest sections. Pamela's improv-isation begins, filling in the rests at first, and then soaring over the choir. When the final fermata is released, I look around at the faces of the choir members. There are few dry eyes, and I have to wipe the tears from my own.*

Music notation, at best, provides only an outline or map of what the composer was audiating at the time of composition. Every choral work, even the most fully notated, has at least some aspects of its performance subject to interpretive decision-making. Traditionally, the responsibility for inter-pretive decision-making has fallen solely on the shoulders of the conductor, the first listener, who then conveys those decisions to the choir. Alternatively, to aid in the development of musical independence, the conductor-teacher should encourage students to generate interpretive ideas, to analyze the musical effect of those ideas, and to select from those ideas for performance. Consider some ways in which this might be accomplished.

First, students might be allowed to explore expressive dimensions of a choral work, such as dynamics and tempo. Does the crescendo really begin at the point where it is indicated in the score, or might it begin earlier? The conductor-teacher should solicit ideas from choir members and try them out with the entire ensemble in rehearsal. What is the best forte sound that the choir can create? Once the forte sound is established, the choir can then determine how other dynamic levels relate to it. To what does the tempo marking *allegro* refer? The choir can give feedback to the conductor-teacher regarding the ease of text enunciation at various tempi. As the choir members generate and analyze these interpretive ideas, they may begin to gain insight into the composer's intentions.

The choir can also have input into the interpretation when the conductor-teacher allows them to change the text of a choral work. Students can write a new text with the same meaning as the original text. This is especially useful when the choir is performing in a foreign language or when younger choirs are performing in their native language about a subject or emotion with which they are not familiar. Although the texts that students write may be functional as translations, students will soon discover that the newly written texts do not fit in the rhythmic context of the original work. Alternatively, students could write an entirely new text, trying to fit in the rhythmic context of the original work that they are performing. In this instance, students can learn a great deal about meter and text accentuation, but they will undoubtedly find that their newly created text does not fit the timbral context of the original work, or that certain tonal motives or word-paintings are not appropriate to the new text. These two ways to change texts are far from mere exercises, for they lead students to discover the essence of truly great choral music: text and music that are seamlessly united.

Physical movement in the choral rehearsal is yet another means to an in-depth understanding of choral works. Some musical practices are closely tied to dance. Contra dances, reels, and jigs, for example, are associated with many fiddle tunes. When students perform these dances, they gain an embodied understanding of meter and tempo. Students may also come to a clearer understanding of phrasing because the movements in these types of dances often change direction at the end of a phrase. Furthermore, because students are physically active, their breathing may become more coordinated with the musical phrase.

Where Learning Sequence Activities are employed, students will already be accustomed to movements that accompany rhythm pattern instruction. These types of movements may easily be transferred to the choral repertoire; students may be asked to rock to the macrobeat and tap to the microbeat as they chant the melodic rhythm of a new choral work. Other more sustained movements may be added as well. Students could be asked to lean into the climax point of a phrase and lean back as the phrase subsides, or they could be asked to draw long arches in the air with their arms to indicate phrase length. Forceful downward movements with the whole body may help emphasize a crusic accent, and a lifting movement will likewise aid in the performance of an anacrusis.

Some students may initially resist any kind of movement in the choral rehearsal. Their reluctance to move is usually an indicator that they are uncomfortable with their bodies (resistance to movement is common during early adolescence). It will help these reluctant students to pantomime motions from daily life. The motions may be as simple as waving to the neighbor across the street, rocking a baby, or rolling a bowling ball. Each of these examples is readily connected with the breath, and each may easily be turned into a macro- or microbeat movement.

Having discovered the marriage of text and tone in choral works, and having had opportunities to change the expressive dimensions of choral works, students will naturally be led to change the tonal and rhythmic dimensions of choral works. Students should be encouraged to experiment with the performance of choral works in tonalities other than the original tonality and in meters other than the original meter. The students should generate ideas for tonal and rhythmic interpretations just as they do for text and expressive interpretations. In their analysis, the students should be urged to ask themselves, "Is this the best possible interpretation of this choral work?"

The students' solo repertoire is often more suitable for purposes of arrangement than works drawn from the choral repertoire. Students can be encouraged, for example, to arrange medleys of familiar songs, including the root melodies, and to describe the unifying devices that they use in their arrangements. It is likely that some students will rely exclusively on text as a unifying device, but if audiation is a priority, students will also look to root melodies and meter to arrange their medleys. They may choose two songs with identical harmonic progressions and arrange them as a duet. They may choose two songs in the same meter to perform, one following the other, and create a modulation between two keyalities or tonalities. It is important to remember that, although music notation can preserve students' arrangements, notation is not vital in the creation or performance of the arrangements. As Gordon points out, "Musicians should be expected to audiate everything they see in notation, but...they should not be expected to put into notation everything that they audiate" (2003, p. 113). Entire concerts of student compositions and arrangements are possible and highly recommended, even for the youngest choir members who have not yet learned to read and write music.

Allowing students to generate interpretive ideas, to analyze the effect of those ideas, and to select from the ideas for performance is a challenging and risky undertaking for the conductor-teacher. He must give up the maestro role and become a coach and mentor in the rehearsal. Individual differences among students must be understood and acknowledged, and the atmosphere for learning must be one that allows each chorus member to feel that his or her contributions to the ensemble are genuinely valued.

## Conclusions

The frame for the choral art lies not in conducting the ensemble but rather in addressing the musicianship of individuals within the choral ensemble. Individuals must be able to learn to use their voices in a healthy and efficient manner, to develop rich music listening, performing, reading, and writing vocabularies through audiation, and to contribute freely and genuinely to musical interpretation. When individual musicianship is addressed in this manner, choir members will reach their highest musical potentials. Choir members who experience this kind of musical achievement will keep singing for a lifetime.

## References

Cooksey, J. M. (1997). Male adolescent transforming voices: Voice classification, voice skill development, and music literature selection. In L. Thurman & G. Welch (Eds.), *Bodymind and voice: foundations of voice education.* (pp. 589-609). Iowa City: The VoiceCare Network, National Center for Voice and Speech, The Voice Center of Fairview/Fairview Arts Medicine Center.

Cutietta, R. (1979). The effects of including systemized sight-singing drill in the middle school choral rehearsal. *Contributions to Music Education, 7,* 12-20.

Demorest, S. M., & May, W. V. (1995). Sightsinging instruction in the choral rehearsal: Factors related to individual performance. *Journal of Research in Music Education, 43*(2), 156-167.

Eisner, E. (2000). Music education six months after the turn of the century. *Arts Education Policy Review, 102*(3), 20-24.

Gordon, E. E. (2003). *Learning sequences in music: Skill, content, and patterns.* Chicago: GIA Publiations.

Henry, M. L., & Demorest, S. M. (1994). Individual sight-singing achievement in successful high school choral ensembles. *Update: Applications of Research in Music Education, 13*(1), 4-8.

Kahane, J. C. (1982). Growth of the human prepubertal and pubertal larynx. *Journal of Speech and Hearing, 25,* 446-455.

Langess, A. M. (1997). Helping children's voices develop in general music education. In L. Thurman & G. Welch (Eds.), *Bodymind and voice: Foundations of voice education.* (pp. 571-581). Iowa City: The VoiceCare Network, National Center for Voice and Speech, The Voice Center of Fairview/Fairview Arts Medicine Center.

*Nadine C. McDermott*

• • • • • • • • • • • • • • • •

BRIARCLIFF MANOR MIDDLE SCHOOL, BRIARCLIFF, NY

# Promoting Healthy Singing: A Necessary Link

While attending a conference session on audiation and Music Learning Theory, I suddenly realized how distracted I was by the clinician's improper vocal technique. It was apparent that this clinician was not a trained singer. The lack of breath support and the incorrect placement of the tongue were causing intonation and projection problems that affected the quality of the clinician's singing voice. The clinician apologized for poor intonation and cited average to low tonal aptitude as the culprit. A trained singer or voice teacher knows that the vocal production problems of the clinician could have been corrected, which would have resulted in a vastly improved vocal performance.

If there is singing involved in any aspect of a musical experience, it is the music educator's professional obligation to know and be able to teach healthy vocal habits, especially because the voice is irreplaceable. Singing is a lifelong skill, and students should have the opportunity to learn and become skilled in using their vocal instrument. By implication, Music Learning Theory teachers should also be teaching and modeling healthy vocal habits.

### An Intangible and Irreplaceable Instrument

"A singer does not have a separate instrument that he can see or touch while making music; the singer *is* a musical instrument" (McKinney, 1982, p. 153). Being able to model proper vocal technique, as well as diagnose vocal problems, is essential to effective teaching and learning of music. That kind of modeling also requires an understanding of the human voice, how it functions, and how to promote correct vocal technique that reflects healthy singing. The voice is an intangible instrument that cannot be replaced and must be treated with care and respect by the teacher and the student.

While implementing a Music Learning Theory component that requires singing, the teacher must be able to monitor the vocal development of the student as well as the development of the student's audiation. The teacher must be aware that improper vocal production can impede progress in demonstrating and eventually developing audiation skills. The student may be able to hear the tonal patterns accurately but may have difficulty producing those patterns vocally. When that occurs, the teacher must have the knowledge and skills to provide assistance in vocal technique, simultaneous with the development of audiation. Learning the guiding principles of healthy vocal production will enhance the teacher's knowledge of singing and modeling, thereby improving the student's singing.

**Holding the Instrument**

"Before trying to play any instrument one should learn how to hold it. Vocally this means posture" (Vennard, 1967, p. 19). The feet should be shoulder width apart, knees slightly bent, shoulders down, arms hanging loosely to the side, and the sternum should be high. In addition, the instrument (voice) needs to be supported by the legs with the pelvis tucked in. The neck, chin, and jaw need to be relaxed. The position of the head is important in tone production. The vocal cords are located behind the larynx. If the neck and head position are out of alignment, this will affect the position of the larynx. To check the position of the head, place the index finger directly under the chin, then lower the thumb to meet the sternum. Adjust the head position so that the index finger and thumb create a right angle. This posture should be sustained while singing so the body will be properly aligned and will allow for adequate breath support.

In addition, the following are several exercises and an image that I have found useful in promoting proper singing posture.

### Exercise to Promote Proper Posture

1. To insure that the chest is in the correct position for singing, raise the arms over the head, and slowly lower the arms to the side of the body. The chest is now in the correct position for singing.

2. To ensure that the legs are involved in the singing process, bend your knees as if sitting down but do not sit down.

## Image to Promote Proper Posture

"Imagine that you are a marionette, hanging from strings, one attached to the top of your head and one attached to the top of your breastbone. This keeps the head erect and lifts the chest, allowing the pelvis just to 'hang' in position." (Vennard, 1967, p. 19)

## The Foundation

"Universally, proper breathing technique is recognized as a fundamental element of healthy and expressive singing. Breath support is the foundation for which all other aspects of vocal development are built" (Nesheim & Noble, 1995, p. 4). While breathing is a natural process, learning how to take a "singer's breath" does not always occur naturally. In developing breath support, the processes of inhalation and exhalation are of equal importance. During inhalation, the breath should be drawn in inaudibly and simultaneously through the nose and the mouth. The air is taken in and moves down into the abdominal area and both the rib cage and abdominal areas move out, without upward movement in the shoulders.

The process of exhalation is often not given adequate attention. Simply taking in a deep breath is not enough. It is knowing what to do with that deep breath and how to properly release it that creates the necessary support for singing. During exhalation, the air should be released with sufficient velocity to maintain a constant, steady, narrow stream. The air "spirals out" away from the body, parallel to the floor. The sternum should be kept high, and clasping the hands in the middle of the chest should be avoided. Immediately following the inhalation process, exhalation must begin without delay. The foundation for the singing tone is now established.

The following are exercises and images that I have found helpful in promoting proper breathing technique.

## Exercises to Promote Proper Breathing

1. To discover how the body reacts while taking a "singer's breath," lay flat on the floor, place one arm on the lower abdominal area and the other arm under the lower back. Inhale inaudibly through the nose and the mouth. The abdominal area will rise toward the ceiling and the back will expand into the floor. Duplicating this same process while standing becomes the challenge.

171

2.  While standing with correct posture, close one nostril. Inhale inaudibly through the open nostril. The lower abdominal area should fill with air and expand out along with the rib cage.

3.  Pretending to sip through a straw, take ten inaudible breaths through the nose and the mouth simultaneously. Exhale on a voiced hissing [s] sound. Avoid letting the rib cage collapse quickly and chest to cave in. Initially you may want to provide straws for the students to use. External tools are often helpful in developing this sensation.

4.  To find the soft palate, look in a mirror while yawning. The soft palate will rise at the beginning of a yawn, creating the lift needed to allow the air stream to move into the head.

5.  To feel the soft palate rise, imagine smelling a pleasant fragrance. The nostrils will flare, and the soft palate will rise.

### Images to Promote Proper Breathing

1.  Imagine having your blood pressure taken. Visualize the nurse pumping the air into arm cuff. The arm cuff expands with each pump of air. This is how the abdominal and rib cage area should respond simultaneously during the inhalation process.

2.  Visualize a water wheel that is kept in motion by the water. The air stream for singing must resemble this motion. This image is helpful when trying to keep the breath flowing while singing. Moving the arms in a circular motion, imitating the water wheel, provides an external image and reminds the singer to keep the air flowing.

3.  Visualize the arc of a basketball being shot. The arc must be high enough for the ball to go into the basket successfully. The voice must have the same arc—"up and over."

### Developing a Healthy Singing Tone

Learning to sing correctly is a lengthy, complex process requiring concentrated study; there are, however, fundamental principles to follow that will promote healthy singing that can be followed by anyone. The goal in developing a healthy singing tone is to produce a supported, free tone that resonates in the head. To achieve this goal, the student must lift the soft palate to create an open space in the back of the throat. In addition, the tongue must be relaxed down behind the bottom teeth. When the palate is lifted with correct tongue placement during the inhalation process, there is a clear path for the tone to move into the head.

The teacher should provide literature and vocalises with appropriate range for the developmental level of the student that promote the development of healthy vocal habits. Start with descending exercises in the middle register, then move into the upper and then lower registers. Literature and vocalises that require singing only in the low register or chest voice should be avoided. Systematically developing the head voice is also recommended.

## Aural and Visual Cues

"The teacher must have a clear-cut conception of good vocal sound to serve as a standard of judgment when hearing sounds which are lacking in some desirable attribute" (McKinney, 1982, p. 13). "The singer cannot hear himself as others hear him" (Kagen, 1950, p. 79). Both McKinney and Kagen support the need for another set of ears—the teacher. The fact that the voice cannot be replaced if damaged is a cause for a conscious effort on the teacher's part to diagnose possible vocal problems. Singing is an extension of speech, and although speaking is a natural process, it is possible to talk incorrectly. There are aural and visual cues that are present if the vocal cords are injured. Look for excessive tension in the body, especially in the neck, and listen for vocal strain while singing and/or speaking. Any tension in the body will eventually creep into the voice. Anyone who has a raspy singing or speaking voice or has frequent laryngitis should have the vocal cords checked by a physician for possible nodules or polyps, as this is not normal. Vennard (1967) defines a nodule as "a knot or tumor produced by friction between vocal ligaments. A polyp is a growth on the mucous membrane of the vocal cord" (p. 241). Complete vocal rest is the prescription that usually follows diagnosis of nodules or polyps on the vocal cords. Using proper breath support in singing and speaking will keep the voice healthy.

## Imagery

"We do not possess the faculty of compelling our vocal cords to flex in any precise manner without first having conceived an image of the sound we wish to produce" (Kagen, 1960, p. 41). Imagery is a successful tool to use in teaching students to develop correct vocal technique. Because the instrument is not tangible, the main guides for the singer are sensations. Singing is kinesthetic as well as a process of metacognition. Knowing what your body is doing and needs to do to produce a healthy singing tone is essential. Imagery assists in the description of vocal tone. Using imagery is an effective tool for all students, regardless of age or experience.

## Articulators and Vowel Formation

"Poor intonation will always be the result of such poor choices of vowel sounds for neutral syllable teaching" (Jordan & Mehaffey, 2001, p. 32). Selection of the vowel and how the vowel is shaped in the mouth are important considerations. "Dee is the syllable of choice because it will keep the vocal sound more high and forward and, hence, improve intonation. Many teachers make the mistake of doing this type of aural/oral teaching on syllables such as 'dah' or 'duh,' which causes vocal placement to be backward and in the jowls" (Jordan & Mehaffey, 2001, pp. 31–32). Intonation can be affected by vowels as well as how the vowels are formed.

The articulators used to form vowels and consonants are the lips, the lower jaw, and the tongue. The singer has direct control of these articulators. The placement of the tongue and shape of the lips are essential in forming vowels. The tongue should be relaxed down behind the bottom teeth and corners of the lips should be in but relaxed. The lower jaw should be relaxed and slightly dropped. To maximize the function of these articulators, they must be free from tension so they can move easily.

## Warm-up

Singing, like a sport, requires a warm-up routine. A proper warm-up with purposeful exercises is essential to developing a solid vocal technique. "It is important that vocal exercises serve to gradually awaken the muscles involved in singing in a manner that does not require premature strenuous activity" (Nesheim & Noble, 1995, p. 3). Approaching warm-ups can be compared to assembling a layer cake. Before vocalizing, the body should be stretched, including the face, neck, and shoulders; also be sure that all the tension in body is released. After the body is relaxed, the breath is the next layer to warm up. Breathing exercises are essential to establish the foundation for the singing tone by increasing breath capacity and vocal support.

The next layer is sound. Siren tones and lip flutters can be used as a means to allow the student to focus on proper breath support, freeing the tone without having to sing a specific pattern of pitches. The final layer is to vocalize on vowels using scale patterns. Now the instrument and the body are ready to participate in the physical activity of singing.

During warm-ups, the teacher should remind students about proper posture, breath support, and tone production. Coaching students during the warm-up process, like a coach speaking to players on the field, allows students to participate in the metacognitive process of a trained singer.

## Making the Link

Acquiring the knowledge and skills to promote healthy singing habits is paramount for a music educator who is not a trained singer but incorporates singing into pedagogy. A teacher who is trained in Music Learning Theory and who is also a teacher of singing can provide an enhanced vocal experience as part of students' training. This knowledge base and the accompanying skills may just be the necessary link that completes and complements Music Learning Theory. It is partly through singing that children learn to discriminate. If teachers of Music Learning Theory help students of all ages to develop vocal technique, their students will become both better singers and better audiators.

## References

Jordan, J., & Mehaffey, M. (2001). *Choral Ensemble Intonation: Method, procedures, and exercises*. Chicago: GIA Publications.

Kagen, S. (1960). *On studying singing*. New York: Dover Publications.

McKinney, J. C. (1982). *The diagnosis & correction of vocal faults*. Tennessee: Broadman Press.

Nesheim, P., & Noble, W. (1995). *Building beautiful voices*. Ohio: Roger Dean Publishing.

Vennard, W. (1967). *Singing: The mechanism and the technic* (Rev. Ed.), New York: Carl Fisher.

Young Hong, A. (1995). *Singing professionally*. New Hampshire: Heinemann.

# *Variation 2:* Instrumental Applications

*Richard F. Grunow*
● ● ● ● ● ● ● ● ● ● ● ● ●
EASTMAN SCHOOL OF MUSIC

# Music Learning Theory: A Catalyst for Change in Beginning Instrumental Music Instruction

Music Learning Theory is a model for teaching and learning music sequentially. It is also a sensible and practical vehicle for instituting change in beginning instrumental music, a profession that adheres more often to fads and long-standing tradition than to empirical evidence. Change that leads to notable improvement can be difficult to achieve, especially when facing resistance from practitioners entrenched in comfortable routines. But, in the end, it is change that secures the future for all endeavors. Consider the following example from the medical profession.

Many years ago I underwent a rather common procedure to remove damaged cartilage from my knee. I spent a day in the hospital in preparation for the operation, and I remained there for several days after the surgery, recuperating from the procedure. Although I cannot recount the details entirely, I do know that I was heavily sedated for a significant period of time and suffered a memorable amount of pain during the ensuing days. When I was released from the hospital my entire leg was bandaged, and I was on crutches for more than a week. To this day I have a noticeable scar from the operation.

Several years ago, some thirty-five years after the initial surgery, I had a similar operation on the same knee. This time I went to an outpatient clinic for a few hours, and I was sedated for only a short period of time. I was on crutches for one day, and three days later I was able to ride a bicycle. Today, I have no scars or pain. In terms of the seriousness of the operation, the surgeon informed me that my procedure was an 8 on a scale of 1 to 10.

This scenario represents a dramatic modification in surgical procedure. Easily added to a list could be any number of new and improved medical procedures that would have been thought impossible only a few years ago. Undoubtedly, those changes stem from experimental research, practical research, and a substantial amount of common sense. Of course, the improvements are also vigorously supported, encouraged, and even demanded by a society with an obvious personal and economic investment in the improvement of health care.

You probably have a sense of where I am directing this discourse, but in case it is not as obvious as I think, ask yourself the following questions: What changes have we witnessed in beginning instrumental music instruction in the last forty years? Are any modifications necessary? Is there a body of experimental research, practical research, and common sense to support change in the way beginning instrumental music is taught? Is it realistic to expect improvements in beginning instrumental music instruction that are as dramatic as those in health care? Will society ever support, encourage, and even demand changes in the way beginning instrumental music is taught?

In answer to the first question—with the exception of improvements in packaging and the use of technology—very little has changed in beginning instrumental music instruction. An old-timer observing in a beginning instrumental classroom today would recognize behaviors and comments prevalent forty or even sixty years ago. "Where is your instrument? How much did you practice? Where is your pencil? How many beats are there in a whole note? How many eighth notes are in a dotted quarter? What are the names of the lines and spaces? You are sharp; pull out. You are flat; push in. You're rushing. You are behind the beat. Hold the note for its full value. Watch me. How do you finger high F-sharp? Breathe from the diaphragm. Use more bow. How many flats are in the key of E-flat? We will be having an extra rehearsal before school on Thursday morning." And from the students we still hear, "Play it for me, so I know how it goes." Before answering the remaining questions, let's examine further the recent tradition in beginning instrumental music instruction.

## Recent Tradition in Beginning Instrumental Music Instruction

Students are typically "recruited" to begin instruction on wind, percussion, and string instruments in the fourth or fifth grade, when they are approximately nine or ten years old. By that time, most students exhibit the physical properties, i.e., finger size, arm length, and height, to manage a traditional music instrument. The enthusiasm to learn to play an instrument is often so contagious that virtually every child expresses an interest, and parents expend a substantial amount of money to obtain the instrument, method book, and accessories. When instruction begins, students are introduced immediately to the chosen instrument and to music notation (the method book). The most pressing issue is to read music and manipulate the instrument in time for the first concert, which is only months away.

With few exceptions, the introductory pages of traditional method books contain fingering charts, music theory, and illustrations of the technical and physical aspects of performing on the instrument—breathing, posture, hand position, articulation, and embouchure. The initial pages of notation are most often characterized by whole notes interspersed with rests. Students begin instruction by associating fingerings with note names—generally the notes that are perceived to be the "easiest" to produce on that instrument—while at the same time being expected to demonstrate correct posture, embouchure, instrument position, breathing habits, intonation, and acceptable tone quality. In addition, they are often required to tap their foot and "count" rhythms based on note values, progressing from large note values (whole notes) to smaller note values (sixteenth notes). The prevailing beliefs are that a) learning about music theory (note names and note values) will enable students to read music, and b) tone quality and the technical/physical aspects of playing an instrument are most easily developed through the performance of sustained pitches or long tones.

Progress with the whole note and rest exercises continues with the introduction of "new notes," gradually leading to performances of "supposedly" familiar melodies. The melodies are usually performed with uncharacteristic rhythms and erratic tempos, due in large part to the manner in which the melodies are notated in the method book. Contributing also to the typical performance is the reality that some students have developed neither the appropriate sense of style nor the technical proficiency to perform at a musical or consistent tempo. A musical context (tonality, meter, and style) and the oral aspects of music (singing and movement) are rarely a part of instruction.

In accordance with tradition, and often because of administrative decree, instrumental music teachers are expected to present a concert with the beginners after several months of the aforementioned instruction. It is imperative that parents are shown a tangible product for their investment, and the ability to "read music" is the most obvious choice. So, the students perform from notation the renditions of the melodies that were learned in class. When recognizable, the melodies usually comprise only Major tonality and Duple meter. Although the applause is understandably enthusiastic and supportive, many parents attend only the portion of the concert in which their child is performing.

Back in the classroom, the eagerness expressed earlier by so many students is beginning to wane, perhaps as soon as the first few weeks or months of instruction. Students are beginning to drop out of the program. By the end of the second year of instruction, it is common for the majority to have discontinued instruction. A substantial number of those who remain after the first two years abandon the program during the middle school and high school years. The students who continue instrumental instruction throughout their formal public school education often comprise less than 10 percent of those who initially began instruction—an unconscionable waste of human potential and a stinging indictment of the profession.

## Continuing the Tradition

The concert tradition that began in the elementary school continues throughout the formal years of music instruction. With the exception of individuals able to perform in small combos or improvise as a member of a jazz ensemble, students are generally limited to performing on their instruments from notation, and then only in concert under the direction of a conductor or with the aid of an accompanist. Relatively few develop the skills to demonstrate independent "music making" during or beyond their formal education. Adding to this disturbing situation is the fact that teachers base their grading heavily on attitude, attendance, and practice time.

Despite the dropout rates and a perceived lack of change, many instrumental music programs thrive with high profiles, huge budgets, and substantial community support—but too often for non-musical reasons. High on the list of rationales is the development of discipline, self-esteem, cooperation, and social skills. Also, we have seen a major campaign recently to advance the notion that "music makes you smarter." There was a time when, "teach your child to blow a horn and he won't blow a safe," was also prominent among the justifications for instrumental music instruction. (That slogan probably lost its popularity because so many prisons have bands.) Curiously, music teachers are some of the most vigorous advocates for keeping music in the schools for non-musical reasons.

Regardless of protestations—for musical or non-musical reasons—music programs, and elementary instrumental programs in particular, are often first to be eliminated or reduced when cuts in the budget are imminent. To schedule instrumental music instruction as a part of the regular school day continues to be difficult, and classroom teachers resist "pull-out" programs that take students from the perceived core curriculum. Rationales notwithstanding, a substantial proportion of society still seems to regard instrumental music instruction as unworthy of inclusion in the core curriculum and, therefore, subject to whimsical budget cuts and political changes of heart.

## Musical Behaviors and a Society "at Risk"

What are the perceived benefits of being in the band or orchestra? Why do students drop out of the instrumental program? Gemeinhardt engaged in research with music dealers, instrumental music teachers, parents, and students to find answers to those and other related questions. According to *The Gemeinhardt Report 3* (Brown, 1990), the following are among the top ten "Benefits of Band/Orchestra": discipline, self-esteem, cooperation, self-confidence, and social skills (p. 15). *The Gemeinhardt Report 3* also cites the following among the top ten "Drop-Out Issues": conflicts with other subjects, fear of failure, boredom, too much competition, and too much time required (p. 17). Although other reasons were somewhat related to music, the report clearly suggests that the perceived benefits of being in the band or orchestra and the reasons students drop out have little to do with musical behaviors.

What are musical behaviors? In 1994, MENC suggested what students should know and be able to do in music. Although not presented in any sequential order, *The National Standards for Arts Education* (Lehman, et al., 1994) identifies nine national voluntary content standards in music for grades K-12: 1) singing alone and with others a varied repertoire of music; 2) performing on instruments, alone and with others, a varied repertoire of music; 3) improvising melodies, variations, and accompaniments; 4) composing and arranging music within specified guidelines; 5) reading and notating music; 6) listening to, analyzing, and describing music; 7) evaluating music and music performances; 8) understanding relationships between music, the other arts, and disciplines outside the arts; and 9) understanding music in relation to history and culture. All students are expected to develop some level of competence within each standard, whether studying instrumental, vocal, or general music. Regardless of the sequence in which content standards are presented, most would agree that the standards suggest musical behaviors conspicuously missing from the "benefits of instrumental music instruction" and the "reasons why students drop out of the program," mentioned in *The Gemeinhardt Report*. How can this be? Based on these findings, one can only draw the conclusion that musical objectives have not been the central focus of beginning instrumental music instruction.

If musical objectives are not central to beginning instrumental instruction, is the musical competence of our society "at risk?" Data from the most recent National Assessment of Educational Progress are inconclusive at best regarding the nation's progress in music (Persky, Sandene, & Askew, 1997). The report also makes it impossible to determine whether musical competence is higher or lower than when the last National Assessment of Educational Progress took place in the 1970s (Lehman, 1999). It is clear, however, that the vast majority of the population does not demonstrate the independent musicianship necessary to continue to participate in society as intelligent consumers and makers of music.

It is time to face reality. Much of what is problematic in keeping music in the curriculum, and the reason that the musicianship of society is clearly substandard, is related directly to the way music is taught—specifically, the ways in which beginning instrumental music is taught. The instruction in most beginning instrumental music classes contradicts common sense and research results related to how children learn music. Some may take comfort in the existence of National Standards and in the inclusion of music in the National Assessment, but I find little solace there. One hundred and fifty years after music instruction was first made an official part of the school curriculum, we are still unable to justify music on its own merits. So much for "educational progress" in music education! Teaching music for non-musical reasons will only support a state of complacency in a profession whose curriculum is in dire need of improvement. Without changes that improve true musicianship, beginning instrumental music instruction will remain at the mercy of current trends and capricious inquiry. The purpose of this chapter is to examine the tenets of Music Learning Theory as a model for improving curricula in beginning instrumental music, thereby leading to its inclusion in the core of the educational curriculum.

**Curriculum**

There are many approaches to curriculum development, each with an abundance of accompanying educational jargon. Any reasonable curriculum, however, should include a) objectives, b) methods, techniques, and materials, and c) measurement and evaluation. In other words, a valid and usable curriculum should contain clear statements of what is to be accomplished, suggested procedures for achieving curricular objectives, and a process to determine the degree to which the objectives have been achieved.

*Objectives*

What are the objectives of instrumental music instruction? For many instrumental music teachers, *The National Standards* represent a new direction in music education, a direction that will ultimately lead to the establishment of music as a respected part of the basic core curriculum. For others, *The National Standards* represent more rhetoric about objectives that are already in place. For example, most beginning instrumental music teachers will say that music reading is perhaps the most important objective (Adderley, 1996). Although many claim that their students are also learning to improvise and to compose, improvisation and composition do not play a central role in most beginning instrumental instruction (Austin, 1988). It is not within the scope of this chapter to discuss in detail each of the National Standards. Still, a more in-depth treatment of reading and improvisation in light of Music Learning Theory could provide insight for the improvement of beginning instrumental music instruction.

READING LANGUAGE AND READING MUSIC: A COMPARISON

Much can be understood about reading music by comparing it to reading language. In language there are four vocabularies: listening, speaking, reading, and writing. It would be inconceivable to expect children to read or to write a language before they have listened to the language and learned to engage in conversation. Children generally listen to language for at least a year before they engage in anything we would recognize as conversation. In the beginning, they speak (babble) in a manner that is difficult to understand; over time, their speech begins to resemble the conversation heard in the environment. If their listening vocabulary is rich, chances are this richness will be reflected in their speaking vocabulary. Perhaps more important, children typically engage in conversation for several years before they are expected to read and write that language. Listening to language is the readiness for speaking language, and both serve as the readiness for learning to read and write language. Not only are the four vocabularies acquired sequentially, they are interactive. Without the sequential and interactive nature of the four vocabularies, the ability to engage in any one of the vocabularies with comprehension will be substantially limited.

A similar sequence and interaction should occur when learning music. Under ideal circumstances, children develop listening vocabularies at home

185

with parents and caregivers providing a rich variety of live music—preferably sung and performed on instruments. At the same time, children sing and move to music with their parents, siblings, and caregivers and go through a babble stage in music similar to the babble stage in language. Such conditions gradually lead to singing and movement that reflect music heard in the environment. Given a rich musical vocabulary supported by an encouraging and interactive environment, children begin to improvise their own songs and chants spontaneously. Those emerging behaviors are not unlike what occurs when children begin to carry on conversations in language. Eventually, children learn to read and to write music in much the same way they learn to read and to write language.

Clearly, a foundation is necessary for learning to read language, and a similar foundation is necessary for learning to read music. Further, reading language requires more than merely saying words with the correct pronunciation; and reading music requires more than "counting" rhythms and relating note names to fingerings on an instrument. Reading involves comprehension. Regarding language, Healy (1990) states

> The ability to "bark at print" is not reading, but many people, including well-meaning parents, think it is. Tests which show that young children's scores are rising may simply be focusing on the "lower level" skills of word reading while neglecting the real heart of the matter: How well do they understand what they have read? Can they reason—and talk, and write—about it? (p. 26)

When comprehending a language, one is able to explain what was read through conversation and writing. The ability to think and make predictions based on an understanding of that language is obviously part of the process.

Similarly, those who comprehend music are able to audiate (think) and make predictions based on their understanding of music.[1] They are able to listen to music with comprehension in much the same manner that one who comprehends language listens to conversation. When instrumentalists read music through audiation, they hear the music before it is played on the instrument, and they also audiate and predict what is not on the page, e.g., tonality and harmonic progression, meter and rhythm functions, and musical style. In contrast, students who are taught to decode notation by "counting"

---

[1] Audiation, a word coined by Edwin E. Gordon, the author of Music Learning Theory, is the ability to hear and to comprehend in one's mind the sound of music that is not or may never have been physically present. Audiation is to music what thinking is to language.

rhythms and by associating note names with fingerings or keys on a musical instrument are not reading with comprehension. To portray such behaviors as anything beyond "lower level" skills would be an exaggeration.

THE ROLE OF IMPROVISATION

Once we know what constitutes reading music with comprehension, the importance of improvisation becomes more obvious. Just as conversation plays a significant role in learning to read a language, improvisation plays a significant role in learning to read music. In fact, evidence exists to support the teaching of improvisation as a foundation for reading music (Azzara, 1993). Unfortunately, improvisation is still viewed by many instrumental music teachers as a "special" gift bestowed on a fortunate few.

In most beginning instrumental classes, unmusical tempos and uncharacteristic rhythms (imposed by early use of notation) demand little of students' senses of tonality, meter, and musical style—requisites for improvisation. Many students demonstrate an ability to sing in tune and move their bodies in an organized manner when they begin instruction on a musical instrument, or certainly soon thereafter. Many would also play by ear (by audiation) and would improvise on familiar folk songs if they were given the opportunity. The focus on being able to read music for the first concert presents a major roadblock to improvising and eventually reading music with comprehension.

In the proper learning environment, it would be difficult to deter students from improvisation. Imagine trying to prevent a child from learning to speak and to carry on a conversation. The instinct to improvise music may be as natural as the instinct for speech in language (Pinker, 1995), and making mistakes is just as indispensable to the learning process. Mistakes are generally not acceptable, however, in the traditional beginning instrumental music classroom.

In many instances, students with the requisite musicianship to improvise are neither challenged nor made comfortable in the current environment for beginning instrumental music. Sadly, those same students often comprise a significant portion of the dropouts. When instruction is appropriate, not only will those students be challenged, but their musicianship will provide a foundation for others whose musicianship is not as well developed. Students should learn as much from musicianship demonstrated by classmates, e.g., intonation, rhythm, style, and characteristic tone quality, as they learn from the teacher. An environment where students are encouraged to play by ear and make mistakes is also an environment in which improvisation will flourish.

In addition to promoting learning, improvisation assists teachers in measuring and evaluating student achievement. In language, we routinely discover one's level of comprehension through conversation. Improvisation should serve a similar function in instrumental music instruction. When students improvise, they are telling us what they audiate, i.e., what they comprehend musically.

Understanding improvisation as an indicator of comprehension certainly calls into question the current penchant for pentatonic and "blues-scale" improvisation designed specifically to ensure that student mistakes are minimal. Although such "failsafe" approaches generally are based on good intentions, students will not express their audiation unless mistakes are possible. Again, imagine learning to speak without being allowed to make mistakes, or, worse yet, having someone correct you on every mistake. When first learning to speak a language, mistakes are inevitable. The role of the parent or caregiver is to provide a model of appropriate language in combination with an encouraging learning environment. The same conditions should exist when young instrumentalists are learning to improvise music.

After students have been taught to improvise and read music with comprehension, they can be easily taught to compose and arrange music, in much the same way that they can learn to write and to compose literature after they have learned to read language with comprehension. Knowing how to evaluate the music of this and other cultures is another natural outcome. When students learn to audiate, they also demonstrate the readiness to make "musical" connections with other arts, other subjects, history, and culture.

*Methods, Techniques, and Materials*

Methods, techniques, and materials are the "stuff" traditionally taught in instrumental music courses at the undergraduate level. Because the difference between method and technique is not clearly defined, the emphasis of those courses is traditionally on materials. The result is a course often lacking relevance and purpose, not to mention consistency. A teacher who demonstrates good method has an understanding of what to teach, when to teach it, and why. Equally important are techniques that provide suggestions for how to teach. For example, a beginning instrumental teacher who understands method begins instruction as students learn to audiate (when) with Major and Minor tonalities and Duple and Triple meters (what) because those are the tonalities and meters that are most pervasive in this culture (why). Because a sense of tonality and a sense of meter are acquired gradually, the teacher should use appropriate teaching techniques (how) to educe and enhance those skills. Teaching materials include method books and instrumental music used to facilitate the methods and techniques employed by the teacher.

Obviously, beginning instrumental music teachers should give high priority to appropriate methods, techniques, and materials. *Jump Right In: The Instrumental Series* (Grunow, Gordon, & Azzara, 2001) includes sequentially ordered lesson plans (method) and more than thirty procedures (techniques) for beginning instrumental music based on Music Learning Theory. The lesson plans and teaching procedures are designed to accommodate individual teaching styles. What follows here are significant underlying principles embraced by Music Learning Theory that should guide instrumental music teachers as they develop appropriate methods and techniques and choose effective materials to meet the musical needs of their students.

*The Audiation Instrument, Executive Skills Instrument, Context, and "Practice."* A student learning to play an instrument based on the tenets of Music Learning Theory will in reality be learning two instruments—the audiation instrument (the instrument in the student's head) and the executive skills instrument (the instrument in the student's hands). Because audiation is to music what thought is to language, it is through audiation that children learn a sense of tonality, meter, and style. If the audiation instrument has not been established previously, the instrumental music teacher must teach those skills in order to provide a context for learning. Without a musical context, the executive skill instrument becomes a mechanical tool with no connection to audiation. In that setting, the student will take only minimal ownership for the music that results, now and in the future.

Fortunately, the executive skills instrument is easier to learn when the audiation instrument supports it. A characteristic embouchure will develop much faster, for example, when a student is audiating an appropriate musical model. Technique or finger dexterity is less of an obstacle when a student can sing the melody being learned. The long-standing tradition of building technique through a regimen of scales and arpeggios will be viewed in a new light when technique is supported by audiation. Breathing correctly to play a musical instrument becomes as natural as breathing in order to speak. For instance, if a person thinks before speaking, enough air will generally be inhaled to express the thought. A similar action occurs when students are taught to audiate before playing a passage on their instrument. Little time will need to be spent teaching students how to breathe or how much bow to use.

Practice also takes on new meaning when the audiation instrument and executive skills instrument are operating in the proper sequence. In other core subjects, students are not instructed to practice. Rather, they are encouraged to "study." If they comprehend the English language and understand the functioning of mathematics, for example, they have acquired a context for the subject matter and "study" becomes a possibility. When students acquire a context for music, they will also be able to "study" music. "Practice" will then be placed in the proper perspective, along with "practice records." Can you recall the last time that a student turned in a "practice record" for English or mathematics?

*Whole-Part-Whole.* The concept of whole-part-whole is perhaps the most obvious common-sense issue embraced by language and also by Music Learning Theory. For example, when learning language, children first hear their parents speak and carry on conversations (whole). As children begin to speak, their first intelligible utterances are generally words or short phrases (parts). Learning the parts is crucial. How much would a child comprehend in conversation without understanding the meanings of words or phrases? Eventually children put the parts together into longer phrases and sentences, forming the whole again. This process continues indefinitely.

So, how does this concept apply to beginning instrumental music instruction? We should start with the whole. We should sing familiar songs for students—hundreds of songs—and play instrumental music for them comprising many different timbres; and we should teach them to sing the songs and play them on their instruments through audiation. To deepen their understanding of the melodies, they should learn the bass line (roots of the chord progression) for each song in addition to the melody. After students have acquired a large repertoire of songs through audiation, teachers will better understand each student's musicianship and will be able to attend more credibly to individual differences.

While learning songs (whole), students also should be taught the parts. In music, tonal patterns and rhythm patterns serve the same function as words in language. Just as language comprehension relies on an understanding of words, so music comprehension relies on an understanding of tonal patterns and rhythm patterns. Patterns based on function are most efficient when teaching students to comprehend music. For example, students should sing tonic and dominant patterns in Major and Minor tonalities and chant macrobeats and microbeats (large beats and small beats) in Duple and Triple meters, because those are the most characteristic functions in those tonalities and meters. After singing and chanting, students should perform the tonal patterns and rhythm patterns on their instruments. Equally important, the patterns must become familiar.

*Familiar versus Unfamiliar.* Imagine reading a book in which all of the words are familiar. That is, you have heard the words before, thought about them, used them in conversation with others, and perhaps used them in your writing. Reading progresses quickly in that setting. In fact, you are able to read silently at a pace that is faster than the time it would take to read the words aloud. You are not restricted to "real time" because you are able to comprehend and retain much of what you read. You can even answer questions and talk freely about what you have read. Contrast that experience with reading a book in which most of the words are unfamiliar. The pace of your reading slows, as well as the comprehension of what you have read. When too many words are unfamiliar, you experience tunnel vision—the brain is overloaded with visual information (Smith, 1997, pp. 25–26). In some cases, you may actually be able to pronounce the words; but comprehension still eludes you, and it is difficult to discuss what you have read.

The same concept applies to reading music. When students are confronted with music notation containing too many patterns that are unfamiliar, they experience a similar tunnel vision. Being unfamiliar with a particular style of music—jazz, salsa, Mozart, country, etc.—may also cause a type of tunnel vision. (A style of music could be compared to a particular dialect within a language.) If the patterns and styles are familiar, reading moves quickly. In many instances, students are able to sing what they have played or are able to play/sing an improvisation that is representative of the melody after they have performed it. Because the music is familiar and students comprehend what they are reading, they are able to read silently (audiate) at a pace that is faster than real time—the time it would take to perform it on the instrument. How do the patterns become familiar?

A style or a pattern in music becomes familiar in much the same way a word becomes familiar in language. First, children should hear music containing those tonal and rhythm functions in the particular style of music. In other words, before students are taught tonic and dominant patterns in Major tonality, they should have heard many songs containing tonic and dominant functions in Major tonality—the listening environment is of the utmost importance. When learning individual patterns, the teacher sings a tonal pattern or chants a rhythm pattern and performs it in duet with the student (teaching mode). Then the teacher sings or chants that pattern and the same student performs it solo (evaluation mode).[2] When the student can perform the pattern solo, that pattern is familiar to the student. Just as

---

2 For additional information on the Teaching Mode/Evaluation Mode, see *Jump Right In: The Instrumental Series – Teacher's Guide for Winds and Percussion* (2001) by Grunow, Gordon, & Azzara (Chicago: GIA Publications), p. 278.

children begin to use a new word in conversation, students will begin to use new patterns in their improvisations. They will also begin to recognize the familiar patterns and styles in the music that they listen to and perform.

When learning to read music, students should learn first to read familiar patterns and series of familiar patterns, then entire melodies. In language, children follow a similar sequence when they read familiar words and phrases, followed by entire sentences. It is important to remember that students do not learn to read, or improve their reading, by attempting to read music that they cannot comprehend. And for the same reason that children are not asked to read individual letters in language, children should not be asked to read individual pitches in music. There is no meaning in an individual letter; there is also no meaning in an individual pitch. The current practice of "reading" music notation through the immediate introduction of individual notes in combination with music theory and instrument fingerings does not lead to reading with comprehension. Tonal syllables and rhythm syllables can also be used to great advantage to prepare students to read music with comprehension.

*Tonal and Rhythm Syllables.* In language we name things to help us think better. Tonal syllables and rhythm syllables serve a similar function when learning to comprehend music. They enable us to store more information and to audiate better. In language, we associate words with things, feelings, places, etc. In music, we associate tonal syllables and rhythm syllables with aural events. Because there is no aural logic inherent in note names (C, D, E, etc.) and note values ( ♩, 𝅗𝅥, ♪, etc.) we are wise to create logic by having students associate syllables with tonalities (Major and Minor), tonal functions (tonic and dominant), meters (Duple and Triple), and rhythm functions (macrobeats and microbeats). For example, DO is the resting tone in Major tonality; LA is the resting tone in Minor tonality. Du de Du de is associated with Duple meter; Du da di Du da di is associated with Triple meter.

Teaching names for tonal functions, e.g., tonic and dominant, and names for rhythm functions, e.g., macrobeats and microbeats, is as important as teaching tonal and rhythm syllables. For example, any combination of DO MI SO is a tonic pattern in Major tonality; any combination of SO FA RE and TI is a dominant pattern in Major tonality. In terms of rhythm, Du de Du Du Du de ( e.g., $\frac{2}{4}$ ♫♩ |♩ ♫| ) is a macro/microbeat pattern in Duple meter, and Du da di Du Du Du da di (e.g., $\frac{6}{8}$ ♫♩· |♩· ♫♩| ) is a macro/microbeat pattern in Triple meter.

In Music Learning Theory, all tonal and rhythm syllables are associated with aural events. Syllables are not determined by note names or note valucs. Also, tonal syllables must be performed within a tonal context, and rhythm syllables must be performed within a rhythm context. Choosing syllables based on aural events as opposed to note names or note values is important,[3] but debating the merits of various syllable systems rarely results in curricular change until a syllable system begins to impede audiation. It is best to experiment with various aurally based syllable systems, then decide which system leads to improvement of audiation (comprehension).

*Same and Different.* Throughout this chapter, I have made reference to comparisons: Major and Minor; tonic and dominant; Duple and Triple; macro and micro; melodies and bass lines. Equally important are the comparisons among various styles of articulations, styles of music, and instrumental timbres. In Music Learning Theory, discrimination learning[4] will be extremely limited unless students are asked to make comparisons. In other words, students will not know what Major tonality is until they can compare it with Minor tonality; students will not understand Duple meter until they have been exposed to Triple meter; students will understand the melody better if they can also sing the bass line, and so on. We know what something is by understanding what it is not.

Unfortunately, most beginning instrumental music method books contain only Major tonality, Duple meter, and music of a similar style. Even if the instrumental teacher is prudent about establishing a context (tonality and meter), students in a traditional setting will still not be able to compare Major tonality with Minor tonality or Duple meter with Triple meter until later in their study. In addition to comparing tonalities and meters, students will benefit by comparing musical styles. For example, much can be gained by performing a familiar folk song in a jazz or classical style. Unless comparisons are possible, comprehension will be limited at best.

### Measurement and Evaluation

In other curricular subjects, students are measured (tested) and evaluated (graded) on criteria that represent the substance of the discipline. In mathematics, for example, students are tested on their ability to add, subtract, multiply, divide, and engage in additional higher order cognitive skills in mathematics. Grades are subsequently assigned based on the

---

[3] For more information on the rhythm syllables used in Gordon's Music Learning Theory, see "The Evolution of Rhythm Syllables in Gordon's Music Learning Theory" (1992) by Grunow.

[4] Discrimination learning is the first of two types of learning in Music Learning Theory. At the discrimination learning stage, the teacher is responsible for teaching. In the second type of learning, inference, students are able to teach themselves. If students are not taught well at the discrimination level, they will have little success in teaching themselves when studying the instrument as a part of formal education or when they complete formal education in music.

students' various levels of achievement. For example, if understanding a specific mathematical problem is the objective, the teacher should use effective methods, techniques, and materials in pursuit of that objective. Measurement and evaluation are the final steps in determining the degree to which the objective has been accomplished. Although measurement also provides information upon which grades may be based, the fundamental reason for measurement and evaluation is for the improvement of instruction. It is of equal importance to the students and to the teacher.

In contrast, traditional instrumental music education tends to be product driven. Contest ratings, the number of all-state participants, the number of trophies assembled in the music room, and often the number of students in the various ensembles attest to the success of the program. In terms of determining individual grades, the most prevalent criteria continue to be attitude, attendance, and practice time (effort).

When the success of the music program is based on group performance, and individual achievement is clouded with non-musical criteria, is it surprising that instrumental music is considered a frill—an extra-curricular activity and perhaps without the intrinsic worth to merit inclusion in the core curriculum? Does that group emphasis also explain why many students do not achieve the independent musicianship necessary to continue performing on their instruments or to participate in society as intelligent makers and consumers of music?

When students are taught according to the principles of Music Learning Theory, they are measured and evaluated on their progress in singing, moving, reading, writing, and improvising.[5] In the process of learning those skills, students will also develop self-esteem, discipline, and cooperation. Those outcomes are both welcome and unavoidable, but they are ancillary to the fundamental reasons for teaching music. They should be a part of every offering in the curriculum. Although attitude, attendance, and practice time (effort) may be reported to parents, those factors are not used as criteria for assigning grades. If developing musicianship also benefits other subject areas, so be it, but it should not be a justification for teaching music.

### Research and Music Learning Theory

It should be evident that a body of research and common sense exists in support of Music Learning Theory as a model for teaching beginning

---

[5] The rating scale is perhaps the most reliable and valid measure of achievement in instrumental music, both in terms of the audiation instrument and the executive skills instruments. For more information on rating scales, see Gordon (2003), pp. 320–323.

instrumental music. Much of the research and common sense applies to many types of instruction; it is not specific to music instruction. Nevertheless, it is Gordon's research that gave rise to Music Learning Theory, and it is his research that impacts most directly on beginning instrumental music instruction. In retrospect, many of his research findings also appear to be common sense, a trait that is characteristic of much good research.

A substantial amount of Music Learning Theory is grounded in Gordon's early research on music aptitude. His findings indicate that music aptitude is normally distributed across the population. In other words, barring some physical disability, every person is capable of learning to sing, read, write, create, improvise, and play a musical instrument to some degree. In light of this information, it is troubling that approximately half the number of students who possess high levels of music aptitude, those who score between the 80th and 99th percentiles on a valid music aptitude test, do not demonstrate high levels of music achievement. Because most music teachers are not aware of the music aptitude levels of their students, approximately 50% of the students with overall high music aptitudes are not encouraged to participate in school orchestras, bands, or choruses. In other words, there are large numbers of students in a typical school that have more aptitude for music than the students who have elected music instruction (Gordon, 2003, p. 51). If those students were attracted to the music program, they would undoubtedly a) benefit from the instruction because of their high aptitude; b) contribute to the learning environment of other students in the class who have less potential; and c) contribute now and in the future to a more musical culture.

Although the pervasive nature of music aptitude certainly is welcome news, without question the greatest attribute of Gordon's aptitude tests is the potential of those tests to assist in attending to the individual differences of students. Aptitude tests uncover what the teacher cannot observe. For example, a student who cannot sing in tune may have high aptitude—the student may not have been previously given the opportunity to sing. What is perhaps most frustrating are those teachers who persuade students to quit because of a perceived lack of musical potential or willingness to put forth the effort.

Gordon's research on developmental and stabilized music aptitude has particular relevance to the beginning instrumental music teacher. It is at nine or ten years of age that students are typically "recruited" for beginning instrumental music. Because music aptitude stabilizes at about nine or ten years of age, the potential to achieve in instrumental music can only be addressed prior to that age. If children who are nine or ten years of age have not achieved a sense of tonality and meter and have not been exposed to many styles of music, the task of successfully initiating those behaviors is an ominous one.

Anyone who has studied Gordon's aptitude tests understands the importance of providing a musical context to achieve the impressive reliabilities and validities that accompany those tests. In spite of that evidence, a musical context is absent in the vast majority of beginning instrumental music classrooms. Teachers rarely establish a sense of tonality or meter for their students, and little attempt is made to provide a context for style. Even when music teachers are so inclined, it is accomplished with great difficulty because traditional materials encourage students to perform individual notes and to perform uncharacteristic rhythms at unmusical tempos.

The *Instrumental Timbre Preference Test* (Gordon, 1984) is the result of Gordon's research on instrumental timbre. For many instrumental teachers, physical characteristics are thought to be predictive of success on a particular instrument, although there is no objective evidence to support that contention. However, Gordon's research does indicate that if a student likes the sound and range of a particular musical instrument, the student will be more successful on that instrument than on one that has a sound and range that the student does not prefer. The purpose of the *Instrumental Timbre Preference Test* is to act as an objective aid to the teacher and parent in helping a student choose an appropriate woodwind, brass, or string instrument to learn in beginning instrumental music.

Research on patterns and improvisation are areas that have also attracted Gordon's research attention. Both are additional examples of common sense applied to music instruction that are largely absent from current practice. Perhaps Gordon's greatest research contribution is that he has opened the door for future researchers to focus on musical behavior, behavior based in audiation.

### Recommendations

Numerous suggestions have been presented for applying Music Learning Theory to various aspects of the music learning process. The following recommendations are directed at areas in which Music Learning Theory could have the most immediate impact: college methods courses, early childhood education and general music classes, and beginning instrumental music instruction.

1.  Methods, techniques, and materials courses at the college level should focus on musicianship, teaching skills, and an understanding of the

INSTRUMENTAL APPLICATIONS

learning process. Future teachers will have little success when teaching students to comprehend music if they lack the requisite musicianship, teaching skills, and knowledge of how children learn music. The measurement and evaluation of musical comprehension should be addressed in all methods courses at the undergraduate level. A course devoted solely to measurement and evaluation—as a readiness for doing research—should also be a requirement at the undergraduate level.

2. Beginning instrumental music teachers should forge supportive relationships with parents, teachers in early childhood, and especially general music teachers. The role those persons occupy in preparing students to begin instruction on a musical instrument cannot be overstated. There is little justification for the separation that now exists between beginning instrumental music and general music. Common sense, and even tradition, suggest that a child should be able to sing in tune and engage in organized movement before performing on an instrument. In many instances, students do demonstrate a sense of tonality and a sense of meter because of effective general music instruction. When most students begin instruction on an instrument, however, they never sing or move again as a part of that instruction. Conversely, the beginning instrumental teacher has every right to ask of the general music teacher, "If children are not learning to sing in tune and move their bodies in an organized manner as a part of general music instruction, what are they learning?"

3. Children should be encouraged to listen to all styles of music of our culture (including popular music), sing that music, and learn to play it by ear on their instruments. It is time that we put aside the myth that students get enough popular music outside of the music classroom. They may be exposed to popular music at times that lacks great depth, however, much popular music is rich in content. Without question, much of the current popular music is richer in content than many of the compositions and arrangements written for beginning instrumental ensembles. Unless students interact through singing and performance, they will not comprehend any music. Exposure is not enough. After all, we wouldn't expect a child to understand a language just by listening to it on TV or radio. They must interact with the language. The same is true for popular music and the music of other cultures. Without interaction, musical choices will be based more on

prejudice than substance. When students are taught to interact and comprehend many styles of music in this and in other cultures, all music will be elevated to a higher level.

4.  The current obsession of beginning instrumental music teachers to perform with notation on the first concert should be replaced with, "We must perform our first concert without notation." Instead of focusing on notation, the instrumental music teacher should engage the students in singing and movement activities while at the same time teaching students to chant rhythm patterns, sing tonal patterns, and perform simple tunes and bass lines on their instruments by ear. The first concert should include singing, movement, and performing by ear (audiation). Most important, the concert should feature students' improvisations of familiar tunes that they have learned to play without notation. The first concert also presents an opportunity for music teachers to engage the parents in singing and movement and to discuss the process by which students learn music.

## Conclusions

Throughout this discussion I have examined the tenets of Music Learning Theory as a sequential model for teaching beginning instrumental music, a model substantive enough to position instrumental music in the core of the educational curriculum. Change is difficult; it is also inevitable. Part of professional responsibility in our discipline is to institute change that will sustain musical integrity. Music Learning Theory is the appropriate catalyst to initiate that kind of change. Otherwise, instrumental music education will be the recipient of misinformation and change that is deemed appropriate for other subject areas.

Two questions posed at the onset of this discussion remain unanswered. I will close by answering them.

*   Is it realistic to expect improvements in beginning instrumental music instruction that are as dramatic as those in health care? When students are taught according to the principles of Music Learning Theory—by a skillful teacher who demonstrates musicianship and an understanding of the learning process—the results are perhaps more dramatic than those in the medical profession. Students demonstrate musicianship at the elementary level that is far beyond most students at the secondary and college level. The evidence already exists. They also demonstrate the potential to become music makers and intelligent

consumers of music during and beyond their formal education. Perhaps the greatest challenge is to attract future teachers who have the requisite musicianship to be effective in applying Music Learning Theory to instrumental music instruction.

- Will society ever support, encourage, and even demand changes in the way beginning instrumental music is taught? Society is demanding change whenever instrumental music is cut from the budget or reduced in the schedule. Because music is perceived as "extra-curricular" rather than basic to the curriculum, the reductions and cuts are not surprising. Any subject that does not have unique offerings will eventually meet a similar demise. If music is to be basic to the curriculum, we must teach what is basic about music. What is perhaps most frustrating is that justifying music in terms of the non-musical objectives only delays the changes necessary for instrumental music to become a valued part of the curriculum. Society will support and encourage change if the result raises the standard of music in the culture—for all individuals. The greatest danger lies in not risking change.

## References

Adderley, C. L. (1996). Music teacher preparation in South Carolina colleges and universities relative to the National Standards: Goals 2000 (Doctoral dissertation, University of South Carolina). *Dissertation Abstracts International, 57*(11A) 4680.

Austin, J. R. (1988). Competitive and noncompetitive goal structures: An analysis of motivation and achievement outcomes among elementary band students (Doctoral dissertation, University of Iowa). *Dissertation Abstracts International, 50*(04A) 0893.

Azzara, C. D. (1992). Audiation-based improvisation techniques and elementary instrumental students' music achievement. *Journal of Research in Music Education, 41*(04), 328-342.

Brown, J. D. (1990). *The Gemeinhardt report 3: Through the eyes of the parent.* Elkhart: The Gemeinhardt Company, 15-17.

Gordon, E. E. (1984). *Instrumental timbre preference test.* Chicago: GIA Publications.

———. (2003). *Learning sequences in music: Skill, content, and patterns.* Chicago: GIA Publications.

Grunow, R. F. (1992). The evolution of rhythm syllables in Gordon's music learning theory. *Quarterly Journal of Music Teaching and Learning, 3*(4), 56-66.

——. (1999). Making connections between early childhood music and beginning instrumental music. *Journal of Music- and Movement-Based Learning, 5*(4), 13-24.

Grunow, R. F., Gordon, E. E., & Azzara, C. D. (2001). *Jump right in: The instrumental series - teacher's guide for winds and percussion.* Chicago: GIA Publications.

Healy, J. M. (1990). *Endangered minds.* New York: Simon and Schuster.

Lehman, P. R. (1999). National assessment of arts education: A first look. *Music Educators Journal, 85*(4), 34-37.

Lehman, P. R., Hinckley, J., Hoffer, C., Lindeman, C., Reimer, B., Shuler, S., & Straub, D. (Eds). (1994). *The school music program: A new vision.* Reston, VA: MENC.

Persky, H. R., Sandene, B. A., & Askew, J. M. (1998). *The NAEP 1997 arts report card.* Washington, DC: National Center for Educational Statistics.

Pinker, S. (1995). *The language instinct.* New York: Harper Perennial.

Smith, F. (1997). *Reading without nonsense* (3rd ed.). New York: Teachers College Press.

*Michael Norman*

• • • • • • • • • • •

DEWITT PUBLIC SCHOOLS, DEWITT, MI

# Developing Thinking Musicians in Instrumental Music

## Introduction

My first year of teaching, as is fairly typical, was wonderful in some respects and horrible in others. As a part of my responsibilities, I taught beginning instrumental music. In these classes, I used a standard, well-respected instrumental method book as my means of sequencing instruction, and yet, as I reflected on my teaching, I began to believe that I was not really teaching music. Rather, I was engaging my students in operant conditioning; they learned that, when they "see this dot," they should "press this button." The mindset in the classroom was "don't ask questions until you're in college studying music." I instinctively knew that what I was doing with my students did not lead to their developing independent musicianship and that it did not encourage reflective thinking. Students were unable to make music without my being present to guide their behavior. This presented an enormous philosophical problem for me, as I had always believed in the importance of developing thinking musicians who could continue to learn independently. I remember having the sixth grade beginning players put their instruments together, set their embouchures, and finger concert B-flat; then I conducted them to play their first sound (which, of course, was a whole note). In response, I heard "BLAAAAAAAAAHEAHHAAHAUHHTspbtspsbtpbsbstb." It wasn't the sound that scared me, although it was certifiably awful, and it wasn't that 105 children were sitting in front of me holding $60,000 worth of metal and wood; what was most unsettling was the students' asking, "Well…how was it?" after they had played their note. I instantly knew that I needed to teach my students to think for themselves musically.

201

Most teachers who have taught instrumental beginners can relate, at least to some degree, to my experience. Underlying our traditional instructional model in instrumental music is the unspoken message that music teachers have "special ears" through which every student's sounds must travel so that they can be judged and corrected. In essence, we have created an external locus of control, rather than giving our students responsibility for their own music making and learning. My goal, as an instrumental music teacher, has become to develop as musically independent instrumentalists as possible. By doing so, the quality of my ensembles has improved, and rehearsals are more efficient and meaningful to the students.

Over the past several years, I have been incorporating principles of Gordon's Music Learning Theory into my teaching and have found them to be tremendously helpful in providing an instructional framework that facilitates the development of musicianship in my students. Also, I have found that using Music Learning Theory has drastically improved my own musicianship as well. As a result of embracing Music Learning Theory in my classroom, the majority of my students are able to improvise fluently, not just in Major but also in Dorian, Mixolydian, and Harmonic Minor. Their improvisations are not limited to Duple meter, but extend to Triple and Unusual meters as well. Improvisation formerly was "mystical" and was only attempted by students with exceptional musicianship and interest. Now all students improvise. In addition, students successfully create music compositions that make sense harmonically, with cadences that create clear pauses/interest points/endings and have melodies that fit the chord structure. They also compose appropriate countermelodies and interesting harmony parts.

## Music Learning Theory as a Framework for Teaching Beginners

Beginning instrumental music using Music Learning Theory is fundamentally different from more traditional approaches. Rather than focusing on learning music notation and individual notes, rhythms, and fingerings, students learn a vocabulary of tonal and rhythm patterns in the context of a tonality or a meter, respectively. They also learn to sing and eventually play songs and the root melodies (the chord-root underpinnings of the harmonic structure) for those songs by ear, singing them first using a neutral syllable and then by associating tonal or rhythm syllables to the patterns in the song. Eventually, they learn to generalize what they have learned by rote from the familiar patterns to unfamiliar patterns and songs.

Once students have developed a practical, audiational fluency through singing and then playing rhythm and tonal patterns, songs, and root melodies, they can bring their knowledge to the reading of music notation.

I begin by showing the students the music notation (symbols) for what they already know. They learn to recognize familiar patterns and songs in music notation. I have found that students are capable of actually hearing the notation in their heads (audiating) as they look at it and that they understand what they are performing from notation in a rich, deep way.

## Warm-ups

My warm-up routine focuses on developing audiational skills, both without and with the use of instruments. Even though an understanding of these warm-ups requires extensive description, all of the following singing activities require a total of only about eight minutes of actual rehearsal time.

Our warm-up begins with a moment of silence in which I ask the students to audiate B-flat concert (which I call B-flat DO) without making a sound. Then, using a well-tuned piano, I play the tonic, dominant, and another tonic chord in B-flat Major concert to establish tonality. At this point, I have either the group or individuals tell me whether they were sharp or flat when they audiated. By using this procedure consistently, most of our beginners understand the concept of sharp and flat by the sixth week of instruction. They learn to audiate tonic within a tonal context.

Next, we identify a pitch to use as the resting tone (tonic) so that we can perform a familiar song in that key and in a specific tonality. In sixth grade, I limit our choices to (all in concert pitch) B-flat DO, E-flat DO, F DO, C LA, C RE, and F SO. Because we use movable DO with LA-based Minor tonal syllables; when DO is the resting tone, we are audiating Major tonality; when LA is the resting tone, we are in Minor tonality; when RE is the resting tone, we are in Dorian tonality; and when SO is the resting tone, we are in Mixolydian tonality. I give our agreed-upon resting tone context by playing tonic-dominant (or subtonic for Dorian and Mixolydian)—tonic on the piano. Then I ask the students to audiate the starting pitch of the familiar song (which may or may not be the resting tone) and sing it. Because they could be asked to audiate the song in any of the four tonalities, this is only successful when students are able to audiate fluently in each tonality. Early in the year, we focus on audiating, singing, and playing in Major and Minor tonalities, adding Dorian and Mixolydian later, first by learning songs, chord root melodies, and patterns by ear in those tonalities. Only after students have a repertoire of songs in each tonality can they begin to change the tonality of familiar songs. After we find the beginning pitch, the students typically sing the familiar song while fingering their "air instruments." At this point, their instruments are either in their cases or in rest position, as all performance is vocal rather than instrumental.

Next, I teach the root melody using the same procedure. Students develop accurate intonation through singing melodies and root melodies. Intonation cannot be developed linearly, as the context for intonation is always vertical. In order to play in tune, students must audiate the harmonic underpinning of a pitch so that the pitch can be fit into the context of a tonality. To develop a harmonic sense in my students, I ask them to learn root melodies of each melody we have sung. Many times, I simplify the root melody to focus only on tonic and dominant underpinnings. I teach the root melody by rote by singing "tonic" and "dominant" on the appropriate pitches for each particular harmonic change in the music. Then, I divide the students into two groups and have one group sing the melody and the other sing the root melody. By putting the melody into a harmonic context, students begin to hear contextually. As a result, they naturally sing and eventually play in tune.

Through singing, we build a repertoire of songs and root melodies, which we will eventually transfer to instruments. This portion of the warm-up is designed to develop audiational skills rather than instrumental technique. I begin with songs that use only tonic and dominant functions in Major and Minor, and gradually progress to subdominant function and the tonalities of Dorian and Mixolydian. Whenever I sing to model for the students, I perform as musically as possible, using expression, phrasing, and articulation. For songs in a connected style, I sing using the articulation syllable "doo," and for songs in a separated style, I sing using the syllable "too." I try to engage my students' musicianship by asking them questions such as: Which type of articulation works best for this song? Why? Is this song in Major, Minor, Dorian, or Mixolydian tonality? Is this song in Duple or Triple meter? How do you know? Can you audiate a root melody for the song? What types of chords are in your root melody? Do you hear any pitches that don't normally fit in the tonality (accidentals)? When the students are more advanced, I ask them to improvise a root melody while I sing the song. I then ask the group why the root melody fits or does not fit with the song. Following this singing, I ask the students to get out their instruments.

While students are getting their instruments out, I sing unfamiliar melodies in order to acculturate the students to new tonalities or meters and to help them to develop an informal vocabulary of songs that we will eventually sing and play. I do not expect them to respond or participate musically other than to listen and to absorb the unfamiliar sounds. The goal is to acculturate them to songs and new meters and tonalities so that the sounds are familiar before I teach those songs, tonalities, and meters in a more direct way. I have found that students benefit greatly when I provide at least fifteen to twenty seconds of silence after performing each song or chant. Though some students may fill this silence with talking or random activity, most of the students are audiating. They are manipulating the new information by trying to sing it to themselves, figure out tonic, associate rhythm or tonal syllables, or identify the tonality or meter. Although this time may seem like a lapse in rehearsal pacing to the casual observer, I am convinced that this is not the case; students need time to process new information before immediately moving on to a new task.

In summary, the following is a list of the singing/listening activities that I perform at the start of every rehearsal with my first-year instrumentalists.

1. Establish B-flat DO.
2. Establish a new tonality, find the starting pitch of a familiar song, and sing the song.
3. Learn or review the root melody for that song, and then sing it with the melody.
4. Review other familiar songs and root melodies, perhaps in new keys, tonalities, or meters, and ask the students questions about those songs.
5. Acculturate the students to the tonalities and meters of the music as they assemble their instruments and prepare to play.

## Tonal Patterns

I use tonal patterns as our physical warm-up on the instruments, and they are presented using a process similar to the one that will be used later as we learn to play rote songs. Students begin by listening to me sing the patterns using a neutral syllable, such as "bum." Then, they echo-sing them using neutral syllables. Next the students echo-sing them using tonal syllables, and then they repeat this while fingering the patterns on their instruments. Students obviously cannot use patterns as an instrumental warm-up until the patterns are familiar to them.

Tonal patterns serve a function similar to that of words in language. In speech we do not attend to the individual letters of words while we are speaking; neither do we attend to the individual notes of a melody. Words operate in specific ways in our language, each serving a specific function. Some are nouns, others are verbs, and so on. The same can be said of the tonal patterns. Each pattern carries with it a harmonic function in the context of a tonality, such as tonic, dominant, or subtonic. Helping students develop a tonal pattern vocabulary is one of the most important pieces in cultivating their musicianship. Once students have a tonal vocabulary, they can create accompaniments and melodies, begin to improvise, and become more sensitive to tonal context, which is the heart of good intonation.

Once students are familiar with a set of patterns and can play them on their instruments, I begin to sing the patterns to the students using solfege and have them reply by singing the name of the tonal function of the pattern (either tonic or dominant) on the tonic or dominant chord root, depending upon the function of the chord. For instance, I might sing "MI-SO-DO," and the students would sing back "tonic" on the tonic pitch. Once most of the students can do this, I sing the familiar patterns without tonal solfege and ask the students to respond by singing the pattern with tonal syllables. Often we will review tonal patterns with tonal syllables so that when students are learning a rote song by ear they can analyze the tonal content of the song using their vocabulary of tonal patterns.

The use of tonal syllables helps my students learn to audiate harmonically in the context of a tonality. For instance, in Major tonality, I teach the students that tonic function "owns" DO, MI, and SO, meaning that any combination, order, or number of those pitches is a tonic pattern. Correspondingly, in Major, dominant "owns" SO, FA, RE, and TI. Students learn a large vocabulary of these patterns in Major and in Harmonic Minor at first.

When presenting tonal patterns, I begin by presenting them in Major tonality. However, after only a couple of class periods, I introduce Minor. Students benefit by working in multiple tonalities because of the value of the comparisons that students are able to make. They learn to understand what something is by experiencing what it is not. By the end of our first year of instruction, students can audiate functions in Major, Harmonic Minor, Dorian, and Mixolydian (tonic, dominant, subdominant, subtonic).

## Rote Songs

After warming the students up with tonal patterns, I move into the instrumental "meat" of the rehearsal. Once students have heard a song a number of times informally and have learned it through singing warm-ups, I present it to them to learn on their instruments. First, I review the song with them by asking them to listen to the entire song (the whole). Then I ask them to echo-sing phrases (the parts), and then I ask them to echo the whole song. When singing, we use the neutral syllable "bum" or the articulation syllables "too" or "doo." After reviewing the song vocally, we repeat this process by playing the parts of the song and then the whole song on instruments. Learning the executive skills (technical skills) necessary to perform a new piece instrumentally typically requires about half a rehearsal period. During this instructional time, we work with executive skills, such as fingerings, posture, or embouchure. I begin with songs that have simple harmonic rhythm, typically only consisting of tonic and dominant functions. For example, "Major Duple" from *Jump Right In: The Instrumental Series* uses only tonic and dominant (Grunow, Gordon, & Azzara, 1998).

After the students have learned to play the melody of the song, I teach them to play the root melody, which they have already sung during warm-ups in a previous rehearsal. After reviewing the root melody vocally, we transfer what the students can already sing and audiate to their instruments. Then we can combine the melody and the root melody, either assigning parts or allowing students to choose which part they prefer to perform. I find that when I give students a choice, the group splits fairly evenly between the melody and the root melody. Although the melody of the song may seem more interesting to perform, many students prefer to perform the root melody because it challenges them audiationally.

## Improvisation

Once students can play several songs and the accompanying root melodies and can demonstrate an understanding of tonal function during tonal pattern instruction, they are ready to begin making some of their own musical choices through improvisation. Traditionally, improvisation has not been a part of most band rehearsals. Instrumental teachers themselves have not been taught to improvise outside of a jazz context, so they do not know how to present improvisation to their students in a general ensemble setting. Many ensemble conductors do not believe that improvisation should play an instructional role in their classrooms, as teaching students to improvise takes time away from concert preparation and the teaching of instrumental technique. However, I have found that improvisation helps students take ownership of their learning and gives them a musical voice. In improvisation lies the power of Music Learning Theory.

When using Music Learning Theory techniques and sequencing, every student can learn to improvise, regardless of his or her intellectual level or music aptitudes. Improvisation activities naturally adapt to individual differences. Students who are advancing rapidly will create more stimulating and challenging improvisations, while students who are struggling can focus on playing chord roots and improvising rhythmically, which will help them develop the understanding of context, intonation, and basic rhythmic skills.

When students are improvising for the first time, I ask that they choose only one pitch from tonic (pick DO, MI, or SO) and the same for dominant (pick SO, FA, RE, or TI). By putting limitations on the students, I am increasing their chances for success and building the self-assurance that allows them to continue to make and explore more choices over time. These limitations eliminate potential failures that might make the students less likely to engage willingly in improvisation in the future. Then we look at the notation of the familiar song that will serve as the basis for the improvisation and identify where the harmonic changes occur in the notation of the song. Although this could be accomplished without using notation, I find that having the notation as a guide in the beginning makes some students feel more confident about their improvisations.

I remind them that only tonic-function pitches can fit in the tonic parts of the piece, and only dominant-function pitches can fit in the dominant parts of the piece. Sometimes, demonstrating a sample improvisation helps the student understand the task and feel more at ease. I then ask the students to sing their improvisations to themselves and finger along while I play the changes on the piano. I pause for about fifteen seconds to allow the students to audiate what they performed and fix or change things that they did not like about their improvisations. Then I play the chord changes again, and they practice their improvisations once more. Finally, they play their improvisations on their instruments.

For their second improvisation, I ask for someone to volunteer to play their first improvisation so that we can use it to demonstrate. Using the volunteered improvisation, I ask the students what they could do to change the improvisation without changing the pitches. Usually, students suggest that they could do rhythm improvisations on each pitch. At first, the students explore rhythms by chanting using a neutral syllable, and, as a class, we decide upon a rhythm that we all like. Then, I ask the entire class to associate the rhythm syllables for the rhythmic improvisation patterns that were selected, and I ask the students to chant the rhythms using rhythm syllables as I play the chordal accompaniment to decide if they work with the song.

When the students are successful at chanting the rhythms, they then sing the rhythms on the chord tones of the original improvisations using a neutral syllable. After they have performed these improvisations vocally, they can transfer them to performance on the instruments. It is important to note that I am not giving the answers to students. Rather, students are listening critically to what they are creating within the tonal structure of the song. Their struggling to find a solution drastically deepens their understanding of how they "fit" musically within the ensemble. Often I have the students perform their improvisations for their peers, and, as a class, we critically reflect on whether each improvisation stayed within the parameters of the harmonic and rhythmic structures of the song.

From these simple beginnings, we move rapidly to using all of the functional pitches within the harmonic structure of the song. Sometimes I eliminate tonal or rhythmic choices for students to improve the quality of their improvisations. For example, when students discover that SO is shared by both tonic and dominant functions, some students choose to stay on that pitch so that they do not have to audiate tonally. By restricting their use of that pitch in their improvisations, I force them to actively engage in harmonic audiation. Also I find that some students get into an improvisational "rut" tonally. By forcing students to explore additional tonal choices, I increase the vocabulary of tonal patterns that they store in their "tonal audiation library." Because, the improvisations are based on tonal pattern functions, with no passing tones/neighbor tones at first, when the students perform their improvisations simultaneously, it creates appropriate chords at the appropriate time in the harmonic structure of the song. As a result, if a student makes the wrong choice, such as performing a dominant function pitch when they should be performing tonic, that student realizes immediately on his or her own that the choice is flawed because of the dissonance that it produces. For the benefit of high aptitude students, as soon as they are able to improvise using tonic and dominant chord tones and with rhythmic interest, I teach passing tones and neighboring tones, which makes their improvisations more interesting because they have more choices of what to include in their improvisations. I have found that this is when my students become interested in composition. Again it is important to note that, if we improvise in Major, we will improvise in Minor very shortly following that lesson. If we focus on a song in Duple meter first, we soon ask students to improvise to a song in Triple meter. We might even change the meter of the song from Duple to Triple so that students experience and improvise within different metric structures while holding the tonal elements constant.

## Rhythm Instruction

Up to this point, I primarily have focused on tonal aspects of music learning. However, rhythm instruction according to Music Learning Theory also differs from more traditional models of instrumental music instruction, which often rely on the use fractions or counting. Because of my experiences with Music Learning Theory, I use movement to help students understand the rhythmic elements of music. Specifically, I focus on helping students feel macrobeats and microbeats, which define meter, and then superimpose the melodic rhythm over the underlying metric structure of macrobeats and microbeats. Although all three of these components of rhythm are necessary for syntactical rhythmic performance, I have found that the concept of microbeats has been the most transformational in my teaching, for it is through the audiation of microbeats that students can truly understand and discriminate among meters. Once students understand and learn to feel through movement how the microbeats group themselves, many rhythmic problems are solved automatically.

I use rhythm syllables with my students, but only after they have experienced meters through movement and have developed a vocabulary of approximately ten rhythm patterns using a neutral syllable. Teaching using a neutral syllable until a group of patterns is familiar forces the students to audiate in a focused manner, but continuing to use a neutral syllable for too long creates confusion and frustration. Conversely, introducing too many patterns before using syllables overwhelms students, because they cannot remember the patterns and discriminate among them. Rhythm syllables give students a way to systematize and audiationally sort the patterns, which helps them remember a larger vocabulary. Eventually, students are taught to recognize in notation what they already know aurally and have already performed using rhythm syllables. This is similar to students learning to read words that they have already heard and spoken.

One of the most important differences in a Music Learning Theory-based approach to teaching rhythm is the paradigm shift from rhythm being about "time" to a new focus on "space." By helping students identify and feel the space between macrobeats through movement, I produce much more rhythmically savvy students. I incorporate a variety of movements when we are audiating rhythms or chanting patterns. Typically we use large body movements (movements that students can feel in their core and that have a feeling of weight) for macrobeats and smaller movements (such as those using toes, hands, and arms) to articulate microbeats. I also help students feel the space between beats by having them move in a flowing way and asking them to superimpose macrobeats or microbeats over their flowing movements in a variety of tempos and meters.

**Repertoire and Concerts**

Using *Jump Right In: The Instrumental Series*, as I do, solves most instructional sequencing concerns in my classroom. However, it is possible to teach according to Music Learning Theory using any method book, as long as one understands how to sequence the repertoire presented in the book and how to present the concepts so that students learn to audiate tonality and meter. At first, repertoire should be chosen based upon its harmonic structure. The following is a sequential taxonomy of harmony that I follow when choosing repertoire: 1) Major and Harmonic Minor tonalities with tonic and dominant functions, 2) Major and Harmonic Minor tonalities adding subdominant function and eventually other functions as the repertoire demands and the students demonstrate readiness, 3) Mixolydian tonality with tonic and subtonic functions, 4) Dorian tonality with tonic, subtonic, and subdominant functions, 5) Lydian tonality with tonic and supertonic functions, and 6) Phrygian tonality with tonic, supertonic, and subtonic functions. Students are experiencing many levels of this taxonomy in each rehearsal; I am constantly exposing students to all other tonalities through informal guidance while I may be focusing only on Major and Minor tonalities in the repertoire that we actually are performing at first.

Incorporating Music Learning Theory into my teaching has had an effect upon concerts, not only in what we play but also in how we approach them. The depth of knowledge of my students and their eagerness to demonstrate what they know is so overpowering that I have had to find ways to allow more individuals and small groups to play on concerts. A typical beginning band concert may include approximately twelve short songs that are performed by the entire band, but it will also include at least as many student small group and individual performances of variations of or improvisations on those songs or independently learned solos that they have taught themselves by ear. Individuals and small groups often perform a song that also was performed by the full band on the concert, but they have changed the meter from Duple to Triple, or vice versa, or the tonality from Major to Minor. They may perform their own arrangement of a song with one student playing the melody and others playing improvised melodies and chord roots. They even perform their own compositions, including the melody as well as harmony parts, the root melody, and sometimes countermelodies. All of this can be performed without music notation or with the notation if the students have progressed to music reading.

One of the problems that I face is the need to limit the number of individuals and small groups showcased on each concert so that the concert is an appropriate length. This is an exciting problem in that it is a result of students being so excited about what they have learned that they all want to perform in front of peers and parents. To do this, I have individuals and small groups perform for the entire ensemble several days before the concert. The students choose fifteen students or ensembles to perform by evaluating the performances and through a teacher-led discussion about appropriate programming. I also have needed to learn how to present improvisations to the audience so that they understand what the students are demonstrating through performance. I have found that having only one section of the band improvise at a time and limiting the use of passing tones and neighboring notes for the group improvisation helps the audience understand what they are hearing. Passing tones and neighboring tones used prudently make the improvisations beautiful and often quite sophisticated aurally, but too many create dissonance that is confusing to the audience.

## Beyond the Beginning

In my school system, I am also responsible for the high school band program. Using Music Learning Theory in this setting has been both challenging and rewarding. The community expects that the marching band will be of high quality and that the concert bands will go to contest and receive outstanding ratings. At first, when I was starting my beginners using Music Learning Theory, I was also teaching as many as six years of students who had no Music Learning Theory background. I had to fight a voice in my head that was saying, "I don't want to do little kid music with my finely trained ensemble."

What lay at the heart of the matter was the simple yet profound difference between technical skill and audiation. While my older students were technically skilled at reading notes and pressing appropriate buttons that corresponded to what they saw in music notation, they could not audiate their part without using an instrument. They also could not identify the tonalities, chord functions, rhythmic functions, harmonies, or keyalities of what they were performing, and they were unable to perform their music or music that they had heard without notation. Although they had developed impressive technical skills, their audiational skills, which are what allows students to make good musical decisions and become independent learners, were sorely lacking. I asked my students to play "Go Tell Aunt Rhody," which was a song that they knew without notation, and only about 40 percent of them were able to produce a recognizable version of the song in a key of their choice. So they could perform the melody of "Go Tell Aunt Rhody" easily from notation, but they could not play it by ear, play it in another key, tonality, or meter, or improvise a harmony part to the melody. They had become "button pushers" rather than comprehensive musicians.

Although I continue to teach my students in the upper grade levels using somewhat traditional rehearsal techniques, I have begun to incorporate the principles of Music Learning Theory into my rehearsal and continue to reflect upon how it could be incorporated at a deeper level. This will continue to evolve as my students who have started within a Music Learning Theory paradigm continue to progress to the upper grade levels.

My older students benefit from many of the same types of activities that I do with my beginners. These can be incorporated into warm-ups or could be used as a break from playing instruments in settings that have longer rehearsals as a result of block scheduling. As with the beginners, I include tonal or rhythm pattern instruction as a part of the audiation development activities using Gordon's tonal and rhythm pattern taxonomies (Gordon, 2003). I also teach students songs and root melodies by ear, and I ask them to figure out how to play those songs and root melodies in other keys, tonalities, or meters. All of these require audiational rather than technical skills and are basic musical operations requiring a deep understanding of the musical repertoire. High school students have a much greater capacity for conceptual (inference) learning than do the younger beginners, who are taught more easily at first using discrimination (rote) learning. Also, they will have developed a music vocabulary as a result of their music experiences in band and beyond. Consequently, they will be able to move to tasks that require inference much more quickly than younger students. They will also find inference activities stimulating and challenging.

When learning repertoire, I try to approach rhythm through movement. When introducing a new piece or trying to fix rhythm problems in more familiar works, I ask students to stand and pulse macrobeats using their heels so that they feel the pulse in their core, or to walk/move through the room to macrobeats with flow while we chant microbeats. Only when students can move to macrobeats and chant microbeats can they meaningfully superimpose melodic rhythm on meter. By physically involving the student in rhythm through movement, I am able to see easily who is feeling the pulse, allowing me to adapt instruction to individual differences.

I also use Music Learning Theory techniques to improve the intonation of my ensemble. Because students have experienced harmonic functions in their audiational warm-ups through tonal patterns, root accompaniments, and improvisation, they are able to approach their repertoire in a much more enlightened manner tonally. I ask all students to learn to sing and play the melodies of their repertoire in several keys, regardless of whether they play the melody in the actual arrangement of the work. I also teach everyone the root melodies whenever possible. This helps the students fit their parts into the tonal structure of the work because they are able to audiate the harmonic context of their part. When students can audiate the harmonic context of their part, they are much more likely to perform in tune. I also use Music Learning Theory techniques to solve other tonal performance problems. For instance, if we are struggling with a modulatory phrase, such as one using a secondary dominant, I can demonstrate for the students what the modulatory chords sound like in the original tonal center and demonstrate their tonal function in the new tonality/keyality.

## Conclusions

Patricia Shehan (1986) has written that "there are no universally acceptable methods in music, but rather a variety of adaptations as diversified as the skills and interests of the multitude of music specialists" (p. 31). Christopher Azzara (1991) writes, "Music learning theory is not one method of teaching music. Rather, it is the outline of logical, fundamental principles for understanding music learning. Because of the open ended nature of the paradigm, it lays the groundwork for a myriad of teaching and learning settings" (p. 107). I wholeheartedly agree. We each need to discover what our students need from us, each according to our individual setting, and how we can meet their needs most efficiently. For me, using Music Learning Theory has revolutionized my teaching and helped me to develop musical independence in my students that enables them to make good musical decisions and engage in music as lifelong learners. Teachers must have the skills and deep understanding of musical content to develop those same skills and understandings in our students. Music Learning Theory has helped me develop my own musicianship, and, in turn, made me a better teacher.

## References

Azzara, C. (1991). Audiation, improvisation, and Music Learning Theory. *The Quarterly, 2*(1&2), 106-109.

Gordon, E. E. (2003). *Learning sequences in music: Skill, content, and patterns*. Chicago: GIA Publications.

Grunow, R. F., Gordon, E. E., & Azzara, C. D. (1998). *Jump right in: The instrumental series* (Rev. ed.). Chicago: GIA

Shehan, P. K. (1986). Major approaches to music education. *Music Educators Journal, 72*(6), 26-31.

*Debbie Rohwer*
• • • • • • • • • •
University of North Texas

# The Application of Music Learning Theory with Senior Citizen Beginning Instrumentalists

Senior citizens represent a sizable and growing population in our country. By the year 2030, the number of older Americans will nearly double, making up 20 percent of the population (U.S. Bureau of the Census, 1993). Armed with more discretionary funds and time than their predecessors, seniors are searching for activities that promote social and cognitive well-being. Not only can these activities make life more enjoyable, but without active involvement, seniors appear to be at a greater risk for physical complications. In recent studies, low levels of affiliation (Welin, Larsson, Svardsudd, Tibblin, & Tibblin, 1992), social support (Falk, Hanson, Isacsson, & Ostergren, 1992), and activity (Foley, Branch, Madans, Brock, Guralnik, & Williams, 1990) were associated with a higher incidence of death for senior citizens.

For many older individuals, participation in musical ensembles can fulfill their need for activity. Musical groups can provide a sense of community as well as a feeling of task accomplishment. Seniors who have sung or played an instrument in their youth often continue musical participation in community groups. For those who have never tried music as a child, or for those who want a second chance at a musical experience, beginner classes are developing that provide an opportunity for musical growth (Coffman & Levy, 1997). Introductory band classes allow seniors to choose an instrument and start from the very beginning, much like the way an elementary student would begin the first days of instrumental instruction.

But seniors are not your ordinary "beginners." While they still need to learn how to hold the instrument and make an initial sound, there are many other components that require special attention. Seniors will be at different psychological, physical, and cognitive levels than the elementary-aged students who normally participate in beginning instrumental music. Our commonly accepted books of songs and activities can appear demeaning to seniors. The normal developmental progress of students is less understood for seniors than for fifth- or sixth-grade instrumental beginners. While there are many unclear factors about the senior citizen as learner, Music Learning Theory can provide a strong musical foundation for the growth of the senior musician. While normal elementary music books may be based on chronological age, Music Learning Theory is based on "musical" age. This allows the new musician to approach learning based on their skills in a non-demeaning and productive way. Armed with the knowledge of Music Learning Theory and an appreciation for the psychological, physical, and cognitive challenges faced by the senior learner, educators can help the new musicians enjoy and learn from their musical experience.

**Understanding the Senior**

An understanding of seniors' well being can help educators work with this age group in a more appropriate and healthy manner. The primary point that gerontologists stress is that there is great variability to the aging process. "While some will experience the effects of biological changes in their 60s, others will not feel their impact until the age of 80 or older" (McGuire, 1996, p. 37). Having a basic understanding of the possible challenges associated with aging can help the teacher address these aspects in context.

The most overt manifestation of aging involves changes in physical functioning. Vision, hearing, breath capacity, and muscle deterioration may all be factors that affect some senior citizens' ability to learn an instrument efficiently. Elderly students may need enlarged music notation, repeated instructions, patience, and regular breaks so that physical concerns do not inhibit learning.

Psychologically, there seem to be few major changes to senior personalities as a result of old age (Kogan, 1990). There may be changes, however, in the way that seniors cope with situations. After many years of experimentation, seniors may be less willing to invest their time or expend their energies on activities that do not completely motivate them. This phenomenon has been labeled in various ways: passivity, introspection, inflexibility, lack of impulsivity, and surrender (Kogan, 1990). Finding what motivates seniors and providing meaningful experiences that encourage their contributions may help seniors stay actively involved in life. Once trust is formed with respect to an activity, any further rigidity can be avoided through sequenced steps in learning.

Cognitive abilities of seniors flourish through sequential learning. While studies note declines in seniors' intelligence test scores (Schaie, 1996), the results may relate more to the seniors' lack of motivation to perform well on a standardized test than their decline in intelligence. Directed learning in a content area of interest to the senior may help improve both memory and understanding (Restak, 1988). By introducing useful concepts in a sequential way, seniors have the chance to exercise and improve their cognitive skills in relation to music.

Once the basics of a subject have been practiced, then problem solving and creative aspects can be addressed. Teachers who provide a sequenced understanding of content, leading to sequenced steps in the creative process, will not only address the musical needs of the seniors, but will also alleviate the concerns of the seniors who are wary of creative activities.

## The Use of Music Learning Theory with the Senior Instrumentalist

While elementary students may be motivated to join musical groups by seeing a shiny saxophone or hearing the marching band play, seniors may have a more pragmatic view of music participation. As one beginning instrumentalist stated, "I'm getting too old to waste time. I want to learn how to play an instrument now so that I can play songs that I know" (Robert Haas, personal communication, February 5, 1998). Whether the seniors join band to learn music, to participate in social relationships (Coffman, 1998), or to seek new challenges (Gibbons, 1979), the senior mindset is different than that of the young beginner. Pages and pages of repetitious musical tasks do little to help the senior musician. In fact, these redundancies may do much more harm by cognitively demeaning and physically tiring an older learner. Sequential instruction based on Gordon's Music Learning Theory can help to avoid many of the normal "lesson book" pitfalls with the senior beginning instrumentalists. Resources provided by *Jump Right In: The Instrumental Series* (Grunow, Gordon, & Azzara, 2001) can help guide this process.

From the first day of instruction based on Music Learning Theory, beginning instrumentalists are asked to think musically. Instead of pushing down random keys or valves while blowing and counting to four, instrumentalists are challenged to use their ears to hear and make musical sounds. Musical phrases in harmonic and metric contexts become the goal of the beginner instead of simply playing single notes devoid of any harmonic or metric reference. Because of the emphasis on sound, beginners are able to concentrate on the concepts of tone quality and phrasing.

In order for beginning seniors to produce refined sounds on their instruments, they must have strong aural concepts of the desirable sound qualities associated with their instruments. The teacher who can produce a high-quality sound on each instrument will be of great help to beginners. For those instruments that the teacher cannot model at a high level, bringing in strong junior high, high school, or collegiate level musicians to model can serve the purpose, while also encouraging multigenerational learning and respect. Recordings highlighting a specific instrument can also be helpful in this process.

Strong aural models provide a constant self-assessment tool for the developing musician. By having a student listen to a model of appropriate quality tone and then aim for that same tone quality in his or her own musical response, development can be quick and efficient. This comparison/reflection component of learning is a healthy means toward the total tone quality development of the senior musician. Playing musically and with a good tone quality is also important to the self-confidence of the older learner. While the young learner may be more patient with a long-term process, older learners may feel less inclined to expend time on an endless pursuit for which they see no quick dividends. The emphasis on sound, then, provides a dual purpose: it provides a solid aural foundation for the learner while allowing the learner to sound impressive quickly.

While the majority of beginner method books ask students to read music notation, put the correct valves or fingers down, blow into the instrument, and keep a steady external beat all at the same time, Gordon's Skill Learning Sequence allows these facets to be developed separately. This provides the learner with the opportunity to concentrate on and improve on one area before combining the skills together. The internalization and automatization of basic abilities gives the learner the comfort to concentrate on higher level topics, such as expressivity, balance, intonation, and other musical concepts.

Addressing each individual's needs in relation to musical readiness is a necessary component of the learning process. With a lifetime of music listening, most seniors have the listening vocabulary to be able to compare sounds, and they definitely have the cognitive readiness to understand basic concepts that lead toward musical development. Tonal and rhythmic readiness can be assessed through singing and movement activities. Singing and movement not only add variety to the lessons, but they also provide a respite from the overuse of the muscle groups used in holding and manipulating an instrument.

While seniors may be more willing to participate in movement and singing activities than the young beginner, care must be taken to keep these sessions brief, depending on the activity. Seniors are pragmatic in their desire to be able to perform for their own enjoyment. A teacher's educational approach must facilitate the enjoyment of music along with skill development when working with seniors. Especially in the early stages, seniors may be less willing to sit for tasks that appear too "schoolish." The teacher has to be ready to improvise tasks depending on the population at hand. For instance, having each instrumentalist conduct can serve as a preliminary check for rhythm readiness. Or bringing in a recording of dance band music or country line dance music and letting the seniors synchronize movements to the music can also be an appropriate, contextual activity that can be used to assess rhythm readiness. Letting the seniors know the potential value of any activity may provide the understanding and motivation needed to improve on the task.

The cognitive abilities of seniors can enable the teacher to be more productive and less redundant by explaining the value of what needs to be done. Autonomous practice can then be used as a learning mechanism. Throughout the teaching process with the senior beginning instrumentalist, the independent capabilities of the learner need to be taken into consideration. The older musician does not need the constant supervision and direction that the younger learner needs. In fact, an overabundance of supervision can be frustrating to the senior, for even though they may be cognitively aware of their deficiencies, they need time to rectify these deficiencies on their own. Especially at the higher levels of musical development, musicians will have less and less need for "a teacher." When the basics are mastered, chamber music can serve a wonderful function for the musicians. Through chamber music experiences, they can make independent decisions, while honing their skills. At this stage, the teacher can best be used as a consultant and a "cheerleader."

## Musical Content and the Senior Instrumentalist

Because Music Learning Theory is not based upon one set of songs, activities and music can be developed that directly relate to the senior musician. "Twinkle, Twinkle Little Star" serves the multifaceted function of being a familiar folk song that has a limited range and a simple rhythm sequence. It can also help teach the sound of a tonic, subdominant, and dominant chord progression, and a stepwise progression with a leap of a fifth. It does not, however, make the seniors feel that they are participating in a task that validates them and their position in life. Self-confidence can be a major factor in adult education, and the content of lessons can be a major accelerator or inhibitor to the process.

Specifically, for the senior, songs that are idiomatic to their generation may resonate with them more than other musical choices. Unfortunately, there are few books available that address this need in the instrumental ensemble setting. Since no method book can be everything to everyone,

| Song | Tonality | Meter | Level | Range |
|---|---|---|---|---|
| A Taste of Honey | Minor | Triple | easier | M9 |
| A Wonderful Guy (*South Pacific*) | Major | Triple | easier | P8 |
| A Time for Us | Minor | Triple | challenging | P11 |
| All the Things You Are | Major | Duple | challenging | M12 |
| Can't Help Falling in Love | Major | Duple | easier | P8 |
| Do-Re-Mi (*Sound of Music*) | Major | Duple | challenging | P8 |
| Edelweiss (*Sound of Music*) | Major | Triple | easier | m7 |
| Fly Me to the Moon | Major | Triple | challenging | P11 |
| Give My Regards to Broadway | Major | Duple | easier | m7 |
| Hello, Young Lovers (*The King and I*) | Major | Triple | easier | P8 |
| I Believe | Major | Duple | easier | M9 |
| If You Go Away | Minor | Triple | challenging | m13 |
| Just in Time | Major | Duple | challenging | m9 |
| Let Me Call You Sweetheart | Major | Triple | challenging | m9 |
| My Funny Valentine (*Babes in Arms*) | Minor | Duple | challenging | m9 |
| Oh, What A Beautiful Mornin' (*Oklahoma*) | Major | Triple | challenging | m9 |
| Que Sera, Sera | Major | Triple | easier | m10 |
| Sixteen Tons | Minor | Duple | easier | P11 |
| Speak Softly, Love (*The Godfather*) | Minor | Duple | challenging | P11 |
| Strangers in the Night | Major | Duple | easier | m7 |
| That's Amore | Major | Triple | easier | M9 |
| The Anniversary Waltz | Major | Triple | easier | M9 |
| The Way You Look Tonight | Major | Duple | challenging | P8 |
| True Love (*High Society*) | Major | Triple | challenging | m7 |
| Where Do I Begin (*Love Story*) | Minor | Duple | challenging | M12 |

*Figure 1.* Example repertoire for the senior beginning musician

external resources are needed that subsidize or replace content that is not useful for a given set of students. While no repertoire list of music appropriate to the senior beginning instrumentalist is applicable to every group, some example songs for beginners are provided in Figure 1. In many cases, the difficulty and range of the piece could be lessened by introducing only the refrain.

Once an appropriate song has been chosen, the teacher must determine the teachable concepts in the piece. For example, a song may be useful for highlighting chord structure or unusual meter. The song can then be arranged or printed for the teacher's use. Later, these printed pieces can be used to give context to the learning of notation.

Music notation programs can be valuable in this process. These programs allow the teacher to be flexible and provide proper content at the proper time for the learning musicians. Melodies can be written in appropriate keyalities and meters for the students. Arrangements can be written that sequentially introduce and reinforce the aural knowledge that the students have learned. The choice of repertoire needs to be planned as far in advance as possible so that longterm goals and appropriate sequencing are organized in a way that is useful to both the teacher and the students. Since senior citizens have a lifetime of music at their disposal, a teacher will have hundreds of songs from which to choose. Having the seniors "aurally request" a song by playing the melody by ear can help the educator plan familiar repertoire for the group. Songs that are familiar and enjoyable can serve as band arrangements, foundations for improvisation, or numerous other musical activities for the senior citizen musician.

From the first day, material can be aurally introduced that has familiar content and can be sequenced appropriately for use as a teaching tool. A song such as "Strangers in the Night" allows the learner to concentrate on tonal steps (see Figure 2). Because the song is familiar and the musicians do not have to read the rhythmic complexities of the song, the rhythm will not be a major inhibitor to the successful performance of the song.

*Figure 2.* Melody to the refrain of "Strangers in the Night"

221

Through tonal pattern practice, seniors will become more accustomed to skips. The musicians can then easily play by ear a melody such as "Can't Help Falling in Love" that has skips of a fifth but is mainly stepwise.

After seniors aurally learn the basic melody to a song such as "Can't Help Falling in Love," aurally adding the roots of the songs to the musicians' musical repertoire can add harmonic interest to the song and help develop harmonic audiation. The instructor can highlight the chord structure of the piece to provide context to the understanding of the patterns and their labels. When teaching improvisation-oriented activities, the seniors can apply the patterns they have learned to add their own accompaniments to the songs (see Figure 3).

The chord progressions from the songs can also be used as fodder for the improvisation of new melodies. Once the "sound" understanding of tonic, subdominant, and dominant have been learned, then singing and/or playing improvisations can become a regular part of rehearsals. Tonally warming the musicians up for this type of activity can be done by asking them to audiate a pitch from the tonic chord, then audiate a pitch from the dominant chord, and then audiate, again, a pitch from the tonic chord. In a group, the musicians can then sing the tonic and dominant chords that they make together. This activity can help solidify the tonal understanding of basic chord progressions, which can lead to the improvisation of new melodies.

*Figure 3.* Melody, chords, and an example harmony part to the refrain of "Can't Help Falling in Love"

Once the musicians are putting their past knowledge into practice through the reading of music, then notation of songs that the musicians learned aurally can be introduced. By not placing a title on the notated songs, the teacher can have the seniors audiate the song before they play it, thereby forcing them to attach the notation to what they can already audiate. Blank staves can be placed under the provided melody so that each musician can document his own newly composed countermelody or harmony line.

## Conclusions

Music educators have the wonderful opportunity of introducing music performance to a growing and almost untapped population: senior citizens. With an understanding of seniors' motivations and challenges, a teacher can organize many different lesson activities that will reach the older beginning musician's needs in an appropriate manner. By using Music Learning Theory as an instructional framework, the teacher can introduce musical ideas in a sequential manner, while also empowering the musical independence of the senior learner.

Listed below are the key points addressed in this article:

- Use songs that provide the necessary musical sequence of learning, but also consider the developmental appropriateness of the material.
- Provide high-quality sound models for the senior beginning musician.
- Provide sequential activities that are musically challenging.
- Give a variety of activities involving movement, singing, and playing, so that the senior doesn't tire or overuse any muscle.
- Try to introduce skill-based activities that will not seem overly "schoolish" to the senior learner.
- Provide settings that encourage autonomous music making for the senior musician.

## References

Coffman, D. D. (1996). Musical backgrounds and interests of active older adult band members. *Dialogue in Instrumental Music Education, 20*, 25-34.

Coffman, D. D., & Levy, K. M. (1997). Senior adult bands: Music's new horizon. *Music Educators Journal, 84*(3), 17-22.

Falk, A., Hanson, B. S., Isacsson, S., & Ostergren, P. (1992). Job strain and mortality in elderly men: Social network, support, and influence as buffers. *American Journal of Public Health, 82*, 1136-1139.

Foley, D., Branch, L., Madans, J., Brock, D., Guralnik, J., & Williams, T. (1990). Physical function. In J. Cornoni-Huntley, R. Huntley, & J. Feldman (Eds.), *Health status and well-being of the elderly: National Health and Nutrition Examination Survey—I. Epidemiological follow-up study* (pp. 221-236). New York: Oxford.

Gibbons, A. C. (1979). Musical Aptitude Profile scores in the elderly and their relationships to morale and selected other variables. Unpublished doctoral dissertation, University of Kansas.

Grunow, R. F., Gordon, E. E., & Azzara, C. D. (2001). *Jump right in: The instrumental series.* Chicago: GIA Publications.

Kogan, N. (1990). Personality and aging. In J. E. Birren & K. W. Schaie (Eds.), *Handbook of the Psychology of Aging* (3rd ed., 330-346). San Diego: Academic.

McGuire, F. A., Boyd, R. K., & Tedrick, R. T. (1996). *Leisure and aging: Ulyssean living in later life.* Champaign, IL: Sagamore.

Restak, R. M. (1988). *The mind.* New York: Bantam.

Schaie, K. W. (1996). Intellectual development in adulthood. In J. E. Birren, K. W. Schaie, R. P. Abeles, M. Gatz, & T. A. Salthouse (Eds.), *Handbook of the Psychology of Aging* (4th ed., pp. 266-285). San Diego: Academic.

U.S. Bureau of the Census. (1993). Sixty-five plus in America. *Current Population Reports.* Special Issue. P25-1092. Washington, DC: U.S. Government Printing Office.

Welin, L., Larsson, B., Svardsudd, K., Tibblin, B., & Tibblin, G. (1992). Social network and activities in relation to mortality from cardiovascular diseases, cancer, and all causes: A 12 year follow up of the study of men born in 1913 and 1923. *Journal of Epidemiology and Community Health, 46,* 127-132.

*Michael E. Martin*
• • • • • • • • • • • • •
SCHOOL DISTRICT OF HAVERFORD TOWNSHIP, HAVERFORD, PA

# Music Learning Theory and Beginning String Instrument Instruction

### The Crucial Role of Audiation

Music Learning Theory can have a greater impact on the performance of beginning string students than on beginning students of any other instruments. This is because the presence or lack of audiation skills are most readily apparent in the performance of string students.[1] The ability or inability to audiate rhythm and meter is readily apparent in performers of all instruments, because no instrument in itself possesses good rhythm or meter; rhythm skills must be brought to the instrument by the performer. However, tonal audiation skills, or lack thereof, are not equally apparent with all instruments. Keyboard percussion instruments and pianos (when properly tuned), for example, are played with good intonation regardless of the tonal audiation skills of the performer. Likewise, players of most woodwind and brass instruments will approximate the desired pitches if they have been taught proper fingering and embouchure. A non-fretted stringed instrument, however, could be said to possess no intonation in itself, except that of the "open" strings when properly tuned. Indeed, a limitless range of poor intonation is possible. Unfortunately, this limitless range of poor intonation is often demonstrated by beginning string students.

---

[1] For a complete definition and discussion of the term "audiation," see Edwin E. Gordon, *Learning Sequences in Music: Skill, Content, and Patterns* (Chicago: GIA Publications, 2003).

225

When asked to list goals or objectives for beginning string students, most teachers include good tone quality, control of the bow in various styles (e.g., détaché, martelé, slur, spiccato), good posture, proper instrument position, proper hand positions, learning to play in tune, learning to tune their own instruments, learning to read notation, learning to perform and read rhythms accurately, knowledge of the fundamentals of music theory, and enjoyment of playing the instrument. Attainment of these goals or objectives requires the development of two types of skills, which hereinafter will be referred to as executive skills and audiation skills. Executive skills are defined as any of the physical skills involved in playing the instrument, such as fingering, bowing, shifting, posture, hand position, and instrument position. Executive skills are what most string teachers have traditionally called "technique." Audiation skills, on the other hand, are those musical skills that are heard inside the mind or felt inside the body of the performer. Audiation skills encompass what many teachers of the past have referred to as "musical ideas," "musical concepts," "musical image," "inner hearing," or "feel" for the music. Yet audiation is much more. Audiation describes the entire process of "thinking in sound."

Music Learning Theory, which explores how audiation skills develop, yields many ideas on how to best develop audiation skills among our students, but it does not tell us how to teach executive skills. Many great string pedagogues have written books, methods, and treatises and produced videos telling us how to best develop executive skills among our students. String teachers should study these methods and approaches to determine the method or approach that works best for them. However, audiation skills and executive skills are equally important when performing on a music instrument, and most existing methods or approaches fail to adequately address the development of audiation skills.

Many great string teachers of the past have referred to the executive skills or "technique" as the tool that is necessary for performers to express their "musical ideas" through the instrument, but what if the students have no "musical ideas" to express? Do we simply continue to teach the mechanics and hope that the musical ideas will follow? We do our students a disservice if we give them only good executive skills without developing their audiation skills. Similarly, our students are not served well if we give them audiation skills without helping them develop good executive skills.

Audiation enables performers to relate what is being played to the resting tone and the tonal functions (e.g., tonic, dominant, subdominant) underlying the music. Also, through audiation performers are able to anticipate the harmonic and melodic structure of the piece in familiar music and to predict it in unfamiliar music. Performers who are able to audiate seem to "automatically" play in tune in any situation. Even if a string is out of tune, the performers' fingers make the adjustment for good intonation, often without conscious effort.

Audiation also enables performers to feel in their bodies the meter and tempo of the music being performed. Through audiation, performers relate the rhythm of the music to the large beats and small beats that formulate the meter of the music. Through audiation, performers are able to anticipate in familiar music and predict in unfamiliar music the rhythmic feel and structure of the piece. Such performers play with rhythmic precision, are able to "stay together" when performing with others, and are able to make the music "flow" with a clear sense of phrasing and form.

Audiation enables performers to recall what they have heard without having to "memorize." They are able to "play by ear," teaching themselves to play familiar music without being bound to music notation. Audiation also enables performers to create and improvise, to "hear" what is seen in notation, and to write what is heard.

Most important, through audiation, students learn to "appreciate" good music and to be able to discriminate the great music from the mediocre. Our livelihood as musicians and, indeed, the perpetuation of culture depend upon the development of musically intelligent audiences.

While teaching audiation skills certainly should be the primary focus of the general music class, many beginning instrumental students in fourth, fifth, or even sixth grade still cannot sing in tune or move their bodies in a rhythmically coordinated manner. This may not be entirely the fault of the general music teacher. Many excellent general music teachers have a limited amount of time in which to teach audiation. Imagine a student receiving no language exposure or stimulation other than a once per week language class. Yet in many educational settings this is nearly the situation with music.

The string teacher must teach audiation skills along with executive skills, coordinating the use of one type of skill with the other. Each beginner enters the class with a different amount of audiation skill, but even students who can sing in tune and move their bodies rhythmically must be guided to apply their audiation skills while playing the instrument. More often than not, students become so involved in the many physical and intellectual skills typically taught in beginning lessons that there may be no music singing or playing in the student's mind (audiation). We must constantly direct the student's attention to the music itself without letting the physical aspects of playing or the intellectual aspects of "music theory" get in the way of the audiation. Audiation is the most important skill that we can teach.

## Practical Application

Now that we have briefly defined audiation and the role it plays among beginning string students, the remainder of this chapter will focus on how to develop audiation skills in beginning string classes and how to combine the teaching of audiation skills and executive skills. The teaching techniques and sequences recommended for teaching audiation skills discussed in this chapter can be used to supplement any string method or approach. An excellent resource is *Jump Right In: The Instrumental Series – Revised Edition for Strings. Jump Right In* is a curriculum for beginning strings that combines the development of audiation skills with elements of the best current approaches for developing executive skills, while allowing the teacher ample flexibility in the area of executive skill development.[2]

## Structuring the Lesson

For optimum development of both audiation skills and executive skills, each beginning string class, lesson, or rehearsal should include the following elements:

A. Appropriate literature
B. Learning Sequence Activities
C. Executive skill development
D. Melodic patterns and songs played on the instrument by ear
E. Use of a cassette tape or CD for practicing at home
F. Musical enrichment (extra challenge for high-aptitude students)

### *Appropriate Literature*

Good literature is an essential part of any beginning string curriculum, and as much teaching as possible should be done through literature. Indeed, one of the ultimate goals of a string teacher is that students will be able to successfully perform a wide variety of literature. Beginning students want to learn to play songs, and most already have a number of simple songs that they can sing from memory. Students can be taught to play many of these songs on their instruments. The first songs that students learn should be those that can be mastered quickly, providing valuable motivation for the students. "Hot Cross Buns" and "Mary Had a Little Lamb," using an open string as the resting tone, are appropriate beginning songs.

---

[2] For further information about the application of Music Learning Theory to beginning string instruction, read Richard F. Grunow, Edwin E. Gordon, Christopher D. Azzara, and Michael E. Martin, *Teachers' Guide, Jump Right In: The Instrumental Series - Revised Edition for Strings* (Chicago: GIA Publications, 2002).

In order to develop audiation skills, it is essential that students experience literature in a variety of tonalities and meters. Major and Harmonic Minor tonalities and Usual Duple and Usual Triple meters must be taught concurrently. Students will not come to fully comprehend one tonality or meter unless they have at least one other tonality or meter with which to compare and contrast. For example, *Jump Right In: The Instrumental Series – Revised Edition for Strings, Book One*, contains songs in both Major and Harmonic Minor tonalities and in both Usual Duple and Usual Triple meters. *Book Two*, in addition to Major, Minor, Duple, and Triple, contains songs in Dorian and Mixolydian tonalities and songs in Unusual and Combined meters. *Solo Books One, Two*, and *Three* contain a total of 300 songs in a variety of tonalities and meters. The teacher using another beginning string method must seek out easy beginning literature in Harmonic Minor tonality and in Usual Triple meter to supplement the literature that is mostly in Major tonality and Duple meter.

Variety of styles is also an important consideration. Songs should be selected that the students can perform in connected styles (détaché or slurred) as well as separated style (martelé). Instructors should be certain to select songs from various cultures, taking into consideration individual students' existing musical knowledge. Generally, folk songs should be used at the beginning level before progressing to "classics." However, there are some tunes from the classic literature that are appropriate for beginners, such as Beethoven's "Ode to Joy."

*Teaching a Rote Song*

In order to foster audiation development, it is essential that students sing a song before they play it. The following procedure for teaching a song by rote will begin the process of audiation upon which the teacher can continually build.

A.  The teacher establishes the tonality of the song by playing a I–V–I chord progression on a piano or other chordal instrument, or by singing or playing a set of tonic and dominant patterns ending on the resting tone. This begins to give the student a tonal framework within which to audiate.
B.  The teacher sings the song for the students without words. Words tend to distract the students' attention from the music itself. Using words, it is also more likely that the students will attempt to sing with a "speaking voice." A very light "doo, doo, doo..." works well, but any neutral syllable that is appropriate to the style of the music may be used.

C. The teacher instructs the students to move their heels to macrobeats (large beats) while listening to the teacher sing the song again. Putting the large beat in the heels allows students to feel lots of body weight on the large beat, making it more effective than tapping the toe.

D. The teacher instructs the students to pat their hands, moving the entire forearm to microbeats (small beats), while listening to the teacher sing the song again. This type of patting allows the students to feel the weight of the hands and arms.

E. The teacher instructs the students to move heels to macrobeats and hands to microbeats while listening to the teacher sing the song again. Students eventually will come to understand that rhythm exists on three levels. The foundational level is the macrobeat. Superimposed upon the macrobeat is the microbeat, and superimposed upon this framework is the melodic rhythm of the song. Students must be able to feel both the macrobeat and the microbeat if they are to be expected to perform with steady tempo and accurate meter.[3]

F. The teacher plays or sings the resting tone for the students and then instructs the students to hold that resting tone in their audiation while listening to the teacher sing the song again. When the teacher finishes singing the song, she asks the students to sing the resting tone that they are audiating. Each student must be constantly audiating a resting tone in order to perform with accurate intonation.

G. The teacher instructs the students to audiate the entire song and to raise their hands when finished. This activity stretches the students' audiation skills and over time produces careful listeners.

H. Students sing the entire song, taking the preparatory breath in the tempo that is established by the teacher. Audiation of what one is to sing takes place during the breath.

I. If students have difficulty performing any portion of the song, the teacher may ask them to echo phrases from the song. The teacher sings the phrase for the students and students echo in tempo without a pause. The teacher should sing for the students but not with the students.

J. The teacher adds accompaniment as the students sing the song. The accompaniment should be provided only after students can successfully sing the melody without accompaniment. The accompaniment should not include the melody. Musical independence is the goal.

---

[3] If students cannot successfully move to macrobeats and microbeats simultaneously, the teacher must plan to spend three to five minutes of each lesson engaging the students in rhythm readiness activities. Suggestions for rhythm readiness activities are found in the *Teachers' Guide for Jump Right In: The Instrumental Series – Revised Edition for Strings.*

K.  The teacher may now teach the words to the song, if desired.

L.  The teacher should then teach a "bass line" for the song, using the same procedure. Learning a bass line for each song and singing in two parts as soon as possible greatly improves the intonation and rhythmic solidity of beginning string classes. It is another way to develop musical independence, and it is laying the foundation for successful improvisation.

*Establishing Tonality and Meter*

Music does not exist in a vacuum; rather, it exists within a framework of underlying tonality and meter. Good intonation comes from audiating the underlying tonality, that is, from audiating the tonal center, or resting tone and the tonal functions (tonic, dominant, subdominant, etc.). Accurate intonation can only occur when the performer is consciously or unconsciously relating the pattern of pitches being performed to the resting tone and tonal functions of the tonality. Steady tempo and meter come from audiating the "feel" or the movement of the underlying large and small beats. Therefore, before engaging in any musical activity, the teacher must establish for the students the tonality and meter to be audiated. For example, before singing a song, the students should not just be given the starting pitch, but should hear a I–V–I chord progression on a piano or guitar, or a few tonic and dominant patterns, played or sung in the tonality and keyality of the song that is to be sung. Students consistently should be asked to keep the resting tone in their audiation. At any point in a piece and at any level of string instruction, the teacher should be able to stop and ask the students to sing the resting tone. If the students are unable to sing the resting tone, even perhaps a subjective resting tone in contemporary music, chances are that the intonation of the group is questionable because, without a resting tone in audiation, the students have nothing definitive to which to tune. In the same manner, before beginning any musical activity involving rhythm, the teacher should demonstrate movement to both the macrobeat and microbeat and ask the students to move to both the macrobeats and microbeats simultaneously. When students are successful, the teacher should instruct the students to stop moving outwardly but to keep moving inwardly. When the teacher detects any inconsistency in tempo or meter, she should immediately ask students to demonstrate outwardly the macrobeats and microbeats that they are feeling.

*Learning Sequence Activities*

In the "whole-part-whole" approach to education, which is fundamental to Music Learning Theory, students are first asked to deal with a "whole." This might be a song students are to learn. When first learning the song, students do not really understand much about the song but are simply immersed in the sound. Let's say the song is in Harmonic Minor tonality, with predominantly tonic and dominant functions. Let's say it is also in Triple meter with predominantly macrobeat and microbeat functions. Later in the same lesson, or perhaps in a subsequent lesson, the teacher begins teaching tonic and dominant tonal patterns in Minor tonality or macrobeat and microbeat rhythm patterns in Triple meter. Students learn to audiate, recognize, perform, and name these functions (the "part"). Now the students are ready to return to the "whole" with greater understanding.

Learning Sequence Activities (pattern instruction) function as the "part" in the "whole-part-whole" approach. The "whole" is referred to as "Performance Activities." Performance Activities involve singing, moving to, and playing songs, études, and literature and working on executive skill development. With the possible exception of singing and moving, these are the types of activities already found in most string classes. Performance Activities take up a large majority of the class time. Learning Sequence Activities, which should only take from five to ten minutes of each class period, involve working only with tonal patterns, void of rhythm, and with rhythm patterns, void of pitch, but with inflection.

Tonal patterns and rhythm patterns, not individual notes, are the vocabulary with which we audiate, just as words, not individual letters, are the vocabulary with which we think. The larger our vocabulary of words, the better we are able to think in language. The larger our vocabulary of tonal patterns and rhythm patterns, the better we are able to audiate in music. Learning Sequence Activities may be thought of as the students' "vocabulary lesson" and make up the part of the class that is most unique to Music Learning Theory.[4]

During Learning Sequence Activities, students learn a sequence of skills using tonal patterns and rhythm patterns in tonalities and meters that have already been experienced during Performance Activities. The following is a brief outline and description of the skill levels taught in *Jump Right In: The Instrumental Series – Revised Edition for Strings.*

**DISCRIMINATION LEARNING:** (Must be taught in this order)

> **Aural/Oral:** The student hears and echo-sings or echo-chants individual patterns without solfege.

---

[4] For a thorough discussion of Learning Sequence Activities, read Edwin E. Gordon, *Learning Sequences in Music: Skill, Content, and Patterns* (Chicago: GIA Publications, 2003).

**Verbal Association:** The student hears and echo-sings or echo-chants individual patterns with solfege and is taught the proper names of tonalities, meters, and functions. Movable DO with a LA-based Minor is the system of tonal solfege that must be used to teach the audiation of tonality. A system of rhythm solfege based on beat function must be used to teach the audiation of meter.[5]

**Partial Synthesis:** The student aurally recognizes familiar tonalities and meters (e.g., Major, Minor, Duple, Triple).

**Symbolic Association:** The student is taught to read and write familiar patterns.

**Composite Synthesis:** The student is taught to read and write series of familiar patterns and to recognize their tonality or meter.

**INFERENCE LEARNING:** (At appropriate times the teacher may "bridge" from a level of Discrimination Learning to a level of Inference Learning.)

**Generalization - Symbolic:** The student reads unfamiliar patterns (sight-reading) and writes unfamiliar patterns from dictation. Symbolic Association is a prerequisite for bridging to this level.

**Creativity/Improvisation:** The student creates and improvises familiar and unfamiliar patterns and writes what has been created or improvised. The teacher may bridge to appropriate creativity and improvisation activities at nearly any time.

**Theoretical Understanding:** The student is taught letter names of lines and spaces, time value names of notes, and other music theory. This level should be delayed until the student has developed strong audiation skills at all previous levels.

Except at the aural/oral level, once the student sings or chants a pattern, he or she may be taught to play that pattern on the instrument. During Learning Sequence Activities, musical content is presented in order of audiation difficulty. For example, tonic and dominant patterns are taught

---

[5] For a complete discussion of both tonal solfege and rhythm solfege, see Edwin E. Gordon, *Learning Sequences in Music: Skill, Content, and Patterns* (Chicago: GIA Publications, 2003).

before subdominant or other more difficult functions; macrobeat and microbeat patterns are taught before divisions or elongations.[6]

New audiation skills are always taught during Learning Sequence Activities. For example, when the teacher wants to begin teaching the students to read notation, that new skill of reading notation is taught first during Learning Sequence Activities when the students have reached the symbolic association level. The students are taught to read tonal patterns or rhythm patterns in Learning Sequence Activities before they are asked to read a song or étude during Performance Activities.

New musical content is always presented during Performance Activities. For example, when the teacher wants to present Minor tonality to the students, she will first teach students a song in Minor tonality. The students will be directed to listen to the song several times and then will be taught to sing the song. Nothing specifically would be taught about Minor tonality because the students are simply immersing in the sound of that tonality in a Performance Activity. In a subsequent lesson, or later in the same lesson, the student would begin learning tonal patterns in Minor tonality during Learning Sequence Activities, following the sequence of skills listed above.

Learning Sequence Activities enable students to return to the literature (the whole) with a greater understanding of that literature. Through discrimination learning sequence, students learn to perform, audiate, recognize, label, read, and write tonal patterns and rhythm patterns characteristic of good literature. Based on the skills taught in discrimination learning, students learn at the inference level to sight read, create, and improvise, all with a good sense of tonality and meter.

## Executive Skill Development

Although Music Learning Theory focuses on the development of audiation skills rather than executive skills, each type of skill helps to reinforce the other. The teacher will find that, as audiation skills are developed, executive skills are easier to teach because the student will realize that proper executive skills are necessary in order to accurately reproduce the music being audiated. For example, students will tend to correct their own left hand positions if they are audiating good intonation. They will realize that proper hand position is necessary in order to play in tune and will more readily make the necessary adjustments. Students who are not audiating

---

[6] For a complete discussion of Tonal and Rhythm Content Learning Sequence, see Edwin E. Gordon, *Learning Sequences in Music: Skill, Content, and Patterns* (Chicago: GIA Publications, 2003).

tend to play with poor left hand position because they do not realize that they are playing out of tune. Similarly, students who are audiating the tone quality they want to produce will tend to adjust the speed and weight of their own bow strokes in order to achieve the desired tone quality. In addition, performance anxiety and related tension are greatly reduced if students are audiating the music that they want to convey to the audience. Freedom, balance, and the ability to engage in continuous fluid movement of the body will hasten the development of audiation skills. Indeed, the audiation of rhythm is the audiation of movement, and free flowing movement must be experienced before it can be audiated.

*Using an Imaginary Instrument*

Students should practice executive skills first using an imaginary instrument. At the first lesson, the teacher should begin to establish proper posture, instrument position, and hand positions by demonstrating with a real instrument while students practice with an imaginary instrument. Real instruments should not be given to the students to take home until at least the second lesson. That way, the teacher has more time to make sure the students are developing proper habits. When the students are using an imaginary instrument, or "air" instrument, they are more likely to observe the posture, instrument position, and hand positions demonstrated by the teacher, and they will also be better able to keep the feeling of "weightlessness," lightness, and natural relaxation once they begin balancing the real instrument. Bow hold should be established with an imaginary bow, and the student should begin moving the right arm with the imaginary bow as songs are sung and rhythm patterns are chanted. All unnecessary tension must be avoided. Students should be taught to think of "balancing" the instruments and bows rather than "holding" them. The body must be well balanced and flexible at all times, able to sway and bend. Each joint in the shoulders, elbows, wrists, fingers, and thumbs must be able to move freely. Freedom and flexibility should be continually monitored by the teacher. The teacher should immediately engage students in shifting games and many flexibility exercises for the bow hand, such as those described in the *Teachers' Guide* for *Jump Right In: The Instrumental Series – Revised Edition for Strings*.

*Developing the Bow Arm*

During the first lesson, students should be taught the two basic styles of articulation: connected style (détaché stroke) and separated style (martelé stroke). Students should be asked to chant microbeats in Duple and Triple meters in both connected and separated styles, using the syllables "doo,

doo..." for connected style and "too, too..." for separated style. Next, the students should be asked to hold the imaginary bows and echo microbeats in both Duple and Triple meters and connected and separated styles on their imaginary instruments.

During the second lesson, before asking students to perform with the bows on real instruments, the teacher may wish to use the exercise of bowing "in-the tube." Students are given a cardboard tube from bathroom tissue or paper towels and instructed to hold their bows in the proper manner and slide the tube over the tip end of the bow. Violin and viola students should hold the tube with their left hand and place the tube on their left shoulder. Cello and bass students should hold the tube with their left hand low and in front of their bodies, parallel to the floor. Students may now practice moving the bow with both connected style (détaché) and separated style (martelé) bow strokes. The tube will help to support the bow, develop a straight bow stroke, and promote loose flexible joints in the fingers, wrist, elbow, and shoulder. This bowing "in-the-tube" technique may be used later to introduce any new bowing, such as slurs, slurred staccato, or hooked bowing. Students should then be asked to echo microbeats in both Duple and Triple meters and both connected and separated styles on their instruments, beginning on a single open string.

In subsequent lessons, as soon as students can chant several macrobeat and microbeat rhythm patterns with rhythm solfege at the Verbal Association level in Learning Sequence Activities, they should begin playing those rhythm patterns, first with their imaginary instruments and then on real instruments. Rhythms should be performed in both connected and separated styles. Violins and violas should begin by using only the middle third of the bow. Cellos and basses should begin by using only the lower third of the bow, where it is easiest to balance. Eventually, students should practice playing these same rhythm patterns in all parts of the bow. The *Teachers Guide* for *Jump Right In: The Instrumental Series – Revised Edition for Strings* contains specific suggestions for introducing slurs, hooked bowings, slurred staccato, portato, pizzicato, spiccato, shifting, and double stops during the first year of instruction. All are presented within a musical context.

*Developing the Left Hand*

Since executive skills and audiation skills must work together, the teacher should strive as much as possible to teach executive skills within a musical context. As students learn new fingerings, after the basic left hand position is established, they should be asked to sing the pitch, using tonal solfege, as it is fingered. For example, the teacher might begin by labeling the open D string as D-DO. (The syllables should always be sung, never spoken.) Students are told that if D is DO, then RE will be performed with the first finger depressed on the D string. Students depress the finger and sing RE. Students lift the finger and sing DO. Next the teacher asks students to sing and finger the pattern DO-RE. Then students are asked to play the pattern DO-RE on their instruments and to place the first finger so that the DO-RE sounds the same as what they just sang. Students are taught to adjust the finger without the aid of tapes or dots on the fingerboards, which simply delay the development of audiation and may become a visual crutch upon which the students rely. Students are then asked to sing and then play RE-DO, DO-RE-DO, RE-DO-RE, etc.

*Jump Right In: The Instrumental Series – Revised Edition for Strings, Book One* contains fingering charts in three Major keyalities and one Minor keyality. The finger placements on the fingering charts are labeled with tonal solfege, not with letter names. Students eventually learn the logic of the finger positions in different Major and Minor keyalities, and they become adept at transposing without the use of notation. For example, students learn that any note on their instrument can be DO. If an open string is DO, then the first finger will sound like RE, etc. If the second finger is DO, then the first finger will sound like TI, etc. Violinists and violists learn that DO and TI always touch and MI and FA always touch. By following this procedure, the fingering patterns and the solfege become wedded to the sound, and the students will be ready to proceed to the next part of the lesson.

## Melodic Patterns and Songs Played on the Instrument by Ear

Music is an aural art, which, for thousands of years, was passed from generation to generation by way of the ear, without the aid of notation. Only within the last several hundred years did performers begin writing down what they had learned or what they had improvised. Today we live in an age that is saturated with entertainment media. If we want music, we no longer sing or play it for ourselves; we turn on the radio or CD player. Furthermore, we have become accustomed to learning with our eyes rather than with our ears. But music, like language, cannot be learned with the eye; it must be learned with the ear. Music notation that we see with our eyes can only serve to remind us of something we can already audiate—something we have learned through the ears.

All good musicians play by ear, whether they are reading notation or not, because the ability to read notation means being able to hear what the written music sounds like before it is played. This is known as notational audiation. Therefore, the ear must be developed before reading; otherwise, the student will not really be reading but will be attempting to "decode" notation. In other words, if a student does not possess a large vocabulary of music learned by ear, then the notation will not have musical meaning for the student; it will only have an intellectual or mechanical meaning, such as what finger to put down or how far to shift. Music "read" in this manner has little chance of sounding musical. Students should learn by ear a large number of songs and bass lines before beginning to read notation.

Once students are able to sing, finger, and play DO and RE on their imaginary instruments and on their real instruments (at perhaps the fourth lesson), the teacher should say the following: "I am going to play a melody for you using only DO and RE. Start on DO and echo what I play." The teacher should then hide his or her fingers from the students and play the melody, asking the students to echo by ear. Melodies used at this stage should be no longer than four macrobeats in length. Students having diffi-culty should be asked to sing and finger the melody on their imaginary instruments and then on their real instruments. Students should NOT sing the entire melody with tonal solfege. D Major, using the open D string as DO, is a good beginning keyality for all of the stringed instruments. After students can successfully echo melodies by ear using DO and RE, and after they have been taught to sing and finger MI (at perhaps the fifth lesson), the students should be asked to echo patterns using RE and MI. Next, the students may be asked to echo melodies using MI, RE, and DO. The teacher might play and ask the students to echo by ear the first half of "Hot Cross Buns" and then the second half of "Hot Cross Buns." Remember that the students should not be able to see the teacher's fingers. Students are then asked to sing and play the entire song by ear. Sixty seconds may be given for students to practice before the entire class is asked to play "Hot Cross Buns" together. Students should be taught many songs and their bass lines following this procedure and be asked to perform patterns and songs on as many strings as possible. As mentioned earlier, students should be taught that any open string can be DO, the first finger on that string is RE, etc. Students could then be asked to echo melodies on any string so long as the teacher establishes which string is to be DO.

### The Importance of the Breath

When echoing patterns and melodic phrases, students must be instructed to breathe in tempo on the last macrobeat before they begin to echo. For example, if the rhythm pattern or phrase to be echoed is four macrobeats in length, students should breathe on the fourth macrobeat and begin to echo on the next macrobeat. This breath should occur whether the students are echoing with voices or with instruments. During the breath students will audiate what they are about to play and will be able to echo the pattern or phrase in the proper tempo.

## Learning New Fingering Patterns and Transposing by Ear

As soon as students are able to perform a few easy songs with the open string as DO (at perhaps the seventh lesson), the instructor should teach a new fingering for DO and the related fingering patterns. For example, the teacher might establish G Major, with DO as the third finger on D for violin and viola, four fingers on D for cello, and two fingers on E for bass. If this note is DO, then the open A string is RE, first finger on the A string is MI, second finger is FA, etc. Students should be taught to play a new song by ear, perhaps "Pierrot," starting on this new G-DO. Once students can play the song in G Major, they should be asked to play the song on as many strings as possible, using similar fingerings. For example, everyone could play "Pierrot" in C Major with the violins, violas and cellos starting on the C-DO on the G string and the basses starting on the C-DO on the A string. Using similar fingerings, the violins should be asked to play "Pierrot" in D Major (upper octave), and the violas, cellos, and basses in F Major.

By perhaps the eighth lesson, students should be asked to take a song that they have learned with an open string as DO and play that song using the new fingering patterns they have learned. For example, violin students might be asked to play "Hot Cross Buns" in G-DO, starting with the first finger on the A string. Students will realize they can play "Hot Cross Buns" using any MI, RE, and DO. Students will be delighted to discover in how many DOs they can play the song. They are learning to connect tonal pattern relationships with finger pattern relationships, and they are learning to use all fingers on all strings. Many simple songs can be played in five or six Major keyalities using this procedure. D Major, G Major, and C Major work well for the heterogeneous string class.

## Minor as Well as Major

As discussed earlier, if students are to understand and audiate tonality, they must learn Minor as well as Major. Harmonic Minor is best, because it includes the leading tone to tonic relationship, making it easier for students to compare and contrast it with Major tonality. Students should learn to sing each song well in advance of the time they will be asked to play it. Students should begin singing songs in Harmonic Minor tonality during the earliest lessons; however, they should not be asked to play songs in Harmonic Minor tonality until they are able to play fluently in at least three Major keyalities. This will give the students time to develop proper hand positions before they are asked to perform the more challenging fingering patterns required in Harmonic Minor tonality. In a carefully sequenced manner for the heterogeneous string class, *Jump Right In: The Instrumental Series – Revised Edition for Strings, Book One* covers D Major, G Major, C Major, and then G Minor. In addition, students are always asked to perform each song in as many keyalities as possible, using similar fingerings on different strings. Hence, some songs on some instruments are performed in E Major, A Major, F Major, D Minor, A Minor, G Minor, C Minor, F Minor, and E Minor.

## Choosing a Tempo

When teaching students to play songs by ear, teachers should be sure to use a musically appropriate tempo. Songs should not be learned at a slow, unmusical, boring tempo and then "sped up." If the student cannot echo the melody at an appropriate tempo, it is likely the student does not have the appropriate executive skill readiness. The teacher therefore should use exercises to improve the dexterity of the fingers and bow until the student has the physical readiness to play the song at the proper tempo. Musicality should never be sacrificed.

## Programs and Recitals

Many teachers are expected to present a program or recital with their beginning students during the first semester of instruction. No notation should be read during this first program. This program should be thought of as a demonstration or an "informance," during which the teacher and students demonstrate or inform the parents about the learning that has been taking place. Students should sing and play as a group many of the songs and bass lines that they have learned by ear. Students (and parents) can be asked to echo tonal patterns, rhythm patterns, and melodic patterns. Students may be ready to demonstrate some simple improvisation activities. Of course, the students should demonstrate proper posture, instrument positions, hand positions, and care and maintenance of their instruments. Short solos may be featured, and each student who wants to play a short solo should be allowed to do so. This can be done very quickly going around the group, with the audience holding the applause until all students have finished. If questions arise regarding why the students are not reading notation, the teacher can explain that music development occurs in the same way as language development and that the students will be ready to read with comprehension only after they develop substantial listening and performing vocabularies.[7]

## The Value of Learning by Ear

Teaching students to play many songs and bass lines by ear, in conjunction with Learning Sequence Activities during the first year of instruction will pay large dividends as the students continue to develop. They will have learned to listen with musical understanding and subconsciously connect the sound with the physical actions required on the instrument. Students will be sensitive performers when playing with an accompanist or as part of a group because they will be aware of the music going on around them and the deep structure of the tonality and meter. Students will adjust intonation, stay together, and keep a steady tempo. They will become motivated as they realize they are able to teach themselves new songs. During this process, tonal memory (audiation) is fostered rather than memorization, which is more of an intellectual or visual process, not necessarily involving sound. Students become musically independent and are able to do more than simply imitate the stronger players in the group. The longer the reading of notation can be delayed, the better the students' audiation skills will be and the faster they will learn to read notation. Learning many songs and bass lines by ear will also prepare students to improvise to the chord progression of a song.

## Use of a CD for Practicing at Home

In order for students to learn to produce characteristic tone quality, style of articulation, and phrasing on a string instrument, they must have a model to hear and emulate. Students should be given opportunities to hear great professional performers either in person or on recordings. Perhaps even more important at the beginning stages, the teacher should model appropriate tone quality and expression during the lessons. When practicing the instrument at home, the student should have a CD with musical examples to echo. These musical examples should demonstrate appropriate tone quality, articulation, and phrasing. These recordings could be made by the teacher, or the teacher should find good performers to make the recordings.

An important component of *Jump Right In: The Instrumental Series – Revised Edition for Strings* is the Home Study CD. This CD contains 1) songs and bass lines for the student to learn to sing, 2) melodic patterns and

---

[7] At the beginning of the year, parents should be given Michael E. Martin, *Parents' Guide, Jump Right In: The Instrumental Series (Revised Edition)* (Chicago: GIA Publications, 2002). This brochure addresses many of the questions that parents will have regarding instrumental instruction based on Music Learning Theory. It is available free of charge from the publisher.

songs played on the instrument for students to learn to play by ear, 3) accompaniments with which the student can sing and play, 4) tonal patterns and rhythm patterns for the student to echo, and 5) enrichment songs for "extra challenge" to be learned by ear. All examples are performed by professional musicians, including artist faculty members from the Eastman School of Music and members of the National Symphony and Rochester Philharmonic Orchestras. Using these CDs, students learn to audiate fundamental aspects of tonality and meter, as well as appropriate tone quality, style of articulation, and phrasing.

## Musical Enrichment

In music, as in any other subject, there are those students who learn faster than others. Extra challenges must be provided for those students. The following are suggested enrichment activities for fast learning students:

- Give students "enrichment songs" or "extra challenge" songs to learn by ear. The teacher should have a set of songs that everyone is expected to learn, as well as a set of optional enrichment songs. Students who successfully learn one or more enrichment songs may be allowed to perform those songs in a concert, recital, or demonstration. *Jump Right In: The Instrumental Series – Revised Edition for Strings* includes twelve Enrichment Songs at the end of the Home Study CD, in addition to the sixteen rote songs that everyone learns.
- Ask students to learn by ear songs that they hear on radio, TV, or recordings.
- Ask students to play a familiar song in a new keyality, a new tonality, or a new meter.
- Establish a checklist for each student to indicate how many songs they can successfully perform without notation. Include spaces to indicate how many different keyalities, tonalities, and meters in which they can perform the song. It is not uncommon for first-year students to learn seventy or more songs, when counting all possible keyalities.
- Ask students to improvise a harmony part to a song. Higher aptitude students will particularly enjoy and excel at creativity and improvisation.
- During Learning Sequence Activities, faster-learning students may be challenged with more difficult patterns or with series of patterns.

In order to teach to students' differences, it is advantageous for the teacher to know the music aptitudes of each student. When a teacher knows the music aptitudes of each student, he or she is able to provide adequate challenges for higher aptitude students, as well as patient guidance for lower-aptitude students.[8]

## Reading and Writing Notation

In music, as in language, we develop four vocabularies, 1) listening, 2) speaking, 3) reading, and 4) writing. The listening vocabulary, which develops first and is by far the largest of our vocabularies, is the foundation upon which the development of the other vocabularies is built. The listening and speaking vocabularies prepare students for learning to read and write with comprehension. In language, our listening and speaking vocabularies are built for five or six years before we begin to read and write. So, too, in music, the listening and performing vocabularies serve as readiness for notational audiation, or reading notation with comprehension. In language, as well as in music, the listening and speaking (performing) vocabularies should be developed as much as possible before reading and writing are begun, for as soon as reading and writing are begun, the development of the listening and speaking (performing) vocabularies is slowed.

The lesson plans in *Jump Right In: The Instrumental Series – Revised Edition for Strings* are written so that the reading of notation is delayed for at least three months and possibly as long as one school year. Before notation is introduced, students should be able to do the following: 1) sing and play by ear several songs and bass lines in at least three Major keyalities and one Minor keyality and in at least Duple and Triple meters, 2) sing, label with solfege and proper names, and play many tonal patterns in both Major and Minor tonalities, 3) chant, label with solfege and proper names, and play many rhythm patterns in both Duple and Triple meters, 4) recognize familiar tonalities and meters when they are heard (Partial Synthesis), and 5) improvise at least tonic and dominant patterns in Major and Minor tonalities, and at least macrobeat and microbeat patterns in Duple and Triple meters.

The reading of notation (a new skill) is introduced first during Learning Sequence Activities at the Symbolic Association level. Students are first shown tonic and dominant patterns in Major tonality, familiar patterns that they have already sung, labeled, identified, and played. The teacher directs the students to look at a pattern; then she sings the pattern and asks the students to sing and then play the pattern. In *Jump Right In: The Instrumental Series – Revised Edition for Strings*, the first page of tonal

---

[8] For a complete discussion of music aptitude testing and its value for adapting instruction to students' musical strengths and weaknesses, see Edwin E. Gordon, *Introduction to Research and the Psychology of Music* (Chicago: GIA Publications, 1998).

pattern reading is in D Major. In a subsequent lesson, the students are shown familiar macrobeat and microbeat patterns in Duple meter. The teacher instructs the students to look at a pattern; then he or she chants the pattern and asks the students to chant and then play the pattern. The measure signature 2/4 is used because of the natural pairing of macrobeats in audiation. After students can read familiar individual patterns, they are taught to read sets of familiar patterns (composite synthesis).

When students have been successful reading the first page of tonal patterns and the first page of rhythm patterns, tonal and rhythm reading may be combined by showing the students a familiar song written in D Major and 2/4 measure signature. The students may then be asked to read harmony parts or other songs or arrangements in D Major and 2/4 measure signature that contain some familiar and some unfamiliar tonal and rhythm patterns. New tonal and rhythm functions are presented in order of audition difficulty. Familiar macrobeat and microbeat rhythm patterns in Triple meter are read first in 6/8 measure signature, again because of the natural pairing of macrobeats in audiation.

Students should be taught to write from dictation, beginning with familiar patterns they have learned to read. After they have learned to write from dictation tonal patterns in D Major and rhythm patterns in 2/4, they could be asked to write a familiar song in D Major and 2/4.

## Enharmonic Patterns and Enrhythmic Patterns

Just as students learn that DO can be any note on their instruments, they need to learn that DO can be written anywhere on the staff, with relationships within the tonality remaining constant. Students should be taught to read and write enharmonic patterns, that is, familiar tonic and dominant tonal patterns written in a different keyality. In *Jump Right In: The Instrumental Series – Revised Edition for Strings*, students are taught to read tonic and dominant patterns in D Major. Later, the students are taught to read those same patterns plus additional patterns in G Major and C Major.

Students must also be taught to read and write enrhythmic patterns; that is, students must be taught that the same rhythm pattern can be written several different ways. Students should be shown that the same familiar rhythm patterns they learned to read and write in 2/4 can be written in 4/4 or 2/2, and the same familiar rhythm patterns they learned to read and write in 6/8 can be written in 3/8 or 3/4. As soon as students have read tonal patterns or rhythm patterns in a given keyality or measure signature, they may begin to read songs or arrangements written in that keyality or measure signature. Students should be taught to read and write patterns and songs

244

that are already familiar to them (which they have already learned to play without notation) before they are asked to read and write patterns and songs that are unfamiliar. Students may also be asked to notate what they create and improvise.

If the proper readiness has been taught, students will learn to read quickly and will read with a good sense of intonation and steady tempo and meter because the notation represents sounds that are already part of the students' listening and performing vocabularies.

**Music Theory**

After students can read, write, create, and improvise in several tonalities and meters, they are ready to learn music theory. Teachers may introduce students to the time value names of notes, the meaning of measure signatures, counting, letter names of lines and spaces, and the meaning of key signatures, scales, accidentals, and intervals. For best audiation skill development, music theory should be delayed as long as possible. Music theory is not necessary for students to learn to audiate, improvise, or read notation. In fact, introducing music theory too early can seriously delay the development of audiation. Students who can audiate will quickly learn music theory. It will serve as an explanation of what they can already audiate. *Book Two* of *Jump Right In: The Instrumental Series – Revised Edition for Strings* contains all of the music theory students will need in order to communicate with most private teachers and orchestra directors.

**Tuning the Instrument**

Tuning the instrument involves both executive skill and audiation skill. Once students can sing in tune, they possess the audiation skill required for tuning. The executive skill for tuning involves being able to play on the string while adjusting the peg or fine tuner. Students should be taught to grasp and turn the peg or fine tuner while bowing or plucking the string and told to listen to the change in the sound as the peg or fine tuner is adjusted. Next, the teacher might establish D Major and ask the students to audiate and sing the resting tone. (It is much easier for students to audiate and reproduce a pattern or a resting tone within the context of a tonality than it is to audiate and reproduce a single pitch.) The students should then be asked to adjust the fine tuner or peg until the sound of the string matches the resting tone in their audiation. Students should frequently be asked to sing the resting tone and to listen for the sound of the string getting "better" or "worse." If turning the fine tuner or peg worsens the sound, students are told to turn in the opposite direction. Most students can easily tell when the sound is getting worse and will reverse directions. It takes a little time and practice for students to learn to stop when the string is exactly in tune, but with a few minutes spent on tuning at each lesson, students learn quickly. Note that the terms "higher" and "lower" should not be used until after notation is introduced. The terms "higher" and "lower" are visual terms and have no meaning for students until they see the relation of pitches on the staff. For a further discussion of tuning the instrument, see the *Teachers' Guide for Jump Right In: The Instrumental Series – Revised Edition for Strings.*

### At What Age Should String Instruction Begin?

There is no correct chronological age at which a student should begin string instrument instruction. Since a string instrument is simply an extension of the players' mind and body, it can play no better in tune than the player can audiate and sing in tune. It can play in no better tempo and meter than the player can move his or her body with consistent tempo and meter. Ideally, then, before beginning instruction on an instrument, the student should be able to sing in tune and move the body in a rhythmically coordinated manner. Just as in language development, each child goes through a "babble" stage in music before he or she has "broken the code" of syntax in the music of the culture. If a child has a high developmental music aptitude and has been exposed to a rich musical environment from the time of birth or before, the child may have emerged from babble and be ready to begin string instrument instruction by age three. Many children emerge from babble around age five. By age nine, most, but not all, children have emerged from music babble.[9]

Parents should not be in a hurry for their children to begin formal instrumental lessons. It is much better to allow the child time to come out of music babble before beginning instrumental instruction. A child who is still in babble will only be able to "babble" or "explore" on the instrument. This babbling or exploration has limited value to students' musical development, because it is inappropriate to correct students who are in music babble or expect them to perform with musical precision. An even worse scenario is the teacher who tries to teach notation and music theory to a child who is still in music babble. Indeed, this may do irreparable damage to the child's audiation development, for once a child has been taught music theory, it is very difficult to teach that child to audiate. The intellectual and visual aspects get in the way of audiation.

---

[9] For more information about the readiness for formal instruction in music, see Edwin E. Gordon, *A Music Learning Theory for Newborn and Young Children* (Chicago: GIA Publications, 2003).

Once children have emerged from music babble, they are ready to benefit from formal instruction. The younger the child, the faster the audiation skills will develop, but executive skills develop more slowly in a younger child. With older beginners, executive skills develop more quickly, but audiation skills are slower to develop. The clever teacher must therefore adapt instruction to both the chronological age and the musical age of her students by proceeding at an appropriate pace in both executive skill development and audiation skill development. In a typical school situation, the teacher will find some students in her class who have not yet emerged from music babble. The teacher must gently try to guide such students through and out of music babble during the early lessons. The early lesson plans in *Jump Right In: The Instrumental Series – Revised Edition for Strings* make accommodation for such students.

## Scheduling and Grouping of Students

When scheduling and grouping students, the teacher should consider the advantages and disadvantages of large-group versus small-group instruction and homogeneous versus heterogeneous instruction. Executive skills are easiest to teach in a small group or private lesson; however, audiation skills are best learned in a large group. One rarely learns to play in tune and with a steady tempo and meter if all playing is done in a private lesson. Students learn to play in tune and with steady tempo and meter when they have to adjust and listen to other performers.

Executive skills are easiest to teach in a homogeneous class; however, audiation skill develops more quickly in a heterogeneous class, where the student hears and must adjust to other octaves and timbres. String students may even be combined with wind or percussion students. Beginning string players can be taught the fingering patterns to play simple songs in B-flat Major, E-flat Major, C Minor, or F Major, if the procedure outlined earlier in this chapter is followed. If students are taught to audiate and are taught the logic of fingering patterns in Major and Minor tonalities, they can learn to play in nearly any keyality during their first year of instruction.

The class should also be heterogeneous with regard to music aptitudes. If the teacher knows the music aptitudes of each student and how to best adapt instruction to students' individual musical strengths and weaknesses, lower aptitude students will learn a great deal from higher aptitude students, while the progress of higher aptitude students will not be slowed.

Ideally, then, students should have both small-group and large-group heterogeneous classes. Three days of instruction per week, on alternate days, are ideal to allow for audiation time between classes. Private lessons should

247

be reserved for students who have already developed substantial audiation skill. The private teacher can then concentrate on technique and literature.

## Summary

- Students must sing and move before they begin playing.
- Students must be physically flexible and well balanced.
- Teachers should establish musical tempos right from the start.
- Instructors must teach the "deep structure" of music, not just the "surface structure." Students should always be aware of the resting tone, the underlying harmonic functions, and the underlying macrobeats and microbeats.
- Optimum learning takes place when both skill and content are taught in a specific sequence. Each step becomes the readiness for the next step. Problems arise if the sequence is confused.
- The most basic skill learning sequence is:
    1. Listen
    2. Perform
    3. Read
    4. Write
- Students should be taught that audiation skill and executive skill are equally important when learning to play a stringed instrument. Audiation is necessary for recalling, performing, reading (notational audiation), writing, creating, or improvising. Executive skill is necessary to reproduce what is being audiated on the instrument.
- Teachers must constantly foster musical independence by:
    1. Singing or playing **for** students, not **with** them.
    2. Hearing each student perform alone at least once in each lesson.
    3. Teaching rhythmically independent harmony parts and rounds.
- Students who are in "babble" must be gently and patiently guided.
- The "Whole-Part-Whole" approach is necessary. The first stage (Performance Activity) is an introduction in which the students gain a vague, general sense of the tonality or meter of a song. In the second stage (Learning Sequence Activity), the students are taught a specific skill using tonal patterns or rhythm patterns in the tonality or meter that was introduced in the Performance Activity. In the third stage, the students return again to the Performance Activity with a deeper understanding of the musical syntax; therefore, they are able to perform with greater precision.
- Students must be taught to discriminate aurally among tonalities, meters, functions, and styles.

- Both tonal and rhythm solfege are essential. Movable DO with a LA-based Minor must be used to teach the audiation of tonalities and functions within those tonalities. A system of rhythm solfege based on beat function should be used to teach the audiation of meters and functions within those meters.
- Students must have a cassette tape or CD with which to practice at home. The cassette or CD must model appropriate tone quality, style of articulation, phrasing, intonation, and meter.

Incorporating Music Learning Theory into beginning string instruction can help any teacher produce students who are keen listeners, sensitive when performing with others, and comfortable playing for themselves and for others, with or without music notation. Instruction that uses Music Learning Theory produces students who hear and correct their own intonation problems and who keep steady tempo and meter. It produces students who are motivated to improve their tone and technique because, through audiation, they have a concept of the sound they wish to make. Incorporating Music Learning Theory into beginning string instruction can also revitalize the teacher who has been looking for a way to teach musicianship and not just technique. Finally, students instructed using Music Learning Theory will become intelligent consumers and discriminating listeners; they will be bored by mediocre music, and they will appreciate great music, because they have been taught to truly understand it.

## References

Bluestine, E. (2002). *The ways children learn music* (2nd Ed.). Chicago: GIA Publications.

Gordon, E. E. (1991). *Guiding your child's musical development.* Chicago: GIA Publications.

——. (1998). *Introduction to research and the psychology of music.* Chicago: GIA Publications.

——. (2001). *Preparatory audiation, audiation, and Music Learning Theory: A handbook of a comprehensive music learning sequence.* Chicago: GIA Publications.

——. (2002). *Rhythm: Contrasting the implications of audiation and notation.* Chicago: GIA Publications.

——. (2003a). *A music learning theory for newborn and young children.* Chicago: GIA Publications.

——. (2003b). *Learning sequences in music: Skill, content, and patterns.* Chicago: GIA Publications.

Gordon, E. E., & Woods, D. G. (1985). *Why use Learning Sequence Activities?* Chicago: GIA Publications.

Grunow, R. F. (Winter 1992). The evolution of rhythm syllables in Gordon's Music Learning Theory, *The Quarterly, 3*(4).

Grunow, R. F., Gordon, E. E., Azzara, C. D., & Martin, M. E. (2002). *Teachers guide, jump right in: The instrumental series revised edition for strings.* Chicago: GIA Publications.

Jackson, B., Berman, J., & Sarch, K. (1987). *The ASTA dictionary of bowing terms for string instruments.* Reston, VA: American String Teachers Association.

Lamb, N. (1971). *A guide to teaching strings.* Dubuque, IA: Wm. C. Brown Company.

Martin, M. E. (2002). *Parents' guide, jump right in: The instrumental series.* (Rev. Edition) Chicago: GIA Publications.

Rolland, P., & Mutschler, M. (1974). *The teaching of action in string playing.* Champaign - Urbana, IL: Illinois String Research Associates.

Young, P. (1987). *Playing the string game: Strategies for teaching cello and strings.* Austin, TX: University of Texas Press.

*Janet Smith*
• • • • • • • • • •
THE INTERNATIONAL SCHOOL OF BRUSSELS, BELGIUM

# Personal Experiences in a String Setting with *Jump Right In: The Instrumental Series*

Every music teacher who uses *Jump Right In: The Instrumental Series* interprets the curriculum and creates different ideas for its implementation. These differences are based on students' musical readinesses, physical readinesses, motivation, and even non-musical factors, such as class scheduling. The following ideas and views come from my experiences using *Jump Right In* in a variety of settings: private lessons, classes in the United States, and classes in an international school in Europe whose student body has over sixty nationalities.

## Readiness for String Instruction

Of all the factors determining success on a string instrument, readiness is the most important. A child must have passed through the preparatory stages of audiation before he or she is ready to begin a string instrument.[1] Otherwise, learning will be limited at best to imitation, with no musical understanding of what is being produced. Most often in a classroom situation, children have the physical readiness and the motivation to begin an instrument but have not been taught how to audiate. Using *Jump Right In*, students progress through the levels of skill learning sequence, beginning with echoing patterns at the aural/oral level. What can be done, however, for the students who are not matching the pitches in the patterns because they are not audiating?

---

[1] A more complete description of these readinesses for instrumental instruction is detailed in *A Music Learning Theory for Newborn and Young Children* (Gordon, 2003).

An instrument is played in tune only to the extent that the person playing it can audiate. Audiation is within musicians, and one of the best ways to develop it is by singing. When students sing, teachers can guide them to develop their audiation skills that can then be applied to their instruments. Learning rote songs is an easy, efficient way to engage students in singing and accomplish several musical goals at once.[2] For students who are not matching pitch, one simple solution can be applied during rote song learning; students should be asked to sing the resting tone of the song during breaks in the song and after the teacher sings the song. For students not singing the resting song on the correct pitch, the teacher can use the following "playback" technique used for students passing through the stages of preparatory audiation. The teacher echoes the incorrect resting tone the student sings and then sings the correct resting tone; the student echoes the resting tone again. I have found that many of my students singing the incorrect tone are, in fact, singing either the SO or the LA below the resting tone. When this happens, the teacher should sing SO-DO or LA-DO. The student is usually successful singing this pattern and, from that point, can immediately echo the single resting tone. Also, if the teacher asks students to sing the resting tone individually by tossing a beanbag underhand to them and asking them to sing the resting tone when they catch it, two things can be accomplished; students have a prop, which makes them less inhibited in singing, and the physical motion of preparation and toss encourages a breath and, thus, audiation before singing.

**Suggestions for Learning Songs by Ear**

In *Jump Right In*, after students have learned to sing several rote songs, they begin echoing melodic phrases on their instrument and progress to learning to play the rote songs by echoing the phrases of the songs. Following are several suggestions that have helped my students learn these rote songs through audiation.

1. The students must always know where the resting tone is. Asking them to stop and sing the resting tone after trying to play a particular phrase often helps students understand the relationship of pitches to the tonality as well as the order of the functions within that tonality.

2. If a student is having difficulty with a part of a song, the teacher should make sure the difficulty is not due to poor technique. If the

---

[2] For more information on rote songs, see the chapter within this book, "Music Learning Theory and Beginning String Instrument Instruction," under the section titled "Teaching a Rote Song."

problem is technique, the teacher should direct the students to work on the executive skill by having them finger the notes on their "imaginary instruments" or their real instruments while singing the difficult pattern. This not only targets executive skills, but strengthens audiation. The teacher should require the use of the "imaginary bow" as well, taking care that students are on the correct strings with the correct arm levels.

3. The teacher should use the "playback" technique when a student plays a phrase with an incorrect note and cannot audiate the correct one. The teacher should echo the incorrect phrase performed by the student and then play the correct phrase. The teacher should ask the student a) if the phrases are the same or different and b) which one is correct. If the student does not know which is correct, the phrase should be audiated again, stopping just after the part where the student is playing incorrectly. This may make the answer clearer.

4. Improvisation is an important part of making music. Just as oral language proficiency requires more than simply repeating what teachers say, music proficiency should require fluency in music. Teachers should encourage students to improvise or "speak" musically. Once students begin to improvise by manipulating the functions through audiation in a context, learning rote songs is much easier, because students comprehend the songs' underlying structure.

5. Students must understand the physical layout of the instrument and how to manipulate it to perform the notes that they are audiating so the lack of executive skills does not hamper audiation. For example, the executive skill of simply removing one finger to produce the next lower note is logical, but a student must also understand how to get to the note below an open string automatically, without having to stop and think about the executive skill.

   This is best learned in a context of audiation instead of by asking students to find the lower note. Any rote song can be used, but I have found that a simple one, such as "Hot Cross Buns," works best. As readinesses, the students should have learned to play the song in D-DO, and will have also learned at least DO, RE, and MI in G-DO. For violin, viola, and cello, this G-DO should be on the D string, and for the bass, this G-DO should be on the E string. I ask the students to echo me, starting on MI, and I play the first phrase while making sure they do not watch my hands. When they need to play DO, some

253

will cross to the next lower string automatically and play it; others will be perplexed. I ask those students to experiment on their instrument to see if there is some note they already know that will work for what they are audiating or if they can figure out some way to play that note. If there are still students who cannot play that note, I ask another student to explain how the note is played. Students are always eager to show one another how to play something, and having a student explain something often makes more of an impact on the students who are learning the skill. After the whole class successfully crosses their strings to play the melody going down, we change the key and play it in a different DO one string over.

## Critical Listening Skills through Enrichment Songs

Enrichment songs can be valuable, not only as a challenging activity for high-aptitude students but also as a way for all students to learn to audiate while listening. One motivational activity I often use in the classroom is a song contest. As there are always a few students who have taken lessons previously and have a high level of technical (but not always audiational) proficiency, it has been necessary to have separate categories for beginning and experienced students. After the students prepare songs of their own choosing that they have learned by ear, they play them for the class. This gives the listening students the opportunity to decide the meter and tonality of the songs and provides a forum to give helpful feedback to the soloists on how to improve. Often the listeners tell the soloist that the macrobeats are not steady; subsequently, the whole class performs the macrobeats with their heels while the soloist plays again, usually remedying the problem. With out-of-tune notes, the listeners suggest that the soloist move his or her fingers until "it sounds right." One benefit of this critical listening and discussion is that the entire class starts to listen more carefully, which improves the students' rhythm and intonation independently. Sometimes a student plays a song in a new keyality. This is an opportunity to figure out the keyality from an audiational standpoint by having the students sing the resting tone, then find the pitch that matches that tone, and, finally, give that pitch a name. Then the soloist is asked to figure out the pitches in the tonality (if this note is DO, where is RE, etc.) Students are thrilled to learn a keyality that nobody else knows!

## Arranging Rote Songs for Performances

A particular advantage of *Jump Right In* is that students need not put aside sequential learning to prepare for a concert. The songs that students have learned by rote throughout the year can be arranged for an enjoyable performance for both the listener and the performer.

Teachers can arrange songs for performance even if the students are not reading music yet. The first step is to decide upon the song(s). The teacher should look at each song and its variations that the ensemble has learned. For instance, if they can play "Major Duple" in G-DO, can they already play it in another keyality? Can they learn it in another keyality before the performance? Do they know the chord root accompaniment? Have they learned a harmony part? Is there an advanced student in the group who can learn or improvise a harmony part? Would a group of students like to compose a melody or harmonies to play as a section using the same harmonic progression as the song? Are there any students who would like to play solos? Would the group be willing to sing the song as part of the arrangement?

After exploring all the possibilities for the rote song, the teacher can begin to plan the arrangement. The written form can be simple—just a map as a reminder of the order of the sections. This map is necessary because the same harmonic progression occurs many times. If a modulation takes place, it is helpful to write a simple modulation for either a small group of students or the pianist and to tell the students that during the modulation students should listen carefully so they can audiate the new DO. Students do not need to be told how many measures are in the piano interludes; rather, they should be encouraged to use their audiation to listen for the end of the phrase played by small groups or the piano.

Figure 1 (on the following page) represents a sample arrangement each student might receive from the teacher. Students should be allowed to write notes to themselves on the paper to help them remember what to do when there are choices such as "melody and harmony, " but no writing of the notes with solfege or on a staff should be allowed.

Students can begin to use markings, such as *piano*, *forte*, *crescendo*, and *decrescendo*, that occur in the music. Since students have learned the songs without notation, they are truly giving meaning to these markings because the markings are a reminder of something that they have already performed in the rote songs. Seeing a song in this abbreviated form makes students aware of the form of the music as opposed to measure numbers, and they will begin to use words such as introduction, interlude, modulation, and coda as they converse with the teacher in the rehearsal. To add interest to the arrangements, new textures that do not require advanced technical skills can be introduced, such as *pizzicato*, *col legno*, and *tremolo*.

| MAJOR DUPLE | |
|---|---|
| SECTIONS OF SONG | NOTES |
| Piano introduction | |
| I   V   I   V | Play roots or improvise tonally |
| I   V   I V I | on macrobeats |
| Piano interlude | |
| Melody in G-DO | Piano |
| Piano modulation to B♭-DO | |
| Melody in B♭-DO | Forte |
| Piano modulation to G-DO | |
| Solos while ensemble plays roots | |
| Melody and harmony | Ritard and fermata at end |

*Figure 1.* Sample rote song arrangement for performance

## Supplementary Games and Exercises for Reading Tonal and Rhythm Patterns

After students have learned to read familiar patterns in the familiar order at the symbolic association level, they may bridge to reading those familiar patterns in an unfamiliar order. The following are several games that can help accomplish this goal.

**Tonal Pattern Games.** Tonality should always be established before the students begin singing or playing and should be reestablished as needed throughout the game. To establish tonality, a I–V–I progression can be played on a piano, or a preparatory sequence can be sung.

*Mix-up:* Students should have their books open to tonal patterns. Each student is assigned a tonal pattern number. The teacher establishes tonality. When the teacher calls the pattern number, the student with that pattern number sings the pattern. If the pattern is sung correctly (with the correct name and the correct pitch), the player is eliminated. If the player sings incorrectly, she advances to the next round. When all have had a turn, round two begins. The teacher assigns new pattern numbers to the students, and the same procedure is repeated. The game continues in this manner until everyone has sung a pattern in tune.

*Speedy:* There are two variations of this game. The teacher assigns students partners by ability level, and one student in each pair is then assigned to Team One and the other to Team Two. Students should have their

256

books open to tonal patterns. The teacher establishes tonality. For the first variation, the teacher says the pattern number, addressing the first pair of students. The student who sings the pattern with solfege syllables and correct pitches first earns a point for his or her team. The game continues pair by pair. For variation two, the teacher says the pattern number. The student who plays the pattern correctly and in tune earns a point for the team.

*Tonal Bingo:* The teacher prepares the traditional Bingo game, using tonal patterns in the place of numbers. Several different Bingo cards should be made for each instrument, with the appropriate clef and key signature placed before each pattern as well as one or two "free" squares. Cards and tokens should be distributed to players. The teacher establishes tonality, then sings one of the patterns from the Bingo cards using a neutral syllable or tonal syllables. The students audiate and read the patterns on their Bingo cards and place a token over the pattern the teacher sang. When a student has filled a row, he or she says, "Bingo." To verify the Bingo, the student must sing each pattern in the Bingo correctly using a neutral syllable or tonal syllables before receiving credit for winning.

**Rhythm Pattern Games.** Meter should always be established before the students begin chanting or playing and should be re-established as needed throughout the game. To establish the meter, the teacher can chant two or more two-macrobeat patterns in the meter and tempo being used. The teacher must establish the meter before each student response as well. This is best done as an introduction and will be referred to below as the rhythm introduction. To chant the rhythm introduction, the teacher says, in meter, "Du de Du, number ___." The pattern number is inserted into the blank. If the pattern is in Triple, the teacher says in meter "Du da di Du, number ___."

*Mix-up:* This game is the same format as the tonal version, substituting rhythm patterns for the tonal patterns.

*Perfection:* There are two variations of this game. The teacher assigns students partners of similar ability level, and one student in each pair is then assigned to Team One and the other to Team Two. Students should have their books open to rhythm patterns. For variation one, the teacher chants the rhythm introduction, including the pattern number, addressing the first pair of students. The student who chants the pattern with correct rhythm syllables and most accurate rhythm earns a point for the team. The game continues pair by pair. For variation two, the teacher assigns a pitch to be played with the rhythm. Then, the teacher says the rhythm introduction, including the pattern number as part of the introduction. The student who

257

plays the pattern with the most accurate rhythm earns a point for the team. To increase the difficulty, different tempos can be used in the rhythm introduction without warning the students. The most difficult tempos are the slow ones.

*Break the chain:* Students sit in a circle on the floor with their books open to rhythm patterns. Each person is assigned to Team One or Team Two. The teacher establishes the meter, and, on the next macrobeat, the first student begins to chant the first pattern. The next student begins to chant the second pattern immediately after the first on the correct macrobeat. Students who perform correctly earn a point for their team. Any student who does not start on the macrobeat, who changes the tempo, or who chants an incorrect rhythm does not earn a point for their team. Every time a student does not maintain the meter or tempo, the teacher must reestablish the meter. To increase the difficulty, different tempos can be used in the rhythm introduction without warning the students. The game continues in this manner, going around the circle several times, so students have several chances to perform correctly. My students find it helpful to rock side-to-side macrobeats and pat their hands to microbeats during this game. When it is time to stop, the team with the most points wins.

*Rhythm Bingo:* This game is the same format as the tonal version, substituting rhythm patterns for the tonal patterns.

## Integrating Students Who Transfer from Other Schools

Integrating students who come into a strings group in the middle of the year and already play a string instrument is not difficult when it is handled in a straightforward manner. An initial private session should be scheduled with the new student. Invite the student to play something from her former class. After some general comments, explain that this class uses a different system. It should be stressed that there is nothing wrong with the student's old system, but that to participate and enjoy the class he or she will need to learn the system that this class uses. Show her the notes in whatever DO is being used most in class at that time, and allow the student to take notes if she desires. Notetaking serves to integrate her as quickly as possible and also prevents overwhelming her at the beginning. The student may wish to write notes on the staff and the corresponding tonal syllables underneath, or simply write the note letters and the corresponding tonal syllables beside them. This step is simply to quickly bridge the gap between one system and another for new students; at no time should the teacher write tonal syllables on paper for established students. Encourage the student to participate when the class sings tonal patterns because it will help him or her catch up to the class faster. Usually it is not a good idea to have the student sing alone during the initial consultation. Have him or her move the heels to macrobeats and pat the hands to microbeats while echoing the macro/microbeat patterns in Duple and Triple meters from *Jump Right In*, and teach the terms "macrobeats" and "microbeats." During this initial evaluation, the teacher should be able to ascertain the student's playing and coordination levels and begin to know the student enough to assign him or her to an experienced player who will become a mentor. The mentor explains the terms learned in verbal association when they are used in class, teaches her new notes in new keyalities, and guides her in class activities. The experienced player can be given a list of the terms to teach to the incoming student, such as tonal, rhythm, Major, Minor, tonic, dominant, audiate, and resting tone.

The incoming student who announces to the beginners, "Where I came from, we're already reading music" may impress students, who then begin to subtly (or not so subtly) drop hints that they think they should be reading too. This is the time to remind them that there is the right time for everything when playing a string instrument and that reading will occur when they have done the necessary things first. In fact, I have found that an incoming student may provide just the encouragement students need by commenting on how much more the *Jump Right In* students are doing than those at her previous school.

In many countries, fixed DO is commonly in use. Changing a child from one solfege system to another is not difficult. The teacher must assure the student that it is fine to keep the other system in private lessons or for when the student moves back to his or her country, and that she is intelligent enough to do both. After experience teaching in countries in which the private lesson academies teach the fixed-DO system with SI in the place of TI, and in which the syllable actually names the note, I have found that students can adapt quickly to a movable-DO system.

## Multiculturalism in Strings Classes

I have had students from both Western and non-Western countries, including India, Pakistan, Zimbabwe, Taiwan, Japan, and Kenya. Some students had no music classes before entering my string classes, but with the proper sequence of skills and content in *Jump Right In*, these students achieved as well or better than students with prior formal music instruction based primarily on Western music.

Working with students for whom English is a second language (ESL) rarely presents a problem when using *Jump Right In*. The fact that, from the

259

beginning, one is making music is perhaps the most elegant thing about Music Learning Theory. Music truly becomes the "universal language" when no spoken language is necessary in order to learn. Language differences become apparent only when the teacher describes physical components of string playing, for example, holding the instrument; much of this can even be accomplished by modeling. At this time, the teacher must take care to speak slowly, demonstrate as much as possible, and write instructions down for reference. ESL students may be assigned to experienced players, who have time to repeat instructions and help give individual attention.

## Strategies for Experienced Players in Beginning Groups

One of the most useful aspects of *Jump Right In* is how it can be adapted to meet the needs of individual students. String players often start studying at an early age, and, thus, in strings classes it is not unusual to have several students who have already taken lessons and possess some technical facility. These students need to be challenged at the same time that the other students are just beginning to learn how to play. Audiation, however, is a skill to which these students usually have not been introduced. The following are several strategies to address this discrepancy.

The most obvious strategy is to use experienced players as role models. Assuming that they play with reasonable intonation and musicality, experienced students can play patterns for the class to echo, leaving the teacher free to help students individually. The role models can be given patterns that the class will echo ahead of time so that they can practice them. This works well with the melodic patterns and also when students are echoing open strings or patterns all on one pitch. The student needs to be given very specific instructions such as: "Play microbeats on TI for four macrobeats, wait four macrobeats for the class to echo, then start again immediately on the fifth macrobeat. Do four sets of patterns." Before the student plays, the teacher should establish tonality to provide a context for the patterns.

Experienced students can also be mentors to other students in several ways. For example, experienced students can be "guardian angels" for a day, to watch for recurring executive skill problems in a less experienced student. An experienced student can also be paired with a student who has been absent from school to help that student to catch up with the rest of the class.

From an audiational standpoint, the possibilities for individual learning are endless. The fact that the experienced students are often free of executive skill problems allows them to focus on audiational challenges. These students can easily teach themselves to play the chord roots while the rest of the class is playing a rote song. First, the teacher should teach the class the chord roots to a few rote songs. Then, while the rest of the class is learning a new rote song through melodic patterns, the advanced players should be asked to play the chord roots themselves, figuring out the harmonic changes through audiation. This gives them an assignment that needs little explanation, leaving the teacher to address the majority of the class.

After the experienced players have sung and played patterns, labeled the functions, and improvised tonal patterns in tonic and dominant, they can begin to improvise harmony parts. They should be guided first to figure out the harmonic changes, then to improvise and play a harmony part at the same time the rest of the class is learning a rote song through melodic patterns. These improvisations can turn into parts of arranged rote songs for performances, as explained previously.

Another means to enrich experienced students in a beginning group is to ask them to prepare an ensemble with minimal teacher guidance, working on the ensemble in another room while the rest of the group rehearses. In this case, they should be given either a rote song or a harmonic progression and asked to prepare harmonies with as much musicality as possible. After a few rehearsals together without a teacher, they should perform for the class. The class can be asked to identify the meter and tonality of the song, sing the chord roots with the song, and discuss musical aspects of the performance.

### Tuning from an Audiational Standpoint

Tuning is often the most chaotic, unmusical part of a strings rehearsal. It can be, however, a logical, organized, audiation-based process if time is set aside at the beginning of each rehearsal to help students think (audiate) in tune, as well as to tune their string instruments.

Because audiating the resting tone of a tonality is necessary for in-tune singing or playing, a logical starting point is to compare an open string pitch with an audiated resting tone. If students are not able to audiate a resting tone, the teacher should sing or play songs in Major tonality for the students. Prior to singing each song, the teacher should establish the proper tonality. During the song, she should stop at various points, sing the resting tone using a neutral syllable or the appropriate tonal syllable, and gesture for the students to breathe and imitate her.

Before actual tuning takes place, it is necessary to practice some executive skills. Students should be guided to move their "imaginary fine tuners" in both directions; for violins and violas this should be done while they are in playing position. After they are comfortable with this, the teacher should "detune" her A string and establish tonality. She then turns

261

her fine tuner while playing the A until the students are satisfied that the played A matches the resting tone they are audiating and singing and tell her to stop tuning. This should be repeated as many times as necessary until the students understand what to do. After the students are able to audiate and sing the resting tone independently from the teacher and they understand the tuning process, they are ready to tune using the following procedure (see Figure 2).

| THE TEACHER | EACH STUDENT |
|---|---|
| 1. Plays a I–V7–I cadence in A Major on keyboard. | 1. Listens. |
| 2. Repeats the cadence. | 2. Audiates resting tone. Sings the resting tone with the group. |
| 3. Repeats the cadence. | 3. Audiates the resting tone. Plays an open A. Compares the open string pitch with audiated resting tone. Adjusts the string accordingly. |

*Figure 2.* Tuning procedure for the A string

When following this tuning procedure, play the appropriate cadence so that the open string being tuned is audiated and sung as the resting tone of that cadence. Repeat the process for each open string as many times as necessary. Instruments can be grouped for tuning purposes as the teacher desires, and resting tones can be sung in the range most comfortable for each student. Singing a resting tone in an octave different from the actual string pitch does not create a problem because students will be audiating a resting tone of the cadence played by the teacher in a context, rather than matching pitches without syntax.

To give students further audiation practice, ask them to guide fellow students in tuning. Play the appropriate cadence for an open string. Then have the students audiate the resting tone. Let one student play and tune her open string, and ask the other students their opinions about the tuning just completed. Students will listen even more closely when they know that they have a voice in the procedures.

As soon as the students are comfortable audiating, singing, and playing resting tones in Major tonality, tuning cadences may be played in different tonalities, such as Harmonic Minor, Aeolian, Dorian, Mixolydian, Phrygian, and Lydian. The teacher should use the appropriate cadence, for example i–VII–i in Dorian tonality. Playing short songs in different tonalities and meters to establish tonality is also an efficient way for the teacher to demonstrate good tone quality and proper posture while allowing students a quick and painless "listening bath" in unusual tonalities and meters. Teachers may encourage more audiation by asking students to audiate, practice, and perform the short tuning songs for the class at a later date.

To save time during the tuning process, teachers may ask students to tune two open strings separately after a particular tonality has been established. The specific strings to be tuned depend on the keyality of the established tonality. For instance, if the keyality established is D, first the open D string and then the open A string may be tuned. Similarly, if the keyality established is A, first the open A string and then the open E string may be tuned. If violas and cellos are in the group, the keyality of C should be established. First tune the open C string and then the open G string.

When students are proficient at tuning one string at a time, they have the readiness to tune two strings simultaneously. This is an opportune time to use audiation to introduce students to the executive skill of playing double stops. The teacher should establish tonality, keeping the keyality the same as the lower string name. For example, to tune the open D and open A strings together, the teacher should establish tonality in the keyality of D. Students first should tune the lower string of the double stop, then play the strings together as a double stop and tune the upper string.

## Conclusion

Due to the nature of string instruments, lack of audiation is immediately apparent in beginning string students. String students cannot approximate pitches as easily as beginning band students, who depress keys and valves (the trombone being the exception); therefore it is imperative that we teach our students to audiate as we concurrently teach executive skills. As more teachers begin to realize the value of teaching string classes through audiation, even more techniques will be created to assist teachers in that goal.

## References

Gordon, E. E. (2003a). *A music learning theory for newborn and young children.* Chicago: GIA Publications.

 . (2003b). *Learning sequences in music: Skill, content, and patterns.* Chicago: GIA Publications.

Grunow, R. F., & Gordon, E. E. (1995) *Jump right in: The instrumental series.* Chicago: GIA Publications.

*Lelouda Stamou*
• • • • • • • • • • • •
University of Macedonia, Greece

# Music Learning Theory, Physiology of Learning, and the Suzuki Philosophy: When Research Meets Philosophy and Educational Practice

In the last fifteen years, research findings in biology and neurophysiology have established the importance of the early years of life for the development of human abilities and talents. At the same time, the continued development of valid research instruments has allowed music researchers to delve deeper into the nature of musical talent and the factors that affect its development. Edwin Gordon, as a part of this effort, has created a body of research on music aptitude and the factors that relate to it. At long last, the effects of music on the process of development are being studied using research techniques that have made the research more widely accepted and valued by the scientific community, as well as by the general population, and these findings concerning the role of music in human development consistently have supported the inclusion of developmentally appropriate music guidance in early childhood and school settings.

These research findings are not surprising to musicians and music teachers, who by experience and instinct understand the positive effects of music on human development. Educators and philosophers of the past often have advocated the importance of music and the necessity of including music instruction at all educational levels, starting as early in life as possible. Almost 2,500 years ago, Plato was describing music as one of the essential elements of education. In his Laws, Plato says that education should start from infancy, with the mothers singing for and dancing with their children. He writes, "nursing and motion should be as continuous as possible" (790c8-9), and it is beneficial when mothers "don't provide stillness but just the opposite, motion; they rock them constantly in their arms, and not with silence but with some melody" (790d9-790e2). According to Plato, the first three years of life are extremely important for a child's future development, because "that is the age when, through habituation, the most decisive growth in the entire character occurs for everyone" (792e2-4).

Shinichi Suzuki, who was born and lived in Japan, is among the most influential music educators of the past century. His teaching method for young children, which he developed in Japan after the Second World War, has spread around the world in less than fifty years. Most Suzuki teachers were not surprised by the research findings on how children learn and on how music affects young children's development, because Suzuki had been advocating this through his teaching methods. As an early childhood music educator, researcher, and Suzuki teacher, I instinctively knew the importance of music in early childhood and was excited when the educational and research communities supported what I already knew and believed. Scientific research converged with and verified existing philosophical values and educational practices, and this convergence has provided the impetus for this paper.

In this chapter, I will compare Gordon's Music Learning Theory and the Suzuki philosophy of Talent Education, while at the same time emphasizing the points of agreement that the two have with one another and with the research on how children learn music and the role of music in early childhood development. Gordon's Music Learning Theory represents some of the most ground-breaking practices in music education that are supported by research, and Suzuki represents more of a philosophical approach to teaching music. Although there are many differences between the two approaches, it is my intention to demonstrate that philosophy and research can balance and complement one another and can be used to advise educational praxis in a natural way, bringing to the forefront common values and truths.

## The Inner Workings of the Brain: Brain and Music Development

The inner workings of the brain have long been a mystery in science. However, in the last several decades, many of the secrets about the way in which the brain develops and functions have been revealed. Two of the most profound discoveries are that the brain uses the outside world to shape itself and that it goes through crucial periods in which the brain cells must have certain kinds of stimulation in order to develop specific abilities (Kotulak, 1996).

Recent evolutions in molecular biology and new imaging techniques have allowed researchers to discover that genes serve as the chemical blueprints of life and establish the framework of the brain. Then the environment takes over and provides the finishing touches (Kotulak, 1996). Scientists have found that the brain goes through four major structural changes: the first during fetal development, the second immediately after birth, the third between ages four and twelve, and fourth during adolescence. Starting from a few cells in the embryo, brain cells multiply at an astounding rate. About 200 billion are created in several months. The genes "hardwire" some of the neurons during the first weeks of fetal development into circuits that command breathing, control heartbeat, regulate body temperature, and produce reflexes.

The brain produces twice as many cells as it eventually will keep. Begley (1996) says, trillions upon trillions of neurons "are like the Pentium chips in a computer before the factory preloads the software. They are pure and of almost infinite potential, unprogrammed circuits that might one day compose rap songs and do calculus, erupt in fury and melt in ecstasy" (p. 56). The job of the cells is to communicate with the body that is developing around them and to be connected with other neurons that have been designated for the same tasks. During fetal development, the connections between neurons, called synapses, increase, reaching 253 million at the time of birth. Depending upon the environmental stimuli, some of these synapses are strengthened, while others die off because of lack of stimulation from the outside world. Brain connections start to die off toward the end of the first year of life, stabilizing at 354 million per speck of brain tissue by age twelve. The trillions of connections that survive the great die-off owe their survival, in large part, to what a child experiences in the first years of life.

The above discussion clarifies the importance of early stimulation for brain development and learning. Early experiences are so powerful, says pediatric neurobiologist Chugani, that "they can completely change the way a person turns out" (Begley, 1996). Proper stimulation at the beginning of life contributes to ability development in a way that can never happen after the first years of life.

Evidence that musical ability is present in all human beings has risen from research in psychology, neurology, psychiatry, and biology (Fox, 1991).

267

Newborns seem to prefer melodies that they learned prenatally, and such melodies can soothe infants after birth (Panneton, 1987). Shaw (1991) found that infants who had received prenatal music stimuli were more responsive to their mothers than infants who did not have any prenatal music stimuli, and Wilkin (1995/96) found that fetuses who were exposed daily to four pieces of music showed more fetal movement and heart rate decelerations to that music than fetuses who had no music stimulation. They also appeared to be more attentive and tended to move more to music after they were born.

Research on the musical development of newborns has shown that infants respond to sound at birth and even before. Newborns distinguish volume, localize a sound, prefer certain sounds to others, and acquire auditory discrimination in the first day of life (Brand, 1985). Pitch and timbre discriminations develop early. Fox (1991) states that what is emerging from reports on early childhood musical development is "a picture of an extremely competent young child, able to discriminate sounds skillfully and to create responses to music through movement and play" (p. 43).

During gestation and the first years of life, musical stimulation will cause the formation of synapses in the brain, especially for music, which, if strengthened, will greatly affect a child's ability to learn music. The sooner a child begins to enjoy a rich music environment, the greater the number of synapses that will be devoted to music learning and cognition. After years of debate on "nature versus nurture" as the source of music aptitude, research in neurophysiology, psychoacoustics, sociomusicology, cognitive psychology, and psychomusicology has supported that music aptitude is a product of both nature and nurture. The proportion that each contributes remains unknown.

## Gordon's Music Learning Theory and Other Research Findings on Music Development

According to Gordon (2003), every child is born with some level of music aptitude. This aptitude is normally distributed among the population at birth. Gordon believes that just as there are no children without intelligence, so there are no children without music aptitude. Although one's level of music aptitude at birth cannot be predicted accurately on the basis of ancestry, there is little doubt that, unless one is exposed early to a rich informal environment in music, one's aptitude for music will start declining and will never reach its potential (Gordon, 2003).

Gordon (1987) has studied music aptitudes and music achievement, which he respectively defines as the potential to achieve and what one has actually accomplished in music, respectively. He hypothesizes that one possesses the highest level of music aptitude, or the most potential, at the time of birth. After that time, rich musical stimulation is needed to keep aptitude levels from decreasing. Gordon (1998) notes, "a good musical environment is essential if one is to be able to realize his or her maximum innate potential, whatever that level may be" (p. 7). He believes that music aptitude at the time of birth is a limiting factor, meaning that "regardless of how favorable children's early informal experiences in music are, their music aptitude will never reach a level higher than that with which they were born" (p. 9).

Music aptitude is developmental, meaning that it can be affected by the quality of the environment during the first nine years of life, with environmental influences being greater when the child is younger (Gordon, 1980; Flohr, 1981; Taggart, 1997). The terms "developmental music aptitude" and "stabilized music aptitude" were introduced by Gordon to define the two periods before and after the approximate age of nine, when the stabilization of music aptitude occurs. Continuing research (Gordon, 2003) has shown that after approximately the age of nine music aptitude is no longer affected by the environment. After this time, although one can keep learning and achieving, his/her music aptitude compared to the entire population will remain relatively constant. This fact is supported by other research findings (Moog, 1976; Petzold, 1966), according to which, at a certain age, the child's development of certain skills levels out. This stabilization apparently is related to the plasticity of the brain during the first years of life. Gordon (2003) says that the level of music aptitude with which a child is born may be, to some extent, a result of prenatal responsiveness to music, as well as the quality of the music environment in utero. His research concerning music aptitude and its development continues to be one of his most important contributions to music education.

Another important contribution is his articulation of the music learning process and what this process should mean for instructional practice. Gordon argues that children should learn music in the same way that they learn their first language. With language, in order for children to be able to use language as adults do, they need to listen to language spoken to them and around them. If that happens, they will develop a listening vocabulary that will allow them to start experimenting with the sounds of language early in the process of development. This experimentation, or language babble, is usually reinforced by adults and is a necessary step to enable children to progress smoothly in the formation of accurate imitations of words and small phrases. Children start developing a speaking vocabulary that becomes richer and more varied depending upon the quality of the language environment around them. In a rich language environment, children will soon move from imitating words and phrases to improvising with language, using the words and phrases that they have learned to create their own sentences. Children need to have well-developed listening and speaking vocabularies before they receive formal instruction in language, which usually happens when they begin school and are taught reading and writing skills.

Likewise, a child's music development needs to proceed through a similar process in order for a child to be ready for formal music instruction, which is instruction that focuses on correctness. Children need to develop a listening vocabulary in music; they need to hear lots of singing and chanting before they will begin to experiment with musical sounds. If the musical environment around the child is rich and playful, the child soon will start experimenting with musical sounds, at first in a way that has little resemblance to music as adults know it. This music babble, if reinforced, will lead to correct imitation of short musical (tonal or rhythm) patterns and phrases. As is the case with language, children will imitate short patterns first and then longer phrases, in the same way that they first imitate words and then small phrases or sentences in language. If guided in a rich, positive, informal environment, children will soon develop a singing and chanting repertoire of tonal and rhythm patterns, and eventually of short songs and chants. They will learn to sing in tune, keep beat, and, eventually, coordinate their breathing and movement with their singing and chanting. When this has occurred, children, having developed the listening and performing vocabularies in music, are musically ready for formal music instruction that will introduce them to reading, writing, and eventually theoretical study of music.

According to Gordon (2003), the more appropriate the early informal experiences in music, the higher the level at which a student's music aptitude will stabilize and, thus, the greater this student's musical achievement can be. Gordon's research findings agree with the findings of other researchers who have studied the effect of early musical experiences on the development of music ability and future musical success. Stamou (January 1998) presents a number of studies that have investigated the influence of early music experiences on musical development. These studies support the importance of early musical stimulation and parental involvement in the development of musical abilities (Brand, 1986; Brokaw, 1983; Doan, 1973; Gordon, 1967; Howe, et al., 1995; Jenkins, 1976; Sloane, 1985; Sloboda & Howe, 1991; Sosniak, 1985; Zdinski, 1991; Zdzinski, 1992).

In this light, some who espouse traditional approaches for teaching music to young children may find these approaches lacking, while others find support for what they are already doing and have found to be successful. In general, Suzuki teachers will find their beliefs about music learning to be supported and justified. However, the incorporation of Gordon's Music Learning Theory within the Suzuki framework can enhance learning for students.

**The Suzuki Philosophy and Method of Teaching**

The Suzuki method of teaching music, founded in Japan in 1945, was introduced in the United States in 1964 and has spread throughout the world since that time. Today, hundreds of thousands of children are being educated through the Suzuki method, not only on violin, for which the method was initially developed, but also on other instruments, such as piano, flute, guitar, viola, cello, bass, and harp.

The idea of Talent Education, which is another name for the Suzuki approach, occurred to Suzuki when he was a young man. The fact that Japanese children, by the age of five or six, were able to internalize Japanese, which is a complicated language, led him to believe that the beginnings of language are acquired through a method that works unconsciously. That was, for Suzuki (1981), a strong indication of the educational possibilities that young children possess, and it instilled in him the belief that "any child has seeds of ability which can be nurtured as far as the capacity of the brain will allow" (p. 5).

Although the word "method" has been widely used in conjunction with Suzuki's work, Talent Education is more than a method of teaching music. Slone (1988) quotes Evely Hermann:

> In the 1960s when the Western String Teachers first went to Matsumoto, Japan, to learn more about the Suzuki Method, they returned home feeling as though they had missed something at the demonstrations which they had attended. Obviously there was more to this teaching method than they understood, for the Japanese teachers were producing fantastic results. Yet when they tried using the method books, they fell short of the desired results. The word METHOD was fully understood, for many methods books were already in print in the United States and in Europe. Little by little the idea began to emerge. This was not a mere method. It was a philosophy. (p. 3)

The goal of Talent Education is the development of a "noble heart" through music, and tremendous love of and respect for each child is central to the way in which teachers and parents work within the Suzuki approach.

271

As Slone (1988) notes, Talent Education is not a cult, nor does it want to be. It is a means of making a major contribution to the life and growth of children. "It is an alternative way of looking at a very imperfect world" (p. 7). The Suzuki approach emphasizes cooperation, unlike traditional methods of violin teaching, in which competition is often reinforced. Of course, this is not to say that there is no competition in Talent Education. However, what Suzuki teachers and parents try to develop is a healthy kind of competition: "the desire to be the best person the individual can be...not the desire to beat someone else" (p. 8).

In a qualitative research study, Collier (1991) examined the experience of twenty-six students who had been involved in Suzuki instruction from their early childhood or early elementary years until high school graduation. The researcher revealed several thematic core components of their experiences evolving from participation in the Suzuki approach. First was the development of significant patterns of interpersonal relationships among parents, teachers, and peers that offered students feelings of security and consistency. Second was the contribution of the Suzuki approach to the development of students' self-esteem, attitudes, values and spirituality that accompanied them in the musical as well as other aspects of their lives. The integration of the Suzuki experience into ongoing adult life was the third theme that emerged from the data. Many of the participants mentioned the development of work habits that they developed as a result of Suzuki instruction that they carried with them into their professional endeavors. They also attributed the development of the ability to isolate difficult tasks and work at them repetitively in small segments until mastered as well as their understanding of the importance of positive reinforcement in dealing with colleagues and employees to their Suzuki education. Collier's study is valuable in revealing the effects of Suzuki instruction on students' non-musical and, to a lesser extent, musical lives. Understanding these experiences enhances teachers' knowledge of the Suzuki approach but also of the values that can be nurtured in an educational environment (Bresler, 1995).

The basic assumption of Suzuki's Talent Education is that every child can learn if given the right environmental stimulation and enough repetition. Although Suzuki formulated his philosophy and approach to teaching music long before the research concerning the effects of music instruction on brain development and on how persons learn music, he was accurate in his assumptions about the way humans develop and learn. Basic principles of Talent Education correspond with what has been learned as a result of the research of neurophysiologists, biologists, and psychologists.

## Intersections between Music Learning Theory and Talent Education

Stamou (Spring 1998) notes that, despite the popularity of the Suzuki approach in the United States and throughout the world, knowledge of the effects of Suzuki instruction on musical development is based mostly on informal observations rather than on research findings. The existing research studies present inconclusive results, in part due to the different methodologies and, often, questionable research instruments and designs employed in the studies.

Gordon's Music Learning Theory, as exemplified by *Jump Right In: The Music Curriculum*, which is based on it, and Suzuki's Talent Education are two distinct approaches to music education. Gordon based his theories in research, whereas Suzuki's work is based in intuition. As Creider (1989) notes, "Gordon is a scientist and not a philosopher" (p. 261). According to her, Gordon's writings are concrete and rigorously logical, following the strict Western academic tradition of research and scholarly publication. He has not been interested in or studied other aspects of children's development outside of their development in music. So, as Creider says, "what is at the core of Suzuki's whole purpose in teaching music to children, that is, creating fine hearts and sensitive human beings, is not addressed in Music Learning Theory in any way" (p. 262).

Although Gordon's Music Learning Theory and Suzuki's Talent Education were developed from different philosophies and cultural backgrounds and aim at different elements in human development, their principles for teaching music to children are similar in many ways. Beyond this, Creider (1989) believes that "when one begins to examine each approach as it relates to the practical issues of how to teach a child music, some interesting possibilities emerge for combining the two" (p. 263).

The importance of the environment during the early years of life was an idea that was fundamental to both Suzuki and Gordon. Both also believed that every child has the potential to achieve musically. The "nature versus nurture" question was discussed by Suzuki, who differentiated between "inborn ability" and "educated ability," much in the same way that Gordon later differentiated between aptitude at the time of birth and the effect of the environment on the development of music aptitude. Suzuki, like Gordon, believed that the brain sets limits as to the extent that the environment can influence ability. As he said, "any child has seeds of ability which can be nurtured as far as the capacity of the brain will allow" (p. 5). That is similar to Gordon's (1991) belief that aptitude at the time of birth is a limiting factor in the extent to which aptitude will develop, regardless of the quality of the environment. Both of these are similar to the way in which

273

neurophysiologists discuss genes as a limiting factor in the amount the environment shapes human characteristics and abilities.

The existence of critical periods for ability development was also a strong component of Suzuki's philosophy and Talent Education. Suzuki (1981) said, "setting a child aside until elementary school age and then saying that now education begins is like taking a withered or withering sprout and suddenly giving it large amounts of fertilizer, putting it in the sunlight and flooding it with water. It is too late for the withered sprout" (p. 12). Within Talent Education, children as young as two or three years old are introduced into the Suzuki environment. Suzuki (1981) refers to a conversation between Darwin and a mother.

> Mother: From what age is it best to educate a child?
> Darwin: How old is your child?
> Mother: My child is a year and a half.
> Darwin: Then you are a year and a half late. (p. 55)

The diminishing influence that the environment has in shaping a child as that child grows older was understood clearly by Suzuki. He says, "humans taking on human form are similar to a plaster sculpture. At first, it is wet and gooey. The plaster soon hardens. After the hardened form is made, nothing can be changed about it" (Suzuki, 1981, p. 86). While this analogy is somewhat exaggerated, it is in some agreement with the recent findings on brain development as well as with Gordon's ideas about developmental music aptitude. Stamou (1999) writes, "there are crucial learning periods during the beginning of life, the 'windows of opportunity,' during which the brain can reorganize itself with particular ease by breaking down or making new connections between brain cells" (p. 2). When these windows close, much of the fundamental architecture of the brain that defines ability is already completed. Gordon (2003) believes that the effect of a rich music environment on a child's music aptitude decreases at an increasing rate as the child grows older and that, by the time a child reaches approximately age nine, his or her music aptitude can no longer be affected by the environment.

Striking similarities also exist between how Gordon and Suzuki describe the music learning process, both believing that it is parallel to language acquisition. Suzuki (1981) argued that music can be learned in the same way that language is learned; this is the reason why his Talent Education was often called "Mother Tongue Education." According to Suzuki, "the best method in the world is hidden within the mother tongue education" (p. 5). If music surrounds the child from the time of birth, or even before, in a positive, reinforcing, rich, and repetitive environment, as usually happens with language, then, by the time they start formal education, children will be able to understand, create, and communicate through language. This belief of Suzuki, which was developed more than fifty years ago, coincides with Gordon's Music Learning Theory, according to which children should be surrounded with music in the same way that they are surrounded with language from the time of birth or before. It also is in line with research findings, according to which the plasticity of the brain during the first years of life will allow an appropriate music environment and an appropriate language environment to create separate neural pathways dedicated to music learning and language learning. These pathways lay the foundation for lifelong fluency in music and in language.

Gordon believes that children must be nurtured in a free, positive, playful environment during the first years of life (Valerio, et al., 1998). He also believes that they should be allowed to interact with the environment as they feel comfortable; they should not be forced to participate, and they should be allowed to explore. Suzuki, too, believed that the quality of the environment has a strong effect on children's emotional and personal development. Suzuki (1981) wrote about the importance of a joyful, non-threatening learning environment in order for learning to take place. He noted that forcing a child who is not ready into formal music instruction is like yelling at a seed to sprout. As he says, "true cultivators know that a seed needs plenty of fertilizer, water, and sunshine. If you hold a seed in your hand and yell, 'Sprout! Sprout! Sprout!' you are being merciless to the seed. The seed will not sprout unless the conditions are right" (p. 15). Those beliefs are supported by research findings in child development and psychology that stress the importance of a non-threatening, positive environment in which play and feelings of love, attention, and security are reinforced. Heyge and Sillick (1998) state that "adults use singing together with gentle touching and handling of [the] baby to develop a secure bond of trust and love and to stimulate the vital neurological development which occurs only at this stage" (p. 12). Gordon and Suzuki would concur fully.

The importance of developing a listening vocabulary as a foundation for music development is evident in both the Suzuki philosophy and in Gordon's Music Learning Theory. Suzuki places emphasis on children knowing by ear the music that they are going to play in the future, and this is the reason that listening to recordings of the repertoire plays such an important role in the Suzuki approach. To Suzuki, developing the listening repertoire is a prerequisite for the development of the performing repertoire, while reading and writing music notation follow much later. When students read and write, they simply are learning the symbols for what they have already listened to and can perform. Similarly, in Music Learning Theory, the listening repertoire forms the foundation for the development of the performing (singing and chanting) repertoire; reading and writing eventually follow and relate at first to what children have already experienced aurally and can produce orally. However, Suzuki instruction can be enriched by the incorporation of Gordon's understanding that a performing vocabulary is developed best through singing, chanting, and moving. According to Music Learning Theory, only after children have sung, chanted, or moved should their performance vocabulary be transferred to an instrument. Singing, chanting, and moving are often neglected in the Suzuki approach. However, a child who cannot sing a song in tune or move to it in tempo probably will not be able to play that song in tune or with a consistent tempo. Many performance problems could be solved if children were able to sing a musical work and move to it with flow and beat before they were asked to perform it on an instrument. If singing, chanting, and moving occur regularly in instruction, then the teaching of fingerings and the rhythm of the song will not be as difficult because children's instrumental performances will be guided by what they are audiating (Grunow & Gordon, 2002). Children will know how a musical work should sound, because they already have developed musical ownership of that work through performance. As a result, they will adjust their instrumental performances to match what they have already performed with their voices and bodies.

Suzuki placed great value on children's learning by rote and listening to and imitating models of musical excellence. Gordon also believes in the importance of rote learning and excellent musical models. According to Gordon, rote learning is necessary for children's music development, as children need to listen to and imitate the singing and chanting of others so that they can develop a readiness to draw from the vocabulary developed during those imitations when creating their own music. Rote learning forms the foundation upon which children build in developing independent, creative musicianship. Because children emulate the musicianship of their musical models, it is essential that these models be of outstanding quality.

The roles of rote learning, however, differ between the Gordon and Suzuki approaches. Gordon views rote learning as necessary readiness for developing an aural/oral understanding of music (audiation) and for developing the ability to improvise and create, which will eventually result naturally in excellence in music performance. Suzuki, on the other hand, primarily views rote learning and imitation as a means through which children learn to reproduce excellence in performance. The Suzuki approach does not move beyond rote learning by encouraging children to use what they have learned by rote as the basis for creating their own music or for making musical decisions with unfamiliar repertoire. As a result, opponents of the Suzuki approach often have criticized it for producing students who are excellent at imitating through performance but do not deeply understand (audiate) what they perform and are not able to generalize what they have learned. By incorporating some of Gordon's ideas about how to develop audiation as a step beyond imitation, Suzuki teachers could guide students into a deeper understanding of tonality, meter, and harmonic function. They also could guide their students to learn to make independent musical decisions based upon what they already know and can do.

## Conclusions

Although Suzuki grounded his teaching approach in philosophical insights and personal beliefs, whereas Gordon also based his on research, it is remarkable how much the two approaches share in terms of beliefs about and principles of teaching music to young children. These principles also align with recent research on the role of music in child development. Educational research, philosophy, and praxis should walk hand in hand, advising and pushing each other forward. Teachers, philosophers, and researchers should work together and inspire one another through their work. Through studying the work of Suzuki, Gordon, and countless researchers who are conducting research on how children learn music and the role of music in child development, music educators can critically examine and improve their own practice and meet the needs of their young students musically and beyond.

## References

Begley, S. (February 19, 1996). Your child's brain: How kids are wired for music, math and emotions. *Newsweek, 327*(8), 54-62.

Brand, M. (March 1985). Lullabies that awaken musicality in infants. *Music Educators Journal, 71*(7), 28-31.

——. (1986). Relationship between home musical environment and selected musical attributes of second-grade children. *Journal of Research in Music Education, 34*(2), 111-120.

Bresler, L. (1995). Ethnography, phenomenology, and action research in music education. *Quarterly Journal of Music Teaching and Learning, 6*(3), 4-16.

Brokaw, J. P. (1983). The extent to which parental supervision and other selected factors are related to achievement of musical and technical-physical characteristics by beginning instrumental music students. *Dissertation Abstracts International, 43*, 3252A.

Collier-Slone, K. The psychology of humanistic life education: A longitudinal study. Doctoral dissertation, The Union Institute, Ohio.

Creider, B. H. (1989). Music Learning Theory and the Suzuki Method. In D. L. Walters & C. C. Taggart (Eds.) *Readings in Music Learning Theory.* Chicago: GIA Publications.

Doan, G. R. (1973). An investigation of the relationship between parental involvement and the performance ability of violin students. *Dissertation Abstracts International, 34*, 5226.

Flohr, J. W. (1981). Short-term music instruction and young children's developmental music aptitude. *Journal of Research in Music Education, 29*(3), 291-233.

Fox, D. B. (1991). Music, development, and the young child. *Music Educators Journal, 77*(5), 42-46.

Gordon, E. E. (1967). A three-year longitudinal predictive validity study of the Musical Aptitude Profile. *Studies in the Psychology of Music 5.* Iowa City: University of Iowa Press.

——. (1980). Developmental music aptitude among inner-city primary children. *Bulletin of the Council for Research in Music Education, 63*, 25-30.

——. (1987). *The nature, description, measurement and evaluation of music aptitudes.* Chicago: GIA Publications.

——. (1998). *Introduction to research and the psychology of music.* Chicago: GIA Publications.

——. (2003a). *Learning sequences in music: Skill, content, and patterns.* Chicago: GIA Publications.

——. (2003b). *A music learning theory for newborn and young children* (Rev. ed.). Chicago: GIA Publications.

Grunow, R. F., Gordon, E. E., Azzara, C. D., & Martin, M. (2002). *Teacher's guide, jump right in: The instrumental series – Revised edition for strings.* (Rev. Edition). Chicago: GIA Publications.

Heyge, L., & Sillick, A. (1998). Music: A natural way to play with babies. *Early Childhood Connections, 4*(4), 8013.

Howe, M. J., Davidson, J. W., Moore, D. G., & Sloboda, J. A. (1995). Are there early childhood signs of musical ability? *Psychology of Music, 23*, 162-176.

Jenkins, J. M. (1976). The relationship between maternal parents' musical experience and the musical development of two- and three-year-old girls. *Dissertation Abstracts International, 37*, 7015.

Kotulak, R. (1996). *Inside the brain: Revolutionary discoveries of how the mind works.* Kansas City, MO: Andrews and McMeel.

Moog, H. (1976). The development of musical experience in children of preschool age. *Psychology of Music, 4*, 38-45.

Panneton, R. K. (1987). Prenatal auditory experience with melodies: Effects on postnatal auditory preferences in human newborns (Doctoral dissertation, University of North Carolina at Greensboro, 1985). *Dissertation Abstracts International, 47*, 3984B.

Petzold, R. G. (1963). The development of auditory perception of musical sounds by children in the first six grades. *Journal of Research in Music Education, 11.*

Plato. *The laws.* Translated, with notes and an interpretive essay by Thomas L. Pangle. (1980). New York: Basic Books.

Shaw, D. (1991). *Intrauterine musical learning: A study of its effects on mother-infant bonding.* Unpublished doctoral dissertation, California School of Professional Psychology, Los Angeles.

Sloane, K. D. (1985). Home influences on talent development. In *Developing Talent in Young People*, B. S. Bloom (Ed.), (pp. 439-476) New York: Ballantine Books.

Sloboda, J. A., & Howe, M. J. A. (1991). Biographical precursors of musical excellence: An interview study. *Psychology of Music, 19*, 3-21.

Slone, K. C. (1988). *They're rarely too young...and never too old "to Twinkle"* (3rd ed.). Ann Arbor, MI: Shar Publications.

Sosniak, L. A. (1985). Learning to be a concert pianist. In *Developing Talent in Young People*, B. S. Bloom (Ed.), (pp. 439-476) New York: Ballantine Books.

Stamou, L. (January 1998). *Effects of parental involvement on children's musical growth: A review of literature.* Poster session presented at the 1998 Midwestern Conference on School Vocal and Instrumental Music, Ann Arbor, MI.

——. (Spring 1998). Suzuki method and philosophy: Selected research findings and implications for teaching. *Sforzando: Michigan Music Educators Association, 10*, 6-8.

——. (1999). The effect of Suzuki instruction and early childhood music experiences on developmental music aptitude and performance achievement of beginning Suzuki string students (Doctoral dissertation, Michigan State University, 1998). *Dissertation Abstracts International, 59*/10, 3769A.

Suzuki, S. (1981). *Ability development from age zero.* Secaucus, NJ: Summy-Birchard.

Taggart, C. C. (November 1997). *A study of developmental music aptitude.* Paper presented at the New Directions in Music Education: Early Childhood Music Conference, Michigan State University, East Lansing, MI.

Valerio, W. H., Reynolds, A., Bolton, B., Taggart, C. C., & Gordon, E. E. (1998). *Music play: The early childhood music curriculum.* Chicago: GIA Publications.

Wilkin, P. E. (Winter 1995/1996). A comparison of fetal and newborn responses to music and sound stimuli with and without daily exposure to a specific piece of music. *Bulletin of the Council for Research in Music Education, 127*, 163-169.

Zdzinsky, S. F. (1991). Relationships among parental involvement, music aptitude, and musical achievement of instrumental music students. *Journal of Research in Music Education, 40*(2), 114 125.

——. (1992). Relationships among parental involvement and affective outcomes in instrumental music. *Southeastern Journal of Music Education, 4*, 155-163.

*Sheryl Iott Richardson*
••••••••••••••••
MICHIGAN STATE UNIVERSITY

# Using Music Learning Theory in Private Piano Lessons

Your mind doesn't register what's in front of your eyes; it's your eyes that register what's in the back of your mind.

— Flesch

## Part One

Most teachers of music have similar goals. We are not looking for fame and fortune, but rather wish to develop self-sufficient students and witness "Eureka!" moments when our students make a musical, technical, or personal discovery, when it seems to them as if this particular discovery has never been made before. While these moments may be fewer and farther between than we would like, they are a guiding force in keeping us motivated in what can be a challenging and exhausting profession. There is also the personal reward of teaching something important and knowing that without us and our commitment to instruction the world of music and the arts would continue to be increasingly undervalued in a society focused on technology and consumerism.

We are, in many ways, living in an exciting time in the world of music education. There is new understanding of how children learn and specifically how they learn music. As teachers and pedagogues, we should pay close attention to this new research and find ways to apply it in our studio piano teaching, both private and group settings. Gordon (2003a) encourages us with these words: "Teachers must be willing to involve themselves in change and. . . teach what they need to learn. . . Students learn best from those who are, themselves, learning" (pp. 27–28).

When I was first exposed to Gordon's ideas in a class being taught by Gordon himself, I had many doubts. Much of it sounded, to my "untrained ear," like the mindless rote-practices of earlier days, when children were taught only in terms of what position their hands should be in and how the song goes. What I gradually came to realize was that despite limited musical acculturation and poor training as a child, my ability to succeed as a musician developed because I could instinctively do much of what Gordon told us that we need to teach. And what is a struggle for me, as a musician and pianist, relates to the skills he was talking about that I have not yet developed—because they are not instinctive for me, and I was not taught that way.

I have found that as I apply his Music Learning Theory to my teaching in private lessons, especially the singing of patterns, use of movement as a foundation of rhythm, and a pervasive use of tonal and rhythm solfege, my students are becoming better musicians. They are able to solve new, complicated rhythm problems and retain what they learned until the next lesson. They are able to hear in their minds what they are trying to play before they play it and are more aware of the tonal and rhythmic structure of their pieces, which has improved their reading of new repertoire, their musical interpretation, and the security of their performances from memory. They "sight-read" and transpose with more confidence and consistency. If we sing melodic patterns using solfege and then practice aural awareness, such as identification of intervals or melodic pattern dictation, they succeed and know they are succeeding before I have even checked their answers.[1] In short, it works!

## Music Learning Theory

Gordon has integrated the most important precepts of child development and learning theory, resulting in a method in which learning occurs through experience, and everything is sequenced so that experience and mastery of one aspect leads easily and logically to the next. This foundation is then built on with elements resembling those of the music learning theories of Kodály, Orff, Dalcroze and Suzuki. As with Kodály and Suzuki, Gordon emphasizes the importance of the child's cultural and environmental experiences before formal music instruction, and the understanding of music's foundation in rhythm and rhythm's foundation in movement has parallels in the philosophies of Orff and Dalcroze.

---

[1] Gordon, in his Music Learning Theory, does not recommend the identification of isolated intervals, but interval identification is a requirement for piano students participating in various testing programs. Therefore, it is a practice in which many piano teachers must currently engage.

Two pillars of Music Learning Theory are audiation and aptitude. Audiation is defined as the ability to hear and understand music through recall (Gordon, 2003a). Audiation is not to be confused with aural perception, which is merely the sensory awareness of sound for which there is no understanding. Perception without audiation is equivalent to hearing an unknown foreign language; you hear the syllables and accents and could possibly even imitate the sounds, but you would not understand what was said or what you were saying.

Aptitude refers to the person's innate ability to learn to audiate. Gordon believes that all children are born with some degree of music aptitude. There has been much debate regarding whether aptitude is a product of nature or nurture, genetics or environment. Gordon (2003b) believes, and I agree, that it is a product of both. While a child is born with a certain potential to achieve, what that child experiences in his environment will either keep that potential at its birth level or allow it to decline. Gordon theorizes that music aptitude stabilizes around the age of nine, at which point the child's aptitude will forever limit or support the student's achievement in music (Gordon, 2003a).

These two pillars—audiation and aptitude—actually stand as one. When discussing aptitude, we are not discussing whether the child will have adept fingers or a commanding stage presence, which reflect achievement or personality, but rather what that child's potential is for hearing and comprehending music through recall or creation. True musicianship—defined as expressive playing that demonstrates awareness of structure, form, and phrase, as well as reliable memory, technical facility, and aural awareness of tone, balance, voicing, and pedal—requires audiation.

## Music as Language and the Building of a Vocabulary

Children need acculturation through appropriate musical experiences before formal instruction begins, without which they will never learn to audiate well, and their musical achievement will be permanently inhibited (Gordon, 2003b). So before any kind of formal instruction begins, the teacher must ensure that children are out of what Gordon terms "music babble." They should be able to move with the music, demonstrating an understanding of its fundamental beats, and to chant simple rhythm patterns. They should be able to echo-sing in response to the teacher's demonstration of short patterns and songs while maintaining tonality and keyality, and should be able to sing the resting tone of a pattern or song sung to them. Acculturation experiences should continue throughout the child's music education, regardless of his or her level of achievement, as there will always be a need to hear music that expands their musical horizons, much as language vocabulary continues to develop into adulthood (Gordon, 2003b).

Music should be taught similarly to language, with the four vocabularies (listening, performing/speaking, reading, and writing) taught in that order. Nothing should be performed until it can be heard and sung. Nothing should be read from notation until its basic elements have been performed, and nothing should be written until it has been heard, played, and read. Teaching is done as much as possible through demonstration and imitation, and rhythm and pitch components are isolated before being involved simultaneously. This increases the pattern's value in building a musical vocabulary and in discrimination learning, the more generalizable the pattern, the more frequently it will be encountered and recognized within other musical contexts (Gordon, 2003a; Walters, 1992).

*Figure 1.* Tonic triad patterns

For example, the tonic patterns in Figure 1 are easily recognized when they appear within pieces, such as those in Figure 2, no matter what the rhythmic context.

*Figure 2.* Excerpts from repertoire containing tonic triad patterns

Last, everything must be taught within context. Rhythms should not be taught as comprising a series of individual durations, but durations should be taught as functioning members of a pattern in the context of a meter. Intervals are not taught as isolated pitches arbitrarily related to one another, but as functional elements of a keyality and modality, i.e., DO to MI in Major, LA to DO in Minor. Melodic intervals are part of a melodic pattern; they are heard, then sung, then performed, then identified, read, written, and finally discussed as theoretical abstractions. Context is always established first; a tonal sequence is sung before a short melodic pattern, and a rhythm sequence is chanted before a rhythmic pattern (Gordon, 2001). Rhythm patterns are always taught with musical inflection to aid in the audiation of meter and so that students' learned music is performed musically.

## From General Music to the Private Lesson

Lowe (2004) has written a series of method books based on Gordon's principles and is well worth the time needed to investigate. It incorporates movement, singing and chanting, and repertoire that can be taught according to Gordon's principles of audiation and stages of Skill Learning Sequence. It would, however, be counterproductive for the experienced teacher to throw out everything that he or she has used in the past, especially to start a late beginner or intermediate student over at the beginning. In this case, components of Lowe's work could be blended with more traditional approaches to teaching. I would, however, strongly recommend its use for beginning students.

The principles of Gordon's Music Learning Theory can be applied, though, in studio lessons in conjunction with many piano or instrumental methods, although this will be much easier with some than with others, and the success of its application will depend greatly on the teacher's understanding and creative application of Music Learning Theory. If you decide to implement components of Music Learning Theory, you may want to write a studio newsletter, informing students' parents of the changes that they will be seeing, not just in how lesson time is spent, but in what might be included in and expected from home practice.

## Learning Sequence Activities

To begin to implement Music Learning Theory, the first change in the traditional lesson plan would be to add a three- to five-minute period of what Gordon calls Learning Sequence Activities. These are patterns sung (if tonal) or chanted (if rhythm) by the teacher. The students either echo the patterns back with the teacher, echo the patterns in solo, or echo them as a group. The teacher should use either tonal or rhythm patterns on any one day, never both.

## Rhythm through Movement and Solfege

According to most of the noted music education theorists of the 20th century (Dalcroze, Kodály, Orff, and Gordon) rhythm has its foundation in movement. "The only way rhythm can truly be understood musically is through body movement and the audiation of body movement" (Gordon, 2003a, p. 69). Therefore, when doing rhythm activities, movement must be incorporated. All students must first be able to perform movement in a free, flowing manner. This is done with the whole body in continuous motion, including the arms, torso, and legs (think tai-chi). Most students can learn everything they need to know by observing and imitating the teacher. A good game for a group class is to keep a balloon in the air while all students move continuously, tapping the balloon to send it back up as needed. If you are teaching an older group of students who are inhibited about moving freely, have them stand in a circle facing outward so that they are not self-conscious about being watched when they move and accompany their movements with music.

After students are capable of free, flowing movement, they should be taught pulsing movement. For this, weight is shifted from one foot to the other with a pronounced side-to-side body motion, each foot-side equaling one macrobeat. The teacher can call attention to demonstration of additional movement or a change in movement by saying "Watch please." Next, arm movement is added from the shoulders, with the arm tapping the microbeats against the sides of the body. For the initial demonstration, the teacher should perform one or two examples of macrobeat/microbeat patterns in Duple or Triple meter.

After pulsing movement has been mastered by the student or group, the teacher can chant short rhythm patterns on "Bah" for the students to respond to while all are performing pulsing movements. The student(s) should begin their response on the next beat after the teacher's pattern without stopping or interrupting the flow of macrobeats in tempo. The teacher should use facial expressions or body language, such as a conducted downbeat, to indicate when to begin. Rhythm patterns should be four macrobeats in length; it is impossible to have a sense of meter with one macrobeat, and anything longer than four macrobeats may be too long for the students to audiate. The teacher first establishes context by chanting the appropriate meter sequence. The sequences for Duple and Triple meter are shown in Figure 3.

*Figure 3.* Duple meter and Triple meter rhythm sequences for establishing meter

When students have several rhythm patterns in their vocabulary, teachers should begin teaching patterns using Gordon's rhythm solfege system, which uses syllables based on beat function rather than time-value names or numerical counting. The syllables used reflect where the duration occurs in the meter. The "big" beat, or macrobeat, is always Du; the microbeats, or equal divisions of the macrobeat are De in Duple, and Da-Di in Triple. Divisions of microbeats are always Ta (Gordon, 2000). (See Figure 4.)[2]

*Figure 4.* Rhythm solfege examples, Duple and Triple meter

With just a little practice, the logic of the rhythm solfege system becomes readily apparent, and using syllables greatly facilitates understanding and accurate, musical performance of rhythm, meter, and tempo. For initial practice on the part of the teacher, start with simple patterns containing only macrobeats and microbeats. Then add patterns with only a few simple divisions of the microbeats until you feel fluent and comfortable. Always have the patterns securely in your vocabulary before teaching them to students.

To teach rhythm patterns using rhythm syllables, pulsing movement should be established, and the rhythm first should be chanted and echoed using "Bah." Later, the rhythm pattern should be repeated using solfege syllables. The student again should respond, first with the teacher and/or group in ensemble, then alone. Responses with others are often imitation rather than audiation, and, while imitation serves as preparation for audiation, it is not audiation itself (Gordon, 2003a). The student must perform the pattern successfully alone for it to become a permanent part of the student's audiation vocabulary (Gordon, 2001). Once several simple

---

[2] For more information about Gordon's rhythm syllable system, see *Learning Sequences in Music: Skill, Content, and Patterns* (Gordon, 2003a).

patterns in the same meter have been taught using neutral and, in later lessons, solfege syllables, a few more patterns in the same meter can be taught. Be careful not to let any one Learning Sequence Activity continue for too long, as the value to learning begins to decline after five or ten minutes in a group setting, and even more quickly in private lessons (Gordon, 2003a).

Gordon's *Rhythm Register Books* and *Tonal Register Books* present a taxonomy of rhythm and tonal patterns in the sequence in which they should be taught with easy, moderately difficult, and difficult patterns for each function. This allows the teacher to tailor the teaching to the student's musical aptitudes so that all students are learning the same function at the same time, such as macrobeat/microbeat patterns (as shown in Figure 5, from Gordon's *Jump Right In: Rhythm Register Book 1*, 1990) or tonic and dominant functions in Major (as shown in Figure 6, from Gordon's *Jump Right In: Tonal Register Book 1*, 1990), but the students with higher musical aptitude can be challenged to perform all patterns, including the more difficult patterns, while those with average musical aptitude can be asked to perform the patterns of moderate difficulty, and those of low musical aptitude can perform the easy patterns. This tailoring of musical instruction to the individual differences of the student is one of the key components of Music Learning Theory and its application in informal or formal instruction.

## Rhythm Pattern Examples

Rhythm Unit 1, Section A, Criterion 1
Chant rhythm sequence in Usual Duple using "bah"
Chant pattern using "bah"
Students chant pattern using "bah"

Rhythm Unit 1, Section A, Criterion 1
Chant rhythm sequence in Usual Triple using "bah"
Chant pattern using "bah"
Students chant pattern using "bah"

*Figure 5.* From *Jump Right In: Rhythm Register Book 1* (Gordon, 1990)

## Tonal Pattern Examples

Tonal Unit 1, Section A, Criterion 2
Sing tonal sequence in D Major using "bum"
Sing pattern using "bum"
Students sing pattern using "bum"

Tonal Unit 1, Section A, Criterion 3
Sing tonal sequence in D Major using "bum"
Sing pattern using "bum"
Students sing pattern using "bum"

*Figure 6.* From *Jump Right In: Tonal Register Book One* (Gordon, 1990)

## Tonal Patterns and Solfege

The singing of tonal patterns in the lesson is beneficial to the building of a tonal vocabulary and the development of tonal audiation skills. Tonal audiation helps the student to recognize the key, mode, and function of the patterns they are playing, which contributes to performing with understanding, security, and musicianship. Tonal audiation is also crucial to the student being aware of the melodic and harmonic structure of their repertoire, and thence to their ability to perform securely without the music, rather than relying on rote memorization practices and kinesthetic memory.

For tonal solfege, the system of movable-DO with a LA-based Minor is used (Gordon, 2003a; see also Bentley, 1959; Heffernan, 1968). This system provides uniformity of syllables across all keys of the same tonality with an easy transition to relative Minor. The key signature then becomes a "DO signature," which makes the theoretical principles of relative keys, when introduced, correspond with the student's listening and performance experience. Movable-DO also makes harmonization and transposition easy and logical (Gordon, 2003a).

Tonal context is established by the singing of a tonal sequence, shown in Figure 7 for Major, Harmonic Minor, and Dorian tonalities.

289

*Figure* 7. Major, Harmonic Minor, and Dorian tonal sequences for establishing mode (Gordon, 2001)

If the teacher is uncertain of his or her own tonal audiation skills, he or she should master the sequence and patterns first before teaching them. Student responses should always be unaccompanied. If the teacher performs the pattern on the piano as the student sings it back, the student is likely to be matching pitch through imitation (Gordon, 1971), which will not develop audiation skill. If the student is apprehensive about performing a tonal pattern without accompaniment, the teacher may play the resting tone for the student for their first response, then sing it to them again for their unaccompanied response. This is an adaptation of Gordon's ideal, but it may be more realistic in a private lesson setting, as the student does not have other students from which to learn as they do in a class. Tonal patterns are two to four pitches in length.

There are several types of tonal activities used in pattern instruction. These include: the teacher singing acculturation patterns or songs in new keyalities or tonalities, the student being asked to sing the first pitch or the resting tone of the pattern sung by the teacher, and the student singing the pattern back in response on a neutral syllable or solfege. All tonal Learning Sequence patterns must be followed by a short pause before the student responds, to give time for audiation, but not enough time for the student to mentally imitate the pattern in its entirety. The response is cued with a breath and a conducted upbeat, with the teacher taking the breath with the student. Gordon (2000) believes that learning and audiation occur on the breath. (However, there is no audiation pause between rhythm patterns, as they would disrupt the audiation of meter.)

Tonal patterns are taught similarly to how rhythm patterns are taught, with tonal patterns first sung and echoed using the neutral syllable "bum," and then using solfege. When students have become adept at this, you may move the activity to higher levels of learning by singing the pattern on "bum" with the student identifying the function of the pattern and whether the pattern is in Major or Minor, or by singing the pattern on "bum" and having the student echo using solfege syllables.

Once a pattern can be read successfully by the student, it is no longer essential to continue singing that pattern using the solfege syllables.

Remember, Learning Sequence Activities are not the goal, but a means to an end: developing the audiation ability of the student so that they can perform, create, improvise, read, and write music with comprehension. When the pattern has become part of the student's music vocabulary, it no longer needs to be "taught." If the student encounters the pattern later and has difficulty reading or performing it, the pattern and syllables can be reviewed quickly by the teacher and the student. Usually this gentle reminder is sufficient to reestablish the pattern in the student's vocabulary (Gordon, 1971).

Learning Sequence Activities can be done in three to five minutes in a thirty minute lesson. Little time is invested, but a large contribution is made to the building of a music vocabulary and to the development of contextual musical understanding. What has really impressed me is how often I turn to these techniques during what might be considered the traditional piano lesson in order to teach and polish repertoire.

## Using Learning Sequence-Type Activities When Introducing New Repertoire

In Music Learning Theory, learning is a Whole-Part-Whole process (Bluestine, 2000; Gordon, 2001). In the teaching of repertoire, this would be represented, for example, by first playing the piece while the student listens, perhaps moving to the beat and following the score (if the student is already reading). The student is then taught the part: some of the rhythm patterns through movement and chanting activities, some of the tonal patterns through singing, and then some of the tonal pattern content on the instrument. After related or isolated patterns from the piece have been mastered by the student (patterns taught do not need to be identical to those found in the piece), the teacher would again play the piece for the student, pointing out patterns that the student already knows or has just been taught. In these situations, tonal and rhythm elements can be used in the same lesson, but again, the tonal elements should be taught first without rhythm and the rhythm patterns should be taught first without pitches.

With careful guidance at the introduction of the piece and "prescriptions" for careful, productive practicing, the student is then prepared to go home and learn the piece with greater comprehension and, therefore, a much greater chance of success. We all know, as musicians and teachers, how difficult it is to correct a mistake once it has been reinforced through practice!

## Rhythm

There are many ways to incorporate moving and chanting into teaching the rhythms of a new piece. To introduce new durations, such as

291

the dotted quarter note, the teacher would first review and then incorporate patterns using familiar durations, in this case using quarter, eighth, and half notes. For example, the teacher, with the student, would establish pulsing movement, and then the teacher would chant, with the student responding "in time" at the end of each measure, with the series shown in Figure 8.

*Figure 8.* Rhythm pattern sequence for dotted quarter note instruction

You have probably noticed in the example above that I am placing the macrobeats on the half notes, creating the feeling of 4/4 measures "in two." This is frequently the case, although it is also possible, especially when the rhythm patterns are more complex and/or include faster durations such as sixteenth notes, for the quarter note to be felt and chanted as the macrobeat.

The teacher can also use pulsing movement with students sitting at the piano. For Duple meter, tapping with both hands: knees (beat 1, Du) - thighs (beat 2, De); or for Triple meter, tapping knees (Du) - thighs (Da) - cross to opposite shoulders (Di). When meter is established, chant the rhythm pattern (never more than four macrobeats at a time) and ask the student to echo, first using a neutral syllable, then using rhythm solfege. Rhythm syllables should never be written into the student's music; they must be heard, felt, audiated, and performed, but never read. They are written in the examples here for your information and guidance.

If the piece includes rhythmic complexity between the two hands, I might devise a series of movement and chanting exercises. For example, to teach tied/syncopated patterns, such as in the piece "Pumpkin Boogie" from the Fabers' Level 2B Lesson Book, excerpted in Figure 9, the teacher and student could go through the following sequence:

Nancy and Randall Faber

*Figure 9.* "Pumpkin Boogie," mm. 4-8, *Faber Lesson Book 2b*

1. The student taps knees-thighs on the Du's while the teacher chants the right-hand rhythm pattern.
2. The student chants and taps the Du's, looking at notation, while the teacher chants the right-hand rhythm pattern.
3. The student chants and points to the Du's in the left hand while the teacher chants the rhythm pattern.
4. The student and teacher tap the Du's together while the teacher chants two measures of the right-hand rhythm pattern for student response.
5. The student taps the Du's and chants the right-hand rhythm pattern while the teacher chants and taps the Du's.

Notice how the activity increases in complexity for the student, but at all times the rhythm components of both parts are present. The student is not being taught by "rote," but through audiation, and learning to read the piece through recognition of what they have already heard, audiated, and performed. This distinction is important, as Gordon's principles, if used correctly, drastically increase the student's musical understanding and literacy, unlike rote practices, in which students learn through mindless imitation without understanding or the ability to apply previous knowledge or skills to the current challenge.

Many beneficial rhythm activities involving movement and chanting are easily integrated into the lesson. Dalcroze, Orff, and Gordon believe that of the two fundamental elements of music, rhythm and tonal, rhythm is more important (Choksy, et al., 1986; Gordon, 2003a; Mark, 1978). A performer unable to audiate tonally can still "decode" notation, remembering fingering combinations and placements to produce individual pitches. Limitations in audiating rhythm will be more obvious because there are no keys or valves to push associated with the time-value names of the notes (Gordon, 2003a). Which is more crucial to successful collaborative performance—the right note at the wrong time or the wrong note at the right time? The listener will be much more forgiving of isolated note mistakes than of interruptions in the flow of rhythm or tempo.

**Tonal**

What many musicians do not realize is that notational forms, from the time of ancient Chinese and Greek civilizations to those now in use, were devised as a way to codify the sounds and physical actions the performers already knew (Walker, 1992). Someone who is able to audiate is able to look at staff notation and match what they see with a mental image of a musical and physical ideal.

In this vein, after the development of aural skills, technique plays a crucial role in improving a student's ability to read and perform music. By technique, I am first referring to how many keys, modes or positions the student is comfortable audiating and performing patterns in. On the piano, "technique" must expand beyond learning to sing and play two to four note patterns to the student being fluent in five-finger patterns, arpeggios, chord progression patterns, etc., appropriate to their level of ability and the technical requirements of their repertoire. These skills first should be taught in groups of few notes, such as cross-hand arpeggios or a scale divided between the two hands. These small patterns then can be expanded and transposed through imitation of the teacher so that encounters with similar skills in score notation serve more as a reference, a reminder of patterns and skills that they already are able to play.

Likewise, it is important that the student be able to play pieces, melodies, and chord progressions in multiple keys. Important melodies or recurring themes and prominent chord progressions or fundamental patterns from their repertoire, such as I–vi–IV–V–I, are excellent sources for transposition, improvisation, and creative "exercises," and should be exploited at every opportunity. Again, the difficulty or scope of the activity can vary to accommodate the level of aptitude and achievement of the student.

If teaching a piece with a variety of scale passages in a certain key, such as Clementi's Sonatina, Op. 36, No. 1, excerpted in Figure 10, the student can be asked to play the G Major scale beginning on G and on B, and the C Major scale beginning on C and E. This can be taught and practiced independently of the piece (i.e., assigned the week before) so that when it is encountered within the repertoire, it is instantly recognizable, both physically and visually.

*Figure 10.* Clementi Sonatina, Op. 36, No. 1, mm. 8-11

Or, similarly, for the various C Major scales from this passage in Mozart's Sonata, K.545:

*Figure 11.* Mozart Sonata K.545, first movement, mm. 5-8

In preparation for either of the above examples, the teacher may even ask the student to practice all of their Major scales starting on each scale degree, devising an appropriate and efficient fingering for each.

The use of solfege can also be incorporated into the learning of repertoire. Exercises can be devised out of measures that contain potentially difficult tonal patterns, such as the Fabers' "Riding the Wind" shown in Figure 12.

Copyright © 1994 by The FJH Music Company, Inc. 2525 Davie Road, Suite 360, Fort Lauderdale, Florida 33317-7424 This edition © 1997 The FJH Music Company, Inc. International Copyright Secured. All Rights Reserved. Printed in U.S.A. Used with permission.

*Figure 12.* "Riding the Wind," *Faber Lesson Book 2b*

The similarities of the three endings of the main theme can be confusing to the student, resulting in misreadings and problems memorizing. Through the use of solfege to identify the different patterns, the student is made aware of the differences aurally first, including recognizing a difference in tonal function, and is better able to recognize, and therefore perform accurately, the three different melody patterns in the correct sequence.

For the student's first encounter with the piece, the teacher could isolate measures 5 through 8, 13 through 16, and 29 through 32, and teach the tonal patterns shown in Figure 13 as follows:

*Figure 13.* Tonal patterns with solfege for "Riding the Wind" pattern instruction

(All student responses occur after a brief audiation pause, as is in Learning Sequence Activities.)

1. The teacher sings the first pattern using a neutral syllable. The student sings it back in response. Repeat for each pattern, then again using solfege syllables.[3]
2. Teacher plays the first pattern on the piano. Student plays it back. Repeat for each of the patterns.
3. Teacher sings one of the three patterns. Student echoes in response. The teacher then shows the student the notation of that pattern in the score, and the student plays while reading the notation.

If the teacher wanted to make this into an inference learning activity, the first pattern could be taught and the second pattern sung on a neutral syllable. The student could then respond on solfege and/or play the pattern on the piano. Or, after teaching the first pattern, the teacher could sing or play one of the other two patterns for the student to perform and then find in the notation. After responding, performing, and/or identifying the pattern, the student would play each pattern several times while reading

---

[3] In my interpretation, "Riding the Wind" is in Phrygian tonality, so the solfege syllables used reflect Gordon's system of movable-DO with LA-based Minor, RE-based Dorian, MI-based Phrygian, etc.

from the notation. These activities involve the first three of the four vocabularies: listening (aural), performing (oral), and reading.

How the teacher responds is important to student learning. Just as a child learns to speak more clearly when the adult repeats his or her words, including mispronunciations, back to them, the piano teacher should first repeat back the student's incorrect response, then repeat the correct pattern for the student to respond to again. In this way, the student learns to compare what they have produced with what they heard. This focuses the student's attention on the music and uses the principle of demonstration and audiation instead of explanation. The student becomes attuned to listening and responding without verbal distractions or the negative feedback of "wrong" or "no" and quickly learns to compare and recognize both patterns. The audiation of both patterns actually improves learning much in the same way that a well-written multiple-choice test teaches as much through the student's reading and consideration of the wrong answers as through the identification of the correct one (Gordon, personal communication, Autumn 2000).

In the lesson, the teacher should encourage the student to continue playing after making mistakes, much as you would want them to in a performance situation, or as we do when speaking and stumbling over a word. If students are audiating, it will not be necessary for them to go back to the beginning of a phrase or song if a pitch or duration is performed incorrectly (Gordon, 2003b). When practicing and correcting errors, the student should always go back to a place just before where the error occurred and perform through where the error occurred. Then the student should go back to the beginning of the piece or section and ensure that the correction has "stuck." The student should also practice the piece in its entirety, with errors disregarded. If we want to build our students' audiation abilities, they must be taught, allowed, and encouraged to play using their audiation skills (Gordon, 2003b).

Other examples of tonal activities that can be used in the introduction and learning of a new piece include the following:

1. Student playing different combinations of parts/hands in blocks and as partners with the teacher, such as: a) student playing accompaniment patterns as block chords chord-hand alone; b) student playing block chords with teacher singing the melody using a neutral syllable or playing it on the piano; c) student playing both the block chords and the melody; or d) student playing any of the above, the entire piece, or a section of a piece in multiple keys.

2.  Singing and playing in isolation a transitional measure that is changed from the exposition to the recapitulation of a sonatina or sonata.
3.  Singing the left-hand part in two-measure sections in Baroque pieces, such as minuets from the notebook of Anna Magdalena Bach.

Any of these tonal and rhythmic techniques can also be used when preparing to play a piece from memory. Some other audiation/memory exercises that can be done to contribute to secure performance from memory, without resorting to rote memorization practices, would include the following:

1.  Audiate the entire piece from beginning to end, away from the instrument and without physical contributions such as finger tapping on a tabletop;
2.  Have starting points throughout the piece at all structural landmarks, but also some more randomly placed or different ones every time the student practices;
3.  Play to a certain point. Stop playing but continue to audiate the piece; then come back in on the instrument, picking up where audiation tells you to;
4.  Play the harmonic progression of the piece in both hands from memory, while singing the melody;
5.  Audiate and play each hand alone, especially the left hand in contrapuntal works or movements.

## Other Applications - Aural Awareness

Learning Sequence-like activities can be useful when teaching aural awareness skills, such as in preparation for a state music teacher association annual testing program. Intervals could be sung using solfege after the tonal sequence is sung, and the harmonic interval could be played and held, as demonstrated in part in Figure 14.

*Figure 14.* Interval patterns and solfege

Triad patterns can be sung to compare Major to Minor, or Major with a doubled root to the dominant seventh. Melody patterns, such as those shown in Figure 15, can be sung for identification or dictation practice.

DO   MI   FA   SO     SO   FA   RE   FA   RE   TI   RE     DO   MI   DO

*Figure 15.* Tonic and dominant function melody patterns for dictation practice

## Sight-reading

For the application of audiation to sight reading, I have written what I call sight-reading snapshots, such as those in Figure 16, for students to practice using the following procedure:

1. The pattern is read and audiated until the student thinks he or she can play it;
2. The student looks at the keyboard and tries to play the pattern as he or she remembers it. The teacher should encourage the student to just "make something up" if he or she is unsure;
3. The pattern is played several times while the student looks at the notation.

The snapshots resemble, but are not always identical to, figurations that appear in their sight-reading pieces (see Figure 17).

*Figure 16.* Sight-reading snapshots, *Student Workbook, Level 3* (Richardson, 2002)

*Figure 17.* Sight-reading piece, *Student Workbook, Level 3* (Richardson, 2002)

These sight-reading exercises encourage the student to read in "chunks," or groups of notes, much as they do when they read language and read words rather than individual letters. The teacher might point to a "snapshot" and ask the student to describe it—a tonic triad pattern, a five-finger pattern with a zig-zag—using whatever language the student is comfortable using. The teacher should then repeat the description in accurate, consistent terminology (Woodruff, 1961). The teacher and student should then play that pattern in a number of keys or positions on the piano while looking at the keyboard and then at the music. Notice the sightreading snapshots have simple melodic rhythms, keeping the two elements separate as much as possible for pattern instruction, so that the tonal pattern in any rhythmic guise will still be recognizable and familiar.

## Theory

Theory should always flow from the student's experience singing, chanting, and performing. Solfege syllables are useful when identifying and writing scales, five-finger patterns, and intervals. Rhythmic movement and chanting help to provide the information necessary to write in missing time signatures, measure lines, or durations. The theoretical activities presented in Figures 18 and 19 help students bridge audiation and technique to theory.

*Activity One:* Teacher says to the students: "Move rhythmically and chant each rhythm (see Figure 18) before adding the bar lines to the following examples. Always check your work by chanting again after adding the bar lines."

*Figure 18.* Rhythm/theory exercises, *Student Workbook, Level 5* (Richardson, 2002)

*Activity Two:* The teacher should ask the students to visualize the five-finger patterns beginning on the note given (see Figure 19), then write the indicated interval. Write the upper note head on the correct line or space; add accidentals as they occur in the five-finger pattern. After completing this exercise, go to the piano and play the five-finger patterns and intervals to check your work.

Major 2nd          Major 3rd          Perfect 4th          Perfect 5th

*Figure 19.* Interval/theory exercise, *Student Workbook, Level 5* (Richardson, 2002)

## Summary

There are, of course, an infinite variety of ways that Music Learning Theory can be used to help in introducing, teaching, and polishing our students', and even our own repertoire. For the teacher who feels ambivalent, just pick one technique—singing melodic patterns, or using free and pulsing movement with students to develop awareness of tempo, meter, and rhythm—and try it with your students. When you witness their improvement and success—their "Eureka!" moment—you will be compelled to branch out and try other things. Before beginning, make sure you are comfortable with the skills and contents you are preparing to teach. Teach yourself first, and then watch your students thrive.

## References

Bentley, A. (1959). Fixed or movable do. *Journal of Research in Music Education, VII.*

Bluestine, E. (2000). *The ways children learn music* (Rev. ed.). Chicago: GIA Publications.

Broder, M. (Ed.). (1960). *W. A. Mozart: Sonatas and fantasies for the piano.* Bryn Mawr, PA: Theodore Presser Co.

Choksy, L., Abramson, R., Gillespie, A., & Woods, D. (1986). *Teaching music in the twentieth century.* Englewood Cliffs, NJ: Prentice-Hall.

Faber, N., & Faber, R. (1994). *Piano adventures: Lesson book 2B.* Fort Lauderdale, FL: FJH Music Co.

———. (1996). *Artist piano sonatinas: Book 2.* Miami Beach, FL: FJH Music Co.

Flesch, R. (1951). *The art of clear thinking.* New York: Harper & Row.

Gordon, E. E. (1971). *The psychology of music teaching.* Englewood Cliffs, NJ: Prentice-Hall.

Gordon, E. E. (1990). *Jump right in: The music curriculum, Rhythm register book 1.* Chicago: GIA Publications.

———. (1990). *Jump right in: The music curriculum, Tonal register book 1.* Chicago: GIA Publications.

———. (2000). *Rhythm: Contrasting the implications of audiation and notation.* Chicago: GIA Publications.

———. (2001). *Reference handbook for using Learning Sequence Activities.* Chicago: GIA Publications.

———. (2003a). *Learning sequences in music: Skill, content, and patterns.* Chicago: GIA Publications.

———. (2003b). *A music learning theory for newborn and young children.* Chicago: GIA Publications.

Heffernan, C. (1968). *Teaching children to read music.* New York: Appleton-Century-Crofts.

Iott Richardson, S. (2002). *Student workbooks, levels 1-5.* Holland, MI: self-published.

Lowe, M. (2004). *Music moves for piano.* Chicago: GIA Publications.

Mark, M. (1978). *Contemporary music education.* New York: Schirmer Books.

Suzuki, S. (1978). *Suzuki piano school, Volume 1.* Secaucus: Warner Bro. Publications.

———. (1981). *Ability development from age zero.* Athens, OH: Ability Development Associates.

Walker, R. (1992). Auditory-visual perception and musical behavior. In R. Colwell (Ed.). *Handbook of Research on Music Teaching and Learning.* New York: Schirmer Books.

Walters, D. (1992). Sequencing for efficient learning. In R. Colwell (Ed.). *Handbook of Research on Music Teaching and Learning.* New York: Schirmer Books.

Woodruff, A. (1961). *Basic concepts of teaching.* San Francisco: Chandler Publishing Co.

*Kenneth R. Trapp*

• • • • • • • • • • • • • •

STRATFORD ACADEMY ELEMENTARY SCHOOL, STRATFORD, CT

# Music Learning Theory Activities for the Keyboard Ensemble Class

Traditional keyboard and piano instruction begins with students naming notes on the staff and identifying keys on the keyboard. Letter names are used to identify notes in relation to the keyboard, and students are encouraged to develop eye to hand coordination. For example, students may be asked to look at a note on the first line of the treble clef staff and identify it as an E. They might then be instructed to play the E key on the piano that corresponds with the written note. Later, they may be asked to look at a note on the space below the first line and identify it as a D and then play the D key on the piano. The note C might be taught next; then those notes could be arranged in a way to notate the song "Hot Cross Buns." With practice, the student may develop the ability to look at notes on a staff and play songs. Little attempt is made to teach students to comprehend or *audiate* the tonality and the meter of the music as the activity is predominantly a visual exercise. Furthermore, students are rarely encouraged to take part in meaningful accompaniment, improvisation, or composition activities.

Keyboard students should bring meaning to what they are playing. Keyboard instruction based on Music Learning Theory teaches sound before sight, allowing students to organize music into patterns that are comprehensible. Students are engaged in singing and moving activities that transfer to keyboard performance. They are encouraged to play songs by ear and develop coordination through accompaniment patterns before they are asked to read notation. Music Learning Theory activities help students develop audiation skills as well as executive skills, which enable them to participate in music activities in a meaningful way. Such keyboard classes provide an excellent environment for students to express their artistry

303

through improvisation, composition, and performance, as well as through reading notation.

Even though traditional methods do not nurture the development of audiation skills, these skills are essential for comprehensive musicianship and musical expression. In this chapter, I will present activities designed to develop the audiation skills of keyboard students in a keyboard ensemble class. I will also present activities to make connections between audiation skill development and the reading and performance of traditional keyboard literature. These activities have proven successful over a thirteen-year period in teaching a middle school keyboard ensemble class as well as with private piano students from ages eight through adulthood.

## Beginning Aural Skill Development

The most effective way for keyboard students to develop aural skills is by singing and moving before keyboard instruction begins. Students should sing many songs in Major tonality and Minor tonality that have the harmonic functions of tonic, dominant, and subdominant. Students should move in Duple meter and Triple meter and perform macrobeat and microbeat patterns. It is important for students to sing alone as well as in ensemble. When students sing alone, the teacher can assess whether they audiate the tonality and meter of the music that they are singing. Furthermore, students who do not achieve at a high level are given an opportunity to hear high achieving students model accurate performances of the music skills and content being taught. Students will learn more from their peers than they will from the teacher.

It is important that the teacher is sensitive to students who may be reluctant to sing alone. Such students could be asked to demonstrate their music achievement when it is time to play solos, rather than when singing in solo. After students who are shy have played their solos, the teacher might ask them to sing only the last note or resting tone of the song that they played. When these students become more comfortable with the idea of performing short, non-threatening solos, they may be asked to sing patterns or an entire song.

In addition to learning the melody of a song, students should learn each song's root melody in order to help them understand the song's harmonic progression. The following procedure may be used to teach students the melody and root melody of songs:

1. Students hear the root melody sung by the teacher while they sing the melody.

2. Teacher sings the root melody alone and the class echoes.
3. Teacher sings the original melody while the class sings the root melody.

The students are then hearing melody and root melody performed simultaneously.

Many keyboard method books provide left hand chordal accompaniment parts to songs. These parts provide harmony for the melody but do not teach the student the process of harmonization. The best way to develop harmonic audiation is to sing the root melodies to familiar songs. By singing melodies and root melodies to many songs, students intuitively begin to understand (audiate) which harmonic functions are used (tonic, dominant, or other), and when the functions change. When students sing melodies and root melodies for many songs, they not only learn to audiate the harmonic structure of familiar music, they also learn to anticipate harmonic change in new music. Students who are taught to sing by rote many melodies and root melodies, such as the following:

**Hot Cross Buns**

**Mary Had a Little Lamb**

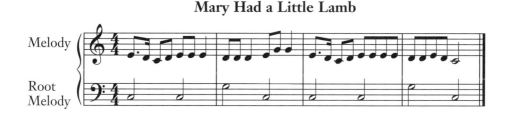

will be able to hear a melody such as:

**Skip to My Lou**

305

and anticipate the following root melody.

The anticipation of harmonic change is an essential skill for listening, improvising, reading, and composition.

While students are developing a singing vocabulary of songs and root melodies in Major tonality and Minor tonality, they should also learn to sing the resting tone DO for music in a Major tonality and the resting tone LA for music in a Minor tonality. When students can successfully sing resting tones in Major and Minor tonalities, they are ready to develop a vocabulary of tonal patterns in Major and Minor tonalities. Students should be instructed to echo-sing tonal patterns in Major tonality that have the functions of tonic (any combination of DO, MI, and SO) and dominant (any combination of SO, FA, RE, and TI) that are first performed by the teacher. They later should echo-sing tonal patterns in Minor tonality that have the functions of tonic (any combination of LA, DO, and MI) and dominant (any combination of MI, RE, TI, and SI). *Jump Right In: The General Music Series* (Taggart, Bolton, Reynolds, Valerio, & Gordon, 2001) has lessons and strategies for teaching audiation of resting tone and tonal patterns.

**Beginning Keyboard Instruction**

Once students are able to sing songs and tonal patterns in Major tonality and Minor tonality with good intonation and are able to audiate resting tones, they are ready to apply those skills to the keyboard in a meaningful way. Singing activities must relate to keyboard activities if aural skills are to transfer to keyboard performance.

The teacher can begin keyboard instruction by projecting an overhead transparency of a keyboard on a screen that the entire class can see. If the lesson is to be played is in C Major the teacher could establish tonality and keyality by playing:

The teacher could also establish tonality and keyality by singing:

If the song "Mary Had a Little Lamb" is being taught in the key of C Major, instruction would be given to place the fingers for the keys of C-DO, RE, MI, and SO. The teacher should always demonstrate correct hand and arm position as well as correct fingerings for each note that is demonstrated. Students should set their keyboards to the minimum volume and sing the syllables as they move their fingers on the correct keys. When students have found the correct keys, they could turn the volume to a comfortable level and prepare to listen to the teacher's performance of the melodic pattern starting on MI. The teacher should prepare the students to echo melodic patterns by singing or playing an introduction that is in the same key, tonality, and meter as the song "Mary Had a Little Lamb." The introduction should also end on the starting note of the melodic patterns as shown below.

Bum, bum, bum.     E - cho me.

Next, the teacher should play a melodic pattern that is the first phrase of "Mary Had a Little Lamb." It is important that the students do not see what keys the teacher is playing when echo-playing melodic patterns but rely on their ears to guide their response. The students should start on MI and attempt to play the phrase they hear being performed by the teacher. *Jump Right In: The Instrumental Series* (Grunow, Gordon, & Azzara, 1989) contains teaching procedures and activities for melodic pattern instruction. Students should be encouraged to learn to play many songs in this manner. As more songs are being played without notation, students will make generalizations, and new songs can be learned rapidly.

Sometimes a student may become frustrated and reluctant to try to play a melody. Often a frustrated student "freezes," playing only one or two notes without finishing the phrase. Many times, the student repeats the same wrong notes on each attempt to echo and is unable to explore different possibilities of how the melody he is hearing could be played on his instrument. An activity that has been helpful to these students is a game called the "different melody" game.

The rules of the game are as follows:

1. The student must play three *different* versions of the melodic pattern that was played by the teacher.
2. None of the student's versions nccds to sound the same as the teacher's, but they all must start on the same first note as the teacher's melody.
3. All student melodies should use the same number of notes as the teacher's. Their melodies should be the same duration.

Students benefit from this activity because they are given permission to play wrong notes and encouraged to continue playing when something does not sound correct. The student is now free to experiment with melodies. The teacher should honor each of the three melodies the student plays, no matter how wrong it sounds. Playing melodies, any melodies, is the goal. Often when this game is played with a student who has trouble matching melodies, his first version is very different, the second version sounds closer to the teacher's version, and the third version sounds very close to the teacher's version.

Most students are excited when they hear that their melody sounds similar to the teacher's. They realize for the first time that they have the ability to make music. Often, the student melodies are musical, even though they are different. The teacher could validate these melodies by playing them back to the student or by notating them and keeping a record of student melodies. If the students have the readiness, they could notate their melodies and play them for the class. Perhaps the class could learn these melodies by rote with the student assuming the role of the teacher.

Once students can play several songs without notation, they can learn the root melodies to those songs on the keyboard. Root melody instruction is similar to melodic pattern instruction, with the exception that root melodies should be played with the left hand in the bass register of the keyboard. It is important that the students are not able to see what the teacher is playing. They should rely on their ears to learn to play the root melodies.

After the root melody of a song is learned, the class can be split into two groups. One group will play the melody to the song while the other group plays the root melody. Both groups should then switch roles, allowing all students to have the experience of playing the melody and root melody. Students should listen to each other to decide if the two melodies performed sound good together and make adjustments if they do not sound muscially appropriate.

Tonal pattern instruction is a powerful technique for teaching students to clearly articulate harmonic functions on the keyboard. Harmonic audiation is transferred to the keyboard when students play tonal patterns that they have sung. Students can be asked to place their hands on a paper keyboard, while the teacher shows the patterns on a keyboard image projected on an overhead screen. Students watch as the teacher demonstrates the correct fingering and hand position for tonic and dominant patterns. The teacher sings while moving his fingers for each pattern. The students should listen and then echo while moving their fingers for the correct keys. An alternative to using a picture of a keyboard is to instruct students to turn the volume down on the synthesizers and sing while moving their fingers and then turn the volume back up to play the patterns.

Students' singing ranges may be different than the keys they are playing on the keyboard. This is especially true at the middle school level, when students' voices may have changed or be in the process of changing. The teacher should determine the most comfortable key for singing and establish that keyality when asking students to sing. When it is time to play the keyboard, the teacher should quickly establish the new keyality for the playing assignment. It is possible that students may be singing in the key of E-flat Major while they move their fingers silently in the key of C Major on the keyboard. When keyboards are set for playing volume, the key of C Major should be established by the teacher to prepare students to transfer their audiation skill to keyboard performance.

## Coordinating Left and Right Hands on the Keyboard

Once the ensemble performance of melody and root melody is achieved, students can begin to play both parts by themselves. The teacher should ask the students to play the melody with the right hand and the root melody with the left hand. The teacher should play both parts simultaneously on the piano, and the students should echo-play.

Some students will have difficulty playing with hands together. A way to address this is to have the student play the melody with his right hand while the teacher plays the left hand root melody. The song should be repeated without a pause as the teacher and the student switch parts, so that the student is now playing the left hand root melody while the teacher plays the right hand melody. This activity can be repeated several times in tempo without pause as the teacher and the student switch roles. When the student can switch from the melody to the root melody with ease, the teacher can ask him to play both parts at the beginning of the next repeat. There should be no break in the flow of the song, and most times the student will begin to play comfortably with both hands.

Another good way to develop steady beat and hand coordination is to play drum patterns on the keyboards. Drum accompaniments can be a valuable component to keyboard ensemble performances. Most keyboards have a percussion setting that turns the keys into drum pads. The best sounds to start with are bass drum and snare drum. The bass drum sound should be played with the left hand, and the snare drum should be played with the right hand. Patterns should be taught in Duple meter and Triple meter, such as:

These drum beats are a good starting point for the rhythmic accompaniment of songs. Once students can play simple rhythm patterns with ease, they can learn to play more difficult patterns and add drum fills at the ends of phrases and the ends of song sections. This left hand/right hand configuration will later transfer to the keyboard when the left hand plays roots on the downbeats and the right hand plays chords on the offbeats as keyboard accompaniments.

Students should be encouraged to play songs in as many keys as possible. By doing so, they learn how music functions in different keys, and they become comfortable with a variety of hand positions on the keyboard. For example, they learn that the sound DO can fall on different keys of the keyboard. A good starting key is C Major. Once several songs can be played in C Major, those same songs should be played in F Major. In addition to songs, tonal patterns that arpeggiate the functions of tonic and dominant should be played in many keys. Once students can play songs in C Major and F Major, songs in Minor tonality should be taught in D Minor and then A Minor on the keyboard.

When audiation skill is being applied to the keyboard in this manner, transposition is a natural process rather than a difficult intellectual exercise.

Students will transpose songs with ease as their ears guide their hands to the correct keys. It is possible for beginning keyboard students to learn a song with the difficulty level of "Joshua Fit the Battle of Jericho" without notation and play melody with the root melody in keys such as D Minor, C Minor, F Minor, E-flat Minor and C-sharp Minor.

## Joshua Fit the Battle of Jericho

Once students can sing songs with root melodies in Major tonality and Minor tonality, they are ready to learn more harmony parts to those songs. The class can be asked to sing the melody and root melody of a familiar song with tonic and dominant harmonic functions. The teacher simultaneously adds harmony by singing DO moving to TI. This harmony part outlines the voice leading for tonic to dominant. After the class has heard this harmony part several times, they will be able to sing it by rote. As they are singing this new harmony part, they will be anticipating the harmonic change in their audiation.

## Mary Had a Little Lamb

311

The class now knows the original melody to the song, a root melody, and one harmony part. When the class is familiar with DO moving to TI, they are ready to repeat the same procedure and learn how MI moves to FA for a tonic and dominant progression.

## Mary Had a Little Lamb

This same procedure should be used for teaching tonic and dominant harmonies in Minor tonality. The syllables for Minor tonality are LA moving to SI and DO moving to RE. For example, here is the melody, two harmony parts, and the root melody to the first phrase of the song "Snake Dance":

## Snake Dance

*Creativity in Improvisation* (Azzara, Grunow, & Gordon, 1997) contains teaching procedures and activities for learning harmony parts to a variety of songs.

When students demonstrate that they can sing melody, root melody, and harmony parts to several familiar songs in Major and Minor tonalities, they are ready to play those parts on the keyboards. The activity should begin with students playing the melody and root melody to a familiar song in Major tonality that uses tonic and dominant harmonic functions. Next, the teacher should ask the class to echo play DO moving to TI for that song. The students listen to how the harmony moves, and then they play. The same procedure should be followed for teaching students to harmonize MI moving to FA on the keyboards.

Once students can play the harmony part with their right hands, they should add the root melody with their left hands. They now are able to play two melodies at the same time, the root and one harmonic voice. The next step is to play both harmonic voices in the right hand and the roots in the left hand. Most students can coordinate the left and right hands easily when they are playing roots and harmony. Students who have difficulty coordinating the melody of a song with the root melody may have their first success coordinating both hands as a result of playing roots and harmony.

Students can now be set up in groups. One group will play the melody to a song while another group plays the harmony and root melody. Another student can play a drum beat that is appropriate to the song using keyboard percussion sounds. The teacher should start the ensemble with an introduction that establishes the tonality, keyality, and meter of the song that students are about to play. The students listen to the teacher's introduction and begin playing at the appropriate time. Their audiation will tell them if they are making music together or if they are out of synchronization. Many songs in Major and Minor should be arranged in this same manner. This type of group interaction will develop the students' abilities to audiate chord progressions as well as ensemble sensitivity.

## Improvisation Skill Development

Improvisation skill development enables students to take ownership of their music making. Improvisation takes place when students perform something that is *different* from what the teacher has performed. Students demonstrate tonal audiation when they sing a different Major tonic pattern (any combination of DO, MI, and SO) than the teacher. Students improvise tonic patterns and then learn to improvise dominant patterns (any combinations of SO, FA, RE, and TI). When students can improvise tonic patterns and dominant patterns, they should improvise two patterns in succession (tonic then dominant or dominant then tonic). By improvising tonic and dominant patterns in succession, students are solidifying the concept of harmonic progression in their audiation and are developing the readiness to improvise to familiar songs. Students should improvise in a Minor tonality in the same

313

manner that they improvise in a Major tonality. The teacher can easily assess the students' ability to audiate when listening to individuals improvise.

Once students can improvise tonic and dominant patterns in a Major tonality and a Minor tonality, they are ready to improvise to the harmonic progression of a song. This activity should begin by singing the melody and root melody to a familiar song. Next, the class should sing the root melody while the teacher sings tonic patterns and dominant patterns on macrobeats, changing function at the appropriate time to fit the harmonic progression of the song. Students then should be encouraged to improvise tonic and dominant patterns as a group and then alone in the same manner. The same procedure should be followed using the keyboards. The following is an example of an improvisation to "Mary Had a Little Lamb."

Students' improvisational vocabulary can be expanded through the audiation of harmonic variations. When students can sing the harmony parts to familiar songs, they are ready to sing and play variations to those harmony parts. Harmonic variation instruction helps students to resolve the chord progressions that they are audiating.

The activity should begin by having students singing the harmony part of DO moving to TI using a neutral syllable to a familiar song, for example, "Mary Had a Little Lamb." The teacher should sing a variation that includes the neighboring tone RE, and students should echo the teacher's variation. When harmonies and harmonic variations are being performed in a meter, it is important to sing using a neutral syllable (Bum or Du) so that tonal solfege is not mistakenly associated with meter. The teacher should sing several variations to demonstrate other possibilities and then ask the students if they hear a different variation of DO moving to TI. It is appropriate to sing tonal syllables during instruction only when they are not in the context of a meter. Students then can be given a chance to improvise harmonic variations as a group and in solo. The same procedure is followed for the harmony of MI leading to FA with the addition of the passing tone RE. Students should be given many chances to improvise in order to make musical sense of harmonic resolutions. After students have

had success with three note variations, they should be encouraged to improvise variations that combine the harmonies DO and TI, and MI and FA.

All of the variations that the class has sung should be played on
keyboards. The improvisational vocabulary of the students now should
include harmonic variations as well as tonic and dominant patterns and
melodies from songs. A relationship thus develops between the song and the
musician. The song leads the musician's audiation through its harmonic
structure, and the musician shapes and reshapes variations of that structure.

Roots and harmony to "Mary Had a Little Lamb" are learned by rote.

Harmonic variation to "Mary Had a Little Lamb" using DO, TI, and RE

Harmonic variation to "Mary Had a Little Lamb" using MI, FA, and RE

Harmonic variation combining DO and TI, and MI and FA with the
passing tone RE

It is possible for students to make a great deal of music as an ensemble and
alone before notation is introduced. The more audiation activities the class
is engaged in before reading begins, the easier it will be for students to read
with comprehension.

315

**Reading Notation**

Reading activities should encourage students to make connections between their audiation skill and the notation. Students will have the most success if they read music that is familiar to them first and later read music that is less familiar. Familiar patterns that the students have performed by rote and improvised should be read from notation before unfamiliar patterns are read. Students should be given many opportunities to read tonal and rhythm patterns separately before an attempt is made to combine tonal and rhythm patterns in notation.

When beginning tonal reading instruction, the teacher should perform familiar tonal patterns from notation as the students read along and then echo. Students should be taught to find DO on the staff and learn how tonal patterns relate to the position of DO. Students also should learn how the resting tone is represented in notation. For example, if notation is being read in F Major, students need to know that there is one flat in the key signature, the first space F sounds like DO, and the music rests on DO. If notation is being read in D Minor, there is still a flat in the key signature, but the music rests on LA, which is represented by the space D below the staff.

When beginning rhythm reading instruction, the teacher should perform familiar rhythm patterns from notation as the students read along and then echo. The teacher should show students how macro- and micro-beats are represented in notation and demonstrate how the meter feels during rhythm reading activities. For example, it is possible for the quarter note to feel like a macrobeat or a microbeat with a 2/4 measure signature. The context of the music should determine how it feels. With a 3/4 measure signature, the quarter note probably will feel like a microbeat, and the dotted-half note will probably feel like a macrobeat.

Once students can read tonal and rhythm patterns separately, they could be shown how these combine in melodic patterns. Students should read melodic patterns that they have played by rote and then read patterns that are less familiar. Songs that the students have sung and played should also be read. While reading familiar songs, attention should be directed to how the rhythmic functions of macro- and microbeats and tonal functions of tonic and dominant are represented in notation. By reading music that is familiar, students are developing the readiness to read music that is unfamiliar.

If a student has difficulty reading a song, the teacher must decide if the difficulty is a tonal problem or rhythm problem and use the appropriate solfege to guide the student's notational audiation. For instance, if a student is reading and singing the song "Skip to My Lou" from notation, and the performance moves with good rhythm but is out of tune, the teacher may instruct the student to sing the resting tone and then to begin again on the note MI. If the rhythm of the song is incorrect, the teacher should establish macro- and microbeats for the student and chant the rhythm patterns that need correction. If the performance is incorrect tonally and rhythmically, then the student is not ready for the reading activity and should sing more songs and root melodies.

## Measuring Harmonic Audiation by Testing

Written tests can help the teacher measure how well students are audiating harmonic progressions. These tests can take many forms. Here are some ideas for measuring students' harmonic audiation.

Students could be presented with a list of ten familiar song titles. The teacher could play or sing the root melody to one of the songs listed. The students would audiate the root melody and write the name of the song that has that same chord progression. This test can also be presented as a reading test in which the students read a root melody and name the song from the list that has the same harmonic progression.

Another testing technique is for the teacher to sing or play the melody of a familiar song while the students look at the notation of four different root melodies. The students should decide which of the notated root melodies has the same harmonic progression.

Students hear this melody and decide which is the correct root melody.

Another way to test students' abilities to read and audiate harmonic progressions is to notate the melody to a familiar song and present four choices of melodies to be used as accompaniments. Students must decide which melody would sound correct as an accompaniment. For example, students could be asked to read the following melody and choose the correct root melody.

Another possibility is to notate one melody that does *not* sound correct and notate three melodies that *do* sound correct as an accompaniment. Students must audiate the three melodies that sound correct and decide which melody does not fit the harmonic progression.

### Incorporating Improvisation Skills into Keyboard Arrangements

By creating arrangements of songs for the keyboard ensemble, students will learn musical form. Arrangements should be created of songs that students have already played solo, for example, "Lightly Row." One student could play the melody during the A section while another student accompanies with the root melody and another student plays harmony. During the B section, the entire class might play the melody and the root melody. On the last A section, the trio ensemble could play again. Improvisation could be incorporated during the next A section. A student could play a solo using tonal patterns and harmonic variations while another student accompanies playing the root melody and another student plays a keyboard percussion part using a drum setting. On the B and the final A section, the entire class could resume playing, and another soloist could be called to improvise on the repeat of the song. An ending could be arranged, during which the keyboard percussion plays the melodic rhythm of the last phrase with the entire ensemble.

### Applying Chord Inversions to the Keyboard

A more advanced keyboard technique is to play chord voicings and melody together with the right hand while the left hand plays the chord roots. Chords should be voiced below the melody. This is a challenge, because the right hand is playing two parts at the same time and must move to different chord inversions quickly. The left hand plays roots that are synchronized with the chords.

To begin this activity, students should sing the melody of a familiar song while they accompany themselves by playing roots and chords on a keyboard. The song should be sung three times while students accompany themselves with the tonic chord starting in a different inversion each time. Proper voice leading should be maintained for each performance. The inversions for the song "Go Tell Aunt Rhody" follow.

This activity should be introduced without notation so that the students' audiation of the harmonic progression helps them decide when to change chords. The same procedure should be used for songs in Minor tonalities.

When students are secure in their ability to accompany themselves in all three inversions, they are ready to play melody and chords in the right hand and roots in the left hand. The chord voicings are played on the macrobeats at the same time as the chord roots as shown below.

The next step would be to add passing voices with the melody that connect the chords. These passing voices can be comfortably played with two notes rather than a three note chord to allow for mobility in the right hand.

As more songs are played in this manner, students can begin to add passing notes in the bass and begin to improvise other accompaniment notes in the right hand. When students demonstrate competence with accompaniment and voicing techniques, they are ready to read the notation for the songs they have played in that manner as well as new arrangements of songs they have not yet played. After they have read arrangements, they will be ready to write their own arrangements.

Students should learn songs that have subdominant harmonic functions in the same manner as songs with tonic and dominant functions as described in this chapter and in *Creativity in Improvisation* (Azzara, Grunow, & Gordon, 1997). After students have sung and played melody and root melody to songs that have a subdominant function, they should apply the same technique to those songs. They should learn to perform tonic, dominant and subdominant harmonies starting in root position for the tonic chord in the following manner.

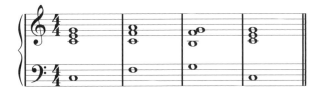

This progression should be played starting in first inversion while maintaining the same voice leading.

The same voice leading should be maintained starting in second inversion.

The steps for applying chord inversion techniques to songs with subdominant harmonic functions are the same as they were for songs with tonic and dominant harmonic functions. These techniques will help students to play a song like "Old MacDonald Had a Farm" without notation in the following manner:

First phrase to "Old MacDonald Had a Farm" melody, roots and inversions

etc.

**Applying Aural Skills to Standard Literature**

Classical piano lessons rarely combine the development of audiation skills with the performance of piano literature; yet, composers of classical music were able to improvise, arrange, and compose musical ideas that resulted from their audiation. Learning rote songs and their harmonies can help students develop musical skills that are transferable to classical repertoire. Students realize through harmonic audiation that there is a deeper structure to the music.

Audiation skill can be taught in the styles of Classical and Baroque music, if students are made aware of resting tones and harmonic progression in the music that they are performing. When students are learning a Clementi sonatina, they should listen and sing the resting tone at the end of each phrase. They should then listen to the music modulate, sing the new resting tone, and find the new resting tone on the keyboard. When this activity is repeated several times, students will learn to anticipate a modulation to the dominant in many pieces in the classical style.

When Clementi sonatinas are first introduced, students should sing the melody and then the root melody. They then should play the melody without notation and add the root melody with the left hand, just as they did with rote songs.

## Sonatina in C Major
Clementi

When this procedure is followed for several pieces, students learn to anticipate the harmonic progression of the sonatina. Students now will bring more meaning to the notated left hand accompaniment because they are audiating the harmonic progression as they read.

Before playing a piece by Bach, students should listen to each phrase and sing the resting tone in the same manner as for Clementi. They will hear the resting tones modulate to many other functions, such as the relative Major, relative Minor, dominant, or subdominant. Students should sing the melody and root melody and begin to play without reading notation. It is reasonable for a beginning student of Bach's music to play with and without notation in the following manner:

## Invention No. 4 in D Minor Bach

Students should be encouraged to learn as many classical pieces as they can without reading notation so that when they read from the notation it will have more meaning. They will be able to make inferences to pieces that are unfamiliar because they will audiate patterns common to most pieces.

## Conclusion

Although Music Learning Theory keyboard activities may seem like a departure from the traditional instruction of reading and playing keyboard literature, they will enhance students' performances and lead to a deeper understanding of the literature. Music pedagogy should move beyond identifying note names and lead students toward music comprehension. In order to comprehend music, students must sing, move, and play songs by ear. Students who are encouraged to perform solo and in ensemble, improvise, read, and compose will be able to express their total artistry as musicians.

## References

Azzara, C. D., Grunow, R. F., & Gordon, E. E. (1997). *Creativity in improvisation*. Chicago: GIA Publications.

Taggart, C. C., Bolton, B. M., Reynolds, A. M., Valerio, W. H., & Gordon, E. E. (2001). *Jump right in: The music curriculum*. Chicago: GIA Publications.

Gordon, E. E. (1990). *Reference Handbook for Using Learning Sequence Activities from Jump right in: The music curriculum* (Revised 2001). Chicago: GIA Publications.

Grunow, R. F., Gordon, E. E., & Azzara, C.D. (1989). *Jump Right In: The Instrumental Series*. Chicago: GIA Publications.

Walters, D., & Taggart, C. C. (Eds.). (1989). *Readings in Music Learning Theory*. Chicago: GIA Publications.

# *Variation 3:* Higher Education Applications

*Joanne Rutkowski*
• • • • • • • • • • • • • •
Pennsylvania State University

# Music Learning Theory and Gordon's Curricular Model in Teacher Education

While the work of Edwin Gordon has influenced the way many music teachers guide children in their growth as musicians, his influence on the way university music majors and future teachers are educated has received minimal attention. Gordon's work can provide much guidance to those of us teaching in higher education. Some examples of higher education applications of Music Learning Theory were provided in *Readings in Music Learning Theory* (Walters & Taggart, 1989). These examples dealt with the college music curriculum (Hobbs, 1989) as well as particular aspects of the curriculum such as teacher education (Dean, 1989) and aural skills courses (Carr, 1989).

Several unique aspects of my approach to teacher education have been influenced by Gordon's Music Learning Theory and his curricular model. I often think about the musicians who would be in my classes if his work were applied in the K-12 music curriculum as well as the total higher education music curriculum. As Hobbs (1989) reflected, "Incoming music majors, having received instruction based upon Music Learning Theory since early childhood, would enter a college or conservatory with highly developed aural/oral and other discrimination skills" (p. 333). However, since this is not the case, and music education faculty typically have limited influence on the total School of Music curriculum, it seems that we must address these issues within the teacher education curriculum. In this chapter, I share how Gordon's work, both his curricular model and Music Learning Theory, has influenced my approach to teacher education.

## Curricular Model

While the curricular model proposed by Gordon (1975, 1984, 2003) is not unique, it is, in my experience, more comprehensive yet simpler to use than others (Eisner, 1985; Reimer, 1989; Runfola & Rutkowski, 1992; Taba, 1962). Furthermore, it is applicable to music curriculum design regardless of students' age level or music setting (general, choral, instrumental, higher education) or curricular level (school curriculum, planned course, course of study for a particular group of students). The first step in Gordon's curricular process (see Figure 1) is a statement of purpose prompted by a series of questions: Why should students receive a music education? Why should this course be offered to students as part of the curriculum? A strong statement of purpose is not grounded in utilitarian justifications but in those points that are unique to music, and it also provides overall direction to the instruction: "if a teacher does not know why he is teaching music, teaching will be haphazard" (Gordon, 1984, p. 206).

The second step in the curricular process is determining the current class achievement as well as the general nature of the students. For a curriculum these issues are broader: What is the nature of the community? What musical opportunities are available to students outside of the school setting? For a planned course or course of study they are more specific: What musical experiences have these students received in school? What is each student's level of music aptitude? What is the musical achievement of the average students in a class? (Gordon, 2003).

The third step involves the specification of music objectives, both comprehensive and sequential. Objectives should contain skill level and content level: "a comprehensive objective is stated in terms of levels of skill and content learning sequences" (Gordon, 1984, p. 208). My experience has shown that most instructional objectives are not specific and deal with mastery of a technique. For example, "Students will clap four-beat rhythm patterns containing whole, half, dotted half, quarter, and eighth notes and rests in a given tempo" (Stauffer & Davidson, 1996, p. 39). This statement deals with mastery of a technique, clapping. A related objective would be, "Upon hearing the teacher chant a familiar Duple macro- and microbeat rhythm pattern on a neutral syllable, the student will be able to recognize the pattern by chanting it back correctly, with appropriate syllables, with consistent tempo and accurate meter." The technique, clapping, is one way

PURPOSE
CURRENT CLASS ACHIEVEMENT
COMPREHENSIVE OBJECTIVES
  Music
  Executive
  Literary
SEQUENTIAL OBJECTIVES
  Method
  Techniques
  Materials
INDIVIDUAL DIFFERENCES
  Aptitude
  Achievement
MEASUREMENT AND EVALUATION

*Figure 1.* Gordon's curricular model

to assist students in accomplishing the objective. Obviously, in order to use the technique, students must master it. However, mastery of the technique is certainly not the objective.

Selection of techniques and materials comprise the next step. Often teachers select a piece of music or a classroom activity and then write the objective. Gordon's model dictates that objectives should be determined first; then materials and techniques should be selected to assist students in accomplishing the objectives. "When method is determined by techniques, materials, or both, rather than by sequential objectives, learning suffers" (Gordon, 1984, p. 210). The organization of techniques and materials in a lesson plan, which is the next step, helps to guide the teacher in the delivery of instruction.

The final step is measurement and evaluation. Decisions regarding students' learning as well as appropriate instruction must be based upon valid measures of appropriate objectives. Too often, "teacher hunches" based on techniques are the basis for making decisions. Valid means of measuring students' accomplishment of objectives are critical but are often not designed or applied. "One of the most serious problems in music education is that teachers rarely measure their students' achievement yet they continuously evaluate it, often using the results to then indirectly evaluate their own teaching effectiveness" (Gordon, 2003, p. 303). It is no wonder that so many teachers have found the recent emphasis on assessment so burdensome.

*Application of model to teacher education.* Gordon's curricular model can be applied when designing a teacher education curriculum. Educators should ask themselves: What is the philosophy of the faculty regarding teacher education? What is the nature of students attending a particular institution? What objectives should be set forth for the students in the program? These objectives should reflect the philosophy of the faculty and nature of the students but also state requirements for teacher certification and accreditation by agencies such as the National Association of Schools of Music (NASM) and the National Council for Accreditation of Teacher Education (NCATE). Valid means for measuring students' accomplishment of these objectives in order to evaluate students' qualifications for certification must be an important aspect of the curriculum. Decisions regarding the establishment of courses and in which courses each objective is best met would then be possible. It is at the course level that decisions regarding techniques and materials should be made. Adoption of Gordon's curricular model by a music education faculty to design teacher education curriculum is, to my knowledge, a rare occurrence. However, I am convinced such an adoption would lead to more effective and efficient teacher education. Teachers prepared through such a curriculum would be better musicians (not just performers) and would be prepared to design instruction to assist their students in becoming better musicians (not just performers).

While application of Gordon's curricular model to a teacher education curriculum is not likely, it is possible, however, for individual faculty members to apply his curricular model within specific courses. A description of how I have used Gordon's model in designing my own courses follows.

I generally teach at least two courses a year in the undergraduate teacher education curriculum at Pennsylvania State University. One, "The Teaching of Music," is taken during the first semester of the student's junior year. The other, "General Music Methods and Materials," is taken by students during their second semester junior year or during their senior year. The first course is a pre-requisite to the other. Both courses are structured around Gordon's curricular model, and students are taught the model as part of the course content. In addition to each of these courses, students simultaneously take a practicum course that focuses on field experience.

All students, regardless of general music, choral, or instrumental specialization, take "Teaching of Music." The focus of this course is to address teaching issues common to all music settings. "An introductory course is needed in the music education curriculum that addresses basic issues common to general music, choral music, and instrumental music (Dean, 1989, p. 345). This course attempts to do so (see Appendix A). Students are presented with Gordon's curricular model on the first day of class as an organizational structure for their own preparation as teachers and also for their use when designing instruction for their students. Philosophical issues are then addressed. Why should all children have access to a music education? Utilitarian and unique music justifications, as well as the limitations of utilitarian justifications, are discussed. We then move on to the nature of the student. In this context, "nature of the student" issues include the nature of music aptitude and achievement (another Gordon influence) and learning sequence issues (how do students learn when they learn music?). Objectives, the next step in the curricular model, are then addressed. This is when students begin to see the relationship among skill and content sequences. I then present techniques for assisting students in accomplishing these objectives. Materials and lesson planning are not specifically addressed in this course, since those issues are setting (general music, choral, instrumental) specific. However, general issues regarding measurement and evaluation of students' aptitude and achievement are discussed. An overview of the content of each class is provided in Appendix B.

"General Music Methods and Materials" is a one-semester course. Typically, students focus on K-6 instruction with me for seven to eight weeks; grade 7-12 instruction is taught by another instructor during the other half of the semester. We begin by revisiting the curricular model and issues from the pre-requisite course (see Appendix C). Then, we start again with philosophy, this time addressing those philosophical issues specifically relevant to general music instruction. The student discussion includes the nature of children's singing voices and the development of the voice through adolescence, as well as means for assessing current class achievement in a general music setting. Then we discuss the selection of objectives based on current class achievement and techniques to accomplish those objectives in the general music setting. The selection of materials is an issue for this particular course, so criteria for selecting repertoire for singing, listening, and moving are presented. The organization of techniques and materials into lesson plans that actively engage these young musicians then becomes important. Finally, valid means of measuring student's achievement, during instruction and at the conclusion of an instructional period, as well as the appropriateness of all aspects of the course of study, are discussed. An overview of the content of each class is provided in Appendix D.

All the steps in the curricular design process become more relevant for these students during the related practicum course taken simultaneously with the methods course. Each student is assigned to an elementary class in a local public school. The pre-service teacher (practicum student) develops and implements a course of study for that group of students over a seven-week period, culminating in the formal assessment of each student's achievement on one objective (see Appendix E).

I have found the application of Gordon's curricular model to my courses to be extremely effective. The students always know where we have been and where we are going, they see the application of the model in their own teaching, and are already moving away from selecting activities based on how they feel. Instead, they are designing courses of study for groups of students based on the current class achievement, selecting materials and activities appropriate for the group of students to guide them to accomplishment of the objectives, assessing the students' learning during and after instruction both formally and informally, and delivering instruction in an engaging and musical way. It has been exciting to see them develop as effective teachers through application of this approach.

## Music Learning Theory

Gordon's Music Learning Theory, including music aptitude issues, has many obvious applications in higher education. In the teacher education program, students should gain an understanding of aptitude and achievement, skill sequence, content sequences, tonal and rhythm solfege, and how these are applied when working with students. They should also be given opportunities to develop their own audiation abilities through music courses offered to them in the curriculum. Ideally, music students would come to us with those skills, but that is usually not the case. "Unfortunately, such a utopian condition does not exist, and despite a growing acceptance of Music Learning Theory as a basis for the music education of children, major improvements in the overall preparation of incoming freshman musicians are unlikely in the near future" (Hobbs, 1989, p. 333). However, in order to teach using Music Learning Theory, future teachers must also develop their own music skills, ideally through the application of Music Learning Theory in their K-12 education and in aural skills (sight-singing, ear training) courses at the college level.

*Music Learning Theory applications in teacher education.* It is clear that future teachers should be taught Gordon's Music Learning Theory and application of that theory in the general music, choral, and instrumental settings. However, I believe the way students are taught Music Learning

Theory greatly influences their acceptance of the theory and their application of the theory in their own classrooms.

A very simplistic description of Gordon's Music Learning Theory might be "sound before sight" and "meeting the individual musical needs of every student." When teaching future teachers the theory, these same basic principles should be applied. In other words, we should "practice what we preach!" Each methods course taught at Penn State has a companion practicum course. The practicum course for "The Teaching of Music" provides a vehicle for me to apply this strategy (see Appendix F). Students experience Music Learning Theory before it is discussed. They participate in informal structured music experiences with preschoolers; I also engage them in Music Learning Theory experiences during class meetings on campus. Therefore, I model Music Learning Theory application for them before we discuss it. Furthermore, students are able to experience informal instruction with young children, which they consistently find very valuable even though their teacher certification is K-12. When we finally discuss Music Learning Theory in class, the students seem to immediately understand because they have already experienced Music Learning Theory.

Approaching the practicum course in this manner also allows students the opportunity to develop their own audiation skills. Many so-called "fine" music students often have difficulty discriminating among various meters and almost always have difficulty discriminating among various tonalities. Only a few have used any kind of tonal or rhythm solfege, and if they have it has usually been a fleeting experience, i.e., "I remember chanting 'ta ta' in elementary school." The practicum course, therefore, not only gives them an experience with Music Learning Theory but it also enhances these future teachers' own audiation skills.

In order to honestly model Gordon's Music Learning Theory, students' individual musical needs should be addressed as well. The *Advanced Measures of Music Audiation* (AMMA) (Gordon, 1989) provides a feasible means for measuring students' aptitudes, and its use in this type of setting is encouraged.

Although I have found this approach to teaching Gordon's work to be quite effective, most of my frustration centers around the students' level of audiation ability when they enter my classes. Toward the middle to end of the semester, it becomes necessary to discuss aspects of Music Learning Theory in class that they have not yet experienced in practicum due to the deficiencies in their own skill and content level achievement. For example, in this one-semester course most students rarely move beyond Verbal Association with tonic, dominant, and sub-dominant function patterns in

Major, Minor, Dorian, and Mixolydian. I often move them to Symbolic Association with tonic function patterns in Major and Minor just to model those procedures. The students also become frustrated and sometimes angry at their low levels of achievement. They always assumed they were excellent musicians based on their high levels of performance and advanced technique on their instruments. An understanding of what they should be able to do and what younger children can do is often a shock to them. More appropriate instruction at the K-12 level, as well as in other courses in the higher education music curriculum, is urgently needed.

## Summary and Conclusions

The future of American music education rests in the hands of those persons currently enrolled in our teacher education programs. It is imperative that they be prepared to offer the best possible music instruction to their students. While the National Standards for Music Education provide some specific goals for K-12 instruction, and, consequently, the teacher education programs that prepare teachers, it must be made clear that they are not curricula. Teachers must be knowledgeable about the curricular design process. If they chose the National Standards as their curricular goals, they must be able to design curricula, planned courses, and courses of study based on those goals. My experience has illustrated the effectiveness of using Gordon's curricular model as a framework for courses in teacher education and preparing students to design instruction based on that model.

I am also convinced that future teachers must initially experience Music Learning Theory when developing their own musicianship before they will be convinced of its appropriateness for their own students. It is my firm belief that these applications of Gordon's Curricular Model and Music Learning Theory to teacher education will deeply enhance the music education of the next generation of children.

## References

Carr, M. A. (1989). The importance of sound before symbol in developing intuitive college musicians. In D. L. Walters & C. C. Taggart (Eds.), *Readings in Music Learning Theory* (pp. 352-364). Chicago: GIA Publications.

Dean, R. A. (1989). Teacher education and Music Learning Theory. In D. L. Walters & C. C. Taggart (Eds.), *Readings in Music Learning Theory* (pp. 343-351). Chicago: GIA Publications.

Eisner, E. W. (1985). *The educational imagination: On the design and evaluation of school programs* (2nd ed.). New York: Macmillan Publishing Company.

Gordon, E. E. (1975). *Learning theory, patterns, and music*. Buffalo, NY: Tometic Associates, Limited.

——. (1989). *Advanced measures of music audiation*. Chicago: GIA Publications.

——. (2003). *Learning sequences in music: Skill, content, and patterns*. Chicago: GIA Publications.

Hobb, W. (1989). Implementing music learning theory within a college curriculum. In D. L. Walters, & C. C. Taggart (Eds.), *Readings in Music Learning Theory* (pp. 333-342). Chicago: GIA Publications.

Reimer, B. (1989). *A philosophy of music education* (2nd ed.). Englewood Cliffs, NJ: Prentice Hall.

Runfola, M., & Rutkowski, J. (1992). General music curriculum. In R. Colwell (Ed.), *Handbook of research on music teaching and learning* (pp. 697-709). New York: Schirmer Books.

Stauffer, S., & Davidson, J. (Eds.) (1996). *Strategies for teaching: General music K-4*. Reston, VA: Music Educators National Conference.

Taba, H. (1962). *Curriculum development theory and practice*. New York: Harcourt, Brace and World.

Walters, D. L., & Taggart, C. C. (Eds.). (1989). *Readings in Music Learning Theory*. Chicago: GIA Publications.

# Appendix A

*Goals for "Teaching of Music"*

## Course Objectives:
To provide prospective teachers with:

1. The opportunity to establish their personal philosophy of music education;

2. An understanding of music aptitude and achievement, their relationship with each other, and the necessity of their consideration in order to design appropriate instruction for students;

3. An understanding of the various components involved in the music teaching process, their attendant learning theories, and appropriate objectives and techniques;

4. An awareness of the nature of special needs students and strategies for most effectively meeting their needs in the music education setting;

5. An awareness of the PA Comprehensive Reading Plan II and the role music education can play in the teaching of reading;

6. An understanding of measurement and evaluation and their important role in the teaching/learning process;

7. An understanding of educational governance;

8. Opportunities to develop their communication skills through the written and spoken word;

9. Opportunities to analyze recorded music from a teacher's viewpoint.

## "Teacher" Objectives:
The teacher will be able to:

1. Effectively express his or her philosophy of music education;

2. Write objectives exhibiting appropriateness of content and sequence;

3. Analyze lesson plans to determine the objectives established by the teacher, including skill and content;

4. Apply tonal, rhythm, and music concept techniques to choral and instrumental settings;

5. Identify a topic of interest in the profession, locate resources pertinent to that topic, and write a paper detailing current thought and understanding of that topic.

# Appendix B

*Daily Course Content for "Teaching of Music"*

#1   Introduction to course; organization of journal
Curricular framework: curriculum, planned courses, course of study

#2   Review curricular framework
Why teach music? Begin philosophy in small group discussion

#3   Nature of the student: what is of concern for teachers?
Gardner's Theory of Multiple Intelligences and its application in the
music setting
Aptitude and achievement; audiation

#4   Revisit philosophy, personal philosophy assignment
Discussion of music education Topic Paper

#5   Continue aptitude discussion; aptitude tests

#6   Music Library and resources

#7   Organization of music learning; discrimination and inference learning

#8   Tonal and Rhythm Literacy Skill Sequence

#9   Review Tonal and Rhythm Literacy Skill Sequence
Discussion: objectives and techniques

#10   Content sequence; Tonal Content Sequence, tonal solfege
Writing Tonal Literacy objectives with content

#11   Tonal Techniques, Assessment tools, using technique charts

#12   Tonal techniques and assessment tools continued
Applying techniques to choral/instrumental settings; meeting
individual needs of students

#13   Documentation of class tonal achievement
Discuss Tonal Technique Application assignment and review for
midterm

#14   Midterm

#15 What is a lesson plan? Task analysis?
Writing a task analysis; discuss tonal/rhythm learning task analysis assignment

#16 Discussion: Rhythm Content Sequence, rhythm solfege

#17 Rhythm techniques, Assessment tools, using techniques charts
(Applying techniques to choral/instrumental settings; meeting individual needs of students)

#18 Continue with rhythm techniques

#19 Review of rhythm learning; documentation of class rhythm achievement

#20 Music Concepts Learning, skill and content sequence
Mode and meter discrimination, objectives and techniques

#21 Music Concepts learning and other concepts; objectives and techniques

#22 Concept techniques

#23 Concept techniques; Use of concept charts, assessment tools

#24 Classroom management issues

#25 Theoretical Understanding Skill Sequence
Development of Independent Musicianship

#26 Finish Independent Musicianship
Pennsylvania Comprehensive Reading Plan II and Music Education
Overview of Lesson Planning strategies

#27 Structure of Education in the USA
What forces guide curriculum? National Standards for the Arts
PDE sequence for school curriculum development and current status

#28 Review of semester; preparation for final exam
Bring your questions!

#29 Final exam

# Appendix C

*Goals for "General Music Methods and Materials"*

*K-6 Portion of Course*

**Course Objectives:**
"Teachers" will be able to:

1. Discuss and implement current philosophies of general music programs, including those of Kodály, Orff, Dalcroze, and Gordon;

2. Identify behavioral characteristics typical of K-6 students;

3. Write outcomes and objectives that reflect the National Standards for Music Education and that are appropriate for K-6 general music students;

4. Select materials appropriate for K-6 general music students, adapting those materials deemed inappropriate;

5. Compose appropriate songs and harmonic concept applications for elementary school students;

6. Plan music lessons for K-6 general music students with appropriate singing, listening/responding, and creating activities;

7. Design and implement a course of study for elementary general music students;

8. Plan elementary school music programs/assemblies;

9. Plan music lessons that account for individual differences among students, including special needs and gifted students;

10. Adapt guitar, piano, recorder, and autoharp instruction to meet general music outcomes.

## Appendix D

*Daily Course Content for "General Music Methods and Materials"*

*K-6 Portion of Course*

#1  Review "Teaching of Music" course materials; developing curriculum
    What to teach in elementary general music
    Review of curriculum design process; course of study
    Elementary teaching experience, name activity
    Setting up your teaching journal

#2  Child and adolescent voices

#3  Selecting song materials
    Compiling song materials for course of study

#4  Continue with song evaluation and compilation of materials
    Composing songs for elementary school children

#5  Task analysis; preparing your lesson

#6  Review task analysis; lesson planning; planning your first full lesson

#7  Guitar, recorders, and autoharp in general music

#8  Review planning and putting together your course of study;
    Classroom management strategies

#9  Teaching use of singing voice; evaluating children's singing voices

#10  Overview of Kodály approach

#11  Evaluating individual student's and class' achievement
     Planning follow-up lessons and using charts
     Informal and formal assessments; grading students

#12  Harmonic concept/independent musicianship development
     Finish discussion of assessment

#13   Overview of Orff and Dalcroze approaches

#14   Creating and listening strategies; addressing individual student's needs

#15   Compare and contrast approaches of Gordon, Kodály, Orff, and Dalcroze

#16   Discussion of MENC strategies and National Standards
Working with classroom teachers
Planning an elementary music "assembly"; integrating curriculum
Review of course

# Appendix E

*Goals for "Practicum: General Music Methods and Materials"*

*K-6*

## Course Objectives:

1. To provide prospective music teachers with the opportunity to observe application of appropriate music lessons with elementary general music students;

2. To provide prospective music teachers with the opportunity to apply various music methods and techniques appropriate for the K-6 general music setting.

## "Teacher" Objectives:

The teacher will be able to:

1. Effectively select, lead, and teach songs and exhibit appropriate strategies for correcting children's performance of songs;

2. Identify various types of singers within the general music classroom setting by observing, and plan appropriate instruction for remediation;

3. Implement appropriate music lessons in a general music setting with elementary school students;

4. Assess class achievement and apply appropriate remediation strategies;

5. Guide listening experiences of general music students;

6. Assess his or her own teaching progress and design strategies for improvement.

# Appendix F

*Goals for "Practicum: Teaching of Music"*

**Course Objectives:**

1. To provide prospective music teachers with an opportunity to observe various components involved in the music teaching process, their attendant learning theories, and appropriate objectives and techniques;

2. To provide prospective music teachers with the opportunity to develop basic music teaching skills;

3. To provide prospective music teachers with the opportunity to observe and interact with children of varying races, sexes, religious beliefs, national origins and socioeconomic backgrounds, particularly children for whom English is a second language and are considered in need of early intervention;

4. To provide prospective music teachers the opportunity to continue developing their own sight-singing and piano skills.

**"Teacher" Objectives:**

The teacher will be able to:

1. Function adequately with "moveable DO" and a rhythm syllable language and apply those systems to vocally sight-read music;

2. Effectively lead, teach, and review songs;

3. Effectively lead informal music activities with young children;

4. Begin to apply "Principles of Learning";

5. Apply procedures for teaching Tonal and Rhythm Literacy and effectively implement an activity applying appropriate task analysis.

*Bruce Taggart*
• • • • • • • • • •
MICHIGAN STATE UNIVERSITY

# Music Learning Theory in the College Music Theory Curriculum

College music theory should offer students the chance to *theorize* about music, to ponder what they hear, to explain how music functions, to create new musical structures based on the understanding of existing ones, to develop an audiational understanding of styles, to understand the relationship between a formal model and an actual composition that seems not to fit the model, to understand the relationship of compositional techniques and aesthetic significance, and to speculate how the human brain processes music. Unfortunately, in the typical music theory curriculum, theorizing is something that students seldom do.

Gordon developed Music Learning Theory out of an analysis of how we learn when we learn music. Typically, in practical application, it has been used primarily for guiding instruction of children in grades K-12. However, a logical sequence that follows Gordon's Music Learning Theory is as important at the college level as at all levels below, incorporating as it does age-appropriate skill learning sequence, tonal content learning sequence, and rhythm content learning sequence into both aspects (written and ear training) of the theory curriculum. Indeed, Music Learning Theory dictates that ear training and written theory be combined. Content and skill instruction must intertwine and reinforce one another; inference must overlap and flow out of discrimination. Before theorizing can occur, students must have the readiness for it. In this chapter, I will discuss several ways to apply Music Learning Theory to the core sequence of under-graduate theory classes, which includes both written theory and ear

345

training, and I will speculate about more comprehensive ways to modify the theory curriculum.

What are the content and skills being taught at the college level, how should discrimination and inference learning occur, and how should we sequence instruction so that students are ready to learn what we present? These questions are seldom asked about the college theory curriculum, with the result being that the sequence of instruction is often ineffective or counterproductive. With no clear instructional objectives based on student abilities and learning characteristics, we should not be surprised that many undergraduates are frustrated by—hate, even—their college theory classes. However, Gordon proposes a general model for music theory instruction that addresses these problems. According to Gordon, theoretical under-standing—true understanding of audiated musical structures—can come only after students have successfully engaged in all other levels of the skill learning sequence. Theoretical understanding, the last level of inference learning, must follow all levels of discrimination learning and the general-ization and creativity/improvisation levels of inference learning.

Unfortunately, the current theory curriculum seldom, if ever, follows this sequence. Indeed, as Gordon points out, the current theory curriculum asks students to "define, offer rules for, and label what is *seen in notation* rather than what is *heard in audiation*"(Gordon, 2003, p. 133). A truly useful college music theory curriculum should start with aural and oral musical structures and introduce notated patterns only as students develop audia-tional readiness. Traditional theory instruction, focusing as it does on notation, tends to look at music from the perspective of the composer rather than the listener, asking what compositional principles govern the structure of a work on paper. Instead, we should be asking what principles and structures govern the experience of the work in audiation. When we analyze a poem, we quickly dispense with its formal, compositional structure (how many lines, what rhyme scheme, and so on) and turn to its meaning, to the aesthetic and affective impact that the words create. A theory curriculum that is based on audiation can also address aesthetic and affective impact in a way that is impossible for a notation-based approach that has no educationally valid sequence of instruction.

Before discussing the college curriculum, we first should examine the assumptions about pre-requisites for college theory and the expectations that we have for college students who have had little or no practical preparation to engage in either the conceptual or aural material they are expected to master in two or three years. Any discussion of the college curriculum should begin with a discussion of all theory instruction that comes before it. Ideally, college theory instruction should be the culmination of eighteen years of theory study; students should start college with aural and conceptual skills that most current undergraduates never attain by the time they graduate.

## Music Theory Before College: The Ideal

To a music theorist, Gordon's Music Learning Theory looks like a music theory curriculum. Children in early elementary school begin with aural/oral and verbal association skills, learning to recognize tonalities and meters, sing tonal patterns and chant rhythm patterns accurately (without and then with syllables), create new tonal and rhythm patterns, identify tonic, subdominant, and dominant functions, and find such patterns in heard melodies. During this time, movement activities serve to reinforce rhythmic and metric understanding and to enhance body awareness and control, which is important for singing and instrumental performance.

Once these skills solidify, children are ready to move on to more conceptual activities (typically by second or third grade). They begin using notation in the context of melodic and rhythmic patterns that they have previously learned, followed by reading and writing unfamiliar patterns. Key signatures are introduced as DO signatures, which are as useful for Dorian or Phrygian as for Major; the treble staff is introduced in the context of syllables and tonal patterns rather than absolute letter names. Meter signatures indicate Duple or Triple only, rather than the conceptual (and perceptually questionable) idea of "simple" versus "compound" meter, or the universal (and often incorrect) idea that each meter signature indicates how many beats are in a measure and which note value carries the beat. Instead, metric notation helps students recognize the rhythmic patterns that they have already experienced aurally and orally.

When students have developed solid skills in Major/Minor and Duple/Triple, they are ready to move on to other tonalities (modes) and meters. By mid- to late-elementary school, students should be working with Dorian, Phrygian, Lydian, Mixolydian, and Locrian tonalities and meters in five and seven, as well as combinations of meters. Only with early exposure to such musical materials will students be comfortable with them when they reach college.

Even as students are working toward the use of symbolic representation, they are developing improvisational skills within a harmonic and metric context. Beginning around second grade, students should be associating syllables with pitches, harmonies, and meters, which allows them to improvise patterns that fit a given harmonic or metric structure. This elementary ability to improvise should lead to more advanced creative activities, including improvisation over more complex harmonic patterns, improvisation in unusual and changing meters, and composition of melodies and longer compositions.

Ideally, a Music Learning Theory curriculum should extend beyond elementary school into middle and high school. Although this could include formal musicianship classes, students are more likely to receive Music Learning Theory-based instruction in performing ensembles. Such instruction would include rhythmic, melodic, and harmonic listening and performance using rhythm and tonal syllables, more advanced improvisation experience, and discussion of such traditional music theory topics as formal structure and identification of chords using Roman numerals and functional description (i.e., tonic, subdominant, "predominant," and dominant). Students in a Music Learning Theory-based ensemble would learn through singing and movement, developing a "theoretical" understanding of their music through a direct experience of the musical materials. They could audiate all that they play and sing, and understand through audiation the rhythmic, melodic, and harmonic structure of their music.

The goal of the college curriculum, then, would be to reinforce, refine, and expand the musical knowledge of incoming students based on their existing audiational skills. Just as students who speak and understand a foreign language can analyze literature in that language, students with a Music Learning Theory background would be fluent in the musical language of compositions, allowing music analysis from an audiational perspective.

Although "analysis" is what we currently ask college music students to do, the nature of music analysis would change if done in the context of audiation rather than notation. Other aspects of the theory curriculum would change also.

The most obvious change would come in the ear training side of the curriculum. Put simply, it would cease to exist. With students who are already fluent in the musical language (able to read it, write it, create with it, understand its syntax and meaning), "dictation" (rhythmic, melodic, and harmonic), identification of chords and intervals, and sight-singing would become unnecessary as a separate course of study. Because students would be accustomed to hearing melodies in terms of scale degree function, harmonic underpinning, and rhythmic and metric context, they could easily hear a melody, translate it into syllables, both rhythmic and metric, and notate it. They then could improvise a harmony to accompany it and compose variations on the same melody to fit the harmonic structure. Likewise, harmonic dictation would be no different from what these students had been doing, in graduated levels, since first grade. A possible difference at the college level would be the use of theoretical terminology to describe chords and chord function and long-range harmonic and melodic structure, but such discussion would fall in the realm of theoretical concepts, which would be built on students' existing conceptual base.

Music Learning Theory students would excel in a traditional college music theory curriculum, in which music is studied as a notational artifact, because they would have the audiational skills necessary to translate notational structures into musical structures. Ideally, however, we would design a new curriculum for those students that allows them to discover theoretical structures through inference learning that grows out of their audiational skills. Because they would not take a separate ear training course, students could be immersed in a rich, performance-based theoretical environment five days a week. The ordering of the curriculum should probably change: rather than starting with intervals, scales, triads, and Roman numeral analysis, these students could start with formal analysis, or even Schenkerian analysis—perhaps an audiational form of Schenkerian analysis that could be accomplished with little notation.

Indeed, the curriculum could be exactly reversed. We might save part-writing and species counterpoint for the last semester as exercises in composition and stylistic analysis. We might follow the Schenkerian ordering of levels and work from the background to the foreground of musical compositions and exercises. Students first might hear and then identify large tonal areas and melodic prolongation, work their way to the middle ground by hearing and labeling more harmonic and melodic patterning, learning to identify more chords, and finally end at the foreground, discussing specific rhythmic, melodic, and harmonic structure and improvising new music to fit those structures. Gone would be the need to teach fundamentals. Gone also would be students' blank stares when they are asked if they hear a certain structure or pattern. Students would be sensitive to harmonic function, they could hear melodic prolongation, they could audiate the harmonic underpinnings of melodic patterns, and they could create new music in specific styles.

These ideas are mere speculation about what could happen in a theorist's dream world. But what about the real world? What should we be doing with our students who can't audiate, who have experienced no discrim-ination learning, much less inference learning, and who have limited listening, singing, or rhythmic skills? In fact, the principles that guide the ideal curriculum should still be in effect for the real-world curriculum. After we help our students develop the readiness for an audiation-based curriculum, we could make drastic changes in content and instructional style.

## Audiation-based Theory Curriculum

The typical college music theory curriculum has at least seven stated or unstated learning objectives:

1.  Students should attain mastery of theory fundamentals, including keys and modes, rhythmic and metric notation, intervals, triads and seventh chords, Roman numeral chord labels, cadential patterns, melodic forms, and harmonization of simple melodies.
2.  Students should learn to write two-voice counterpoint (typically species counterpoint), four-voice chorale-style counterpoint, and simple Baroque counterpoint.
3.  Students should be able to analyze tonal music for key, harmonic progression, and all common formal structures.
4.  Students should be able to identify and use in written work typical chromatic chords and progressions.
5.  Students should be able to compose simple compositions in the characteristic styles of musical periods and genres.
6.  Students should have the following ear training skills: identifying and singing all intervals, triads, and seventh chords, as well as writing melodies, rhythmic patterns, and chord progressions from dictation.
7.  Students should be able to sing a melody from sight, typically using moveable-DO syllables in all clefs.

These learning objectives are common to most theory programs in the United States. Some place more or less emphasis on one skill or another. Some add improvisation, keyboard skills, expanded twentieth century materials, and orchestration to the list. Some programs integrate ear training, sight-singing, and keyboard skills into a single class, while others teach these skills in separate classes.

In most cases, however, student readiness in terms of conceptual and especially audiational skills is not taken into consideration in the sequence of instruction. First year students typically start with a rudiments class that focuses on musical components—scales, intervals, chords, cadences—from a notational and aural perspective. Most programs use textbooks that cover these fundamentals with copious notated examples that few if any students can audiate, and that few students take the time, or have the ability, to play on the piano. As the semesters pass, students see more and more complicated musical structures (in notation, in their texts) and learn increasingly elaborate musical components—expanded cadence structures, phrase structure, encyclopedic lists of chord functions, chromatic harmony—that they continue to learn conceptually but not through audiation. Formal analysis typically comes last; the discrete components (which few students can audiate) are strung together into a musical architecture that few students can perceive except as a discrete passage of conceptual elements.

This early focus on "nuts and bolts" is equivalent to an English literature program teaching its students the fine points of grammar and syntax before checking to see whether they can understand the language in written or spoken form, or whether they have actually read a book or short story. In fact, an English literature course for illiterate students would, by necessity, start with oral presentations of literature. Reading and writing would follow as students acquired the necessary readiness skills.

Unfortunately, most music students already have experienced notation, which leads theory instructors to assume that they read it with comprehension (that is, audiate it) as well. But reading music without audiation is like singing an Italian aria phonetically without understanding the words. A poor performance is the inevitable outcome. Just as singers must go beyond mastery of diction in a foreign language to gain a true understanding of what they are singing, theory students should go beyond mastery of note reading to gain a true audiational understanding of musical structure.

An audiation-based theory curriculum can retain the objectives of the typical theory curriculum, although the objectives' importance will shift as we modify the presentation. Thus, identification of isolated intervals will be a less important ear training goal than understanding where intervals fall in diatonic music and hearing those intervals in terms of scale degree and voice leading. An encyclopedic knowledge of chord function will be less important than an audiated understanding of harmony and voice leading.

How can we modify the existing theory curriculum to teach to our students' abilities and give them the readiness they need for abstract inference learning? We can make several changes immediately; others would require a more fundamental overhaul of class sequence.

The first change we can make is to cut back on the use of notation in the early semesters. Perhaps eliminate the notation-bound text. We can follow Gordon's sequence of instruction, beginning with discrimination learning (teaching skills, content, and pattern by rote) using aural/oral, verbal association, partial synthesis, symbolic association, and composite synthesis, leading to inference learning that allows students to *theorize* about music.

We should first establish that students can hear *with audiational comprehension* the musical structures that we are teaching. The first semester should be devoted, as much as possible, to aural/oral, verbal association, and partial synthesis instruction, with bridging movement (temporarily skipping levels of learning) to inference learning when appropriate. The traditional separation of instruction into written theory and ear training would not be appropriate here because of the absence of notation. Using tonal and rhythm syllables, students can learn to hear and sing intervals, triads, seventh chords, melodies, simple chord progressions, and rhythmic patterns. The instructor should sing all of these using a neutral syllable and asking the students to sing them back. A shift to non-notated melodic "dictation," in which students learn to identify scale and harmonic function, tonal patterns, meter function, and rhythmic patterns through syllable association, can be instituted immediately by any aural skills class. Likewise, asking students to learn intervals and chords through singing is much more beneficial than merely asking students to listen and guess passively.

An initial emphasis on aural/oral activities is easily introduced into any aural skills class; yet it is a teaching tool that is seldom used in the college classroom, perhaps because instructors feel that they must hurry their students through the "easy" material so that they can spend more time with the "hard" material. What they do not realize is that, without mastery of material at the aural/oral level, students have little or no chance of succeeding at higher levels, *regardless of the amount of time spent on those activities*. The typical college ear training class has the "haves" (those who can easily master the material) and the "have-nots" (those who never master the material). No amount of drill, computer-assisted or otherwise, can help the have-nots achieve at higher levels of learning if they have not mastered the lowest levels of discrimination learning.

Even without notation, a first-semester class can cover nearly as much material as is covered in a traditional theory class. Students can learn about melodic structure, cadence types, chord function, consonance and dissonance, even, to some extent, species counterpoint, in a purely aural/oral and verbal association context. A more extensive reordering of the instructional sequence would allow students to learn about larger formal structure and stylistic characteristics of musical periods in the first year. As a general rule, even in a traditional class, students will learn theoretical structures much better if they experience them aurally and orally first.

The use of tonal and rhythm syllables is essential in such non-notated instruction. We can teach most theoretical concepts using syllables, including intervals, chords, and cadence structures. For example, in a Major key, the interval from DO to any diatonic note above is always a Major or perfect interval; a perfect authentic cadence in Major always has SO-DO in the bass. Because Music Learning Theory places a strong emphasis on learning harmonic function, students will develop an early audiational understanding of tonic, subdominant, and dominant functions, which makes teaching about cadence type or phrase structure simple.

Gordon's Learning Sequence Activities can be adapted to the college ear training class as part of this sequential instruction. Because college students learn faster than the young students for whom the Learning Sequence Activities are intended, some of the criteria can be changed or eliminated from the sequence. The early criteria can be covered quickly, because most students will have few difficulties with them. They are important to include, however, because some students will have difficulties with even the earliest criteria, such as singing the resting tone or first pitch of a pattern. Identifying such students early is important; they can either be given extra instruction or, if necessary, be advised not to pursue music as a major. Such information is better given earlier than later.

Learning Sequence Activities can be integrated into the first-year college theory classroom as easily as into classes in primary and secondary school. They can be taught in the first ten minutes of every class and used as the foundation upon which other instruction is built. The instructor should keep track of student achievement, individualizing instruction. An aptitude test (specifically, Gordon's *Advanced Measures of Music Audiation*) can help the instructor meet the needs of both advanced and struggling students. Students with high aptitude and high achievement can be given extra challenges in pattern instruction (longer patterns, more inference activities); students with high aptitude and low achievement can be given extra help to raise their achievement levels; and students with low aptitude (and, presumably, low achievement) can be given extra help, including tutoring. (Often, low-aptitude students who experience frustration with their low scores will come to the instructor for career advice. Knowing a student's aptitude score can help the instructor guide the student toward realistic musical and professional goals.) With aptitude scores for the class, the instructor can effectively govern the pace of instruction to meet the needs of the most students.

Some levels in the skill learning sequence might seem less relevant than others in the college theory curriculum. The oral/aural level will be appropriate for many but not all students; some will have had sufficient oral/aural preparation prior to college. Symbolic association discrimination learning might seem less useful for most students because most already read music. We should note, however, that recognizing note names and durations is not necessarily the same as reading music; even knowing which buttons to push on an instrument for each note name is not necessarily reading music. Our goal for our students should be mastery of the generalization-symbolic level of learning; that is, reading unfamiliar music at sight and audiating it—knowing what it will sound like before they play it or sing it. Even the simplest symbolic association (reading familiar patterns) at the discrimination learning level is important for first-year students. In addition to building audiational skills, it paves the way for later theoretical instruction. Fluency in recognizing tonic, subdominant, and dominant patterns in Major and Minor keys will greatly assist in analyzing harmonic structure in a written score. Mastery of the discrimination learning level of music reading is essential preparation for the inference learning level.

Theory instructors can be unaware of significant problems being experienced by many students in class. Students can often satisfy the narrow requirements of a class, receiving a high grade even, without mastering the fundamentals that should support such learning. In an ear training/sight-singing class, for example, students can learn to take melodic dictation and sing prepared songs using syllables, but not be able to sing back simple tonic, subdominant, dominant patterns at the generalization-verbal level. Because theory teachers tend not to follow a sequence of instruction that moves from discrimination learning through inference learning, they never know about such gaps in their students' abilities; most would be astonished, in fact, that many of their best students cannot achieve at the inference level. In teaching and measuring a small set of skills, many of which have little to do with the practice of music in the real world, we fail to teach fundamental skills that might actually be useful. Even though the early stages might seem unnecessary, following Gordon's sequence of instruction will ultimately lead to better skills.

Throughout Gordon's Music Learning Theory, syllables, both tonal and rhythmic, play a vital role. In the theory curriculum proposed here, syllables must take the place of notation in teaching concepts. What syllables should be used? For rhythm syllables, this question is easy; for tonal syllables, the answer is less clear. Because few theory programs use rhythm syllables, there is little disagreement about which system is best. Most often, ear training instructors use no syllables at all, or they use a home-grown system of words ("opportunity" for unusual paired meter, "Saturday Sunday" for 3 + 2 usual combined meter, for example). We can adopt Gordon's rhythm syllables with little controversy. For tonal syllables, on the other hand, instructors are passionate about which system is best.

The most common choices are moveable DO with DO always being the tonic (so-called "DO-based" Minor, but also DO-based Dorian, Phrygian, etc.), moveable DO with different syllables on tonic, depending on tonality (so-called LA-based Minor, but also RE-based Dorian, MI-based Phrygian, etc.), and fixed DO, in which all C's (including C-sharp and C-flat) are DO, all D's are RE, and so on. The first two are most common in college theory classes in the U.S (Taggart & Taggart, 1994). Fixed DO is used primarily at music conservatories that follow the French system of solfege instruction. Although its proponents argue passionately in its support, we will not consider fixed DO here, because it is much less common than moveable-DO systems, and because it is not useful in teaching the skills in Music Learning Theory.

Typically, music theorists blanch when considering the possibility of something other than DO being the tonic. They object strongly to singing the tonic triad in Minor as LA, DO, MI, because (they argue) it does not reflect the commonalities between harmonic function in Major and Minor. To some extent, this argument is valid. We do want our students to focus on the resting tone (tonic note) and tonic and dominant triads, hearing all notes and patterns in a consistent harmonic context. To someone accustomed to DO-based Minor, changing the tonic and dominant to LA, DO, MI, and MI, SI, TI, respectively, is disorienting. Some general concepts, such as cadence types, or specific patterns, such as the augmented sixth chords (LE, DO, MI, FI, for the German augmented sixth) can be taught most easily when the syllables stay the same. Particularly when a non-notated approach is used, it is better for students to remember that SO, DO is an authentic cadence, no matter what. To have to learn two cadences (SO, DO in Major, and MI, LA in Minor) for a musical pattern that is identical in Major and Minor is an extra complication that would be good to avoid, if possible.

LA-based Minor has some significant advantages over DO-based Minor, however. In addition to the consistency of having the half step always fall between MI-FA and TI-DO, the most striking advantage comes with singing at sight. Using DO-based syllables, students must analyze music before they can sing it in order to know where to insert ME, LE, and TE in Minor (or, even worse, where to insert RA, ME, LE, and TE in Phrygian), because the notation does not reflect these alterations. Students must know ahead of time what tonality a piece is in before they can sing it. This is a cumbersome and unnecessary level of complication to what should be a simple process. Using LA-based Minor (and MI-based Phrygian, etc.), students assign syllables to notes based on the key signature. As they sing, the tonality will emerge. If a Minor piece modulates to Major, the tonic will smoothly modulate to DO.

The conceptual problems created by differences between Major and Minor syllables are only problematic if viewed through theorists' eyes (and heard through theorists' ears) in the context of current practice. If we accept the premise that our students now are not learning as much as we think they are, it becomes easier to change our approach. I suspect that with a complete shift of paradigm, as proposed here, to one that focuses on heard and performed structure before notated and conceptual structure, we could easily adopt LA-based Minor in all we do. Students who are accustomed to LA, DO, MI, as the tonic in Minor will have a different understanding of Minor, but it will not seem inconsistent to them if it is all they know. Being able to hear half-steps—which are the key to functional tonality using the diatonic scale—and having an audiational understanding of how the difference in half step placement changes the tonality of music, are skills worth fostering. Furthermore, with strong skills that result from following Gordon's instructional sequence, students should find it easy to switch to the more theoretical DO-based Minor when necessary.

**Outcomes**

In the course of incorporating Music Learning Theory into the theory curriculum, we would do well to assess the true value of music theory to music students. Theorists are often accused (by students and, sometimes, by faculty in other disciplines of music) of making busy-work for students, forcing them to spend at least half of their college career on a subject that has no relevance to the rest of their musical life. They argue that they will never need to know how to write correct voice leading in four parts, write a two-part invention, analyze the harmonic structure of a Chopin mazurka, or discover the pitch-class sets of a Schoenberg piano piece. They might even argue that they will never need to identify intervals and chords, write melodies and harmonies from dictation, or sight sing using syllables that they never quite master. Although we might dismiss such complaints as being inevitable with any required subject, we should ask ourselves whether there might be a grain of truth in them. These activities might be more useful if our students had the proper skills to carry them out with musical understanding.

Perhaps we focus too much on outcomes without considering the learning process that leads there, and we lose a large percentage of our students as a result. Surely there is value in knowing how to write a two-part invention if it is done creatively through an audiated understanding of Baroque style, rather than as a mechanical exercise in filling in a template. Even if one considered circling and labeling pitch class sets in Schoenberg to be unmusical, no one could argue against an audiated understanding of sonorities in Schoenberg. And a complete fluency with musical syllables that allows comfortable sight-singing in all tonal styles through audiation is perhaps one of the most useful skills of all to a musician.

So our desired outcomes may not need overhauling, just the way we get to them. If we want our students to compose in Baroque SATB style, we should give them the musical skills that allow them to infer the rules through study of the style rather than simply teaching them rules to follow, as if it were musical paint-by-number. Reliance on such rules is perhaps the least musical approach we can take, because most of our students have no audiational understanding of why they are following the rules. When we play for them obvious parallel fifths, for example, most students simply look blank when asked if they hear a problem. This is because there is nothing inherently wrong with parallel fifths; we hear them all the time in various musical styles. Parallel fifths are only incorrect in a specific, narrowly defined style. Students must be able to hear in that style, must have an audiated understanding of conventional structures, before they can recognize divergence from the style. Although we can teach them to paint by numbers, no number of rules or amount of memorization can bring them to the level of inference learning through audiation that is necessary to understand the music.

Quite frankly, we are wasting our students' time by teaching them rules without audiation. We satisfy ourselves that our students are learning because they are able to produce acceptable product in the form of technically correct part-writing exercises and analyses, and a few of our students will have sufficiently high music aptitude to learn to audiate the structures and styles being discussed on their own. I suspect that many students at most undergraduate institutions never experience significant, useful musical learning.

Perhaps this realization should embolden us to make significant changes in the curriculum. Perhaps anything that follows an educationally sound sequence of instruction is better than what we have now. We might find that, by focusing on more skills but fewer concepts using Music Learning Theory, our students ultimately end up learning more. So, for example, knowing the rules for resolving diminished seventh chords might not prove as useful as audiating resolution tendencies for chords in general and figuring out intuitively (inferring) how the tendency tones in diminished seventh chord must resolve. Perhaps being given a template for writing a two-part invention is not as useful as learning the stylistic characteristics of inventions through listening and performance, and, eventually, writing an invention based on that audiated stylistic understanding.

What would such a curriculum look like? In its early semesters it would consist primarily of skills development as described above. By the second year, discrimination learning would give way increasingly to inference learning. Students would explore musical styles through listening and composition. Eventually they would be ready to look at scores while listening to music, and, finally, while audiating the music. Because they would have a strong audiated understanding of musical style, they could easily follow key changes and formal progressions in the written score because they could compare them to an audiated model.

Teaching this way is scary, because it means temporarily postponing topics from our long laundry list of instruction, topics that we think must be covered by the end of four semesters. Even changing the aural skills curriculum to include less dictation activities and more aural/oral, verbal association, and symbolic association activities at the beginning worries some instructors, because they see the goal of harmonic dictation of Bach chorales looming above them, and they feel that they must start climbing if they are going to reach their goal. Unfortunately, as in mountain climbing, failing to bring the right equipment means that we may never reach the top. Spending time to ensure that our students have mastered the basics will ultimately save us time and, more important, take them farther.

For music theory to be about theorizing, our students must have the fundamental skills necessary to hear and perform musical structures rather than read them in notation with little musical understanding. Such theorizing would prove useful to performers, educators, and scholars alike. Performers could explore ways of expressing musical structures discovered through analysis; educators would have the necessary skills to teach a skill-based curriculum; and scholars would be better equipped to compare and contrast musical styles in their research. In all cases, learning abstract theoretical concepts about music cannot occur without the necessary skills that must begin with the aural/oral level of discrimination learning.

## References

Gordon, E. E. (1989). *Advanced measures of music audiation.* Chicago: GIA Publications.

——. (2003). *Learning sequences in music: Skill, content, and patterns.* Chicago: GIA Publications.

Taggart, C. C., & Taggart, B. (1994). Sightsinging systems in use: A survey of college music theory programs. *Southeastern Journal of Music Education, 6,* 194-209.

*Bruce Dalby*
• • • • • • • • • •
UNIVERSITY OF NEW MEXICO

# Music Learning Theory Methods in the Undergraduate Music Theory and Ear Training Curriculum

## Introduction

For many young musicians, university music theory instruction represents the first systematic attempt to learn to understand the music they have spent many years singing or playing. These students' musical training prior to college has emphasized imitation—or, at best, the aural/oral level of skill sequence—with little attention to audiation development through appropriate instruction in higher level skills. These students may have learned to "recite" music with technical proficiency but without comprehension of its tonal and rhythmic characteristics, much as one might pronounce the sounds of a language without understanding the meaning of the words.

The music education profession seems not to question this state of affairs. It is considered acceptable for students to spend the elementary and secondary years of music instruction learning the "mechanics" of music, such as instrumental and vocal technique, decoding music notation, ensemble skills, and other abilities necessary for the successful functioning of school bands, orchestras, and choruses. Aural musicianship, namely the ability to comprehend the tonal and rhythmic characteristics of music, is viewed as a specialized skill for students who decide to major in music at the post-secondary level, and the freshman year of college is considered an appropriate time to begin its development.

Proponents of Music Learning Theory would prescribe a much earlier commencement of aural skill learning. At nine or more years past their music aptitude stabilization point, most entering freshman have missed the optimum "window of opportunity" for developing audiation skills. As Gordon reminds us, remediation is not possible.[1] Compensatory audiation instruction may be beneficial, but these students cannot regain the potential for music achievement that a richer musical upbringing would have permitted.

Responsibility for the enormous task of aural skill development at the university is delegated to the music theory faculty, and most freshmen begin the catch-up process in a music fundamentals class. Unfortunately, traditional music theory practice is founded on philosophical and methodological assumptions that are significantly at odds with the tenets of Music Learning Theory. The two fields differ not only about what to teach, but how, and in what sequence to teach it. From a Music Learning Theory perspective, the traditional music theory and ear training curriculum is neither an appropriate nor an efficient treatment for students' aural deficiencies.

There have been few opportunities to conduct university ear training instruction according to proper skill and content sequence. Traditional methods are well established, and their adherents are hesitant to question the status quo and give unbiased consideration to other approaches. Among the limited number of university professors who are knowledgeable about—and supportive of—Music Learning Theory, few are in a position to influence the theory and ear training curriculum. Little is known, therefore, about the effectiveness and appropriateness of a Music Learning Theory-based undergraduate ear training curriculum.

Since 1998 I have taught beginning undergraduate ear training using Music Learning Theory sequence and methods with first-year music education majors at the University of New Mexico. In this chapter, I compare traditional music theory and Music Learning Theory-based approaches to ear training, describe my ear training curriculum, make some preliminary evaluations of its effectiveness, and offer recommendations for further efforts in this direction.

## Music Learning Theory and Traditional Music Theory Approaches Compared

The differences between Music Learning Theory and traditional music theory approaches to ear training are numerous. In *Readings in Music Learning Theory*, Roger Dean provides a partial list of questionable music

---

[1] See Edwin E. Gordon, *Learning Sequences in Music: Skill, Content, and Patterns*, p. 233.

theory practices.[2] Among these are the use of inappropriate tonal and rhythm solfege systems and the practice of explaining "time signatures" and "key signatures" on the basis of theoretical analysis. These differences need not be revisited here, as they are general ways in which Music Learning Theory methodology is distinguished from various other approaches to music teaching, and are well documented elsewhere.[3]

Dean also addresses the following traditional music theory practices that contrast more directly with Music Learning Theory principles:

*Notation is used in an attempt to explain aural phenomena, thereby denying the independence of the ear from the eye.* Although inappropriate approaches to notation are common in music education, the emphasis on notation in traditional theory curricula is particularly pervasive. To a considerable degree, students continue to be taught to understand music through their eyes and intellect instead of through their ears. The result in many cases is further delay in the development of audiation.

*Primarily diatonic passages are stressed initially in sight-singing and dictation exercises at the expense of developing the student's ability to discriminate among pattern functions.* The logical orientation of music theory suggests that diatonic (stepwise) tonal patterns are easier to understand than patterns involving skips and are therefore the most appropriate starting point for initial ear training instruction. In contrast, Gordon advises music teachers to sequence the introduction of tonal patterns according to their frequency of occurrence in music literature and their audiational difficulty as determined by research. Gordon's research points to arpeggiated tonal patterns in the most familiar tonalities and tonal functions as the best starting place for tonal pattern instruction.[4]

*Tonal patterns and rhythm patterns are combined in initial dictation and in sight-singing exercises.* Tonal and rhythm content are kept separate in Learning Sequence Activities due to young children's inability to conserve musically. In other words, children are apt to confuse a change in rhythm content for a change in tonal content, and vice versa. There has been little study of the audiation abilities of undergraduates or of appropriate ear

---

[2] See Roger A. Dean, "Teacher Education and Music Learning Theory," *Readings in Music Learning Theory*, pp. 348-49.

[3] Gordon's explanations of tonal and rhythm solfege, including his criticisms of other systems in use, are found in Chapter 4 of *Learning Sequences in Music*. Discussions of meter classification and issues of time signature versus measure signature terminology are in Chapter 7. Tonality and keyality as they relate to traditional definitions of key signatures are discussed in Chapter 6.

[4] See *Learning Sequences in Music*, pp. 206-207.

training methodology for their unique combination of musical and intellectual maturity. It is clear, however, that the musical age of many freshmen lags far behind their chronological age. Until the conservation abilities of aurally deficient undergraduates can be better determined through research, the prudent course is to conduct Learning Sequence Activities with them in the same manner as that recommended for younger children, that is, with tonal and rhythm content kept separate.

To Dean's list of questionable music theory practices, I would add the following:[5]

*Study of theory begins before, or at best concurrently with, ear training.* Students are taught the *why* of musical elements before they have necessarily acquired the ability to understand those elements aurally. According to Music Learning Theory, it is essential to teach theoretical concepts only after audiation skills are well developed, just as language teaching addresses grammar—the theory of sentence construction—only after children have learned to think, speak, improvise, read, and write in their native tongue. Most undergraduates would benefit from an extended period of strictly aural/oral instruction before acquiring theoretical information.

*Musical elements tend to be studied out of context.* In Music Learning Theory, context is of supreme importance. In the tonal realm, for example, students are continually guided to audiate tonal elements in relation to a tonality, resting tone, and tonal functions. While contextual awareness is also an objective of music theory instruction, its logical frame of reference dictates first an extended step-by-step study of isolated musical elements. Much time is spent analyzing decontextualized notes, intervals, scales, and chords before students are required to audiate those phenomena in relation to a melodic phrase or chord progression. Tonality is not usually established before tonal elements are sounded, nor is meter established before rhythm patterns are played. Instead of movement activities designed to develop a kinesthetic awareness of rhythm, mathematical analysis is employed to develop an intellectual understanding of rhythmic relationships. Furthermore, intervals and chords are often treated as if they are always the same, regardless of context. The intervals SO-MI and RE-TI, for example, are both descending Minor thirds, but they are audiated very differently if heard as members of tonic and dominant functions, respectively, in Major.

---

[5] While there are undoubtedly theory instructors whose teaching is more congruent with Music Learning Theory principles, these generalizations are based on analysis of prominent theory texts and provide a representative picture of traditional practice.

Learning Sequence Activities are the Music Learning Theory equivalent of interval, scale, chord, and rhythm pattern studies in traditional music theory classes. Under both models, students learn to isolate the parts of music for close aural scrutiny. The differences in how this process is carried out, however, are striking. The tonal and rhythm patterns used in Learning Sequence Activities are derived directly from music literature that students have already listened to and sung. Properly taught, students develop a strong aural/oral foundation for tonal and rhythm content before engaging in detailed study of the elements of that content through Learning Sequence Activities. This tight linkage between the musical whole (literature, songs) and musical parts (tonal and rhythm patterns) is maintained throughout all levels of instruction. Students always experience new content (a new tonality or meter, a new tonal or rhythm function) in music literature. Their initial experience with new content is then followed closely by systematic analysis of that content through tonal and rhythm pattern instruction in Learning Sequence Activities.

In music theory classes, the connection to music literature is more tenuous. Ear training instruction generally commences immediately with the study of intervals, scales, chords, and rhythm patterns. Students do not usually listen to and sing songs containing specified content before commencing to analyze that content through various exercises. There is also little or no rote learning of literature. Further, the emphasis on singing from notation[6] lessens the likelihood that exercises and songs will become a part of the student's aural/oral foundation.

*Only Major and Minor tonalities are examined.* Rarely is consideration given to other tonalities such as Dorian, Mixolydian, and Lydian. Much of folk, popular, and classical music is thus ignored. Perhaps worse, students miss out on the tonal audiation development that is a natural outcome of exposure to a wide variety of contrasting tonalities.

## The Music Learning Theory-Based Ear Training Program

Beginning in the 1998-99 academic year, first-year music education majors met in special sections of ear training for each of the first two courses in the UNM music theory sequence. The ear training component of these courses met three times per week for fifty minutes—an excellent schedule for formal audiation training.[7] These students also received traditional instruction in written music theory from a different instructor two days per week.

---

[6] Sight-singing and sight-reading are the commonly used terms in the music theory world. Gordon's objections to the use of these terms can be found in *Learning Sequences in Music: Skill, Content, and Patterns*, p. 114.

*Classroom Activities*

Unlike other members of the music theory classes, the students in the Music Learning Theory ear training group purchased supplemental materials specifically for the ear training component. There were many resources I wished to use, but I had to be selective in order to limit the extra cost to these students. The choice was a difficult one: I could select materials to support Learning Sequence Activities or Classroom Activities, but not both. The Tonal and Rhythm Pattern Cassettes from *Jump Right In: The Music Curriculum* would have been an excellent resource for students to use in practicing Learning Sequence Activities, but I decided instead to focus on the music literature to be used in Classroom Activities. I considered it essential that class members have access to a rich variety of authentic musical materials to bolster their aural/oral foundation. The CD collections of familiar folk songs from *Jump Right In: The Instrumental Series* seemed ideally suited to this purpose. Each CD consists of 100 songs in various tonalities, keyalities, meters, and styles performed by top-flight wind and string instrumentalists with rhythm section accompaniment. The students also purchased some of the written materials coordinated with the folk song CDs.

A variety of Classroom Activities and related homework assignments were facilitated by the combination of aural and written materials from the folk song collections shown in Figure 1. Solo Book 1, which is coordinated with the *Simple Gifts* CD, contains the most simple, familiar songs, and is thus suitable for the most basic activities. These songs provided the content for most of the Classroom Activities during the first semester and much of the second semester. Activities included singing melodies and root melodies (individually and combined), harmonizing songs vocally, analyzing harmonic progressions of songs using related tonal patterns, analyzing rhythmic characteristics of songs using related rhythm patterns, improvising to song chord progressions, and engaging in rhythmic movement activities. During the second semester, students also used Volume 1 for in-class and out-of-class transcription exercises—or dictation, as it is more commonly called in traditional music theory. This process worked well, as students had the CD and writing book for this volume but not the reading book.

---

[7] Gordon considers three music class periods per week optimal for younger children, beyond which students reach a point of rapidly diminishing audiation learning returns. "Students need unstructured time to audiate what they have learned in music, just as they need unstructured time to think about what they have learned in other subjects." See Gordon, Edwin E. and David G. Woods "Reference Handbook for Using Learning Sequence Activities, Revised Edition" from *Jump Right In: The Music Curriculum*, p. 22.

| VOLUME | CD | PURPOSE | BOOK | PURPOSE |
|--------|-----|---------|------|---------|
| Solo Book 1 | *Simple Gifts* | General listening and singing exercises | Writing | Transcribing exercises |
| Solo Book 2 | *Don Gato* | General listening, singing, and reading exercises | Reading and Writing | Reading, writing, and transposing exercises |
| Solo Book 3 | Not used | | Reading | Music reading ("sight-singing") exercises |

*Figure 1.*

Solo Book 2, which is coordinated with the *Don Gato* CD, was also used for general listening and singing exercises. In addition, students acquired both the reading and writing books for this volume, which made possible a wide variety of notation-based activities. These included initial melodic reading exercises, early practice in writing melodic material in various keyalities and clefs (direct copying without transposing), and transposition assignments.

Solo Book 3 was most suitable for music reading exercises. The songs in Volume 3 are somewhat less familiar, on average, than those on the other two volumes, providing a better measure of whether students are actually reading music notation or just using the notation as a general reminder of melodic material they already know. Students purchased the reading book for this volume but not the CD. Music reading activities commenced late in the first semester and continued throughout the rest of the year.

Although the tonal and rhythm content of these materials is quite basic, they proved suitable for this group of students. Audiation skills at the beginning of the fall semester, as measured by students' performance on Gordon's *Iowa Tests of Music Literacy*, were rudimentary. Tonally, for example, the majority of these students upon entering the Music Theory I class could

THE DEVELOPMENT AND PRACTICAL APPLICATION OF MUSIC LEARNING THEORY

not aurally identify tonic and dominant functions in a simple folk song. Some students had fairly well-developed rhythm audiation, but many others were unable to distinguish between Duple and Triple meter, let alone identify various rhythm functions. The successful progress of this group of students is evidence that the instrumental series solo book materials are appropriate for initial use in college level ear-training instruction.

*Learning Sequence Activities*

I had latitude to use whatever methodology I wished for the special ear-training section, but these students had to be prepared to rejoin their peers in the traditional theory group for further coursework following their year with me. Because only two semesters were available to address major content objectives of both Music Learning Theory and traditional music theory approaches, the manner of selecting and sequencing tonal and rhythm patterns for use in Learning Sequence Activities was a crucial decision. A "pure" approach to Music Learning Theory calls for using the tonal and rhythm patterns found in the Tonal and Rhythm Register Books from *Jump Right In: The Music Curriculum* and delivering them according to students' music aptitude. After considerable thought, I decided this course of action would be unrealistic. Experiences at Pennsylvania State University during the 1980s support this judgment.[8] Learning Sequence Activities were used in the musicianship courses in the undergraduate music theory curriculum there. These classes completed two of twenty-one tonal and rhythm units from Book 1 in five weeks. At this pace, three semesters would have been needed just to get through Book 1. A modified approach was needed that would lead to faster progress while still remaining as true as possible to authentic Music Learning Theory procedures.

I concluded that the situation called for compromises similar to those found in *Jump Right In: The Instrumental Series*, in which all students study the same tonal and rhythm patterns. I used patterns from the instrumental series supplemented by others of my own choice. Although I did not deliver patterns according to students' music aptitudes and in the sequence prescribed by the register books, I followed all other principles of content and skill sequence. New tonal and rhythm content was always introduced in the recommended sequence. With regard to skill sequence, any given tonal or rhythm pattern was always experienced first at the aural/oral level, then verbal association, and so on.

---

8 See Maureen A. Carr, "The Importance of Sound Before Symbol in Developing Intuitive College Musicians," in *Readings in Music Learning Theory*, pp. 352-64.

Music reading commenced midway through the first semester, and Book One and Ensemble Book One from the instrumental series proved suitable for students' first experiences with notation. These books include several sets each of notated tonal and rhythm patterns that students had already practiced at lower skill levels before attempting symbolic association. In-class reading and writing exercises with these patterns were supplemented by work with different patterns of the same tonal and rhythm functions, plus patterns for other functions found in the solo book songs but not included in the instrumental series books. Because the instrumental series books use a limited range of keyalities, students were also assigned to write out some of the tonal pattern sets in all Major and Minor keys. These materials were useful for various in-class reading and writing exercises.

*Coordination of Classroom Activities and Learning Sequence Activities*

I was careful to observe Gordon's rules for coordinating Classroom Activities and Learning Sequence Activities. These rules provide an elegant framework for effective, efficient audiation instruction. Although my experience with Music Learning Theory to this point was considerable, I had had little opportunity for sustained audiation teaching. It was satisfying, therefore, to be able to guide the students through a wide variety of properly sequenced activities. New content (a new tonality or tonal function, a new meter or rhythm function, etc.) was always introduced in a song. Singing the melodies and root melodies of the song established basic aural/oral familiarity with the new content. Subsequent close analysis of new content through Learning Sequence Activities provided the basis for higher level activities with the same songs upon returning to classroom activities.

The following sequence illustrates an approach to teaching the tonal structure of the first four macrobeats of "Go Tell Aunt Rhody" by referring to relevant tonal patterns previously taught in Learning Sequence Activities (Figure 2 shows the notation for "Go Tell Aunt Rhody" in C Major):

*Figure 2.*

- Teacher establishes tonality by performing tonic-dominant-tonic in C Major at the piano (see Figure 3):

*Figure 3.*

- Teacher sings a segment of the song (melodic pattern) using a neutral syllable, gesturing at the end of the segment for students to echo.
- Students sing the song segment.
- Teacher sings the tonal pattern MI-DO, then provides an appropriate gesture[9] indicating for students to echo the pattern.
- Students echo the tonal pattern.
- Teacher repeats the melodic pattern with students echoing.

Tonal characteristics of other sections of the song can be analyzed in the same manner. The rhythmic content of songs can also be revealed in similar fashion using related rhythm patterns (in this case, the rhythm pattern would be Du, Du de, Du, Du). Similar study of more complex songs becomes possible as the class progresses through higher levels of tonal and rhythm content.

In my experience, university students' reactions to activities of this type are similar to those of younger students: attention and concentration are high, and there is genuine interest in learning to understand the under-lying tonal and rhythmic structure of music literature. Music Learning Theory provides students with the necessary sequence, establishing proper readiness for introducing new content or a new skill applied to content previously practiced at lower skill levels. When these processes are conducted thoroughly, classes can undertake subsequent verbal analysis of music (theoretical understanding) with greater effectiveness. In the above example, the teacher might note the presence of the passing tone RE in the initial melodic pattern from "Go Tell Aunt Rhody" outlined by the tonal pattern MI-DO. If students first learn to audiate musical passages through

---

[9] For information about proper procedures, timing, and gestures for Learning Sequence Activities, see Robert Harper, "General Techniques for Teaching Learning Sequence Activities" in *Readings in Music Learning Theory*, pp. 105-128.

an appropriate methodology, such theoretical analysis has the potential to further enhance overall musical understanding.

*Content*

I covered a wide range of content during the two-semester ear training program, including the following tonal functions: 1) Major tonality—tonic, dominant, subdominant, supertonic, submediant, and secondary dominants built on RE ($V^7/V^7$) and LA ($V^7/ii$); 2) Minor tonality—tonic, dominant, subdominant, and tonic and dominant of the relative Major; 3) Dorian tonality—tonic, subdominant, and subtonic; and 4) Mixolydian tonality—tonic and subtonic. Rhythm content included macrobeats, microbeats, divisions, elongations, ties, and rests in Usual Duple, Usual Triple, and Unusual meter. I also taught ties and rests in Duple and Triple meter.

*Coordinating with Written Theory Activities*

Students began the study of traditional music theory immediately in the companion written theory class. Some violations of ideal learning sequence were necessary, therefore, to help the students in the Music Learning Theory group relate the audiation activities of the ear training class to the processes and terminology taught in music theory. For example, because traditional music theory approaches typically prescribe considerable study of scales and intervals, I spent time analyzing scales and intervals in relation to the tonal syllables and tonal functions we were studying in ear training.

Traditional music theory courses focus primarily on music of the "common practice" era of the Western art music tradition. Although this music shares most of the tonal and rhythmic characteristics of the familiar folk songs used in the Music Learning Theory ear training group, there are a few important differences. For example, folk songs generally do not use the cadential six-four chord found so frequently in the compositions of common practice composers such as Haydn and Mozart. Also, the half cadence in common practice music differs somewhat from the use of secondary dominant chords (such as $V^7/V^7$) found in familiar folk songs. Differences of these types were quite easily clarified using standard Classroom Activity and Learning Sequence Activity processes.

Part writing rules of the common practice era also comprise a significant component of music theory instruction. Although these rules are often taught through a strictly theoretical process, their audiational basis can be revealed through appropriate aural analysis. For example, the stepwise downward movement of the seventh of the dominant chord to the third of the tonic chord in an authentic cadence was familiar to class members as the result of tonal pattern instruction in Learning Sequence Activities and the vocal harmonization of simple songs in classroom activities. It was a relatively simple matter to relate that aural experience to the appropriate part writing procedure.

*Student Evaluation*

Student progress was measured by in-class quizzes every other week. These quizzes included both individual performance and written response tasks. Individual performance tasks included the following: a) singing song melodies and bass lines, b) echoing tonal and rhythm patterns at verbal association, generalization, and improvisation skill levels, c) reading tonal and rhythm patterns and melodic phrases, and d) improvising to chord progressions from the songs. Although performance tasks are arguably the most important to evaluate, limitations of class time necessitated considerable emphasis on notated responses, in which the entire class answers each quiz item for later checking by the instructor. Written tasks in quizzes were similar to the "dictation" exercises used in traditional ear-training classes. In Music Learning Theory terminology, these are generalization tasks in which the student hears a musical example (a tonal pattern, rhythm pattern, melodic pattern, complete melody, chord progression, or chordal accompaniment) sounded at the piano or with a neutral syllable and then identifies the example in notation.

**Evaluations and Recommendations**

Although the ear training program described in this chapter is relatively new, and no formal research has yet been conducted to measure its effectiveness, I can offer some preliminary evaluations. First, and not surprisingly, entering undergraduate music majors display a wide range of audiation abilities. Music achievement pretesting—as well as curricular efforts over six semesters—supported this assessment. Some students progressed through all levels of skill and content undertaken in the class with little difficulty, while others struggled with the most basic aural discriminations. In light of what Gordon tells us about developmental and stabilized music aptitude,[10] audiation development should be considered a "use it or lose it" proposition. Students who miss out on early opportunities to develop aural skills are apt to be at a lifelong disadvantage.

---

[10] See Chapter 3, "Music Aptitudes and Music Achievement," of *Learning Sequences in Music: Skill, Content, and Patterns.*

Individual differences aside, diligent students in the Music Learning Theory ear training classes made significant progress in improving their audiation abilities. Many students performed very well with an ambitious set of content and skill objectives. I have no objective support beyond anecdotal evidence for the long-term practical effectiveness of the ear training program, but I have been encouraged by the readiness with which most of the participants entered an introductory improvisation course required of music education majors at the University of New Mexico. Many of these students were beginning improvisers, yet made excellent progress in developing skill and fluency in improvising to the simple folk tunes used in the class.

Due to differences in the student populations, instructors and course objectives, it is difficult to make comparisons to students in the other ear training sections. "Winning the argument" about ear training methodology is not as easy as running a simple experiment for a year or two and comparing post-test scores. The relatively brief instructional period of two semesters is a further factor bearing on the question of the effectiveness of the aural training. Given the considerable audiation deficiencies that many freshmen bring to their first semester of university ear training, a four-semester sequence of Music Learning Theory-based instruction might be required for the majority of students to achieve proficient levels of aural skill.

The importance of individual practice is clear. University ear training must play "catch-up" relative to a daunting number of content and skill objectives, and class time alone, for most students, is inadequate to the task. As stated earlier, the majority of class materials supported Classroom Activities. Providing appropriate individual practice aids for Learning Sequence Activities was a particular challenge. Students enrolled during the first semester of this program (Fall 1998) were assigned to work with the cassette tapes from *Jump Right In: The Instrumental Series*, which include recorded series of tonal and rhythm patterns at the aural/oral and verbal association skill levels. These materials were of some benefit, but their effectiveness was limited by a lack of user feedback and a somewhat narrow range of tonal and rhythm content. This problem led me to begin developing *Audiation Assistant*, a computer-based program for individual practice with tonal and rhythm patterns. Students worked with a primitive early version of this software beginning late in Fall 1998 and served as beta users of the evolving product during subsequent semesters until the final version 1.0 of *Audiation Assistant* became available in Spring 2000. Results of this training with *Audiation Assistant* were promising and pointed to the potential further usefulness of technology-assisted instruction in accord with Music Learning Theory principles.

The future of the Music Learning Theory ear training program at UNM is clouded somewhat by shifting curricular and staffing issues. For example, the initial plan was for graduates of my ear training program to be assigned for their second year of ear training to an instructor whose philosophy and methods were compatible with Music Learning Theory principles. Unfortunately, this instructor was later reassigned, and his curriculum was replaced by another based on fixed-DO tonal solfege, a dire prospect for students immersed for a year in moveable DO. The search for a compatible continuation of instruction for this group of students is, therefore, an ongoing issue. Problems of this sort reflect the minority position of the Music Learning Theory philosophy. One hopes that with continuing exposure to effective models of the Music Learning Theory approach, the rest of the music education profession will gradually come to value audiation development as a prime curricular goal in every music classroom.

## References

Dalby, B. F. (2000). *Audiation assistant*. Chicago: GIA Publications.

Gordon, E. E. (1991). *Iowa tests of music literacy*. Chicago: GIA Publications.

——. (1997). *Learning sequences in music: Skill, content, and patterns*. Chicago: GIA Publications.

Gordon, E, E., & Woods, D. G. (1990). Reference handbook for using Learning Sequence Activities (Rev. ed.). *Jump Right In: The Music Curriculum*. Chicago: GIA Publications.

Grunow, R. F., Gordon, E. E., & Azzara, C. D. (1993). *Jump right in: The instrumental series*. Chicago: GIA Publications.

Taggart, C. C., & Walters, D. L. (Eds.). (1989). *Readings in Music Learning Theory*. Chicago: GIA Publications.

*Warren Henry*

UNIVERSITY OF NORTH TEXAS

# The Application of Music Learning Theory in the University Methods Class

## Introduction

Music teacher education places university professors in the unique role of providing a foundation of knowledge and skills upon which students' professional careers as music teachers will be based. Often, the professor chooses content reflective of his or her own philosophical foundation, areas the professor deems necessary for a successful future in music education. The wealth of information available for music educators, combined with the requisite musical skills needed for classroom teaching, can become overwhelming as professors make decisions regarding what to teach or what not to teach. Ultimately, this affects curricula and, thus, the future work of music teachers.

The scope of course content areas may include, for example, the National Standards, curricular development, lesson planning, learning theories, and teaching methodologies. Musical skill areas often include piano proficiency, conducting, error detection, and sight-singing. Additional but often overlooked skill areas must also include competency in teaching. This includes not only teaching a lesson with appropriate sequencing, monitoring, transitions, and closure, but also developing musical skills in a sequenced manner appropriate to the learner.

In light of limited instructional time, professors in teacher education programs must give careful consideration to the *process* of sequential instruction in order to have a successful *product*—the effective music educator. A review of literature by Verrastro and Leglar (1992) identified presage as an additional consideration for teacher education programs. They define presage as an attempt to predict "professional effectiveness on the basis of personal qualities, academic standing, aptitude, or intellectual and musical competencies" (p. 676).

Gordon's Music Learning Theory, identified by the Music Educators National Conference as one of five major approaches to music education (Shehan, 1989), focuses on such content and skills as aptitude, audiation, sequence, pattern instruction, and improvisation, all of which reflect the components of presage, process, and product. The benefits of incorporating Music Learning Theory into methods classes are twofold. It can enable both the professor and preservice teacher to explore presage, process, and product and how they affect 1) the musical development of children and 2) the teacher's effectiveness in a teaching setting.

The following sections will examine the practical application of Music Learning Theory in the methods classroom and its relationship with the educational components of presage, process, and product.[1] Each component is examined in the context of music teacher education.

## Music Learning Theory: Presage to Process

A distinguishing component of Music Learning Theory is pattern instruction, the teaching of a taxonomy of rhythm patterns and tonal patterns sequenced according to difficulty at various skill levels.[2] Tonal pattern instruction is separated from rhythm pattern instruction, each of which serves to build a music language vocabulary. For the first few classes of the semester, the professor can present pattern instruction for the students, eventually having the students assume the teaching role.

In a methods class, students can engage in pattern instruction. Depending on the class size and available space, small groups can be created to provide more teaching opportunities. Student-led pattern instruction places students in a teaching role, thereby allowing the professor to evaluate the student's potential in the areas of leadership, singing accuracy, aural skills, and pacing (presage). Although pattern instruction takes as little as five minutes, some professors may want to request cassette or videotape assignments. Consider the following assignment:

---

[1] For additional information on Music Learning Theory in the college curriculum, see Hobbs (1989).

[2] See *Jump Right In: The Music Curriculum* (1986).

**Example 1:** *Tape Assignment:* On a cassette tape, perform a series of twelve tonal patterns, using an equal number of tonic, dominant, and sub-dominant patterns. Do not start and stop the tape.

Rather than hearing students only in class throughout the semester, this type of assignment could provide an opportunity to hear all students individually and provide written feedback. Admittedly, students could write down the patterns beforehand and then sing them to the recorder. However, pattern competency, including other aural competency skills, must ultimately be demonstrated live in a final aural exam.

Songs and chants of various tonalities and meters, which are essential to Music Learning Theory, give children opportunities to make comparisons and therefore better understand the complexity of tonalities and meters. "The rationale is that learning what something is not is part of learning what it is" (Walters, 1992, p. 542). College students without a rich aural background may find various modal and rhythmic songs initially difficult to perform, in large part, according to Hobbs (1989), due to their own limited abilities to audiate. He states:

> That is the case despite the advanced level of their instrumental technique, the beauty of their voices, their intellectual understanding of music rudiments, and even their advanced but mechanistic music reading ability. Of still greater concern to post-secondary instructors and administrators should be the fact that many of those aurally immature students leave our institutions with degrees in hand, but with little improvement in ear-related activities. (p. 333)

Proficiency in performing patterns and songs of various tonalities and meters is another criterion upon which to assess each student's musicianship, and therefore his or her potential as a music educator. Elliott's (1995) praxial philosophy of music education suggests that an accurate assessment of students' musicianship and musical knowledge can only be measured through their own music making. He states:

> *Our musical knowledge is in our actions; our musical thinking and knowing are in our musical doing and making.* In other words, a performer's musical understanding is exhibited not in what a performer says about what he or she does; a performer's musical understanding is exhibited in the quality of what she gets done in and through her actions of performing. (p. 57)

Therefore, requiring college students to become familiar and proficient with song literature of different tonalities and meters a) improves students' aural skills and, therefore, their musicianship, b) challenges students and allows them to experience what their students will experience, and c) develops an attitude that classroom music or beginning instrumental music can be more than a series of unrelated activities that have no musical value.

Music education students' images of beginning instruction are often inaccurate. Generally, the perception, both for instrumental and vocal students, is one that is characterized by trivial games, amusical three-note songs, and little application or need for musicianship. Music Learning Theory activities can address these misperceptions. Consider the following activity, which is appropriate for older elementary students (assuming readiness) while at the same time challenging for college students.

> **Example 2:** *Activity:* Ask college students to stand in a circle and pair off in groups of two. The activity is similar to call and response. The first person sings a tonic pattern, and the second person responds with an improvised tonic pattern. Repeat the process with a sub-dominant pattern, dominant pattern, and finally a tonic pattern. Have each group perform until all students have participated. This activity can also be applied in an instrumental methods class.

When college students' musicianship is challenged in new ways, they realize that children can meet these *same* challenges, and thus develop a new understanding and appreciation for the process and possibilities of elementary instruction. These activities should be followed by discussions and examples of how to sequence instruction in order to achieve this skill level (process). Other areas of discussion should include how these activities may fit with approaches such as those of Orff, Kodály, or Dalcroze[3] as well as meet content expectations for the National Standards.

The National Standards were developed in part to bring continuity to music education across the United States; they are written under the framework of nine content standards for grades K-4, 5-8, and 9-12. Specifically, the standards were designed "to guide reform in PreK-12 music as America moves toward the 21st century" (MENC, 1994, p. 3). Clearly, if the standards are to have an impact on the future of music education, teacher education programs must weave the standards into course syllabi and model how the standards can be applied in school music

---

[3] For application of Music Learning Theory with Suzuki, Orff, Kodály, or Dalcroze, see Walters, D. L. and C. C. Taggart (1989).

programs. Music Learning Theory activities are an effective means by which to comply to the suggested content and achievement standards.

For example, Content Standard #3 is described as "Improvising melodies, variations, and accompaniments." The activity suggested in Example 2 would meet the K-4 Content Standard #3a: "improvise 'answers' in the same style to given rhythmic and melodic phrases." (MENC, 1994, p. 14). An extension of this activity (see Example 3) could included improvising simple harmonic accompaniments, meeting the 5-8 Content Standard #3a: "improvise simple harmonic accompaniments" (p. 18). This can be very challenging for preservice teachers who have missed these opportunities in their own musical training. It is critical for methods instructors to realize that many music educators who are expected to teach to the standards may themselves still need to master those skills they will be teaching.

> **Example 3:** *Harmonization Activity:* 1) Ask class to sing "Home on the Range." 2) Identify the function of the underlying harmonies. 3) Split class in half. One group sings the melody, and one group sings the newly discovered bass line.[4]

Another critical component of Music Learning Theory is movement and its relationship to music. Gordon suggests classroom learning experiences based on the elements of movement identified by Laban (1971): time, weight, space, and flow. Most college students are uncomfortable and inhibited when asked to move freely. However, if movement experiences are introduced simply with gradual progressions to more complicated exploration activities, methods students will become less inhibited and begin to realize the connection between music and movement. College students have often commented on their improved conducting skills after exploration of time, weight, space, and flow. More important, if future music educators are to use movement for musical development,[5] then they themselves must first be comfortable with expressive movement so that they can model for their students.

## Music Learning Theory: Process to Product

Central to these exercises is the study of how persons learn. Questions regarding such issues as sequence, motivation, assessment, and retention

---

[4] An excellent resource for activities of this kind may be found in Azzara, C. D., R. F. Grunow, and E. E. Gordon (1997). *Creativity in Improvisation.*

[5] K-4 Content Standard #6e: "Respond through purposeful movement to selected prominent music characteristics or to specific music events while listening to music" (MENC, 1994, p. 15).

should be at the core of the Music Learning Theory curriculum. However, preservice teachers tend to spend many hours in the practice room developing their expertise as a performer and not enough time engaged in pedagogical inquiry and problem-solving.

Music Learning Theory provides an excellent framework from which to develop effective teaching skills. Structuring Learning Sequence Activities for preservice teachers throughout a sixteen-week methods class can establish effective teaching behaviors that will last throughout their careers. For the purposes of this paper, discussion of effective teaching behaviors will be limited to readiness, sequence, and motivation.

## Readiness

Consider this example. Teacher: "If it's 25 degrees Celsius in Kalamazoo, Michigan, what would it be in Fahrenheit?" Student: "Gee, I can't answer that cuz I don't even know how far it is from Kalamazoo to Fahrenheit."[6] In this instance, the student is not ready to learn because of a lack of basic knowledge. Musically, consider how often we observe new teachers asking students to demonstrate skills for which they are not ready. For example, teachers may ask students to identify and sing the solfege syllables of a tonal pattern. Identification is simple, because it can be "mathematically" calculated (line-space-line-space). Singing the pattern, however, is more difficult and often unsuccessful, leaving new teachers baffled. They fail to realize that their students do not yet have the requisite aural foundation (audiation readiness) necessary to perform the pattern accurately; their students cannot yet think in sound.

Determining readiness is sometimes defined in the education literature as task analysis. Simply stated, a task analysis breaks the learning process down to its component parts and sequences the steps necessary to complete the task. This enables the teacher to select an objective with the appropriate level of difficulty; the student must achieve each step before continuing to the next step. *Jump Right In: The Music Curriculum* (Taggart, Bolton, Reynolds, Valerio, & Gordon, 1999) incorporates necessary readiness and serves as an excellent model for preservice teachers. The curriculum provides many sequential activities appropriate for the music classroom. Children's musicianship is developed through activities using songs, games, movement, and listening examples. Also included are tonal and rhythm units, each designed to meet several criteria. Only when each criterion is met can the student move to the next unit.

---

6 Adapted from Cummings, C. (1990), p. 49.

## Sequence

By giving methods classes the opportunity to experience these units and developmentally appropriate activities, preservice teachers develop an understanding of the importance of readiness, a concept upon which teaching sequences are built (Walters, 1992). Music Learning Theory is an excellent model for sequential learning and provides a springboard from which to make comparisons with other learning theories, such as those suggested by Piaget, Bruner, and Gagné. When students experience the step from partial synthesis to symbolic association, for example, they are forced to think about the process and how it can affect the quality of a child's music education. Eventually, the concept of sequence becomes cemented and ultimately is transferred to all aspects of teaching. The result, or *product*, is a teacher who effectively demonstrates an understanding of process by sequencing instruction based on readiness, which, in turn, motivates students to learn.

## Motivation

Motivation is perhaps one of the most important aspects of teaching, for without it, students can become listless, disinterested, and detached from the subject matter. Students direct their attention to subjects with varying degrees of intensity. According to Cummings (1990), the teacher's dilemma is "to get students to direct their attention toward school tasks with an acceptable degree of effort" (p. 125). Atkinson (1964) argues that internal motivation, or intrinsic motivation, is a combination of a student's expected success and the value of the task. In other words, students will not exert any effort if they feel they have no control over their success. Moreover, if the value of the task is questioned ("Why do we have to do this anyway?"), student effort will diminish.

The sequenced patterns of Music Learning Theory can help explain theories of motivation for preservice teachers. Pattern instruction is also skill development, sequenced in small steps. When students successfully achieve each skill level, their feeling of self-worth increases, and their perception of self-ability improves. The sequence of pattern instruction facilitates incremental musical growth, with each step as an opportunity for individuals to experience success. Effective instruction (awareness of sequence and readiness) controls motivation, and when preservice teachers apply this knowledge in a contextual setting, their own motivation for teaching increases.

When instruction is individualized, teachers can better serve the needs of students. Perhaps one of the greatest strengths of Music Learning

Theory is that it focuses on each student as an individual. Preservice teachers do not typically think of individualizing instruction. In fact, the label "classroom music" or "group lessons" implies the antithesis of individualized instruction. Focusing on the individual learner, however, is necessary, because elementary music classrooms contain children with a wide variety of skill levels and aptitudes. Early childhood music programs are becoming more common, but they are still not the norm for preschool children. Future early elementary music teachers will face groups of children, some of whom may have had five years in a music development program and some of whom have had little experience with music. The disparity among students increases with each grade level as many students begin some type of instrumental instruction. Clearly, the need to focus on students individually is critical to effective teaching. Preservice teachers must understand this responsibility.

Gordon has designed several aptitude measures,[7] each of which is designed to determine the musical potential of individual students. The data from these tests allow teachers to tailor their instruction to each individual. This gives teachers a realistic understanding of what to expect. With this knowledge, instruction can be tailored to suit the needs of each student. Pattern instruction is designed with easy, medium, and difficult patterns specifically for this reason.

Practicum teachers often have failed lessons because their objectives do not match the skill levels of all students. For example, the teacher may give each student an opportunity to play a complex rhythmic ostinato while others play the melodic line. One student may have the skill and aptitude to successfully complete the task while another student may not. The result is frustration for the student, teacher, and peers, which could have been avoided if the ostinato had been tailored to meet the individual's skill level. Rather than asking "Why aren't they getting this?," the preservice teacher should be learning to make pedagogical decisions based on students' aptitude and skills. Failure to recognize individual differences among students can result in wasted time for both the teacher and learner.

## Conclusions

In *Music Matters: A New Philosophy of Music Education*, David Elliott (1995) states: "The future of music education—and, perhaps, the future of education itself—lies in facing our problems as challenges, in supporting our fellow practitioners, and in inducting new teachers into our practice so

---

[7] See *Audie* (1989), *Primary Measures of Music Audiation* (1979), *Intermediate Measures of Music Audiation* (1982), and *Music Aptitude Profile* (1988).

that all students in all schools can achieve the profound values of music education" (p. 310). The methods class is only one step in a learning process that continues throughout one's professional career. However, it is a setting in which attitudes and habits are formed, which means methods instructors need to be judicious with their curricular choices.

Certainly central to any teacher education program is the attention to presage, process, and product. Is the student suited for teaching, and does the student "have what it takes" to succeed (presage)? Are curricula and course content sequenced appropriately to set students up for optimum success (process)? Finally, is the new teacher (product) from the teacher education program representative of what the university expects of its graduates?

These questions, although directed toward teacher education programs, are the same questions that can be asked when designing methods curricula for classroom use. Music Learning Theory is one means of exploring the ideas of presage, process, and product. It places musicianship at the core, while still attending to individual needs and shows students that readiness and sequence directly affect teaching success. With this foundation, students will be capable of successful teaching in whatever area they choose to teach.

## References

Atkinson, J. W. (1964). *An introduction to motivation.* Princeton, NJ: Van Nostrand.

Azzara, C. D., Grunow, R. F., & Gordon, E. E. (1997). *Creativity in improvisation.* Chicago: GIA Publications.

Cummings, C. (1990). *Teaching makes a difference.* Edmonds, WA: Teaching.

Elliott, D. J. (1995). *Music matters: A new philosophy of music education.* New York: Oxford University Press.

Gordon, E. E. (1979). *Primary measures of music audiation.* Chicago: GIA Publications.

——. (1982). *Intermediate measures of music audiation.* Chicago: GIA Publications.

——. (1988). *Music aptitude profile.* Chicago: GIA Publications.

——. (1989). *Audie: A game for understanding and analyzing your child's music potential.* Chicago: GIA Publications.

Hobbs, W. (1989). Implementing Music Learning Theory within a college curriculum. In D. L. Walters & C. C. Taggart (Eds.), *Readings in Music Learning Theory* (333-342). Chicago: GIA Publications.

Laban, R. (1971). *The mastery of movement.* London: London MacDonald and Evans.

Music Educators National Conference (1994). *The school music program: A new vision.* Reston, VA: Music Educators National Conference.

Shehan, P. K. (1986). Major approaches to music education: An account of method. *Music Educators Journal,* 72(6), 26-31.

Taggart, C. C., Bolton, B., Reynolds, A., Valerio, W., & Gordon, E. E. (1999). *Jump right in: The music curriculum.* Chicago: GIA Publications.

Verrastro, R., & Leglar, M. (1992). Music teacher education. In Colwell, R. (Ed.). *Handbook of research on music teaching and learning* (pp. 676-696). New York: Schirmer.

Walters, D. L., & Taggart, C. C. (Eds.). (1989). *Readings in Music Learning Theory.* Chicago: GIA Publications.

Walters, D. L. (1992). Sequencing for efficient learning. In R. Colwell (Ed.). *Handbook of research on music teaching and learning* (pp. 535-545). New York: Schirmer.

# Appendix

## Sample Activities/Assignments

1. *Activity:* Give each college student a tennis ball. As the class bounces their tennis balls to the big beat, the teacher (leader) chants rhythms on a neutral syllable to be echoed by the class. Allow individuals to call the rhythms for class. Variations: Leader calls the rhythm, and the class or individual improvises a response. Rhythms may be chanted with a neutral syllable or with rhythm mnemonics. Rhythms may be chanted in duple, triple, and mixed meter.

2. *Activity:* After discovering the harmonic structure of a simple folk song, ask the class to improvise a new melody using the same harmonic structure. Next, assign each phrase of the song to an individual and have him or her perform the improvised melody. Follow this activity by having individuals improvise the entire song while the class sings the bass line. Be sure to perform songs in Major and Minor/Duple and Triple.

3. *Activity:* Teacher sings a tonic pattern, class echoes; teacher sings a dominant pattern, class echoes. However, if the teacher sings a Minor tonic pattern, the class (or individual) sings the pattern in Major. If the teacher sings a Major tonic pattern, the class (or individual) sings the pattern in Minor. For the dominant patterns, the class (or individual) improvises a different dominant pattern.

4. *Assignment:* Choose three folk songs. On a cassette tape, perform each song as written, followed by two more performances of the same song sung in a different mode. A total of at least five modes should be represented.

*Colleen Conway/M. Christina Schneider*
● ● ● ● ● ● ● ● ● ● ● ● ● ● ● ● ● ● ● ● ● ● ● ● ● ● ● ● ● ●
UNIVERSITY OF MICHIGAN/SOUTH CAROLINA DEPARTMENT OF EDUCATION

# Music Learning Theory and Instrumental Methods Curricula

## Introduction

Instrumental music teachers in university music education programs must be properly prepared to ensure the future success of instrumental music in the public schools. However, college graduates often enter the music education profession without the necessary understanding of how children learn music (Dean, 1989; Hobbs, 1989). In addition, although many of these graduates are considered fine performers, they often lack the necessary tonal and rhythm skills to teach others. Many graduates are not able to guide students through music development, nor can they accompany a simple folk song, diagnose problems in a rehearsal, conduct a musical ensemble, or improvise (Hobbs, 1989). In discussing the effects of the Music Educators National Conference (MENC) National Standards for K-12 music instruction on teacher education, scholars (Hope, 1995; MENC, 1994; Shuler, 1995) have reiterated the need for teachers to posses the following: strong tonal and rhythm skills; the ability to create, evaluate, and improvise music; and the knowledge to accurately measure and evaluate music perform- ances of students. An understanding of Music Learning Theory and the ability to audiate will provide preservice teachers with specific techniques for instructing students in the content areas outlined in contemporary learning standards. College methods professors should incorporate Music Learning Theory into instrumental methods courses so that preservice teachers develop their audiation skills and improve their independent musicianship. By experiencing Music Learning Theory as a part of their own learning process, preservice teachers will be better prepared to guide their future students through the same process. In this chapter, we address this need and discuss the practical application of Music Learning Theory in the undergraduate instrumental methods course curriculum.

A successful instrumental music teacher must have an understanding of how children learn music and an understanding of how to organize classroom lesson and rehearsal activities to best facilitate this learning. Therefore, the focus of the instrumental methods curriculum should be the development of music skills and concepts (i.e., audiation skills, rhythm learning, tonal learning) as well as discussion of non-music topics (i.e., scheduling, budgets, instrument repair). Too often, the balance between the development of music skills and non-music topics is too heavily placed on the latter. In addition to developing music skills, presenting teaching techniques, and discussing the administration and organization of an instrumental program, methods course instructors must also design class activities that allow preservice teachers to build the thinking and decision-making skills necessary for success in teaching (Atterbury, 1994; Barry, 1996; Conway, 1998a; Gromko, 1995; & Robbins, 1993). University faculty can use Music Learning Theory in instrumental methods curricula to help students meet all of these methods course goals, while also developing a variety of teaching techniques that will help students become more successful as teachers.

**Instrumental Methods Curriculum Designs.**

A variety of curriculum designs are used to meet certification requirements for instrumental music education. Most programs include some combination of general teaching methods courses, instrument methods courses (e.g., brass class, string class), elementary instrumental methods, secondary instrumental methods, and music education beginning instruments ensemble. Due to the fact that the time allocated to these courses and the curricula presented in each course is different from university to university, it is impractical to establish universal recommendations for the specific curricular inclusion of Music Learning Theory into the instrumental music education program. However, the instrumental music education instructor who recognizes the need for Music Learning Theory in the instrumental curriculum can determine the most suitable place for its incorporation.

Methods curricula often include anecdotal information regarding classroom survival based on the public school experience of the instructor. Although this information is valuable, methods course instructors should also provide students with specific techniques for teaching and opportunities

386

for students to practice these techniques for better understanding. This may best be accomplished by incorporating a skills session into the instrumental methods curricula, so that students may practice being both teachers and students. Students may practice techniques for teaching songs by rote, delivering tonal-pattern instruction, delivering rhythm-pattern instruction, and guiding improvisation development in this setting.

## Prerequisite Skills for Instrumental Music Education Students

Although most undergraduate instrumentalists are capable of performing music on their instruments from notation, these students may or may not be able to audiate notation. To become a successful music educator, the preservice teacher must be able to sing, chant, move, and audiate. In the ideal university setting, basic musicianship course instructors (ear-training and sight-singing) use Music Learning Theory to advance the musicianship of undergraduate students (Hobbs, 1989). Students then enter the instrumental methods sequence equipped with strong audiation and improvisation skills that prepare them to understand the ways that children learn music and to perfect their techniques for guiding students' audiation development. However, in many situations the instrumental methods instructor may need to offer skill sessions outside of the instrumental methods class or may need to incorporate skill sessions into the instrumental methods class activities so that students may acquire fundamental music skills.

Gordon (2003) suggests that adult musicians who have not had a strong music environment as children or who do not possess average or high music aptitude may not yet have guided themselves through the types and stages of preparatory audiation. Thus, undergraduate music majors who either cannot accurately sing songs or tonal patterns with a sense of tonality or who cannot accurately chant rhythm patterns with a sense of internal pulse or meter have not left the acculturation, imitation, or assimilation types of preparatory audiation. For those students, methods course instructors may need to provide skill sessions that incorporate movement activities using flow, space, weight, and time while establishing a listening vocabulary. Students should also receive rote-song, root-melody, tonal-pattern (both in Major and Minor tonalities), and rhythm-pattern instruction (in Usual Duple meter, Usual Triple meter, and Unusual meters) through the incorporation of those types of movement activities. Once preservice teachers are capable of singing (imitating) tonal patterns while coordinating their breathing and flowing movement and have developed a broad listening vocabulary, they will have developed the readiness to begin

Learning Sequence Activities as presented in *Jump Right In: The Instrumental Series* (Grunow, Gordon, & Azzara, 2001).

Concurrent with delivering rote-song, root-melody, tonal-pattern, and rhythm-pattern instruction, the instrumental methods instructor must introduce the development of executive skills, mouthpiece placement, instrument hand positions, and articulation styles on instruments. Although music and movement activities may be necessary in the beginning of the semester, preservice teachers will develop quickly the ability to coordinate their breathing and flowing movement while singing and chanting, so that the methods course instructor will later be able to use the time first devoted to vocabulary development for other purposes.

## Preservice Teachers Delivering Learning Sequence Instruction

The methods course instructor must present and discuss with students the types and stages of preparatory audiation as well as the types and stages of audiation. Preservice teachers who experience the music development process themselves through developmentally appropriate instruction will understand from personal experience how students learn music. Those preservice teachers will be capable of bringing meaning to Music Learning Theory and the teaching techniques recommended when teaching is based in Music Learning Theory.

In addition to listening vocabulary readiness as found in *Music Play* (Valerio, Reynolds, Taggart, Bolton, & Gordon, 1998), Learning Sequence Activities and music content, as found in *Jump Right In: The Instrumental Series* (Grunow, Gordon, & Azzara, 2001), and improvisation development, as found in *Creativity in Improvisation* (Azzara, Grunow, & Gordon, 1997), preservice teacher instruction opportunities and development of preservice teacher reflection skills need to be an integral component of the methods course curriculum. Preservice teachers are ready to teach Learning Sequence Activities when they are a) capable of coordinating songs and chants with their breathing and flowing movement, b) capable of performing a repertoire of rote songs and root melodies in a variety of keyalites and tonalities, and c) capable of improvising tonal patterns, rhythm patterns, and melodic patterns vocally and instrumentally.

Preservice teachers should begin presenting teaching techniques by designing informal movement activities to assist student development of listening vocabularies in a variety tonalities and meters and should choose rote songs and root melodies to teach their peers both vocally and instrumentally. Most important, preservice teachers should practice delivering tonal-pattern instruction and rhythm-pattern instruction to their peers. This may also serve as compensatory education for any student still in need of more aural-oral (listening and speaking vocabulary) development, while it serves as practice of the teaching techniques needed when using Music Learning Theory in the beginning instrumental classroom.

One of the most important ways that students learn is through watching, listening, and imitating behaviors that are modeled in their environment. Future band and orchestra directors must feel comfortable serving as music models for their students by performing notated music and improvisations vocally and instrumentally. Preservice teachers who receive instruction through Music Learning Theory prepare for this when their instrumental methods instructor serves as a music model during class sessions and when they are encouraged to incorporate modeling into their own teaching.

Preservice teachers who teach through modeling are practicing the teaching technique that is most fundamental to music: nonverbal instruction. That is, preservice teachers are teaching music using music. Air speed, articulation, tone quality, and style are no longer taught through verbal instruction but, instead, are given musical meaning through performance. Topics such as embouchure, finger and hand placement, and posture are positively reinforced through the visual instead of the verbal. Both preservice teachers and their future beginning instrumentalists determine how to improve their own performances by listening and watching a music model.

## Diagnosis of Performance Problems

Teachers may use their knowledge of audiation development as a guide for diagnosing performance problems, both in ensemble and individual performances. The inability to produce a "clean" attack is one sign that students have not yet been guided through the assimilation stages of preparatory audiation. Students are not yet capable of coordinating their breathing and body movements in tempo while audiating accurate pitches. The preservice teacher must determine if the problem is a lack of rhythm readiness or a lack of tonal readiness among students (due to individual differences it may be a little of each) and then provide supplemental audiation activities based in movement. In a similar manner, brass and woodwind students who are unable to produce pitches in high or low registers are probably having difficulty audiating those pitches. Preservice teachers should be encouraged to develop a repertoire of tonal patterns that includes octave (register) changes so that they can help those students with difficulties to sing and improvise tonal patterns that include those pitches that were previously difficult to perform.

Poor intonation is a common instrumental performance problem caused by students' inability to audiate. Preservice teachers should develop several audiation activities that help serve as a "tuner" for an ensemble. Performing the melodies found in notation vocally is one way that this may be accomplished. Oftentimes, students perform in one keyality with better intonation than in another. This may be due to executive skill difficulties or an inability to establish immediately the tonal center in the new keyality. Performing familiar rote songs in the keyality of concern is one technique for improving the executive skills and audiation skills among students. In addition, students may be encouraged to silently hear a change of keyality inside their heads and then to sing and instrumentally perform a tonic pattern in the new keyality without teacher assistance. Poor intonation may also occur because students are not yet performing on their instrument with a characteristic tone quality. Examples of poor tone quality and good tone quality as demonstrated by the teacher will help students determine the elements of good tone quality.

Part-singing is another way of helping students learn to balance and blend within the ensemble. Students who can sing the main melody, root melody, and a harmony or countermelody by ear are capable of performing these melodies on their instruments with good intonation. When students can perform both the bass line and the melody line, they become more sensitive to the ways that music blends together. Students who have strong awareness of melody and harmony or countermelody can make performance decisions more effectively. In this way, students can be more actively involved in the ensemble performance preparation.

Preservice teachers can use their knowledge of rhythm development to diagnose the causes of specific rhythm problems among students. Students who perform notated rhythm patterns incorrectly may not yet have these rhythm patterns established in their listening vocabulary. Students who have the rhythm patterns already established in their listening vocabulary may not yet have these rhythm patterns established in their reading vocabulary. Tempo problems are often a result of internal pulse problems among students. Typically, slower tempos are more difficult for students to audiate than faster tempos. Instrumentalists who perform all music at one tempo may possess subjective internal pulse in a particular meter at a particular tempo but may not possess the objective pulse set for the ensemble by another. As suggested here, an understanding of Music Learning Theory can assist the preservice teacher with problem diagnosis and many of the decisions that are typically made in the instrumental instructional setting.

## Applications of Music Learning Theory to Other Traditional Components of the Methods Course

Preservice teachers who have a foundation in Music Learning Theory rely on a method based on research when making decisions about many aspects of the instrumental music program. Decisions made by teachers regarding recruitment, lesson grouping, scheduling, literature selection, concert planning, motivation, classroom management, lesson planning, evaluation, and curricula should facilitate student learning. Many times, young teachers base decisions solely on their own public school learning experiences or their student teaching experience. Those two experiences clearly are not sufficient for making decisions regarding student learning.

*Jump Right In: The Instrumental Series Teacher's Guide* (Grunow, Gordon, & Azzara, 2001) offers several important suggestions for recruitment based on Music Learning Theory. First, the teacher should administer a music aptitude test and the *Instrument Timbre Preference Test* (Gordon, 1991) to guide student instrument choice based on knowledge of the students' strengths and weaknesses. Also, recruitment demonstrations should include singing and moving for those attending the demonstration as well as those on the stage. Finally, when possible, first-year instrumentalists should be used as models in the recruitment demonstration. Methods course instructors also need to discuss musical age versus chronological age with regard to the appropriate age to begin instrumental instruction, as well as various formats for recruitment demonstrations. Additionally, they should address the need for communication with parents, making connections to the work of the general music teacher, and instrument placement procedures. Many of these topics may be addressed in the methods course with outside readings, written assignments, or through out-of-class discussion groups so that class time is reserved for music teaching techniques.

Lesson grouping and scheduling decisions made by teachers should reflect an understanding of techniques for teaching to individual differences. *Jump Right In: The Instrumental Series Teacher's Guide* suggests that optimal student instruction occurs twice a week in small group lessons that include mixed instrumentation and heterogeneous grouping of music aptitudes. A solid knowledge of Music Learning Theory will prepare the teacher to teach with mixed instrumentation and mixed ability levels in the same class. Carefully selected tonal and rhythm patterns may be presented to individual students during Learning Sequence Activities so that instructors teach to the individual differences within each class, thereby allowing students to progress individually through the stages of music development. When using Music Learning Theory, it is not necessary to teach all instruments in one group (e.g., the "flute group"), nor is it desirable to have all the "best flute players" in the same group.

The preservice teacher who has an understanding of the importance of audiation will choose literature for future ensembles based on the ensembles' ability or inability to audiate. Literature should be analyzed for musical content (e.g., Major tonality with tonic, subdominant, and dominant functions in Usual Duple meter) and for opportunities that may be given to students for improvisation, vocal performance, or music enrichment. Concerts may include duets and chamber ensembles performing melodies with root melodies and countermelodies that students have learned aurally.

In the traditional instrumental methods course, students study intrinsic and extrinsic motivation, and the instructor often provides examples of each for instrumental music education. The instructor also provides classroom management suggestions, while students study various discipline strategies. Teachers with Music Learning Theory backgrounds understand how children learn music, and are thus well equipped to present motivating class activities. Understanding students' differences will also allow the teacher to tailor learning activities to the needs of each child so that each child will be motivated to learn. If activities are too difficult or too easy, student motivation will suffer concurrently with classroom discipline.

Preservice teachers who sequence music content in a developmentally appropriate manner may be better able to determine the types of music achievement that should occur in the instrumental classroom and when it should occur. Teachers should reflect and develop specific music criteria that may be used to objectively measure each student's music achievement. In this way, the teacher may better evaluate each student's performance based on music achievement and not on non-music criteria.

## Use of Music Learning Theory to Develop Thinking and Decision-Making Skills

Once preservice teachers have achieved a balance between their skills as musicians and their understanding of how individuals learn and should be taught music, they must learn to adapt what they have learned in different teaching situations. The decision-making and thinking skills needed for this application of knowledge must be fostered in the methods course as well.

Students who study Music Learning Theory must be made aware that, in many teaching situations, they may be the only person in the school or district who understands music development. Activities in the methods course should use problem-solving techniques to discuss how to integrate Music Learning Theory into traditional instruction. Case studies, journals, class debates and teaching simulations may be used as resources for developing these types of problem-solving activities (Conway, 1997, 1999a, 1999b; Robbins, 1993).

*Jump Right In: The Instrumental Series* is perhaps the most instructive method book for beginning instrumental students. However, even in teaching situations that require use of a traditional method book, a teacher can learn to modify Music Learning Theory to support traditional instruction. Through careful decision-making and reflection on teaching, the preservice teacher will learn to modify Music Learning Theory for use in any music context. As the teacher reflects on his or her own teaching, Music Learning Theory provides a model for viewing music learning. The reflective teacher asks, "Are my students audiating?" If they are not, that teacher will modify instruction so that students will audiate and learn music more effectively.

Many traditional method book authors use folk songs as a curriculum. If the methods course instructor has music education students analyze the songs (and their corresponding root melodies) in these various method books for content—Major tonality with tonic and dominant functions, Minor tonality with tonic and dominant functions, Major tonality with tonic, subdominant, and dominant functions, and Minor tonality with tonic, subdominant, and dominant functions—these books may be used and Music Learning Theory can still be incorporated. This analysis may also be repeated with Duple and Triple meter. Students should be encouraged to develop a repertoire of songs from the method book aurally before using music notation to read the song.

Most traditional method book authors introduce whole notes and whole rests in the beginning of the book. Preservice teachers who understand internal pulse development know that vocally or instrumentally performing sustained pitches or sustained silence is more difficult than vocally or instrumentally performing microbeat rhythm patterns or division rhythm patterns that define a particular tempo and meter. Preservice teachers should be encouraged to reorder method book examples to avoid any developmentally inappropriate sequences of notation.

Once preservice teachers have sequenced the notated examples in a method book based on music content difficulty and rhythm pattern difficulty, they should introduce improvisation. Tonal pattern instruction and rhythm pattern instruction may be incorporated into instrumental classes by preservice teachers as supplemental material so that students develop their improvisation skills. Students may sing and audiate songs along with corresponding root melodies from the band method book or orchestra method book. They may then perform those songs and the corresponding root melodies in the presented keyality and in different keyalities. When students are capable of performing aurally a repertoire of songs from the method book with the corresponding root melody aurally, of improvising tonal patterns, of improvising rhythm patterns, and of improvising melodic patterns, they may write the chord changes over the melody in the method book. Finally, preservice teachers should guide their students in improvising counter-melodies for those songs.

The development of preservice teachers is a challenge. In most universities, the methods course instructor is primarily responsible for guiding the preservice teachers' teaching skill development and for guiding the preservice teachers' knowledge of non-music topics. Despite this instruction, many preservice teachers are not prepared to become successful music educators. Preservice teachers must first sing, move, audiate, and improvise themselves so that they may successfully guide the music development of others. Because preservice teachers must possess those skills to be successful teachers and because many preservice teachers do not possess those skills initially, the methods course instructor must be responsible for guiding the development of the preservice teacher's listening, speaking, moving, and teaching vocabularies as well.

The instrumental methods course must include instruction regarding preparatory audiation, audiation, modeling, diagnosing performance problems, and notation sequencing. In addition, the methods course instructor should include the development of organizational skills, administrative skills, and reflective thinking. Methods course instructors must decide what skills are necessary for preservice teachers to become successful music educators. Those professors must then determine what musical abilities serve as the necessary readinesses for achieving those skills. In many cases, the musical abilities must be addressed in the method course as well. Only in this manner will the methods course instructor effectively enable preservice teachers to teach themselves how to become successful music development guides, and, thus, become successful music educators.

# References

Atterbury, B. W. (1994). Developing reflective music educators. *Journal of Music Teacher Education, 4*(1), 6-12.

Azzara, C. D., Grunow, R. F., & Gordon, E. E. (1997). *Creativity in improvisation.* Chicago: GIA Publications.

Barry, N. (1996). Promoting reflective practice in an elementary music methods course. *Journal of Music Teacher Education, 5*(2), 6-13.

Conway, C. M. (1997). *The development of a casebook for use in instrumental music education methods courses.* Unpublished doctoral dissertation, Teachers College, Columbia University.

———. (1998). Reflection and the music methods course. *Southeastern Journal of Music Education, 8.*

———. (1999a). The development of teaching cases for instrumental music methods courses. *Journal of Research in Music Education, 47*(4), 343-356.

———. (1999b). The case method and music teacher education. *Update: Applications of Research in Music Education, 17*(2), 20-26.

Dean, R. (1989). Teacher education and Music Learning Theory. In D. L. Walters and C. C. Taggart, (Eds.), *Readings in Music Learning Theory.* Chicago: GIA Publications, 343-351.

Gordon, E. E. (1991). *Instrument timbre preference test.* Chicago: GIA Publications.

———. (2003). *Learning sequences in music: Skill, content, and patterns.* Chicago: GIA Publications.

Gromko, J. E. (1995). Educating the reflective teacher. *Journal of Music Teacher Education, 4*(2), 8-13.

Grunow, R. F., Gordon, E. E., & Azzara, C. D. (2001). *Jump right in: The instrumental series* (2nd Ed.). Chicago: GIA Publications.

———. (2001). *Jump right in: The instrumental series teacher's guide* (2nd Ed.). Chicago: GIA Publications.

Hobbs, W. (1989). Implementing Music Learning Theory within a college curriculum. In D. L. Walters and C. C. Taggart (Eds.), *Readings in Music Learning Theory.* Chicago: GIA Publications, 333-342.

Hope, S. (1995). Teacher preparation and the voluntary K-12 music standards. *The Quarterly Journal of Music Teaching and Learning, VI* (2), 14-21.

Music Educators National Conference (1994). *National standards for arts education.* Reston, VA: MENC.

Robbins, J. (1993). Preparing students to think like teachers: Relocating our teacher education perspective. *The Quarterly Journal of Music Teaching and Learning, IV* (1), 45-51.

Shuler, S. C. (1995). The impact of national standards on the preparation, inservice professional development, and assessment of music teachers. *Arts Education Policy Review, 96*(2).

Valerio, W. H., Reynolds, A., Taggart, C. C., Bolton, B., & Gordon, E.E. (1998). *Music play: The early childhood music curriculum.* Chicago: GIA Publications.

# *Variation 4:*
# Current Trends and Implementation

*Christopher D. Azzara*

EASTMAN SCHOOL OF MUSIC

# Understanding Music through Improvisation

One of the most important skills presented in Music Learning Theory is improvisation the spontaneous expression of audiation.[1] Improvisation is necessary in music education because it is through improvisation that students express their musical thoughts and feelings in the moment of performance.

Unfortunately, although the process of making all art involves creativity and improvisation, improvisation is missing from much of music education. To rectify this problem, music teachers should change the model from which they work and gain a deeper understanding of music through improvisation. Music Learning Theory can provide a basis for this change.

## The Importance of Learning by Ear

In language, individuals develop four vocabularies: listening, speaking, reading, and writing. Musicians nurture similar vocabularies, and improvisation in music plays the role that speech and conversation play in language. While learning to improvise music is not exactly the same as learning to speak and converse, the process is similar. For example, as a child you are surrounded by the sounds of your native language. You babble for a period of time and eventually begin to say the same words and phrases that you hear spoken by your parents and siblings. You associate words (names) with people, things, feelings, and desires. Eventually you begin to make statements and ask questions that are your own. You begin to interact verbally. You are improvising in language. And, in most cases, you continue to improvise for

---

[1] Audiation is a central component of Music Learning Theory. It is the ability to hear and comprehend in one's mind the sound of music that is not or may never have been physically present (Gordon, 2003).

several years before you learn to read or write. Just imagine trying to teach a child to read if the child cannot carry on a conversation.[2]

Learning to improvise music is a similar process. First, students should listen to music that is characteristic of their culture, e.g., folk songs, jazz, and classical melodies. Next, they should interact musically with others and begin to make up melodies and rhythms of their own. The earlier this process begins, the better. When surrounded by a musically rich environment, children have a chance to develop their improvisational skills at a young age. Young children naturally play with the materials at hand.

As a part of their music instruction, students should sing and play by ear many melodies and bass lines in as many different tonalities and meters as possible. The objective is not to memorize the tunes. After all, individuals do not memorize speech as children. Rather, the objective is to learn so many melodies and bass lines that students begin to hear and predict harmonic progressions and generate their *own* melodic lines. Hearing harmonic progressions and generating melodies from within are fundamental to improvisation.

At the same time that students build a vocabulary of tunes, harmonic progressions, and a feeling for musical style, they should build a vocabulary of tonal patterns, rhythm patterns, harmonic patterns, and names for the tonalities, meters, and functions in the melodies that they sing and play. Tonal and rhythm syllables help individuals remember many tonal and rhythm patterns. The names for tonalities, meters, and functions provide an aural classification system. For example, in Major and Minor tonalities, students begin by learning tonic and dominant functions; in Duple and Triple meters they learn macrobeat, microbeat, and division functions. With a rich aural background as a foundation for learning to read, students will develop skill in reading notation with comprehension because they have the perspective of improvisation. That is, when students read, they should be able to hear the melody and also the harmonic progression—before playing the music on an instrument. Harmony is a result of two or more melodies coming together and interacting. Learning a large repertoire of music by ear and developing a melodic sense of harmonic progression by ear are the heart of improvisation. Thus, well-developed improvisational skills will improve student musicianship and allow for more spontaneous music making in general.

**Whole-Part-Whole**

To be able to improvise expressively, individuals should a) actively listen to improvised music; b) learn a repertoire of tunes by ear; c) develop a

---

[2] For further information on how children acquire language, see Pinker (1995).

melodic sense of harmonic progressions by ear; d) learn the tonal, rhythmic, and stylistic vocabulary of music by ear; and e) take the risks necessary to improvise. By nature, children are eager to improvise. Early stages of improvisation include spontaneous unchoreographed movement to music and the spontaneous singing and harmonization of familiar tunes. When students are learning to improvise, start with the *whole* (learn tunes by ear); learn *parts* (patterns and phrases) in context; then return to the *whole* (the tune) with even more understanding, for the whole is greater than the sum of its parts. All of this should take place first at the aural/oral level of learning.

By learning many melodies, bass lines, and harmonic progressions in a variety of styles, tonalities, and meters by ear, students develop an understanding of how melodies combine to create harmony. For example, students may wish to start with a repertoire in Major and Minor with tonic and dominant harmonies and continue by learning tunes with subdominant, mediant, submediant, supertonic, other harmonic functions, and more chromatic harmonies. Students should also learn songs in other tonalities, such as Dorian and Mixolydian. Learning a large repertoire helps individuals invent new musical lines when improvising. While memory plays a part in learning, the idea is to learn the music—have ownership of music in the same way that it is possible to have ownership for language when speaking. The more tunes a person knows, the easier it is for them to learn unfamiliar melodies by ear. Ultimately, it becomes easy for them to create more melodies. In this way, individuals place unfamiliar music into the context of the familiar.

Although improvisation is a creative activity, there are differences between "creativity" and "improvisation." Improvisation involves specific "limits." These guidelines provide a framework for the performer, e.g., the tonality, the harmonic progression, the meter, and the form. Creativity involves fewer restrictions than improvisation. Challenging these limits by playing inside and outside of the understood guidelines results in creative improvisation. Many improvisers and composers find that they are most creative when given certain limits.

### Learning to Improvise (Combining Learning Sequence Activities with Classroom Activities)

The following provides an outline for combining Classroom Activities and Learning Sequence Activities, two fundamental components of Music Learning Theory, with the goal of learning to improvise.[3]

---

[3] For further information, refer to Azzara, Grunow, & Gordon (1997) and Grunow, Gordon, & Azzara (2001).

*Learning Repertoire by Ear.* The aural/oral level is fundamental to improvisation. It is essential for students to experience a variety of styles of music at the aural/oral level. This includes learning to sing a large and varied repertoire of music by ear. For example, the students should learn to sing "Long, Long Ago," which represents one of the many songs commonly learned in school music settings. The suggestions presented here will provide opportunities for a deeper understanding of these songs.

## Long, Long Ago

The students should learn the song by rote, without notation. Teach the tune using neutral syllables such as Doo, Too, Ba, or Da. Instrumentalists can practice the connected and separated styles of articulation by singing the melody on the neutral syllable "Doo, Doo, Doo, Doo" or "Too, Too, Too, Too." Then students should learn to play the song by ear in many keys, beginning with familiar keys. Learn the words to the song and perform with expressive phrasing and dynamics.

*Learning Bass Lines by Ear.* Students should learn to sing the bass line of the song by ear. This will help them develop an understanding of the harmonic progression. For example, teach the bass line to "Long, Long Ago." Instrumentalists first should sing the bass line and then learn to play it by ear in many keys. Begin by learning bass lines that incorporate the roots of the harmonic functions (Azzara, 1999).

## Long, Long Ago
### Bass Line

*Additional Techniques for Developing Musicianship.* When learning tunes, use the following techniques to develop musicianship and check for comprehension. *Technique #1 -* Sing the entire tune except for the last pitch. Audiate the last pitch. Sing the last pitch aloud. If the pitch is the resting tone, name the tonality (DO = Major; LA = Minor; etc.). *Technique #2 -* Sing the tune "inside" your head (audiate without singing aloud). Now, sing the tune again "outside" so that others can hear it. *Technique #3 -* Sing the melody while audiating the bass line. *Technique #4 -* Sing the bass line while audiating the melody.

*Initiating Improvisation.* To initiate improvisation, have the students improvise responses to musical phrases performed by another individual. For example, students should respond to the following musical phrases with an improvised musical phrase using a neutral syllable such as "Doo" or "Too."

1. The teacher might sing:

A student's response might be:

2. The teacher might sing:

A final response might be:

Also, students could improvise responses to familiar songs, for example, "Long, Long Ago." The teacher sings a phrase of the song and the students sing an "answer" following the harmonic progression of "Long, Long Ago." For example:

1. The teacher sings:

A student's response might be:

2. The teacher sings:

A student's response might be:

Eventually the students should be able to improvise both the antecedent and consequent phrase for the harmonic progression, which is being audiated during improvisation.

**Echoing, Naming, and Improvising Rhythm Patterns and Tonal Patterns**

Tonal and rhythm pattern instruction will greatly improve aural skills, including the ability to audiate rhythm functions and tonal functions (harmonic progressions) in music. Therefore, several minutes (five to ten maximum) of each lesson should be devoted to tonal and rhythm pattern instruction.

*Rhythm Patterns.* Rhythm patterns help to define meter and provide a basis for understanding rhythm and meter. Develop a vocabulary of rhythm patterns in many meters. Establish the meter and begin by chanting rhythm patterns using a neutral syllable - "Bah" (aural/oral). For example:

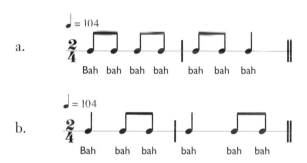

The students should echo patterns while moving to the large beats (macrobeats) with their heels and the small beats (microbeats) with their hands.

Next, chant the same patterns using rhythm syllables (verbal association). Learning rhythm syllables will help students develop a system for organizing and comprehending meter and rhythm functions. For example:

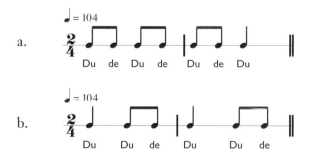

Encourage students to *feel* the macrobeats and the microbeats rather than visualizing the notation. Students should use their ears and bodies, not the notation, to understand the distinct rhythm differences. For example, have the class listen and move to a performance of a familiar tune. Ask, "Where do you feel the large beat? The small beat?" This will indicate the meter and function of the rhythms in the music. Sometimes individuals will feel different macrobeats because some individuals will feel macrobeats that are spaced farther apart than others do.

At this point, it becomes possible to name the large beats and small beats without referring to notation. In Duple meter, the syllable associated with the macrobeats is:

In Duple meter, the syllables associated with the microbeats are:

In Triple meter, the syllable associated with the macrobeats is:

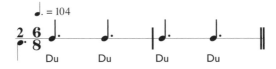

In Triple meter, the syllables associated with the microbeats are:

Students should respond to the teacher's patterns with improvised patterns using a neutral syllable or rhythm syllables. Students will experience success improvising rhythm patterns using a neutral syllable (improvisation – aural/oral). It will be helpful to define the guidelines of the rhythm improvisation by using rhythm syllables when improvising (improvisation – aural/oral using rhythm syllables as a technique).

For example:

Consider the following pattern that includes both macrobeats and microbeats in Duple meter.

Now, ask the student to perform a different macrobeat/microbeat pattern using rhythm syllables. For example:

Improvising patterns must also be done in the context of phrases. Improvise a phrase of macrobeat and microbeat patterns in Duple meter. For example, audiate the following phrase of macrobeat/microbeat patterns in Duple meter.

Now, have the students perform different phrases of macrobeat/microbeat patterns using rhythm syllables. A possible response:

Continue this procedure using other rhythm functions and other meters.

*Tonal Patterns.* Tonal patterns should be taught in the context of harmony and tonality. Students should develop a vocabulary of tonal patterns in many tonalities. The teacher should establish tonality and begin by singing tonal patterns using a neutral syllable such as "Bum" (aural/oral). For example, in Major students should echo tonic and dominant patterns.

Bum bum bum   bum bum   bum bum bum bum   bum bum bum bum bum

Next, students should echo the same tonal patterns using tonal syllables (verbal association). Learning tonal syllables will help individuals develop a system for organizing and comprehending tonality and harmonic functions. It is critical that the patterns always be sung with syllables and not spoken. This will help the student make a musical connection to the sound of the syllables.

DO MI DO   RE SO   SO FA RE TI   DO SO MI DO MI

It will be easier to learn harmonic functions if the tonal syllables have inherent logic. When syllables have logic, it is possible to name the tonalities and the functions of the tonal patterns from an aural perspective. For example, DO is the resting tone in Major tonality; any combination of DO, MI, and SO is a tonic pattern in Major; and any combination of SO, FA, RE, and TI is a dominant pattern in Major tonality. Combinations of FA, LA, and DO are subdominant in Major. The same idea applies to Minor tonality. For example, LA is the resting tone in Minor tonality; any combination of LA, DO, and MI is a tonic pattern in Minor tonality; and any combination of MI, RE, TI, and SI is a dominant pattern in Minor tonality. Combinations of RE, FA, and LA are subdominant in Minor tonality. (Remember to always *sing* the syllables; do not say the syllables.)

Now, ask students to respond to patterns with an improvised pattern using a neutral syllable and tonal syllables. As with rhythm patterns, students may experience some success improvising tonal patterns using a neutral syllable (improvisation – aural/oral). However, it will be helpful to define the guidelines of the tonal improvisation by using tonal syllables when improvising (improvisation – aural/oral using tonal syllables as a technique). For example, the teacher should say to the students: "Listen to the following tonic pattern in Major."

DO MI DO

"Now, using tonal syllables, perform a different tonic pattern." A possible response:

"Listen to the following dominant pattern in Major."

"Now, using tonal syllables, you perform a different dominant pattern." A possible response:

Also, it is important to improvise series of tonal patterns in the context of progressions. For example, improvise a series of tonic and dominant patterns in Major tonality. Say to the students, "Audiate the following tonic-dominant-tonic progression in Major."

"Now, using tonal syllables, you perform different patterns for the same progression." A possible response:

Continue this procedure using other tonal functions and other tonalities.

## Using the Partial Synthesis and Generalization-Verbal Levels of Learning to Develop Musicianship for Improvising.

The *partial synthesis* level of learning is valuable for teaching students to recognize for themselves the tonalities or meters that are established when familiar tonal patterns or familiar rhythm patterns are performed in a series. A familiar pattern is a pattern that a student can perform alone. Synthesizing series of familiar tonal patterns or familiar rhythm patterns in the larger context of the tonality or meter helps students to have an understanding of how patterns relate and interact with each other in a series. It also deepens a student's sense of tonality and meter.

At the *generalization-verbal* level of learning, students are asked to repeat the teacher's performance of familiar and unfamiliar tonal or rhythm patterns using tonal syllables or rhythm syllables instead of the neutral syllable that the teacher used. Also at this level of learning, students name the tonalities or meters that are established when familiar and unfamiliar tonal or rhythm patterns are performed in a series. These activities add depth and dimension to audiation skill and improve overall musicianship.

**Harmonic Patterns and Time Patterns**

Students also should learn harmonic patterns. A harmonic pattern includes two or more simultaneous sounding pitches that progress from one to the next with the tonic chord as a reference. The following is an example of a tonic-dominant-tonic harmonic pattern:

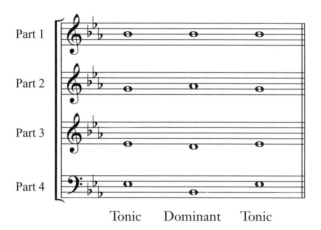

The following is an example of a tonic-subdominant-tonic harmonic pattern:

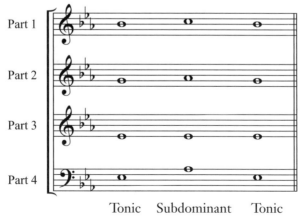

A harmonic pattern is audiated as a sonority in a linear sequential fashion. Students should develop a vocabulary of many harmonic patterns in the context of a variety of tonalities and meters. With an understanding of harmonic patterns, students can improvise melodic patterns (combined tonal and rhythm patterns) over different harmonic pattern progressions.

In addition to developing a vocabulary of harmonic patterns, students should develop skill with time patterns—two or more durations of fundamental pitches on a harmonic pattern, each being audiated as a chord root. Time patterns will help students develop a sense of when the harmony changes.

## Improvising to Harmonic Progressions

### Rhythm Improvisation Using Bass Lines

Students should be asked to improvise rhythms to the root of the harmonic functions of familiar bass lines. For example, students may have already learned the bass line to "Long, Long Ago." Now, have students improvise rhythm patterns using only macrobeats and microbeats on a neutral syllable such as "Bah" to that bass line. (For this example, the quarter note equals the macrobeat.) For example:

## Long, Long Ago

### Rhythm Improvisation Using Four-Part Harmony

Students may also engage in rhythm improvisation while singing four-part harmony. Use the following suggestions.

Have a group of students sing the following four parts together. Give each student the opportunity to sing each part.

Part 1 — SO — SO — SO
Part 2 — MI — FA — MI
Part 3 — DO — TI — DO
Part 4 — DO — SO — SO

Become familiar with the harmonic progression of a tune containing the same harmony (in this case, tonic and dominant harmony). Harmonic progression is defined here in a linear sense by how the harmony changes (tonal elements) and when the harmony changes (harmonic rhythm) (Azzara, 1993). For example:

**Long, Long Ago**

Ask students to improvise rhythm patterns to the harmonic progression of the tune while singing the assigned pitches. For example:

## Improvising Melodies

Students should improvise tonal patterns to the harmonic progression of "Long, Long Ago" on each macrobeat. (For this example, the quarter note equals the macrobeat.)

Now, have students improvise tonal patterns to the harmonic progression of "Long, Long Ago" using macrobeats and microbeats. (Again, for this example the quarter note equals the macrobeat.)

You may find it more musical to feel half notes as macrobeats and quarter notes as microbeats for "Long, Long Ago." Either is correct and results in a different musical interpretation of the song. Every tune has its own macrobeat-microbeat feeling. When half notes are the macrobeats, an improvisation using macrobeats would sound like this:

When quarter notes are microbeats an improvisation using microbeats would sound like this:

At this point students should improvise melodies and countermelodies using passing tones, embellishments of notes, and other rhythm functions.

These melodies will come naturally as your students gain more experience and learn more tunes. Continue this procedure with a large repertoire and in many musical styles. It is critical that students learn many harmonic progressions. The goal is to develop aural skills that can be expressed spontaneously.

**Additional Suggestions for Improvisation**

Developing a large musical repertoire by ear is important to the improvisation learning process and will provide a basis for developing skill with patterns. For example, the readiness for acquiring skill with tonic and dominant patterns in Major tonality is to develop a repertoire of Major songs containing tonic and dominant functions. The following are suggestions and ideas for continued development as an improviser.

1. Embellishing the melody of a tune:
   - Rhythm variation: keep pitches of the melody the same and improvise rhythm variations.
   - Tonal variation: embellish melody with upper and lower neighbors and passing tones.
   - Expressive variation: change dynamics, phrasing, tone, and/or style of articulation.
   - Use silence and space: perform rests and long notes as you create and develop the motives that you are improvising. This will provide opportunities for interaction with other performers.
2. Embellishing harmony parts and countermelodies:
   - Rhythm variation: keep pitches of the harmony part the same and improvise rhythm variations.
   - Tonal variation: embellish harmony part with upper and lower neighbors and passing tones.

415

- Expressive variation: change dynamics, phrasing, tone, and/or style of articulation.
- Use silence and space.

3. Embellishing chord tones:
   - Perform sustained chord-tone lines (for example, when working with a tonic and dominant progression in Major, sing the following parts: Part I, DO-TI-DO; Part II, MI-FA-MI; Part III, SO-SO-SO) with Part IV, the bass line of a tune.
   - Rhythm variation: keep pitches of the chord-tone melody the same and improvise rhythm variations.
   - Tonal variation: embellish chord tones with upper and lower neighbors.
   - Expressive variation: change dynamics, phrasing, tone quality, and/or style of articulation.
   - Use of silence (rests).

4. Listening to improvisers and learning improvised solos by ear:
   - Think of the improvised solo as a tune/song.
   - Add these solos to your repertoire of tunes.

The above procedures should be repeated for many tunes in many styles, tonalities, and meters. Begin with repertoire that is in Major and Minor tonalities using tonic and dominant harmonic functions; then work with Major and Minor repertoire with tonic, dominant, and subdominant harmonic progressions. Continue with ii–V7–I progressions, V7/V, and other harmonic progressions, as well as repertoire in other tonalities, such as Dorian and Mixolydian.

**Measuring and Evaluating Improvisation**

Teachers should provide students with specific feedback regarding improvisation skill and content. Consider using the following criteria when assessing improvisations.

The improviser:
- Demonstrates motivic development through tonal and rhythm sequences.
- Demonstrates effective use of silence and space.
- Demonstrates a sense of style.
- Demonstrates an understanding of tension and release through resolution of notes and rhythmic variety.
- Embellishes notes and performs variations of themes.

416

## The Relationship between Improvisation and Learning to Read and Write Music with Comprehension

While learning to read is important to an individual's music education, many times music teachers ask their students to read the notation for music without first asking them to think and "speak" musically. Reading music is the ability to hear and comprehend music in your head when looking at a page of notation, just as you can read and comprehend the words on this page. Improvisational skill is related to music reading because it allows individuals to express their thoughts and ideas about what they have read with their own musical ideas in much the same way that individuals paraphrase what they have read in language.

Reading music involves comprehension, just as reading language involves comprehension.[4] It is much more than just "sounding out" melodies and rhythms printed on the page. Music educators must deepen their definition of what it means to read music. There is more to music reading than relating fingerings to note names and mathematics to rhythm without comprehending the tonality and meter of music. Music reading means that an individual can hear and comprehend the music in his or her head without the sound being physically present and without the aid of an instrument. Music reading also means that an individual can look at notation and audiate the "invisible" notes (e.g., other musical lines implied by the notation, but not written down).

To determine students' comprehension, teachers should ask students to "paraphrase" what they have read through singing, moving, creating and improvising. In language, we ask students to "state it in their own words" and not only to repeat what they have seen on the printed page. "Performing" the words does not necessarily constitute reading with comprehension. In addition to performing the notes they see, music readers should be asked to do something different from what is on the printed page by making musical inferences through the process of creativity and improv-isation. For example, students should be able to interact musically with similar tonal and rhythmic functions to indicate that they comprehend the harmonic and rhythmic structure found in the reading excerpt. Through improvisation, our students can begin to "know" what they are performing. Students may also wish to document their ideas in composition. Expressing comprehension of reading through improvisation and composition is a way for students to express their own musical thoughts. It is important to remember that notation is the documentation of creativity; therefore,

---

[4] For further information on reading with comprehension, consult Smith (1985) and Healy (1990).

reading notation should reflect an understanding of the creative process (Azzara, 1993).[5]

## Suggested Activities for Connecting Improvisation to Reading and Writing Music – Symbolic Association, Composite Synthesis, Generalization Symbolic, and Theoretical Understanding

The following activities should help connect improvising to reading and writing music.

*Symbolic Association–Tonal Reading.* Incorporate improvisation activities when teaching symbolic association – tonal reading to your class.

Directions:

1. Indicate to the students that in G Major, G indicates tonic and D7 indicates dominant. Tonic patterns include any combination of DO, MI, and SO and dominant patterns include any combination of SO, FA, RE, and TI. The arrow points to DO.

2. After the students read the following familiar patterns by singing them using tonal syllables and by performing them on their instruments, ask the students to improvise different patterns than those written with the same tonal functions.

3. Also, for each pattern, students should be asked to improvise a different pattern with a different function in response to reading the notations of the patterns.

*Composite Synthesis – Tonal Reading.* Incorporate improvisation activities when teaching composite synthesis – tonal reading to your class.

Directions:

1. Ask your students to read the series of patterns below by singing them using tonal syllables and by performing them on their instruments.

---

[5] For further information, see Azzara (2002).

2. Next, ask your students to improvise different patterns for the same harmonic progression.

*Symbolic Association – Rhythm Reading.* Incorporate improvisation activities when teaching symbolic association – rhythm reading to your students.

Directions:
1. After the students read the following familiar patterns by chanting them using rhythm syllables and by performing them on their instruments, ask the students to improvise different patterns with the same rhythm function of those written.

2. Also for each pattern, students should be asked to improvise a different rhythm pattern with a different function in response to reading the notated patterns.

*Composite Synthesis – Rhythm Reading.* Incorporate improvisation activities when teaching composite synthesis – rhythm reading to your class.

Directions:
1. Instruct your students to read the series of patterns below by chanting them using rhythm syllables and by performing them on their instruments.

2. Next, ask your students to improvise a different series of patterns in the same meter.

## Generalization Symbolic

Improvisation will also help students comprehend unfamiliar patterns when reading. For example, when students can read familiar tonal patterns like this:

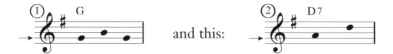

and this:

they should have the opportunity to make the inferences necessary to read unfamiliar patterns such as:

When students can read familiar rhythm patterns like this:

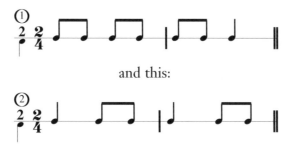

and this:

they then should have the opportunity to make the inferences necessary to read unfamiliar rhythm patterns such as:

In many instances, students will have improvised these unfamiliar patterns and now can see what they look like in notation.

## First Composition – Singing and Playing

As a part of symbolic association – writing, composite synthesis – writing, and creativity/improvisation – symbolic (writing), students should document tonal and rhythm patterns they have heard, read, and improvised.

Students should also document their creativity through composition. Provide guidelines for first compositions, but also give the students the opportunity to compose with fewer limits described to them. In improvisation, students interact, create, and develop ideas in the moment of performance. Composition differs in a temporal sense in that composers can create and develop ideas at liberty throughout a work in progress. They can "go back" to work through an idea or "move ahead" and make adjustments as necessary. The following is a typical "First Composition" assignment (Azzara, Grunow, & Gordon, 1997; Grunow, Gordon, & Azzara, 2001).

### First Composition

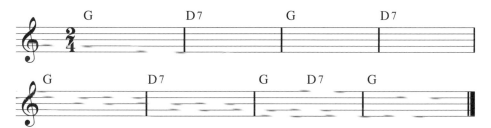

Give the following directions to your students:
a.  Indicate for your instrument that G is DO.
b.  Start on DO; end on DO.
c.  Use only tonic and dominant patterns. Do not use passing tones.
d.  Use only macrobeats and microbeats (quarter note = macrobeat; eighth notes = microbeats). Do not use any other rhythm functions.
e.  Use the chord progression that is indicated.
f.  Use only the pitches in the octave between the SO below G-DO and the SO above G-DO.
g.  Be prepared to sing and play your composition in class.

The harmonic progressions of other familiar songs may be used in future assignments. As the audiation skills of the students develop, it also may be suggested that they use, for example, subdominant and multiple tonal patterns and division and elongation rhythm patterns. When the original songs are brought to class, each student's creation should be read and sung by the class. Then it should be read and performed on instruments by the class. The teacher should be prepared to help students find the correct key signature and DO for each instrument, if ensemble performance is to take place. More advanced students may write two-, three-, four-, and five-part arrangements of their songs for various vocal and instrumental combinations. Many of these compositions will be suitable for performance at concerts. When students audiate what they listen to, improvise, read, and write, music theory begins to make musical sense. With a musical context, theoretical terms and information are useful tools for teachers and students when talking about music objectives and concepts.

## Conclusion

Music Learning Theory is an explanation of how we learn when we learn music. With that explanation comes an understanding of method (*what*, *why*, and *when* we teach music). Music educators should articulate their objectives clearly, teach musical behaviors sequentially, and list the criteria for measuring and evaluating musical performances. Method and the appropriate teaching techniques, objectives, and measurement tools provide teachers with sequential curriculum and an awareness of individual differences among students. Music Learning Theory is useful for defining and implementing these goals.

Improvisation should be at the center of music teaching and learning. Throughout history, improvisation has played a vital role in music.[6] For example, Bach, Mozart, and Beethoven, were all improvisers. Today, however, improvisation is practiced almost exclusively by jazz, folk, and popular musicians. With the exception of some general music activities and a select number of students in jazz ensembles, improvisation is missing from the heart of most school music curricula. Yet, improvisation is a higher order thinking skill. Through improvisation in the music classroom, teachers can deepen their understanding of the learning process, because it is through improvisation that students express their musical ideas. This can be accomplished in the context of all musical styles. When incorporating improvisation, teachers have a perfect window to discover and teach to individual differences, student comprehension, and audiation.

Improvisation provides a way for students to expand their minds and express themselves with and without notation. Educators must develop methods and techniques that have direction and that incorporate improvisation into the core of the curricula. Music Learning Theory can provide the underpinnings to help teachers develop appropriate methods and techniques as well as to help teachers understand their students' individual needs. If improvisation is to become a more vital aspect of music programs, educators will need to revise current curricula. As a result, teachers and students will improve their musicianship and develop a more intimate relationship with music.

---

6 For further information, see Ferand (1961) and Azzara (2002).

# References

Azzara, C. D. (1993). Audiation-based improvisation techniques and elementary instrumental students' music achievement. *Journal of Research in Music Education, 41*(4), 328-342.

——. (1999). An aural approach to improvisation. *Music Educators Journal, 86*(3), 21-25.

——. (2002). Improvisation. In R. Colwell & C. Richardson (Eds.), *The New Handbook of Research on Music Teaching and Learning* (pp. 171–187). New York: Oxford University Press.

Azzara, C. D., Grunow, R. F., & Gordon, E. E. (1997). *Creativity In Improvisation Book 1, Book 2, and Getting Started.* Chicago: GIA Publications.

Ferand, E. (1961). *Improvisation in nine centuries of Western music.* Arno Volk Verlag, Hans Gerig KG, Cologne.

Gordon, E. E. (2003). *Learning Sequences in Music: Skill, Content, and Patterns.* Chicago: GIA Publications.

Grunow, R. F., Gordon, E. E., & Azzara, C. D. (2001). *Jump Right In: The Instrumental Series – Teacher's Guide for Winds and Percussion–Revised Edition.* Chicago: GIA Publications.

Healy, J. M. (1990). *Endangered minds: Why our children don't think and what we can do about it.* New York: Simon and Schuster.

Nachmanovitch, S. (1990). *Free play: Improvisation in life and the arts.* Los Angeles: Jeremy P. Tarcher.

Pinker, S. (1995). *The language instinct.* New York: Harper Perennial.

Smith, F. (1997). *Reading without nonsense.* New York: Teacher's College Press.

*Eric Bluestine*

●●●●●●●●●●●

DECATUR ELEMENTARY SCHOOL, PHILADELPHIA, PENNSYLVANIA

# Music Learning Theory and Aesthetic Education

I once had a friendly argument with a colleague (a fellow Gordon Music Learning Theory advocate) who believed that aesthetic music education was unnecessary. "You never hear about aesthetic *driver* education, do you?" he asked. "And yet if I wanted to, I could teach a course in aesthetic driver education. I could focus on the aesthetic pleasures of country driving versus city driving, the aesthetic pleasures of driving with the windows rolled down on a sunny day, the difference in comfort between driving a Rolls Royce and a Geo Metro. But such teaching would be absurd. Why is aesthetic music education any less absurd?" I suspect that some readers may be asking the same question. Perhaps some readers are wondering if a chapter about aesthetic education belongs in a book about Music Learning Theory. Aren't the topics mutually exclusive?

My primary purpose in writing this is to make the case that aesthetic education is a necessary and natural outgrowth of Music Learning Theory. My second purpose is to present a critique of the philosophical insights of Bennett Reimer, a prominent music education philosopher and an advocate for aesthetic education. I will argue that, although many of Reimer's insights are intriguing, they are insufficient for creating a music curriculum based on aesthetic education and must be supplemented. My third purpose is to offer practical suggestions to teachers interested in coordinating aesthetic education with Music Learning Theory.

In short, I believe that advocates of aesthetic music education should focus not on "the education of feeling" (Reimer, 1989, p. 53), but on the following topics: the violation of expectations, the relationship between repetition and variation, the use of metaphor in poetic and musical creation,

425

the difference between prosaic symmetry and aesthetic balance in music, the function of ambiguity in musical structures, and the relationship between art and artificiality. The challenge for me has been to redefine aesthetic music education as an outgrowth of Music Learning Theory and the whole-part-whole learning process. The understanding of musical aesthetics takes place during the final "whole" of the process. Therefore, before I discuss aesthetic music education in practical terms, it seems prudent for me to devote a few pages to the whole-part-whole process.

## The Whole-Part-Whole Process[1]

Walters (1992) summarized the three stages of the whole-part-whole process as follows: 1) introduction—overview of the whole; 2) application—specific study of the parts (patterns); 3) reinforcement—greater understanding of the whole. Typically, the process works like this: students learn a song by rote or they listen to a piece of music for the first time; then they hear and sing or chant patterns (though not necessarily the same patterns found in the rote song); finally, students return to the rote song or the piece of music with a greater understanding of its structure.

Here is a more detailed example of a lesson structured according to the whole-part-whole process. Suppose you wanted to teach your students that a particular Baroque aria—Handel's "The Trumpet Shall Sound" from *Messiah*, let's say—is in ABA form. The A sections are in Major tonality; the B section is in Minor tonality. How might you go about teaching the form of this aria? Instead of expecting your students immediately to understand the form of a complex piece of music, you could first present ABA form to them in a short, manageable construction—a series of patterns such as those in Figure 1.

You might teach the form of the aria using the whole-part-whole approach as follows.

*Whole #1—(Introduction):* First, play the aria for your students. Let them hear it several times. Let them physically move to it and even sing fragments from it. They should be able to recognize the aria and that its various sections are different from each other even if they don't yet have a sophisticated understanding of its structure.

*Part—(Application):* Next, teach patterns. At this level, students will learn to understand the syntax of patterns in a series. (Gordon calls this level of learning partial synthesis.) Here are some things you need to know:

---

[1] This chapter was written in 1999. This section and the next, in which I critique Reimer's work, were incorporated into my book *The Ways Children Learn Music* (Chicago: GIA, 2000).

426

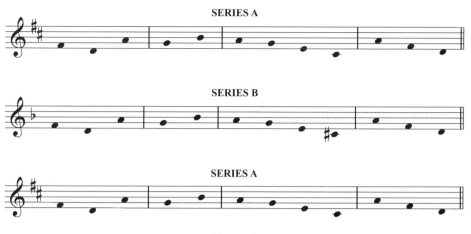

*Figure 1.*

1.  The series of patterns you teach (such as those in Figure 1) need not be from the aria you are teaching. The patterns should, however, have tonic, dominant, and subdominant functions—the same harmonic functions of patterns found in Handel's aria.

2.  Each series should be made up of patterns you have already taught by rote. (Imagine how difficult it would be for most students to audiate patterns in a series if they had not audiated and performed them first as *individual* patterns.)

3.  Students should know the harmonic function (tonic Major, subdominant Minor, etc.) of each pattern in series A and B.

4.  The tonal patterns should be performed with a consistent tempo but with as little reference as possible to any meter.

5.  As you sing, you should put a small amount of space between pitches and a bit more space between patterns. (The vertical lines are not bar lines. They show the separation of the patterns.)

6.  You do not need to establish tonality; the series of tonal patterns itself provides the syntactic context.

7.  You should not use tonal solfege. Theoretically, that tool has served its purpose and the students will have internalized the syllables. Use a neutral syllable instead.

8.  You should teach the tonality of each series by rote. Students should not be made to infer anything.

Sing series A and B, announcing "A" and "B" before you sing each one. Then teach your students the tonality of each series. Next, sing each series, one after another, in ABA order, announcing the letter of each series before you sing. Finally, rearrange the different series and sing series B at the beginning or at the end. If your students can recognize series B in its different locations—if they can audiate both Major and Minor tonalities—then they are ready to understand the form of the aria.

*Whole #2—(Reinforcement):* And now the fun begins! What do you feel like teaching? Of course, you'll teach your students that the aria they have been studying is in ABA form. (Some of your students may figure this out for themselves. If some cannot, just ask them to audiate and sing the resting tone, DO or LA, at the end of each section.) Beyond that, what else might you do? You could play an aria that your students have never heard before and ask them to identify its form and the modulations that take place. You could ask them to make up their own series of patterns in ABA form. Why not have them compose their own arias?

These activities may sound too ambitious; and actually they *are* too ambitious for students who have not had the benefit of pattern instruction as the "part" of the whole-part-whole learning process.

## A Critique of Reimer's Work

Reimer (1994) has asked, "Is there no area of compatibility or complementarity between contemporary cognitivist curricula and the extreme specificationism of Gordon's learning theory?" In other words, Reimer is asking if he and Gordon see eye to eye on anything. In my opinion, they agree on quite a lot. Here, for instance, are seven philosophical positions they share:

1. Music is not a language.
2. Music should be taught to everyone, not just a privileged few.
3. Music should be taught for its own sake, not to enhance the study of English, math, or social studies.
4. Students should be exposed to music from a wide variety of styles, cultures, and time periods.
5. Musical meaning resides in music itself, not in extra-musical associations.
6. Students should not be taught to perform merely through imitation; they should be encouraged to make artistic decisions as they prepare for a performance.
7. Children should be taught according to a whole-part-whole learning process.

In spite of these admirable philosophical insights, Reimer's ideas about aesthetic education have had almost no influence on my teaching and thinking. In his book *A Philosophy of Music Education* (1989), he says virtually nothing about tonality, meter, form, counterpoint, harmony, timbre, texture, tempo, melody, or style. Perhaps he deliberately avoids discussing the elements of music so that he can focus on philosophy. Yet, he overlooks the fundamental philosophical topics that I mentioned in the introduction to this chapter.

Reimer focuses on the notion that aesthetic music education should be the education of feeling. He writes (1989).

> The major function of education in the arts is to help people gain access to the experience of feeling contained in the artistic qualities of things. Education in the arts, then, can be regarded as the education of feeling. (p. 53)

I am compelled to challenge the logic of this statement on three grounds: the education of feeling is impossible, unnecessary, and unethical.

Why is the education of feeling impossible? Reimer (1989) writes,

> Let us call all the possible category words [such as "love," "fear," or "anger"] emotions. And let us call what takes place in our actual subjective experience feelings. Feelings themselves—experienced subjectivities—are incapable of being named, for every time we produce a name, we are producing a category. . . (p. 47)

The distinction Reimer makes between emotion and feeling is crucial for music teachers: We can name emotions; we cannot name feelings. But every bit of musical content we teach (such as tonic Major, *fortissimo*, Duple meter, binary form, etc.) has a name. In fact, we could not teach musical content without naming it. Imagine trying to teach specific musical styles, dynamics, timbres, forms, meters, and tonalities without naming them. Impossible! But if we accept the idea that feelings evoked by music are examples of musical content, then we can neither name the content we intend to teach, nor teach that content; if we cannot name feelings, we cannot teach feeling. Notice I did not say that students cannot *learn* to feel, only that we cannot *teach* them specific feelings.

Consider the following example: if we establish Major tonality and sing tonic and dominant patterns using a neutral syllable, our students will learn to audiate and sing those patterns. If they continue to sing using nothing but a neutral syllable, then most of our students will become confused about how the patterns interrelate and function in context. More specifically, we should teach our students that when they sing DO, MI, and

SO in any combination, they are singing tonic Major patterns; when they sing TI, RE, FA, and SO in any combination, they are singing dominant Major patterns.

I am not suggesting that we teach tonic and dominant as theoretical concepts; naming patterns and theorizing about them are two different things. At this early stage in their music education, students do not need to understand music theory, that is, why DO, MI, and SO belong together (and why DO, MI, and FA do not). I would not subject my first and second graders to a theoretical explanation of scale degrees, the circle of fifths, or the overtone series. If our task is to help students become independent musical thinkers; then we must give them tools (tonal and rhythm solfège) to help them *think musically*. Eventually, they will be able to theorize, that is, to think about music.

My point is that students must *name* and *categorize* patterns to understand them in greater depth. In short, although we can teach our students to understand tonic and dominant harmonic functions and that dominant chords resolve to tonic chord, we *cannot* teach our students the particular feelings that such a resolution evokes because, as Reimer points out, such feelings are too complex to be named. The education of feeling is not only impossible; it is also, fortunately, unnecessary. Students can learn to audiate a dominant-tonic cadence without undergoing introspective soul-searching about the feelings such a cadence evokes.

Even if the education of feeling were possible and necessary, is it something we want to do? Consider two of Beethoven's symphonies. Reimer, to his credit, would probably advise us to move past the simplistic idea that Beethoven's Fifth Symphony evokes anger and that his *Pastoral* Symphony evokes joy. But what if I focused on Beethoven's *Pastoral* Symphony, first movement, fourth measure, as seen in Figure 2? How is that half cadence supposed to make me feel in that context? Unsettled? Restless? In fact, it does. But I feel more than that. I want the music to move on, but I also want to linger on the dominant chord in the fourth measure and hold that fermata forever. If I accepted the notion that dominant chords convey nothing but a sense of tension and that tonic chords convey nothing but a sense of resolution, I would be denying the complexity of my feelings.

This, I believe, is what we do to students when we attempt to teach them musical feeling. Supposedly we try to heighten their musical sensitivity, but actually we have our own "emotional agenda." We want our students to tell us that dominant chords convey tension and tonic chords convey resolution and satisfaction. If students tell us anything different, we view this answer as wrong.

*Figure 2.*

## What Is Aesthetic Education?

Let me return to the friendly argument with my colleague that I began to describe in the introduction. You may recall that he asked, "If aesthetic driver education is absurd, why is aesthetic music education any less absurd?" I responded that his basic premise was wrong. You never hear about aesthetic driver education, not because it's absurd, but because it's impossible. The word *aesthetic*, according to Webster's Dictionary, means "appreciative of, responsive to, or zealous about the beautiful." A drive through the country may be an aesthetically pleasurable experience, but it— the drive itself, the road, the scenery—is not an aesthetic *product*. It follows that you can experience the aesthetics of driving, but you cannot *teach* the aesthetics of driving: there's simply no product to teach—no work of art; no organized plan; no beginning, middle and end; no manipulation of elements resulting in a self-contained, artistic whole. "To write a symphony is, for me, to construct a world," wrote Gustav Mahler (Machlis 1977, p. 452). I submit that *every* piece of music is a "world," an entity.

For the opposite reason, you could not teach the aesthetics of, say, shoelace manufacturing. Unlike a drive through the country, a shoelace is a product that serves a practical function, but it has no artistic, aesthetic qualities. No shoelace maker ever agonizes over aesthetic choices about a shoelace's length, width, or material.[2] The shoelace maker has little choice about such matters. He cannot make his shoelace out of steel, 75 feet long and 8 inches wide. He has practical problems to solve: his shoelace must be long but not so long that people trip over it; it must be flexible but not easily broken; it must be narrow enough to fit inside those little holes.

A piece of music, on the other hand, is not a series of prosaic problems a composer solves but a series of artistic choices he makes. These artistic choices, taken together, form an aesthetic product. I should add that these choices are neither right nor wrong; such descriptions are inappropriate. A composer manipulates pitches, durations, dynamics, instrumental timbres,

---

[2] I have been told that there are decorated, neon shoelaces, which are, I suppose, aesthetic products, but I'm thinking about standard "dress" shoelaces for this particular example.

and other musical elements so that those elements interact to form a unique, integrated, artistic whole.

Leonard Bernstein (1959) put it this way.

> [A composer is] always probing and rejecting in his dedication to perfection, to the principle of *inevitability*. This somehow is the key to the mystery of a great artist: that for reasons unknown to him or to anyone else, he will give away his energies and his life just to make sure that one note follows another inevitably. The composer, by doing this, leaves us at the finish with the feeling that something is right in the world, something checks throughout, *something follows its own laws consistently*. [Italics added.] (p. 93)

Certainly, we should teach our students to understand tonality, meter, tempo, harmony, counterpoint and other musical elements. But we should not stop there. If we do stop there, our students may never learn the qualitative difference between the construction of a sonata and the construction of a shoelace. We should go on to teach our students that each piece of music is an artistic product made up of a composer's choices about musical elements that interact cooperatively to form an integrated whole. That is as close as I can come to a definition of aesthetic music education.

## Aesthetic Music Education in Practice

Last December, just before Christmas vacation, I played Handel's "Hallelujah Chorus" for my fourth and fifth grade students. They had heard the opening phrase many times before (most of them started to sing along as soon as I put the tape on), but they did not know the rest of it. When it was over, they applauded. (They get carried away sometimes.)

Then a student raised her hand and mentioned that the word "hallelujah" was sung in so many different ways. I asked her what she meant, and she said that the rhythm kept changing. She chanted various examples, some of which appear in Figure 3.

"That's called melodic rhythm," I reminded her. (The class had heard the term before.) "Let's listen to the first minute of the piece again," I told my students, "and try to hear all the different ways that Handel sets the word 'hallelujah.'" I played the tape of the piece until it reached the fughetta with the words "and He shall reign forever and ever."

Then I stopped the tape and asked them to chant, one at a time with a neutral syllable, the "hallelujah" rhythms they heard. I began playing a series of macrobeats on a hand drum, and I told the students to pat Duple microbeats; then I called on one student at a time to chant the melodic

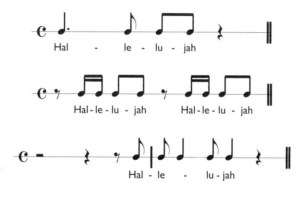

*Figure 3.*

rhythm of the "hallelujah" they were audiating while the rest of us continued to perform underlying macro- and microbeats: Bah—Bum **Bum** Bah; Bah-Bah **Bum** Bah.

"Who can chant their pattern with Dus and Du-Des?" I asked. Some of the students could do it. I continued playing macrobeats, they continued patting Duple microbeats, and, one at a time, they chanted various patterns: Du—de **Du** de; de-ta-**Du**-de. I told them that my favorite rhythm pattern is in the bass part about one minute into the piece: Hal-le-**lu**-jah-Hal-**le**-lu-**jah**, or de-ta-**Du**-de-ta-**Du**-de-**Du**. "Too hard!" my students complained.

Up to this point, I had simply been teaching a lesson in melodic rhythm. Let me explain a few things about the lesson before I move on.

1.  I moved from the entire piece to portions of the piece, from the whole to the parts.

2.  I set up a metric context (Duple meter) before I asked children to chant patterns. Then the students performed macrobeats, microbeats and the melodic rhythm of the "hallelujahs" at the same time. This is one of the basic tenets of Music Learning Theory: pattern instruction is meaningless unless students hear and perform patterns in an explicit tonal or metric context.

3.  I separated the tonal and rhythmic elements and asked students to chant rhythm patterns without pitch. I wanted to focus on rhythm without confusing the children with tonal elements.

4.  I was not teaching the rhythm patterns by rote; the students were teaching themselves. This is an example of a level of skill Gordon calls generalization-aural/oral.

5.  When I asked students to chant with rhythm syllables, I was moving them, with only some success, to a level of inference learning Gordon calls generalization-verbal.

After this, my lesson took an unusual turn. "Let's sing the opening phrase," I told my students. (Most of my fourth and fifth graders can sing a high D.) I played the introduction, and they came in with the soprano line, shown in Figure 4.

Hal - le - lu - jah    Hal - le - lu - jah    Hal - le - lu - jah    Hal - le - lu - jah    Hal -

le - lu - jah

*Figure 4.*

After they finished singing the opening phrase, I asked them, "How could Handel have written that differently?" Blank stares. "What else could Handel have done?" I asked again. No one responded. Finally I said, "Maybe he could have written this." I played the melody in Figure 5.

My students groaned after I played it. "That's terrible," one of them said.

"Tell me what I did to change it," I said.

One student raised his hand. "You changed the rhythm," he said.

"What do you mean?" I asked. "Did I change the tempo, the meter, or the melodic rhythm?" Sheer terror on the kids' faces!

"Okay, let's start with tempo." I asked them to show macrobeats by making big circles with their arms, starting from the shoulder. They were to pat their knees on the macrobeat and then start the circular motion all over again. Once they established a consistent tempo (with my help), I played Figure 4 as they kept the beat. I told them to keep going and then I played Figure 5. I said, "Ready. . . And . . . Stop." They stopped, and I asked them if their beat had changed. They said it hadn't.

Hal - le - lu - jah    Hal - le - lu - jah    Hal - le - lu - jah    Hal - le - lu - jah

*Figure 5.*

"What about the meter?" I asked. I asked half the class to pat macrobeats while the other half patted microbeats. Some children were able to use both hands and perform macro- and microbeats at the same time.

"What kind of microbeats are these?" I asked. They all agreed the microbeats were Duple. "Keep moving your hands while I play the two 'hallelujah' phrases." When I was finished, I asked the class if the macro- and microbeats were the same for both phrases. Everyone agreed both phrases were in Duple meter.

They were now certain that I had changed the melodic rhythm, not the tempo or the meter. "Which 'hallelujah' did I change?" I asked them. Most of them knew that I changed the melodic rhythm on the third "hallelujah."

"Now let me ask you again," I said. "What else could Handel have done?" This time they knew what I was asking: I wanted them to come up with their own variation of the opening "hallelujah" phrase. Their task was to change Handel's melodic rhythm while maintaining the original tempo and meter. They offered several versions, including this one (Figure 6).

*Figure 6.*

"Why do you suppose Handel chose the version he did?" I asked. "Why didn't he choose one of yours?" This question led the class into a profound discussion about musical aesthetics. These are some of the topics they touched on: the violation of expectations, the relationship between repetition and variation, the relationship between symmetry and balance. Many students, though not all, concluded that Handel chose the version in Figure 4 because he wanted to surprise listeners on the third "hallelujah." The first two hallelujahs set up a pattern; the third one changes the pattern. Many students, though not all, thought the versions in Figures 5 and 6 were dull because they repeated too much.

"Now we're going to hear the piece all the way through," I told them. "And this time I want you to focus on the different ways Handel sets the word 'hallelujah,' the way he repeats phrases, and the way he does *not* repeat phrases. See if there are any moments that surprise you."

Perhaps you are thinking that this last direction was very general. I agree; but then again, the study of Handel's "Hallelujah Chorus" is endless, and this will not be the last time they study the piece. At any rate, this was, for better or worse, a lesson in aesthetic music education.

Let me go over a few things that happened.

1. I built my lesson according to a whole-part-whole plan.
2. I steered clear of a discussion of feelings and emotions. Such a discussion would have diverted the students' attention from the music they were studying, and, therefore, from musical aesthetics.
3. I did not tell them I liked Handel's version best; and I did not ask them which version they liked best. Such information would have been irrelevant to my lesson. I accepted their opinions openly and willingly if they chose to offer them.
4. My lesson was not one of aesthetic music education until I asked my students the questions, "How else could Handel have composed this phrase?" and "Why do you think Handel chose the version he did and rejected the others?"
5. First, my students correctly identified the musical elements in the three examples that were the same (tempo and meter), and the musical element that changed (the melodic rhythm). Second, they improvised various phrases using Handel's original raw material. Finally, they were ready to discuss Handel's artistic choices. Had my students not first generalized and improvised, they would not have been prepared to discuss musical aesthetics.
6. Notice that during the first half of the lesson I focused on what Handel did; during the second half, I focused on what Handel *did not do but could have done*. Perhaps you believe the second half of my lesson was completely irrelevant. You may be thinking, "All we should care about is what Handel did; who cares what he *might* have done?" Yet, that is the basis for aesthetic education.

"But is this really formal instruction in musical aesthetics," you may be asking "or is it merely informal guidance?" I must make an important distinction at this point: by eliciting responses from my students about the intrinsic musical elements in Handel's music, I was, in fact, instructing them about musical aesthetics; but students may have aesthetic reactions to music even when they receive informal guidance. Let me offer the following example.

Most of my kindergarten students are still in tonal and rhythm babble—that is, they lack a sense of tonality and meter—and I am giving them informal guidance. One of the songs I sing for them during their music class is shown in Figure 7.

*Figure* 7.

I tell my students to stand in front of their chairs facing me, and as I sing this song for them, we move in place in a continuous, flowing manner. When the song ends, my students and I freeze. Then I sing the song again and we start moving, and when the song is over, we freeze again. Then I say to my students, "I'm going to sing the song again, and this time, no matter when the music stops, I want you to stop moving completely, like a statue. When the music starts again, you can move again." (It's quite a sight to see a group of twenty-five kindergarten children instantly freeze!)

What I do not tell them is that I might stop singing the song at any point, and they still have to freeze, even if the moment in the song is the "wrong" place to stop. For instance, I might choose to stop singing at the end of measure two, on the dominant. When I do that, typically the children will laugh. Then I'll continue singing and stop at the end of measure six, again on the low dominant. Once again, the children laugh.

But the interesting thing is that they do not know *why* they are laughing. And I certainly would not dream of launching into a discussion with them about symmetry, balance, and the violation of expectations in music. It seems clear to me, though, that their laughter is an aesthetic reaction. What is even more interesting is they tend *not* to laugh if I stop singing at the end of measure four. There is something about my stopping at the end of measure four that is less funny, or less surprising, than my stopping at the end of measure two or measure six. I strongly suspect that the students' reaction has to do with the symmetrical nature of the song.

If you sing it, you will notice that it is in Major tonality and that it is multimetric. Also, you may notice as you sing it that you group the eight measures into two four-measure units. Children, whether they realize it or not, are doing the same thing. The first two measures are paired with the next two measures; because measures five and six are a literal repeat of measures one and two, the listener expects to hear a literal repeat of measures three and four. In other words, the music sets up the listener to expect measures five through eight to be identical to measures one through four as in Figure 8. (The only difference between the first four and the last four measures is the necessary final cadence on the tonic.) When children do not hear a literal repeat where they expect it—either because the music has changed or because I stop singing altogether—they laugh.

*Figure 8.*

The song in Figure 7 is surprising for several reasons. You may notice as you sing it that the last two measures probably violate your expectations and cause the song to be asymmetrical. Suppose I had created the song in Unusual Paired meter throughout. Perhaps I could still have avoided a dull, literal repeat of the first four measures by composing something like the song in Figure 8. In fact, I sang the song in Figure 8 once for my kindergarten students, just to see their reaction. They were as bored as I was. There is something captivating about the asymmetrical structure of the song in Figure 7. Once again, the laughter of children as they hear Figure 7—but not Figures 8 and 9—reveals their level of interest in the music. Perhaps it is fair to say that the song in Figure 7 is a balanced work of art in spite of its lack of symmetry.

*Figure 9.*

**Conclusion**

My primary purpose in writing this chapter has been to show how aesthetic education may function cooperatively with Music Learning Theory. To do justice to this topic, my chapter should have been twice as long as it is. I should have discussed, in practical terms, each topic about aesthetic education that I mentioned: the violation of expectations, the relationship between repetition and variation, the use of metaphor in poetic and musical creation, the difference between prosaic symmetry and aesthetic balance in music, the function of ambiguity in musical structures, and the relationship between art and artificiality. I was able to touch on only a few of these topics here, but I hope I have been able to offer at least a coherent, if incomplete, introduction to aesthetic music education.

I have also tried to present a balanced appraisal of the ideas of Bennett Reimer, since he has written so much on aesthetic education. I will conclude with his description of the *Jump Right In* curriculum as "a series of readiness exercises and songs connected to them as if the songs were, themselves, more elaborate audiation exercises" (1994). Up to a point, Reimer is correct. In a general music class, teachers treat songs (and recorded musical examples) as audiation exercises *and* works of art. We should not apologize for this. If we taught "active listening," as Reimer (1991) advocates, by playing recordings of music without teaching audiation, then each music classroom would become like a radio station, and each music teacher would become a glorified disc jockey.

Reimer's claim that users of the *Jump Right In* curriculum—and, by extension, proponents of Music Learning Theory—treat pieces of music merely as audiation exercises is simply wrong. Still, I believe Reimer has, inadvertently, discerned a disturbing trend: perhaps we have focused too much of our energies on the first "whole" and the middle "part" of the learning process. The literature on Music Learning Theory, including my own writing, bears this out. Hardly anything has been written on the final "whole" of the learning process; almost nothing has been written about teachers and students relating pattern instruction to the audiation of larger forms of music. This is unfortunate, because the eight levels of Gordon's Skill Learning Sequence apply not only to pattern instruction but to complete works of music. Consider the example I used earlier in this paper: Students can learn the form of a series of patterns *and* the form of a Handel aria at the partial synthesis level. (A student's music education should not end, however, simply because he or she understands the form of a Handel aria. He should also learn that the aria is an aesthetic product made up of a series of artistic choices.)

In short, my experience leads me to believe that a) aesthetic music education is a natural outgrowth of Music Learning Theory, and b) aesthetic music education cannot occur unless students have sophisticated audiation skill. The audiation of functional patterns is, indeed, a means to an end; and it is time we shifted our attention to the final "whole" of the learning process by relating pattern instruction to complete works of music and by teaching musical aesthetics. Only then will students be able to take full advantage of the foundation that pattern instruction offers them.

# References

Bernstein, L. (1959). *The joy of music*. New York: Simon and Schuster.

Gordon E. E. (1991). "A Response to Volume II, Numbers 1 and 2 of the Quarterly." *The Quarterly, II* (4), pp. 62-72.

Machlis, J. (1977). *The enjoyment of music: An introduction to perceptive listening*. New York: W. W. Norton and Company.

Reimer, B. (1989). *A philosophy of music education*. Englewood Cliffs, New Jersey: Prentice Hall

——. (1991). "Aesthetic Education: What It Means and Why It Matters." (Audio Tape No. 3019 in *Voice Of Experience*). Reston, Virginia: Music Educators National Conference.

Reimer, B., & Gordon, E. E. (1994). *The Reimer/Gordon debate on music learning: Complementary or contradictory views?* (Audio Tape Stock #3004, ISBN 1-56545-052-3). MENC National Biennial In-service Conference in Cincinnati, Ohio.

Walters, D. L. (1989). Coordinating Learning Sequence Activities and Classroom Activities. In D. L. Walters and C. C. Taggart (Eds.). *Readings in Music Learning Theory*. Chicago: GIA Publications.

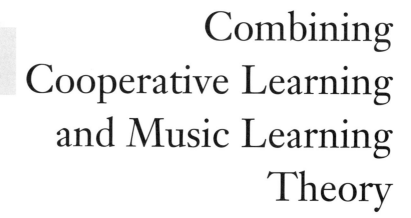

*Richard M. Cangro*

THE HARTT SCHOOL
UNIVERSITY OF HARTFORD COMMUNITY DIVISION

# Combining Cooperative Learning and Music Learning Theory

## Introduction

After taking some courses and workshops in Music Learning Theory, I decided to broaden the horizons of my middle school band by including some musicianship activities during rehearsals. These activities were designed primarily to develop each student's inner musical instrument. As a result of these musical experiences, I hoped my students would improve their levels of understanding of tonality and meter, which in turn would improve the ensemble's intonation, rhythmic precision, communication, concept of sound, and sense of style. I decided to start a rehearsal by singing a classical melody and having the students learn that melody by ear. I hoped that after singing and playing the melody by ear we could discuss topics, such as tonality, meter, harmony, dynamics, phrasing, and expressiveness, with a depth of musical understanding. With these goals in mind, I bravely stood in front of the group at our first rehearsal of the year and asked them to sing an easy melody. This became one of the longest lessons I have ever endured, as well as a turning point in my music education philosophy.

After I sang the first phrase to the group, ignoring the faces of bewilderment, I asked the students to sing the melody back to me. I received nothing but silence in return. I sang the melody once again and asked them to sing it back to me, but they would not make a sound. Beginning to see the tremendous challenge I was undertaking, I altered the lesson plan and asked the students to perform a phrase from the melody on their instruments.

441

Being aware of their musical abilities, I felt confident they would be able play the melody by ear without much effort. After giving them sixty seconds to figure out the notes and rhythms individually, I asked for volunteers to perform the first phrase for the group. No one would volunteer to play a solo in front of his or her peers for fear of making a mistake. I asked the band to perform all together, and finally I received a trepidatious response from the students. Playing by ear was more of a challenge than I had anticipated. The band played the melody timidly—unsure of the pitches, key, tonality, and rhythms. It was as if I had paralyzed their abilities to perform on their instruments. It was curious to me that after learning and practicing an instrument for approximately four years these students could not confidently perform an easy melody by ear. This lack of student success caused me to reflect on the process of teaching musicianship effectively during band rehearsals.

When students were asked to perform on their instruments in solo, they did not respond well. However, when I asked the students to perform as a group, they responded much more positively. The students felt safer when performing with others. I realized my tasks needed to be group activities that encouraged students to participate with a level of comfort not present when playing alone. However, I could not monitor individual learning when the entire band performed together. It is extremely difficult to hear the musical progress of an individual when every other person in the band is playing at the same time. After rethinking my lesson format, I planned an experiment for the next lesson. I would give them a short list of familiar melodies, divide the band into smaller groups, and assign each group to learn one song by ear. I made everyone in each group responsible for checking each other's mastery. I gave them five minutes to complete this task, which culminated with each group performing a song for the whole ensemble. Realizing the freedom of this activity, the students began to come alive and work together in choosing a song, helping each other learn the melody, and even adding notes and harmonies to their arrangements.

Given this new freedom to explore music with their instruments, my students began experimenting with the melody by playing it as a round, ornamenting it, applying root melodies or bass lines, and improvising new melodies. They were actually applying many of the musical concepts that they had learned from performing band repertoire. The results were splendid! Each group performed their arrangement. Some were good, some humorous, and all revealed musical abilities that helped guide me as to what musical skills the next lesson should focus on developing. With high levels of participation and enthusiasm, students came alive by acquiring ownership for something that they created in music. They laughed and learned at the same time while creating, performing, and responding to music.

As a result of collaboratively working in smaller groups on this task, the students were able to discuss aspects of instrumental performance, such as balance and dynamics, intelligently. Phrases such as "How does that go?", "I can't hear myself," and "Who is playing the melody?" ignited musical discussions. Expressiveness and musicality, as well as technique, were all expressed at differing levels according to individual musical differences. Students made musical decisions, helped each other through difficulties, and successfully collaborated; the group effort became the driving force.

Observing my students develop their independence by making musical decisions became the catalyst for my further investigation into cooperative learning and how it can be used in instrumental music education. As a result of improving my cooperative lessons each year with members of this band, their performance level has increased, as well as their levels of musical understanding. Ensemble sections have become more cohesive; students listen to each other and the other sections; students have become more aware of balance and dynamics; and an overall awareness of meter has become more evident throughout the ensemble. Consequently, the band can learn and perform appropriate literature more quickly and more expressively because of newly acquired strategies that enable students to collaborate and engage in musical thinking.

**What Is Cooperative Learning?**

Cooperative learning can be broadly described as students working together to accomplish a common goal. The Roman philosopher Seneca advocated cooperative learning through such statements as *"Qui docet discet,"* which translates, "When you teach, you learn twice" (Johnson & Johnson, 1992). Cooperative learning in the public school setting can be traced as far back as the 19th century. During the common school movement of the 1830s and 1840s, the modern American schools began to take form with one-room schoolhouses simultaneously addressing various educational levels. Older students helped younger students learn their assignments by teaching the material to them, while the teacher facilitated and guided groups and individuals. Similarly, Maria Montessori (1870–1952), an advocate of collaborative and cooperative learning, developed an instructional paradigm whereby students are responsible for their learning through peer collaboration and inquiry, with the teacher functioning as a facilitator (Lillard & Schachar, 1988).

John Dewey (1859–1952) founded the Laboratory School at the University of Chicago in 1896 with the purpose of studying student-peer relations. He advocated teaching methods that provided for social interaction in knowledge acquisition and illustrated the interdependence of society through practical, experiential group activities. In *Democracy and Education* (1916), Dewey states, "The social environment consists of all the activities of fellow beings that are bound up in the carrying on of the activities of any one of its members. It is truly educative in its effect in the degree in which an individual shares or participates in some conjoint activity. By doing his share in the associated activity, the individual appropriates the purpose which actuates it, becomes familiar with its methods and subject matters, acquires needed skill, and is saturated with is emotional spirit" (p. 22). In cooperative learning settings, students see other students in various stages of mastery of a cognitive task, while supporting and helping each other to achieve. Each cooperative group, in essence, becomes a microcosm of the whole class in academic achievement, gender, ethnicity, and race. As a result of working cooperatively, individuals become enabled to learn actively together, while the teacher becomes a facilitator in the learning process, fostering independence through student-to-student interaction.

Student-to-student interaction in small, heterogeneous learning groups, with individuals helping each other, is common to all versions of cooperative learning. The predominant cooperative learning models share some form of the following five components (Johnson & Johnson, 1986, 1990; Devries & Slavin, 1978; Kagan, 1997):

1. *Positive Interdependence:* Each student is responsible for his or her own learning and the learning of the other group members. Individuals are dependent on each other to reach a shared goal.
2. *Individual Accountability:* Each student demonstrates mastery or completion of a task or assignment.
3. *Face to Face Positive Interaction:* Individuals support and assist each other's learning.
4. *Social Skills:* Groups demonstrate effective communication, trust building, and conflict resolution.
5. *Group Processing:* Peers assess task mastery and completion for the group.

Kagan (1997) describes careful structuring of cooperative learning activities so that all students are able to participate, elaborate, and contribute to the group, increasing their understanding through verbal

---

## PIES

**Positive Interdependence**
- Each group member's success is contingent upon every other group member.
- "Is my gain, your gain?"

**Individual Accountability**
- Each group member is accountable for their learning and each other's learning.
- "Is individual performance required?"

**Equal Participation**
- Each group member has a turn to participate and must contribute something.
- "Will each group member have a turn and be able to contribute something?"

**Simultaneous Interaction**
- Each person in a group participates in turn, one after the other in sequence.
- "What percentage of students are overtly active at once?"

---

*Figure 1.* Four Basic Principles of Cooperative Learning as described by Kagan (1997)

processing. He describes four basic principles that must be present in effective cooperative learning situations: positive interdependence, individual accountability, equal participation, and simultaneous interaction (see Figure 1). Positive interdependence occurs when the gains of the group or team are positively correlated with each individual's achievement in that group. Individual accountability requires some kind of performance by each student within a group demonstrating a level of mastery. Equal participation necessitates that each student be given the opportunity to contribute to the group task to the same extent. Simultaneous interaction describes the percentage of students overtly active at the same time. For example, simply giving a task to a group with no structures or roles is labeled "group work," not cooperative learning, according to Kagan. Group work lacks individual accountability and frequently lacks equal participation. Johnson and Johnson (1990) state that many studies in cooperative learning that fail to find a transfer of learning from group to individual most likely suffer from a lack of positive interdependence, individual accountability, higher-level tasks, and discussion of the material being learned. Johnson and Johnson further state that studies consistently found group to individual transfer of learning when the following considerations were made: a) carefully structuring positive interdependence and individual accountability within the cooperative condition, b) requiring students to discuss the material they were learning, and c) using higher-level tasks.

In music, individual accountability, discussion, and higher-level tasks are all common aspects of an effective music program. Developing both group musicianship and individual musicianship during instruction requires learning strategies that address skill development in a way that leads to musical independence by engaging as many individuals as possible. By having structured student interaction in the music class, a teacher facilitates learning through active engagement in the musical process, with opportunities for application of musical skills and concepts with immediate feedback. Cooperative learning strategies offer music educators the flexibility to develop many aspects of music learning for students, as well as ensemble performance goals.

## Cooperative Learning and Music Learning Theory

Incorporating cooperative learning strategies into the Music Learning Theory learning sequences and activities (Gordon, 2003) is an effective way to engage students actively in developing audiation at every level. Paired with direct instruction, cooperative learning can further address individual student musical needs by allowing students the opportunity to learn from each other. By having opportunities to listen, interact, coach, and assess each other's musical performances in a small, cooperative learning group, students further internalize musical concepts through experiential learning in a comfortable, close-knit setting with their peers.

In Music Learning Theory, through Learning Sequence Activities, students observe, listen, interact, process, verbalize, and perform musical thoughts and patterns with the goal of musical comprehension. As soon as students develop the listening and performing vocabularies necessary at the aural/oral skill level, they are ready to use these musical skills to communicate cooperatively and learn with their peers, reinforcing audiation. After developing an aural/oral tonal and rhythm vocabulary, students can be guided to bridge to inference learning (generalization—aural/oral or creativity/improvisation—aural/oral) through cooperative learning strategies that powerfully develop audiation through student interaction. When students have the opportunity to develop their audiation cooperatively through observation, reflection, and discussion of a musical performance, learners are able to internalize musical concepts and skills. Working collaboratively requires students to reflect, process, and verbalize thoughts, making generalizations and elaborations that they share further with their peers in their own words. Making generalizations and elaborations requires students to understand the relationship between new knowledge and prior knowledge, which is an effective way to improve depth of comprehension.

Each Learning Sequence Activity can be expanded and reinforced with a cooperative learning strategy. Coupling direct instruction with cooperative learning strategies enables a teacher to present musical skills and content effectively and then provides an opportunity for students to respond and audiate at their own individual rate of comprehension. Facilitating student learning through cooperative learning activities, in turn, enables the teacher to address individual musical strengths and weaknesses by allowing students to simultaneously perform, interact, and help each other.

## Lesson Planning for Cooperative Learning

*Modeling*

When planning to include cooperative learning strategies in music instruction, a number of issues should be considered. Students need to learn how to interact appropriately in a learning situation. In most classes, students are asked to remain quiet and listen to the teacher. In cooperative learning settings, students must talk to each other, work through difficulties, and work toward completing the shared goal of their group. For successful cooperative learning lessons, the teacher needs to model for the class how groups should interact, how to help and coach others, how to stay on task, and how to monitor time limits.

*Classroom Management*

With cooperative learning, one of the most useful classroom management tools for teachers is a quiet signal. This signal is used to bring a large group to attention quickly and effectively. In cooperative learning settings, students are busy working and interacting in small groups, many times with a higher than normal noise level. Because of this, the teacher must establish a quiet signal before cooperative learning activities begin.

When students are working and see the signal, whether it is a placard or a raised hand by a teacher, they should be trained to respond quickly so that classroom management is maintained and the transition to the next step in the lesson is seamless.

When students are working cooperatively in groups, it can be difficult for them to hear one another. One suggestion is to ask students to use six-inch voices when working in groups. This means that students can speak within a listening range of six inches from their mouth. This strategy reduces the noise level considerably. Instrumental music classes have a unique problem, in that students use instruments to express their musical ideas. When not speaking or singing, instrumentalists should conform to the "one player at a time" rule. Only one player in each group should be allowed to play at a time. This will preserve an acceptable sound level in a band or orchestra rehearsal room. Depending on the activity, there will be times when groups need to perform together on their instruments. It is up to the teacher's discretion to decide how long this should occur and at what point in the activity.

An effective strategy for teachers to use in cooperative learning activities is a time limit. Structuring tasks is vital in the management and effectiveness of cooperative learning. Teachers must carefully predetermine the amount of time to be devoted to certain tasks when students are working cooperatively. Too much time on a task may create discipline problems. Not enough time on a task may cause students frustration, as they will not be able to complete a task. It is important to establish time limits that promote effective use of time and learning.

## Grouping Students

Grouping three to five students according to their skills level is crucial in the cooperative learning process. Four-member groups are optimal in most learning situations. Student groups should be balanced, displaying a normal distribution of abilities. When students are grouped with others of like skill level, problems may occur, such as apathy, competing for leadership within a group, lack of social cohesion, and off-task behavior. All of these problems defeat the purpose of cooperative learning. Each cooperative group should contain a distribution of high-, average-, and low-achieving students with high, average, and low music aptitudes. Heterogeneous ability groupings foster heterogeneous musical ideas and opinions that can cause individuals to think, compare, and refine their musical ideas and opinions based on the various responses from their peers.

### Cooperative Learning Models in Action

Several different cooperative learning strategies are available. The strategies described below are effective in various learning situations, including in a performing ensemble. Some models are designed for small group instruction, while others work best in large classes, such as a band or orchestra. Depending on the outcome desired by the teacher, the model should be chosen carefully, taking into consideration classroom management, logistics, and group dynamics.

Timed-Pair-Share (Kagan, 1997) works well with short tasks. Students first think silently of an answer to a question or problem posed by the teacher. After a specified length of time, students pair up with a partner to discuss and compare ideas, with a specified length of time given to each student to talk through their ideas. After some time, the pairs share their combined ideas with the class.

This model is effective with all grade levels and class sizes and affords each student extra time to think and generate ideas. Students have an opportunity individually to process a posed question or task, compare and elaborate ideas and solutions, and receive immediate feedback from peers. A variation of this model, adapted for instrumental music, might be Think-Pair-Square-Share. The "square" may consist of a section or family of instruments. An overall sense of interdependence and peer coaching should be pervasive among the cooperative pairs and groups. A sample activity for this approach follows.

### Instrumental Music Application

**Objective:** The learners will develop the ability to sing and perform in Minor tonality.

**Cooperative structure:** Timed, Pair, Square, Share

**Material:** "Twinkle, Twinkle Little Star"

**Skills developed:**
- Understanding of Major and Minor tonalities
- Application of tonal understanding by transforming a song in B-flat Major tonality into G Minor by singing and performing the song on an instrument.

**Procedures:**

**Direct Instruction—Whole Class**

1. Students sing "Twinkle, Twinkle Little Star" in B-flat Major tonality.

2. Students perform "Twinkle, Twinkle" by ear together on their instruments in concert B-flat Major.

3. Teacher establishes Minor tonality (G-LA) and asks students to sing "Twinkle, Twinkle" in G Minor.

**Task**

Cooperative groups (by section) work together to perform Minor "Twinkle, Twinkle" by ear, demonstrating correct tonality, key, and rhythm.

| Steps | Cooperative Groups | Timer |
|-------|--------------------|-------|
| *Think* | Individuals think and finger the song silently. | 30 seconds |
| *Pair* | Individuals pair up with a person in the group and discuss the song—fingering together and correcting each other without playing their instruments. | 90 seconds *(45 seconds for each student)* |
| *Square* | Students pair up with others in section. Each person takes a turn playing a phrase of the song while group members listen, learn, and coach. | 4 minutes *(1 minute per student)* |
| *Share* | Individuals/sections perform song for band. | 5 minutes **Total - 11 minutes** |

**Closure:** Teacher has entire band perform "Twinkle, Twinkle" in G Minor.

For further assessment, the teacher may call on individuals from each section to perform the song to check for comprehension. A reflection worksheet may also serve as a self-assessment.

Pairs Check (Kagan, 1997) involves a team of two pairs of students who are given a task. Each pair of students works on a problem. One student in the pair works while the other coaches and monitors the progress of the first student. After switching roles and completing several problems or questions, the pair should compare their answers to those of the other pair. If the pairs agree on the answers, they provide positive reinforcement to each other. If the answers are different, a discussion should ensue until the pairs arrive at a consensus. Results are then discussed in the class, with all pairs of students exchanging answers and solutions. An example of this strategy follows.

## Classroom Music Application

**Objective:** The learners will develop the ability to read and notate tonic and dominant tonal patterns in Major tonality

**Cooperative structure:** Pairs Check

**Material:** Major tonic and dominant tonal patterns

**Skills developed:**
- Understanding of Major tonality
- Reading and notating music

**Procedures:**
### Direct Instruction—Whole Class
1. Students echo-sing Major tonic and dominant tonal patterns.

2. Students improvise Major tonic and dominant tonal patterns with their voices.

3. Students read and sing Major tonal patterns from notation.

### Task
Cooperative pairs work together to compose, notate, and perform Major tonic and dominant tonal patterns.

| Steps | Cooperative Groups | Timer |
|-------|-------------------|-------|
| *Think* | Individuals compose and then notate two tonic and two dominant tonal patterns. | 4 minutes |
| *Pair* | Individuals pair up with another person in the group, and the partners check each other's patterns, correcting each other. | 60 seconds |
| *Check* | Students pair up with others and check each other's patterns, correcting each other. | 4 minutes **Total - 9 minutes** |

**Closure:** Teacher has groups perform their notated patterns.

For further assessment, the teacher may call on individuals from each group to perform some tonal patterns to check for comprehension.

Roundtable/Round Robin (Kagan, 1997) is a brainstorming activity that requires a minimum of three students in a group. It may be implemented in either spoken or written form. In written form, one piece of paper is passed around the group with the intent of having each individual respond to a question or problem with a short answer or comment. This procedure generates a list of responses for discussion or review by the whole group. The spoken version (Round Robin) is similar to the written; students pass around ideas verbally but do not keep a written record of their individual responses. An instrumental application of this strategy follows:

### Instrumental Music Application

**Objective:** The learners will develop the ability to perform, from notation, songs in Minor tonality.

**Cooperative structure:** Round Robin

**Material:** Minor "Twinkle, Twinkle" and "Minka, Minka"

**Skills developed:**
• Performing by ear a song in Minor tonality
• Reading and performing from notation music in concert G Minor

**Procedures:**
  **Direct Instruction—Whole Class**
  1. Teacher reviews Minor tonality by having students sing Minor "Twinkle, Twinkle Little Star."

  2. Students perform Minor "Twinkle, Twinkle" on their instruments as a group.

  3. Teacher reviews key and tonal patterns for concert G Minor and then explains that students will perform "Minka, Minka" from a worksheet, demonstrating a steady beat and accurate performance of all tonal and rhythm patterns.

**Task**
Students separate into their assigned cooperative groups to work on "Minka, Minka"

| Steps | Cooperative Groups | Timer |
|---|---|---|
| *Think* | Individuals think and finger the song silently. | 60 seconds |
| *Round Robin* | Taking turns, each student performs four measures of "Minka, Minka" from notation, while the other group members coach and give suggestions for tonal and rhythm improvements. | 4 minutes *(1 minute per person)* |

**Closure:** Teacher has entire band perform "Minka, Minka."

For further assessment, the teacher may call on individuals from each group to perform some or all of "Minka, Minka" to check for comprehension.

Teams-Games-Tournaments (Slavin, 1992) is a basic cooperative-competitive model that challenges individuals to perform better after practicing with the members of their group. The group works together to ensure that each member knows the assigned material. After practicing together, team members split up to compete at tournament tables with members of other teams whose past performance is at a similar level of competency. Students earn points for their team based on how well they do at their tournament tables. Individual progress can be measured through rating scales specifically designed for the material. Students who understand how to use the rating scales may serve as judges at the tournament tables. Performers may be measured on aspects of performance, such as steady beat, correct pitches, posture and hand position, or correct rhythms.

Group Investigation (Sharan and Shachar, 1988) is one of the most independent models of cooperative learning. Students form their own groups and then decide what they will study, how they will go about obtaining the information, and how to present their findings to the class. This model requires a certain level of maturity and should be used with older students. The group assigns responsibility to each individual to do his or her share in completing the project. In instrumental music, students may use this model to complete an arrangement or composition assignment. Students could choose the instrumentation, style, and harmony based on the group's level of music understanding. Jazz combos and student-run chamber ensembles naturally engage in Group Investigation by working independently to learn and perform their piece.

## Summary

All of these models can be used effectively in conjunction with Music Learning Theory to develop and enhance audiation. Choosing an appropriate cooperative structure requires careful thought about the content and skills that need to be addressed in a curriculum. Once a teacher is able to clearly define what students are expected to accomplish and to what extent, selecting a cooperative learning model becomes a simple matter.

## Assessment

Clear objectives with measurable outcomes are part of effective instruction in any subject. Diagnosing difficulties and prescribing solutions for students shapes how a teacher plans for future learning. One main goal of cooperative learning in any subject area is to improve learning for each individual through student interaction. Even though students are working together, the teacher should formally assess only levels of achievement gained by the individual. Assessing group work can undermine the integrity and effectiveness of cooperative learning. Student interaction in small groups does not guarantee that all members are participating and contributing equally. It would be unfair to grade a group of students on efforts that are assumed to have been equal. Equal participation should be carefully monitored in planning and implementation of cooperative instructional strategies so that one student does not do all the work, with the group receiving credit. Group assessment should focus mainly on how well the

**Name:** _____

After thinking, fingering, and practicing, complete the following by checking the appropriate box.

**1. I can perform "Molly Malone" with a steady beat.**

| Always | Frequently | Sometimes | Rarely | Never |
|--------|------------|-----------|--------|-------|
| ☐ | ☐ | ☐ | ☐ | ☐ |

**2. I can perform the song with the appropriate group of notes for concert E-flat Major.**

| Always | Frequently | Sometimes | Rarely | Never |
|--------|------------|-----------|--------|-------|
| ☐ | ☐ | ☐ | ☐ | ☐ |

**3. I can accurately perform the dotted-quarter eighth note patterns in the song.**

| Always | Frequently | Sometimes | Rarely | Never |
|--------|------------|-----------|--------|-------|
| ☐ | ☐ | ☐ | ☐ | ☐ |

**4. How did you and your group operate?**

(Circle the number that best describes how the group cooperated.)

| | Always | Frequently | Sometimes | Rarely | Never |
|---|--------|------------|-----------|--------|-------|
| • I shared my ideas with the group. | 5 | 4 | 3 | 2 | 1 |
| • I listened to the others. | 5 | 4 | 3 | 2 | 1 |
| • One person talked the most in our group. | 5 | 4 | 3 | 2 | 1 |
| • We contributed equally to solve our problems. | 5 | 4 | 3 | 2 | 1 |
| • I helped my partner and/or others in my group. | 5 | 4 | 3 | 2 | 1 |

*Figure 2.* Example of a reflective worksheet to be completed individually

group cooperated on a task. Achievement through cooperative learning should be assessed individually.

Many assessment opportunities become available when implementing cooperative learning strategies in music. Examples of formal and informal measures of student performance, such as peer-assessments, individual and group reflective worksheets (see Figure 2), and guided practice with peer coaching/assessing become integrated easily in lessons that include structured cooperative learning. With proper guidance, immediate feedback from peers can quickly and effectively address difficulties that arise in student performances, leaving the teacher to facilitate learning among many independent, interdependent groups. As a result of the teacher facilitating student interaction, individuals develop ownership for assessment tools that measure their music learning, as well as acquire skills to independently diagnose and prescribe solutions for musical difficulties. Furthermore, when students can assess cooperatively and improve musical performance through the use of measurement tools, higher levels of musical comprehension are addressed and applied.

## Conclusions

Classroom instruction that includes appropriately structured cooperative learning activities provides opportunities for multiple students to respond simultaneously to a question, diagnose difficulties, prescribe solutions to peers, learn and apply concepts through various multiple intelligences, and monitor varying levels of achievement within the group. Cooperative learning strategies, used within the context of a Music Learning Theory curriculum, give students powerful opportunities that effectively develop audiation to its fullest capacity. Individuals in cooperative groups receive immediate attention to their learning needs from their peers, creating a class with a high proportion of student engagement and on-task behavior. Teachers who engage their classes through cooperative learning activities can create active music learners and independent music makers, developing a foundation of social and musical skills for their students that will last a lifetime.

## References

Devries, D., & Slavin, R. (1978). Teams-Games-Tournaments (TGT): Review of ten classroom experiments. *Journal of Research and Development in Education, 12*(1), 28-38.

Dewey, J. (1916). *Democracy and education.* New York: Macmillan.

Gordon, E. E. (2003). *Learning sequences in music: Skill, content, and patterns.* Chicago: GIA Publications.

Johnson, D. W., & Johnson, R. T. (1986). *Circles of learning: Cooperation in the Classroom* (Rev. ed.). Edina, MN: Interaction Press.

——. (1990). *Cooperation in the classroom.* Edina, MN: Interaction Press.

——. (1992). Implementing cooperative learning. *Contemporary Education, LXIII*(3), 173-181.

Kagan, S. (1997). *Cooperative learning* (2nd edition). San Clemente, CA: Resources for Teachers, Inc.

Lillard, P. P. (1996). *Montessori Today: A comprehensive approach to education from birth to adulthood.* New York: Schocken Books.

Sharan, S., & Shachar, H. (1988). *Language and learning in the cooperative classroom.* New York: Springer Publishing Co.

Slavin, R. (1992) *Cooperative learning: Theory, research and practice.* Boston: Allyn and Bacon.

*Herbert D. Marshall*
• • • • • • • • • • • • • •
University of Michigan

# World Music within the Context of Music Learning Theory

That world music appears in this collection of readings is testament to the increased awareness music educators have of music beyond the Western classical tradition and the willingness of Music Learning Theory practitioners to adapt instruction to meet current trends. In this chapter I will a) offer a rationale for the inclusion of world music as repertoire in classrooms and ensembles, b) propose criteria for selection of world music, and c) suggest techniques for teaching world music.

## A Rationale for World Music

If there were a Music Learning Theory creed, one of the first statements would be "we believe in teaching a variety of tonalities and meters." Another prominent belief is that "students learn best what something is by hearing what it is not." By expanding your repertoire to include music of other cultures, you may accomplish both of these goals.

For example, consider the deep structural elements of typical Western classical music along with folk and popular music in the United States. If, by observation or acclimation, we agreed upon a general set of musical elements present in typical U.S. school repertoire, then where might we find complementary, contrasting, stimulating music? Figure 1 may serve as a musical compass for the teacher seeking to diversify his or her repertoire. Some of this information is gleaned from Nettl, et al. (1992) and Titon (2002), but most is from personal experience. When choosing music for your classroom, listening to recordings is essential. Recordings by individual artists and collected by scholars in series are available in stores and online. A particularly good source is *World Music – The Rough Guide* (1994), which publishes recordings and commentary on traditional and contemporary music from around the world. It is like a travel guide for your audiation.

The examples in Figure 1 are particularly useful for students in discrimination levels of learning. Primary students will benefit most by hearing and moving to recordings. They will benefit from immersion in music of other cultures, both by becoming familiar with those musics and by comparing them to Western music. Once a listening vocabulary is established, middle elementary students should have many opportunities to sing, play, and move to the music of other cultures. World music offers many points of departure because of the frequent use of ostinato and layering, which allows us to individualize instruction by attending to the difficulty of the layers and assigning them to students accordingly.

When students are ready for inference learning and have already learned to read music notation, a comparison of music notation systems would be appropriate. An interesting audiational challenge might be to give advanced students a familiar piece of music in an unfamiliar system of notation, such as the tonic SO-FA system borrowed from Europe and still widely used in South Africa or the pitch-set and gong-cycle notation in gamelon music. The students might be asked to infer the rules of the alternate notation system by audiating the familiar piece.

A third creed statement for Music Learning Theory practitioners—borrowed from Pestalozzian methodology—might be "young people learn music best in an active, experiential manner." Unfortunately, in the Western tradition, the boundaries between the performer and the audience are rigid. Performers are often in formal dress—instrumentalists are hidden behind stands, and singers stand shoulder-to-shoulder on narrow risers. Movement is severely restricted. Communication with the audience is in the style of classical theater, in which the audience is behind an abstract fourth wall, unseen and unheard. Audiences learn their role quickly and wait politely to applaud at prescribed intervals. If the music moves them, they dare not sing, clap, or move for fear of breaking concert etiquette. This is particularly difficult for children, who naturally react physically to music. Thus, the very audience we seek to cultivate and inspire is often left at home to avoid disruption.

This is not the case in many parts of the world; in many cultures, music is still a communal activity. Often there is a leader who starts pieces

| Element | U.S. Tendency | Possible Contrast | Potential Sources[1] |
|---|---|---|---|
| Meter | Duple and Triple | Unusual[2] | Eastern European, Greek, Yemeni, North and South Classical Indian |
| | Monometric | Polymetric (including music that accompanies movement in which the meter of the music and movement is diferent) | Many cultures in sub-Saharan Africa, some Latino and gamelon examples |
| | Unitemporal | Multi- and Polytemporal | Native American aerophone[3] and vocal, Roma chordophone and vocal, some complex call-and-response songs in African and African American culture, Chinese instrumental music, Hebrew, Islamic, and Western liturgical chant |
| | Unimetric | Multimetric | Dance "medleys" made up of seamless chains of tunes in different meters found in Celtic, Middle Eastern, and Mediterranean cultures |
| Tonal | Equal Temperment | Many other tunings using half steps and whole steps, use of microtones | Particularly chordophone and vocal music of the Middle East and Southern Asia, many examples using Balinese and Javanese gamelon instruments—makers tune each "orchestra" in a unique way, often to the overtones of the largest gong |
| | Major and Harmonic Minor tonality | Mixolydian, Dorian, and Aeolian | British, Welsh, Scottish, Celtic, Russian, and some Scandinavian |
| | | Lydian, Mixolydian | Serbian, Hungarian |
| | | Phrygian | Roma, Mediterranean, and Middle East |
| | | Pentatonic | Asian, some children's and folk music of African and Latino cultures |
| | | other, e.g. *sléndro* and *pélog* scales in gamelon music | Other pitch sets found and documented from Eastern European, Middle Eastern, Chinese, and Indian |
| | Tertian and Vertical Harmonies | Drones | Classical Indian, Middle Eastern |
| | | Heterophony | Celtic, gamelon, Peking opera |
| | | Complex layering of pitched motives | Equatorial Africa—especially forest cultures, Shona culture, gamelon |

*Figure 1.* Resources for structural elements of music

[1] For brevity, this list includes general regions where the reader is likely to find appropriate examples; it is not exhaustive.

[2] For definitions of these terms, see *Learning Sequences in Music: Skill, Content, and Patterns* (Gordon, 2003).

[3] To describe instrumental music, Curt Sachs and Erich von Hornbostel devised a classification system using the terms aerophone, chordophone, membranophone, and idiophone. They are more useful and inclusive than the traditional Western classical families.

or organizes events, but everyone participates, as in music of Zimbabwe's Shona people. A Shona mbira (thumb piano) player will begin a melody but may be joined by a multi-generational ensemble of singers, dancers, hand-clappers, and percussionists (Turino, in Nettl, 1992). The mbira players provide a lilting, mesmerizing foundation for an event with complex layers and timbres. Perhaps a similar communal music activity could be experienced by our students and their families as an outgrowth of what happens in the classroom. Mbiras are relatively inexpensive and can be used in general music activities. Tones are produced by plucking small strips of metal that vibrate. The instruments can be tuned by changing the length of these strips. In this way, students can create a pitched ostinato pattern over which can be layered non-pitched instruments or vocal lines.

Re-enacting spring, harvest, and wedding rituals from other cultures demonstrates the use of music to unite people and mark milestones in life, such as dance and panpipe events in Andean culture (Turino, in Nettl, 1992). These rituals can be recreated for North American students, noting that the seasons are in the same sequence but occur in different months, thus acknowledging the temporal differences between Northern and Southern Hemispheres. Panpipes are readily available and inexpensive, but are more difficult to tune. Recorders in the lower range are an appropriate substitution and are part of a long tradition of flute playing in Latin cultures.

While representing the role of music in culture, one must not ignore other concurrent forms of expression. What Westerners have separated into performing arts—music, dance, drama—remain integrated in many other cultures. For example, traditional vocal music of the Zulu and Xhosa people is intrinsically linked with movement. The Hindi word *sangita* refers to music, movement, and dramatic storytelling (Capwell, 1992). The Peking opera tradition is an example of the symbiotic state of music, dance, and drama in which vocalists use stylized movement to communicate a story, masked characters mime traditional roles in sync with music, and musicians accompany and enhance the performance with sensitivity, flexibility, and meticulous timing. Perhaps if children in our classrooms were allowed to participate in communal music music making and were encouraged to express themselves through arts in an integrated way, making music rather than consuming music would be more commonplace.

World music is worth studying on the basis of its own musical value. Beyond this, world music is an opportunity to open learners' minds to the diversity and commonality of the earth's human inhabitants.

> Ethnomusicology is indeed a remarkable field because it deals with human beings through our music, which is perhaps our most personal form of expression. If we can learn to appreciate and understand the music of a culture, then perhaps we can learn to appreciate its members as human beings and respect them as individual—and they can learn to appreciate and respect us. (Olson, 2002, p. 107)

For a Music Learning Theory practitioner who feels that diversity and tolerance are priorities (or curricular mandates), world music may be a means through which to accomplish these goals while having students experience stimulating and compelling music. Western music that focuses on diversity tends to do so through lyrics; many of the songs feature instructive poems about diversity set to music that is placid and predictable. Diversity and tolerance are implicit in world music, and the educator should use music of other cultures to open students' minds to issues of diversity, choosing the salient points upon which to focus based on the maturity of the students and the needs of the curriculum.

## Selecting World Music

As far as anthropologists know, all cultures on Earth communicate through some form of language, profess belief in a higher power, and make music. As long as there has been immigration, there has been an exchange of music between people of different cultures. When choosing music for use in a classroom, it is important to consider music as representing a culture rather than a country. In that way, music helps define human experience rather than symbolize a geographic place or current political abstraction.

Throughout history and across vast regions of the planet, colonial powers have drawn haphazard political boundaries that divided people who share a common culture, such as the Tswana people in Southern Africa. Many tribes coexisted in the semi-arid regions of southern Africa. When the English and Dutch found gold and diamonds in this region, they quickly scrambled to claim the natural wealth and establish boundaries. Part of the Tswana people found themselves in north-central South Africa, mining riches from the earth for Europeans. Most of the Tswana remained in what is now Botswana. They have a common culture but live in separate countries.

Colonial powers have also aggregated people with little in common, such as the many Native American tribes within the United States. Native Americans, who had the misfortune to inhabit valuable land, were summarily relocated to less valuable land, such as the Cherokee who walked from western Georgia to Oklahoma. In this way, tribes with different languages and lifestyles were forced to subsist in new and shared locations, all under the aegis of the United States government. Although they lived in common country, their cultures were disparate. Musical examples and lesson plans for teaching music of Native Americans, African Americans, Asian Americans, and Hispanic Americans can be found in *Teaching Music with a Multicultural Approach* (Anderson, 1991). When studying the music of these cultures, students should be made aware of the contexts from which the music came.

More than political boundaries, geographic features are important as factors in commonality among peoples, as in South America, where those who live in mountain regions tend to share musical styles that are different from plains dwellers and from coastal dwellers. Cultures in similar habitats—weather, food, dwellings—often exhibit similar styles regardless of political affiliation. Thus, the first precept when choosing non-Western repertoire is to select music of a people, culture, or tribe, not necessarily of a country or other political entity.

As travel became faster, safer, and more affordable, musicians borrowed musical elements, instruments, and performance practices from other cultures. This became especially apparent in the 19th century, for example, in Debussy's use of whole tone scales from Asia, Orff's facsimiles of gamelon instruments, and Copland's use of Mexican folk songs. These examples are not world music but the borrowing of non-native harmonies, timbres, and tunes filtered through a Western composer for Western consumption.

World music, when used in the classroom, should be as authentic and close to the source as possible in order to represent the culture in an honest and respectful manner. An indigenous musician, transmitting music, meaning, and culture in a personal and powerful manner, captivates learners and makes an enduring impression. Such musicians should be a regular part of school music classrooms. The United States is fortunate to harbor excellent examples of world music as well as accomplished performers of this music (Lornell & Rasmussen, 1997). Along with the myriad print and electronic resources at our fingertips, the most authentic sources may be persons in our communities who agree to pass on music and lore of their culture (Robinson, 2002). Thus, the second precept is to invite a "culture-bearer" to share music with us and immerse our students in a diverse repertoire of musics and music practices.

Finally, we must examine the deep structure of the music. What about the musical content is new, intriguing, or instructive to Western ears? A Western-sounding tune with non-English lyrics is not the best choice for use in our classrooms because no musical rationale for including non-Western music are being met. While it may be a reasonable goal for our students to learn to sing in a Romance or Germanic language, in doing so they will encounter very few new sounds—certainly few new meters or forms—singing or playing commercially available music produced in Western Europe.

For many years, ethnomusicologists have been gathering examples and describing musical experiences throughout the world. Recently, music educators have begun to infuse, enhance, and broaden their students' experiences with music from other cultures. What these scholars seem to share in common with Music Learning theorists is a desire "to show ways of valuing music on its own terms; of recognizing that diversity is a strength of humanity, and that fear of the unknown may hold us back from experiences that would enrich, develop, and excite us" (Floyd, 1996, p. 1). Because we learn what something is by hearing what it is not, the third precept is to select music on the basis of meter, rhythm, form, tonality, harmony, melody, timbre, and tuning system; this opens our students' ears and stands as a powerful example of, or in strong contrast to, the musical content in our Western canon.

## Techniques for Teaching World Music

Like Western classical music, some world cultures revere a refined and complex musical genre, such as the classical music of China and Southern India. These must be learned through years of study with a mentor or guru. However, in much of the world, there exists folk music that is not taught formally but is learned in an informal oral tradition, by exposure and experience.

The teacher should attempt to present music of another culture in a manner that most nearly approximates the way in which a musician from that culture would learn it because the way music is transmitted is an important component of its function in society. Examples of music's role in society may be found in *Music in Cultural Context: Eight Views on World Music Education* (Campbell, 1996).

While the time required for musical immersion is not easily found in today's music classrooms, the process of aural/oral transmission is an efficient and natural procedure to teach traditional music. Few cultures of the world rely on a piano and notation—two very Western conveniences or curses, depending on your point of view—to teach and learn music. We should strive to comprehend pieces well enough that if stranded on an island, we could share music with the native population using only our voices, bodies, and brains to transmit musical ideas. Notation should not be needed, as it is not a part of music transmission in many cultures.

Whether I am learning music from Tswana, Celtic, Venezuelan, Lithuanian, or Taiwanese culture-bearers, the procedure for learning music is remarkably similar.

1. The culture-bearer appears to audiate the piece to be taught.
2. He looks at me with intent, as if telling a personal story or important message.
3. He sings or plays the entire piece, maintaining that focused, intent look.
4. He checks for understanding and gives me some background about the piece.
5. He repeats and breaks the piece into parts as necessary.
6. We conclude with either a solo performance by me, or a performance together.

When I, in turn, pass on the music I have learned, I try to do justice to my culture-bearers by teaching the music with the same intensity, care, and process with which it was taught to me.

You will note similarities between the process above and Music Learning Theory techniques, such as the rote song procedure and the early childhood methods of immersion. That is logical and appropriate, because when the learner has not experienced the music of another culture, that learner is in babble, hearing new music in a new context and likely exhibiting a wide-eyed audiation stare! Teaching this repertoire is a perfect opportunity for expert modeling from the teacher and deep audiation from the learner. While Music Learning Theory practitioners are sometimes criticized for teaching Western music by rote, no one seems to question teaching non-Western music by rote, and the aural/oral transmission process that is central to Music Learning Theory is culturally authentic in many non-Western cultures.

When teaching songs with movement, as in the sub-Saharan African tradition, movement should be incorporated from the beginning of the process. The body, through movement, will teach the learner the rhythmic structure of the music while the mind analyzes the tonal structure. As the text may be the biggest challenge, consider teaching, but not refining, all the musical elements, then teaching text. While learning text, the learners continue to audiate and organize the musical elements. Then, when we integrate text, music, and movement, all three elements usually fall into place.

Adapting Western instruments to play non-Western parts may be difficult. Barred instruments found in Orff-based classrooms are easily modifiable for use in gamelon music (particularly using the Javanese *sléndro* scale) and Eastern African and Latin marimba ensembles. Flutes, recorders, and double reeds can replicate many of the wind sounds found in world music. You may retune your violins, autoharps, and dulcimers; scavenge an assortment of sticks, stones, shells, and gourds; and collect a variety of one- and two-headed drums of different shapes and sizes. Assembling the immense assortment of chordophones, idiophones, and membranophones may seem daunting, but remember that music in much of the world is made with what is readily at hand. Many of the instruments can be made by you and your students.

In Trinidad, carnival music played on African membranophones was banned out of fear by the British in 1883, so the Trinidadians fashioned different lengths of bamboo, which they hit with sticks, to form "tamboo bamboo" bands. By the late 1930s, metal refuse, such as pots and pans, car parts, and especially old oil drums, were plentiful. Oil drum tops were cut off and fashioned into eight-pitch tuned pans and played with mallets. By 1945, steel pan bands were the dominant sound in Trinidad (Mason, 1998). This is an example of the power of folk music to overcome political and material challenges—a drive we may emulate in our classrooms.

Another challenge, which is linked to selection, is finding vocal music that is developmentally appropriate. Simple toddler games and songs with limited ranges are common in many cultures, and because of their sharp contrast to Western music, students will find them compelling. For it is more difficult to find repertoire similar to our progression of carefully graduated literature for upper elementary and middle school students. This is not a bad thing; it just requires flexibility and creativity. For, if we are honest, I think we will admit that much of the music created for school ensembles is contrived and insipid. Students can't wait to get to "real" music.

In cultures in which polyphonic choral music is a community event, people of all ages and abilities participate. Young people join in as soon as they are ready. Their progression through different parts and roles in music-making parallels their growth into mature roles in the society. The closest Western example I can think of is the bluegrass song "Daddy sang bass, Momma sang tenor, me and little brother would join right in there." Thus, pieces from other cultures naturally may have numerous parts: high female, low female, high male, low male. Because we tend to segregate music participation by age, much world music needs to be adapted or arranged to fit

467

school ensembles and help our students maintain healthy vocal habits.

The well-known Zulu piece "Siyahamba," for instance, is often performed in three treble parts, but the melody can stand alone or be expanded by adding tenor and bass parts. One of the best-known pieces from Venezuela is "Alma Llanera," which is often heard in a traditional setting of treble voices in duet and male voices imitating instrumental accompaniment. The duet will be as effective and evocative in any voicing with vocal, instrumental, or no accompaniment. Just like "Amazing Grace," "Shenandoah," and "Silent Night," a "sturdy" tune from another culture will hold up through many different treatments and will still communicate through a sensitive and artistic musical performance.

## Conclusion

Since I began studying and performing world music, I have struggled to incorporate it into my traditional lessons in a way that would enhance my students' experience and respectfully share music of other peoples in a manner that is musical, meaningful, and authentic, yet stop short of delivering an ethnomusicological thesis. The three precepts for selection of world music literature discussed in this chapter are the result of study and experimentation: 1) select music of a people, culture, or tribe, not necessarily of a country or other political entity, 2) invite a "culture-bearer" to share music with us and our students, and 3) select music on the basis of meter, rhythm, form, tonality, harmony, melody, timbre, and tuning systems that opens our students' ears and stands as a powerful example of, or in strong contrast to, the musical content in our curricula.

If we follow the advice above, then teaching world music becomes easier. We must teach in a manner consistent with the way music is transmitted in that culture, and do our best to be musical, authentic, and compelling. I have visited foreign countries and learned music in several cultures. The prevailing attitude from my hosts was joy that visitors were interested in their music, and insistence that their music, culture, and good wishes be shared.

## References

Anderson, W. (1991). *Teaching music with a multicultural approach*. Reston, VA: MENC.

Broughton, S., Ellingham, M., Muddyman, D., & Trillo, R. (Eds.) Burton, K. (Contributing. Ed.). (1994). *World music: The rough guide*. London: Penguin.

Campbell, P. S. (Ed.). (1996). *Music in cultural context: Eight views on world music education.* Reston, VA: MENC.

Capwell, C. (1992). The music of India, in *Excursions in world music.* Englewood Cliffs, NJ: Prentice Hall.

Floyd, M. (Ed.). (1996). *World musics in education.* Aldershot, England: Scholar Press.

Lornell, K., & Rasmussen, A. (Eds.). (1997). *Musics of multicultural America: A study of twelve musical communities.* NY: Schirmer.

Mason, P. (1998). *Bacchanal! The carnival culture of Trinidad.* Philadelphia: Temple University Press.

Nettl, B., Capwell, C., Wong, I., Turino, T., & Bohlman, P. (1992). *Excursions in world music.* Englewood Cliffs, NJ: Prentice Hall.

Olson, D. (2002). *The Garland encyclopedia of world music, vol. 10,* Ruth M. Stone. (Ed.). NY: Rutledge.

Robinson, K. (2002). *World musics and music education: Facing the issues.* (Reimer, Ed.). Reston, VA: MENC.

Titon, J. (Ed.) (2002). *Worlds of music* (4th ed.). Belmont, CA: Wadsworth Group.

The author is indebted to generous musicians on five continents who have shared their thoughts and their art. The ideas and suggestions found here are due in part to the lectures and guidance of two wise and talented educators: Robin Moore, Temple University, and Kathy Robinson, Eastman School of Music.

*Helena Rodrigues*

LISBOA, PORTUGAL

# Music Learning Theory in Portugal - Adding Revolutionary Footnotes to Portuguese Music Education

All the philosophers have just added footnotes to what Socrates has said.
— Bertrand Russell

## Introduction

As a student searching for bibliographic resources during my master's degree, I came across some books written by Edwin Gordon. I found Gordon's work at first to be strange, then unfamiliar, and finally compelling. I became fascinated by his recommendations for teaching and by the meticulous research he had done to support his ideas.

In 1994, it was my great fortune to meet Gordon and to invite him to Portugal to present workshops in Lisboa, Braga, Coimbra, and Aveiro. In 1997, Gordon was joined by Richard Grunow, who lectured on Music Learning Theory as applied to instrumental music instruction, and, since then, Edwin Gordon has been visiting Portugal almost every year. His lectures, which have focused on Music Learning Theory, evaluation and measurement in music education, psychology of music, musical guidance for young children, and research methodology have had a profound impact on music education in Portugal.

471

Many teachers and music students attended the seminars and, subsequently, have been studying his writings in-depth. Several programs have developed to provide early childhood musical guidance to Portuguese children as a result. In my dissertation, I studied the adaptation of *Intermediate Measures of Music Audiation* (IMMA) for use in Portugal. Gordon's books *Learning Sequences in Music* (Gordon, 2003b) and *A Music Learning Theory for Newborn and Young Children* (Gordon, 2003b) have been translated into Portuguese by Fundação Calouste Gulbenkian. In addition, articles by and about Gordon have been published in Portuguese.

Historically, Portuguese music education has been influenced by pedagogues like Willems, Orff, Wuyttack, Ward and, to a smaller extent, Schaffer, Kodály, Suzuki, and Dalcroze. In the last eight years, Gordon's ideas have been shaping Portugese music education, even though some of Music Learning Theory's components—like the use of "movable DO"—are difficult for us to adopt. This chapter contains my reflections about the introduction, growth, and development of Music Learning Theory in Portugal.

### "Copernician" Footnotes

I believe that a "Copernician" aspect of Music Learning Theory is that it suggests a change in the focus of music education from "how to teach" music to "how children learn" music. *How Children Learn When They Learn Music*, a 1968 monograph by Gordon, called for a new look at teaching music. His focus on how children learn music is different from the traditional view of teaching in Portugal, which has been more teacher- than student-focused and is concerned primarily with what the teacher should teach.

Gordon has been critical of traditional teaching methods, which favor imitation and do not enable musicians to act independently. He believes that we should be able to "possess" music in the same way that we "possess" language, communicating original ideas in both mediums.

This type of criticism has made us question the value of what we have been teaching in Portugal and has helped us to recognize that much of our teaching has centered on imitation, repetition, music notation, and music theory. This has resulted in a lack of musical ownership and musical independence in our students. It has also resulted in few students finding their personal voices in music and expressing their own musical ideas. For example, I have seen many advanced music students and professional musicians who recognize the importance of traditional, high-level music achievement but do not adequately apply their high standards to the development of independent musicianship in their students. They do not ask their students to play by ear, to create an accompaniment to a familiar song, to create a harmony part to a melody, to transpose, or to play in the style of Mozart, Bach, or other composers. Why does this occur? Too often, teachers have focused heavily on teaching about music and not on helping students acquire the tools needed to express themselves musically. They teach students to be "musical reporters" rather that to be musicians who are creative and expressive. Understanding the deep structures in music and being able to express oneself musically is fundamental to being musical. As with swimming, walking, or speaking, if we have really learned music, it is a part of us and always will be. Music is not only something we do; it is a part of who we are.

The more one understands the denotative aspects of communication, the more one can appreciate them. Within art, several realities (the understandable and the ineffable) coexist. The ineffable is person-dependent and varies from individual to individual. Therefore, music instruction should focus on what can be taught. As our students engage in what can be taught, they can use what they have learned to express their own musical ideas, using their own musical mediums, through interpreting musical works, creating their own music, theorizing about music, or listening to music with a rich, deep understanding of what they hear.

Reading music notation and understanding music theory are important to learning music, but they are only a small part of a solid music education. To be valuable, they must be taught at the appropriate time and in the right way in relation to the development of other musical skills that are perhaps even more important. Appropriate sequencing of instruction is key in Music Learning Theory, so when specific skills are taught is crucial to the successful development of musicianship. Underlying this entire discussion is a fundamental question, and in the answer to this question lays the philosophical and practical foundations of Gordon's approach to music education: what does it mean to learn music? Gordon's answer to this question is expressed in the term *audiation*, which he defines as "hearing and comprehending in one's mind the sound of music that is not or may never have been physically present" (Gordon, 2003a, p. 361). Gordon believes that audiation is to music what thinking is to language.

Although there is some connection between audiation and the meaning Edgar Willems (another pedagogue who has greatly influenced music education in Portugal) attributes to inner hearing, the new word coined by Gordon has forced us to consider the meaning of "to learn music" from a new perspective. To truly understand the word audiation, we must contemplate the "musical thinking" processes that underlie specific musical behaviors and achievements. In fact, there are many musical achievements for which the underlying processes can be mainly imitative. Playing an instrument and even singing can occur through imitation without musical understanding. Also, music reading can be nothing more than the decoding of signs in the same way that reading a foreign language is possible using a phonetic key. In reading like this, however, the reader would not understand the meaning of what he was reading.

Audiation requires musical comprehension. This comprehension can occur without the use of music notation since it belongs purely to the realm of the syntactical organization of pitches into tonalities and durations in meters in cognition. Audiation points to the need to attend to the processes behind certain musical products. Mathematics teachers, for example, want their students to know more than just the correct answers to arithmetic problems; they want their students to understand the reasons behind the answers. Without understanding these reasons, students will not be able to generalize their knowledge to the solving of new problems.

Another important component of Music Learning Theory is the distinction between discrimination learning and inference learning. In discrimination learning, imitation plays a crucial role; through imitation, students learn a vocabulary of tonal and rhythm patterns, and learn to associate tonal or rhythm syllables with those patterns, as well as to read them. With this vocabulary as a foundation, students can learn, independent of a teacher, new patterns and new musical ideas through generalizing what was learned by rote during discrimination learning to the new situation. Imitation and recognition, which occur in discrimination learning, indicate readiness for inference learning, in which students teach themselves. Gordon believes that preparing our students for inference learning should be the primary aim of teaching, because when students can teach themselves, they have become autonomous and independent musicians.

In Portugal, we traditionally have focused too much on discrimination learning and have not enabled or encouraged our students to teach themselves and perhaps surpass our own skills as musicians. Children should be engaged in creativity and discovery—which, at first, might be more appropriately called exploration—as soon as possible. However, first they must have a musical vocabulary to explore and with which to create.

Gordon's emphasis on music in early childhood was new for many teachers in Portugal, and after his seminars several early childhood music initiatives took place in our country. For instance, *Bebé Babá* (Rodrigues & Rodrigues, 2004) is an inovative educational project designed for parents and babies that is deeply influenced by Gordon's work.[1]

---

[1] For more information, see www.musicateatral.com.

Gordon's introduction of the concept of musical age being different from chronological age also changed music teaching in Portugal. Prior to Gordon's visit, a student's chronological age was the primary guidepost for determining the content of music instruction. There is growing awareness now that this might not be appropriate.

Gordon's eight types of audiation also deserve attention in Portugal. Perhaps, as they are understood, music educators in Portugal will see the need to put into practice what other pedagogues have been advocating about the need for "sound-before-sight-before-theory."

Much of Portuguese music education traditionally has focused on interval training. Therefore, the establishment of Gordon's pattern taxonomy and a skill learning sequence makes possible a foundation for the development of new teaching methodologies in Portugal that would focus on the patterns within a syntactical context rather than intervals in isolation. The concepts of a functional pattern rather than an interval, approaching tonal and rhythm skill development separately, and need for the establishment of tonal and rhythm syntax are also new to Portuguese music education.

Learning Sequence Activities, or pattern instruction, are at the core of Music Learning Theory. I have identified three teaching techniques incorporated as a part of teaching Learning Sequence Activities that facilitate the development of audiation in my students. The first concerns tonal pattern presentation techniques. Performing tonal patterns with *staccato* articulation and leaving silence and breath before gesturing for students to echo the tonal patterns activates audiation. This small detail makes a large difference in terms of audiation when compared to many of the imitation activities that are normally used in Portuguese music education. It also highlights the connection between breath and music, which is central to a musical performance.

The second technique relates to the matching of the difficulty level of each pattern in Learning Sequence Activities to the musical strengths and weaknesses of each student, while at the same time maintaining the integrity of the skill learning sequence. I had never seen such a systematized way of individualizing instruction to the needs of individual students.

The third technique relates to the second. Gordon believes that students only take ownership of a pattern when they have sung or chanted it in solo. However, students are not asked to sing alone until they have demonstrated that they are able to perform the pattern with the teacher. When they do perform in solo, the teacher gestures to them immediately before they are to sing or chant the pattern, "surprising" everyone at the last moment. Everyone in the class must be attentive, because no one knows who will be called on next. Techniques such as these are useful to any educator, even those outside of music.

Gordon's approach to rhythm is also new to Portuguese music teachers, in that it focuses on how rhythm is attached to movement and to the audiation of meter, rather than on how it is notated. In addition, musicians in Portugal have been discussing the meaning one attributes to tonality and meter. For example, there are situations in which different listeners, both of whom are good musicians, will audiate the same piece of music in different ways. Neither is wrong, as the musicians are constructing their own musical meanings in their audiation. However, this conflicts with the traditional way of teaching in Portugal, in which it is assumed that there is only one right answer.

Using the moveable-DO system, as advocated by Music Learning Theory, is difficult for teachers in Portugal. Fixed DO has been used in Portugal for a long time, and changing traditions is difficult. How does one cope with a student body that has been taught in a different system or that attends two different music classes, each using its own approach to tonal verbal association? Nevertheless, Gordon has helped Portuguese teachers recognize that our solfege system is illogical, because it gives the same names to different relationships within a tonal system. Many of us have developed our own relative systems in the face of fixed DO, even though fixed DO is the official Portuguese system. Teachers are beginning to accept the logic underlying Gordon's choice of syllables; both rhythmically and tonally, his methods reflect musical structure, musical functions, and musical syntax.

The skill and content sequences that Gordon proposes are interesting to teachers in Portugal. Most mainstream music education discourse in Portugal defines goals without specifying expected levels of achievement of those goals. On the other hand, Music Learning Theory suggests possible outcomes that are specific and can be measured. For example, the *Iowa Tests of Music Literacy* (ITML) is a good match as a measurement tool with Gordon's educational taxonomy. Learning Sequence Activities also are examples of sequential teaching tools, means of individualizing instruction, and evaluation tools that can be used to improve instruction. The measurement tools that Gordon has developed are unique in the context of Portuguese music education in terms of their psychological foundations, depth and breadth, and procedural rigor. Gordon's theories are based on empirical research and have an achievable final goal, which could be roughly summarized as "to improve instruction." By giving direction to music teacher thinking in Portugal, Music Learning Theory is allowing each teacher to express him- or herself through teaching. Although there is a common way in which students learn, keeping in mind individual differences, there are several ways to facilitate that learning. Music Learning Theory gives teachers direction but also leaves choices for the teacher. It provides an underlying structure, over which individual teachers can be creative, enhancing the learning experiences for their students.

**Conclusions**

Knowledge of music education methods is a small part of teacher education. In fact, even though they have a strong foundation in theory, many teachers are unable to put that foundation into practice successfully. Teachers need to discover what will help them improve their teaching individually and pursue that knowledge. Having a strong methodological base will not only improve the quality of music teaching in Portugal, it will help Portuguese music educators feel more comfortable and successful in their teaching. In Portugal, music teachers, as individuals, choose the methodology that they find most compelling. Therefore, Portuguese music educators must know as much as possible about teaching methods so that they can use the methods that best fit with their personalities, mediums of musical expression, personal styles, and teaching settings, while they first and foremost consider the needs of their students.

What will be the trajectory of the development of Music Learning Theory in Portugal? Whatever its course, instructors here will continue to study, evaluate, and apply Gordon's Music Learning Theory in their teaching. We are fortunate to have had the opportunity, through seminars, to have Gordon's direct instruction, and we hope to continue these dialogues as we continue to improve music education in Portugal.

**References**

Bluestine, E. (1995). *The ways children learn music.* Chicago: GIA Publications.

Gordon, E. E. (1968). *How children learn when they learn music.* Unpublished manuscript, University of Iowa.

——. (2003a). *Learning sequences in music: Skill, content, and patterns.* Chicago: GIA Publications.

——. (2003b). *A music learning theory for newborn and young children.* Chicago: GIA Publications.

Rodrigues, H., & Rodrigues, P. (2004). *Bebé Babá – Explorations in early childhood music.* Chicago: GIA Publications.

Rodrigues, H., Rodrigues, P., & Nunes, P. (2004). *Bebé Babá – Da musicali dade dos afectos à música com bebés.* Porto: Campo das letras.

*Kristin Slocum Kreiss*

• • • • • • • • • • • • • • •

NORTHVILLE PUBLIC SCHOOLS, NORTHVILLE, MI

# Writing a Music Curriculum Using Music Learning Theory

As we have entered the new millennium, the field of education seems to be wrestling with curricula. This is reflected in the call for National Standards in various "core" subjects as outlined in Goals 2000. In the past, many music departments have not been pressured to have a written curriculum for their programs, but in most districts across the country this is no longer the case. Music education was a leader in the movement toward National Standards with the development of standards in arts education (dance, music, theatre, and visual arts) in 1994 (Music Educators National Conference, 1994). As a result of these standards, many districts are now calling for music departments to develop or update their curricula. If you are just starting to incorporate Music Learning Theory into your teaching, you may need to modify or write your curriculum to reflect this change.

## Why Is a Curriculum Necessary?

Sadly, music programs in many school districts are still considered "frills" or "specials." As a result, many music educators find themselves constantly defending the importance of their programs. Unfortunately, many administrators and music educators alike are using extra-musical reasons for justifying the inclusion of music in the schools, citing articles in music education publications that link music participation to higher SAT scores or discussing techniques for using music to teach multiplication tables or dinosaur facts. While these are worthy utilitarian outcomes, they should not be our primary reason for teaching music. A music curriculum should

479

outline the musical objectives of our programs and will help dispel the myth that we only "sing songs" or "play instruments" in music class. Such a music curriculum can be used to make music teachers responsible for each student's *music* education. To be viewed as an essential part of each student's education, music educators need to be held accountable for their own subject area, as are our colleagues in other subjects (Walker & Soltis, 1992).

So, in order to explain the importance of music in every child's education, music educators need to be clear about their own philosophies of music education. What is music education, and why is it important? It is only after we answer these questions that we can begin to outline our objectives for our programs.

A music curriculum should be logically sequenced; this will ensure that our students are learning the right skills at the right time (Sidnell, 1973). A child would never be taught how to read before they could speak. Unfortunately, many music programs are designed to teach exactly that way; students are taught to read notation before they can sing in tune or move to macrobeats or microbeats. Designing a music curriculum that follows a research-supported sequence on when and how children learn to do these things will help avoid such problems. Music Learning Theory provides such a sequence and lends itself to serving as a foundation for an appropriate music curriculum. A music curriculum that is well sequenced simplifies lesson planning by outlining what to teach and when it should be taught. Designing lesson plans according to such a curriculum takes much of the guesswork out of deciding which objective(s) to focus on in a lesson.

Too often in music education, there is poor communication among K-12 teachers in the music program. Elementary music teachers follow their own method, teaching objectives that they deem important without regard for what their fellow elementary music teachers are doing. This leaves middle and high school music educators in the dark about what students already know and are able to do. These secondary teachers often end up reteaching skills to get all of their students "on the same page." With a unified music curriculum, the entire music faculty would be following the same sequence. Elementary teachers would know what was being taught across the district, and middle and high school teachers could *continue* the education of their students, rather than stepping backward.

A unified music curriculum that reflects what is being taught in the music classroom will help when evaluating the music program (Sidnell, 1973). The curriculum will show the appropriate level of students' music achievement, as well as where they are headed. It will also ensure that students are progressing in the proper sequence. Thus, a curriculum can be a useful reference in evaluating individual students, teachers, and programs as well.

A music curriculum is an essential tool for music educators at all levels; "success in education is almost never the result of sheer luck," but rather, "the outcome of careful planning" (Steller, 1983, p. 68). Music programs that are using Music Learning Theory need to be sure that their curriculum reflects this method. The rest of this essay will outline how to go about writing a new curriculum using Music Learning Theory.

**Getting Started**

When starting the curriculum-writing process, there are many things to consider (Walker & Soltis, 1992). Does the district have a mission statement that must be included in the curriculum? Should the curriculum reflect the National Standards? Is there a state curriculum guide or syllabus that should be consulted? All of these questions can be answered at a meeting with music faculty and appropriate administrators. At such a meeting, the responsibility of consulting various resources can be delegated, then discussed at a subsequent meeting. It is helpful to use a variety of resources when writing a curriculum to ensure that your curriculum is well rounded.

It is also imperative that the faculty agree upon the method that will be used in the music program. It would be helpful at this point to differen-tiate between method and technique. Gordon (2003) defines method as "**why** we teach **what** we teach **when** we teach it" (p. 28). Conversely, technique "refers to **how** we teach" (Gordon, 2003, p. 28). Technique is a teaching device used to achieve an objective. Often, music curricula reflect the techniques used rather than what is being taught when, and why. A music curriculum should reflect method, not techniques. This is not to say that good technique is not valuable. In fact, it is essential. No music curriculum, no matter how well written, can be successful without high-quality lesson planning and instruction (Doll, 1993). There are many effective teaching techniques that can be used to accomplish an objective efficiently, but the method needs to remain consistent and appropriate.

It is for this reason that Music Learning Theory lends itself to serving as a foundation for writing a curriculum. Music Learning Theory is a method that tells us when our students should learn what they learn musically. Using Music Learning Theory as a basis for the curriculum can ensure a valid method, yet allow for various teaching techniques to be used when working with students toward the achievement of sequential objectives.

The music faculty should familiarize themselves with the method before beginning to write the curriculum, with one or two teachers serving

481

as "method parliamentarians" to ensure that the method is used consistently in the written curriculum.

## Organizing and Writing the Formal Music Curriculum

Once the faculty agrees on a method and various sources have been consulted, the faculty must decide how to organize their curriculum. A curriculum needs to be logically organized so that it is useful to the music faculty. There are many ways in which to organize a curriculum, but certain components seem to be universal. I recommend using the following categories: a) rationale/philosophy statement, b) comprehensive objectives, c) description of current program and assumptions, and d) sequential objectives. When writing the curriculum, it is important to write the sections in this order as well to ensure horizontal and vertical consistency.

### Rationale Statement

Most curricula begin with a rationale statement, sometimes called a philosophy statement. This should be an explanation of why music is an essential aspect of each student's education (i.e., historical, social, cultural, and/or aesthetic benefits of music) (Sidnell, 1973).

As in any subject area, music teachers should have their own individual philosophy of music education. The music faculty will need to discuss their personal philosophies in order to develop a district philosophy that is acceptable to all members of the faculty (Walker & Soltis, 1992). One music teacher should be designated to take the ideas of the faculty and consolidate them into a rationale for the district's music program. Choosing one author will help to ensure that the rationale statement flows well.

### Comprehensive Objectives

Following the rationale statement should be comprehensive objectives, which are what students will accomplish as a result of completing the district's music program (Brandt & Tyler, 1993; Gordon, 2003). This may be the most difficult, although not the most time-consuming, section upon which to reach agreement; however, "you cannot build a road if you do not know its final destination" (Sidnell, 1973, p. 32). It is helpful to realize that these objectives *should* be broad and all-encompassing (Doll, 1993).

Two simple objectives can serve as your comprehensive objectives as well as being a mission statement of sorts for your program: 1) overall music literacy through audiation and 2) appreciation through understanding (Gordon, 2003). All sequential objectives should be stepping stones toward these overall goals.

*Program Description and Assumptions*

It is helpful to include a description of the current program to use as a reference when evaluating the curriculum as well as the music program itself. The assumptions would outline district-wide information, such as: 1) method (Music Learning Theory), 2) syllable system, tonal and rhythm (it is strongly recommended that the entire district use the same syllable system), 3) music textbook series used in the district, and 4) general repertoire, which may fall into three sections: elementary general, instrumental, and choral.

*Sequential Objectives*

The final and most complex section of the curriculum should be sequential objectives, which are the *methods* that will be followed to accomplish the comprehensive objectives (Gordon, 2003). These are the more specific skills that students need to develop to accomplish the comprehensive objectives. Sequential objectives will need to be organized into categories for clarity. These categories can vary to reflect the philosophy of the music department. The music department may decide to organize their sequential objectives by: a) the elements of music, that is, melody, harmony, rhythm, tone color, texture, and form (Reimer, 1989); b) the various ways to "music," performing, improvising, composing, arranging, and conducting (Elliot, 1995); c) the National Standards in music education (Music Educators National Conference, 1994); d) the levels and sublevels of Music Learning Theory's Skill Level Sequence, i.e., aural/oral, verbal association, partial synthesis, etc. (Gordon, 2003); e) categories outlined in the district's music textbook series; f) categories outlined in the state music curriculum; or g) by categories of their own that incorporate some or all of the ideas listed above.

While the categories used for organization are the choice of the music department, the sequence of the individual objectives must be supported by research and consistent with how children learn music. If the sequence is carefully developed, gaps in the learning process can be avoided (Sidnell, 1973, p. 35). Gordon (2003) outlines a specific sequence for skill acquisition in music in his Music Learning Theory; *discrimination* (aural/oral, verbal association, partial synthesis, symbolic association, composite synthesis), then *inference* (generalizion, creativity/improvisation, theoretical understanding).

Writing the sequential objectives will be the most time-consuming section of the curriculum writing process. As stated earlier, the sequential objectives should reflect the *method*. The categories and subsections shown in Figure 1 may help to organize the sequential objectives (Taggart, 1995).

*Audiation Skills*

Music Learning Theory follows a whole-part-whole approach that is reflective of the approach used to teach language. Before children speak, they are saturated with words and language; they develop a vast listening vocabulary. They then begin to experiment with speech, finally uttering their first word. Children learn more and more words, which then are used in sentences. By the time children are asked to read, they can already communicate through speech, improvising sentences and paragraphs. In general, we do not need to think about the proper sequence for teaching a child to speak; the method is a natural part of all cultures.

Gordon's Skill Learning Sequence outlines a similar sequence for learning music (Gordon, 2003). Gordon (2003) defines two types of learning: discrimination (rote learning) and inference (guided learning with unfamiliar content). Children must have discrimination learning before they can successfully engage in inference learning. Discrimination learning includes the following levels: aural/oral (rote songs, tonal and rhythm patterns using neutral syllables), verbal association (associating given syllables with patterns already learned), partial synthesis (beginning to put patterns in a musical context), symbolic association (reading and writing familiar patterns), and composite synthesis (reading and writing of familiar material in context). Inference learning includes the following sublevels: generalization (applying learned skills to a new situation), creativity/improvisation (tonal and rhythm patterns, both oral and written, with or without syllables), and theoretical understanding (the "why?", music theory) (Gordon, 2003).

*Whole-Part-Whole*

As stated above, Music Learning Theory follows a whole-part-whole approach. Students are introduced to content (e.g., tonalities, meters, macrobeats, microbeats, harmonic function) in Classroom Activities (Whole). Then skill and content are learned through pattern instruction, using Learning Sequence Activities (Part) (Gordon & Woods, 1992a, 1992b, 1992c). The learned skill and content are then applied to song and/or chant materials in Classroom Activities (Whole). For example, students in a second grade music class learn "Hush, Little Baby" in Major tonality, and Duple meter, as well as a large vocabulary of other songs and chants in a variety of meters and tonalities (Whole). In a subsequent lesson, these same students echo specific Duple rhythm patterns using rhythm syllables at the verbal association skill level (Part). These rhythm patterns do not need to be taken directly from the song; students need only to have

A. AUDIATION
  1. Content
     a. Tonal (includes harmony)
        • Resting tone, etc.
        • Tonic/dominant, etc.
        • Major/Minor, etc.
     b. Rhythm
        • Macro/microbeats, etc.
        • Duple/Triple, etc.
  2. Skills (Gordon 1997, p. 90)
     a. Discrimination
        • Aural/oral, verbal association, partial
          synthesis, etc.
     b. Inference
        • Generalization, creativity/improvisation, etc.
  **Recommended technique: Learning Sequence Activities

B. CLASSROOM ACTIVITY SKILLS
  1. Singing
  2. Chanting
  3. Playing instruments
  4. Movement/dance
  5. Creating/improvising/composing
  6. Life skills

C. CONCEPTS
  1. Expressive elements
  2. Tone color
  3. Form

*Figure 1.* Categories and subsections of sequential objectives

been introduced to the meter in previous song material. In yet another lesson, students echo a Duple rhythm pattern using rhythm syllables to form a chanted ostinato for another Duple meter song (Whole).

### Learning Sequence Activities

Many music educators are incorporating elements of Music Learning Theory into their teaching but are apprehensive about using Learning Sequence Activities (Gordon & Woods, 1992a, 1992b, 1992c). In their publications, Gordon and Woods set up a series of tonal and rhythmic patterns to be taught using the skills and content as established in Music Learning Theory. The difficulty levels of each set of patterns are identified so that instruction can be individualized to each student's music aptitude (potential to achieve) and achievement (accomplishments). The difficulty levels of the patterns in these books have been studied thoroughly. Instead of using Learning Sequence Activities, many music educators choose to teach patterns that they create, sometimes using a standardized set of patterns, sometimes improvising patterns during teaching. This is not ideal. The method may suffer as a result. That is, teachers may teach a type or stage of audiation that is not appropriate for the students because they do not have the readiness (Gordon, 2003).

The application of skills obtained during Learning Sequence Activities should be included in Classroom Activities. For example, creating tonic patterns in Major tonality is a skill taught in Learning Sequence Activities. Creating a tonic ostinato for a song in Major tonality could be taught in Classroom Activities, but only *after creating patterns has been taught in Learning Sequence Activities*. Children learn songs in Major tonality. Creating Major tonic patterns is learned through Learning Sequence Activities. Then students create a tonic ostinato for a song in Major tonality during Classroom Activities.

The method for teaching children to be musically literate is not as ingrained or automatic as it is for teaching children to speak. Gordon argues that music educators have put the cart before the horse for decades, even centuries (Gordon, 2003). That is, music educators have been teaching children to read notation and to compose and improvise without their first having the ability to audiate tonality and meter, that is, to audiate the syntax of music.

It is difficult for music educators to create instructional sequence without intense study of Music Learning Theory. However, Learning Sequence Activities (Gordon & Woods, 1992a, 1992b, 1992c) are based in research and are sequenced and appropriate for the way in which children learn music. By using these activities, teachers will ensure that the teaching method is both appropriate and efficient.

Another reason to use Learning Sequence Activities is that they help to individualize instruction to the needs of each student. Each tonal and rhythm unit has patterns at three difficulty levels: easy, medium, and difficult. Using these difficulty levels in relation to the music aptitude and achievement of the students will facilitate individualizing instruction. If a child has high music aptitude and achievement, the teacher may give the child the easy, then, assuming correct responses, the medium and difficult patterns. By using patterns that coincide with the student's aptitude, the teacher is individualizing the difficulty levels to what is appropriate for each child.

Also, using Learning Sequence Activities will make sure that students are being evaluated consistently. The activities are designed so that the teacher can keep track of each student's progress at all times. The patterns are notated at the top of a seating chart to be filled out by the teacher. The teacher notes the student's rhythm or tonal aptitude on the chart and gives patterns accordingly. Correct responses are noted on the seating chart according to the difficulty level reached. For example, if a child has low tonal or rhythm aptitude and is successful with the easy pattern, the teacher would put one check mark under the student's name. If the children have high tonal or rhythm aptitude and are successful with the easy and medium patterns, they receive two checks, and the teacher can evaluate their achievement accordingly. Having these records will help in evaluating the students, completing report cards, and adapting instruction.

Often, music educators who do not fully understand Music Learning Theory see Learning Sequence Activities as just singing and chanting patterns, which seems almost unmusical in nature. On the contrary, these activities provide the groundwork for skill development through the audiation of tonalities and meters (musical syntax). These activities include listening, performing, creating, improvising, reading, and notating, all of which are outlined in the National Standards (Music Educators National Conference, 1994). For all of these reasons, Learning Sequence Activities should be integral to formal music curriculum, as these activities will guide and apply to the rest of the curriculum.

*Classroom Activity Skills*

This category should include skill objectives that are not specifically addressed in Learning Sequence Activities. For example, reading music notation is included in Learning Sequence Activities; therefore, it should not be included in this category. However, singing partner songs, a performance skill used in Classroom Activities, is not outlined in Learning Sequence Activities, so it could be included here as a sequential objective.

Within this category might be several general subsections: a) Singing, b) chanting, c) playing instruments, d) moving/dance, e) creating/improvising/composing, and f) life skills. Each of these subsections should include a list of related sequential objectives.

*Singing.* This subsection specifically should address singing skills that were not addressed as tonal skills in Learning Sequence Activities. In the elementary general music program, this could include, for example, singing in solo, singing in a group, singing simple ostinati, and singing partner songs. At the secondary level, this may include singing in four-part harmony, blending, and range.

*Chanting.* Like singing skills, this subsection should address chanting skills not included as rhythm skills in Learning Sequence Activities. Many of these skills may be parallel to singing skills, but should be discussed separately in this subsection, because chanting skills are more related to rhythmic aptitude and are therefore separate and distinct from singing skills, which are more related to tonal aptitude. For example, objectives might be chanting rhythmic ostinati to a familiar song in the elementary classroom or asking a section of a jazz band to chant an appropriate rhythmic accompaniment to a familiar tune.

*Movement/Dance.* Moving is fundamental to rhythmic audiation (Gordon, 2003). This subsection should focus on teaching children to move their bodies in continuous, fluid style as a readiness for discrete movement (i.e., moving to macro/microbeats). Children must be able to move to macrobeats and microbeats to truly understand meter. This subsection should also include bilateral and alternating macrobeat and microbeat movement, both alone and with a partner. Also, students will need to gain kinesthetic experience with flow, weight, space, and time to audiate rhythm and style. Any body percussion or ostinati objectives should be included here, as well as any movement responses to form, style, etc. Also, folk dance skills can be developed under this subsection. Dance objectives may include specific movements, such as do-si-do or promenade, as well as entire dances, such as square dancing or dancing for a show or jazz choir.

*Playing Instruments.* The use of classroom instruments in the elementary program (e.g., maracas, tambourines, rhythm sticks, xylophones, etc.) and how these instruments will be played (e.g., bilateral or alternating bordun, macrobeat resting-tone ostinato) should be addressed in this subsection, as well as any movement that will serve as instrument readiness. This subsection is also where any technical objectives of an instrumental (band or orchestra) program should be outlined. If any instruments are to be used in the choral program, the objectives should be reflected in this subsection.

*Creating/Improvising/Composing.* Again, only objectives not outlined in Learning Sequence Activities should be included in this subsection. In Learning Sequence Activities, creating, improvising and composing relate to specific skills and content. The sequence in this section should incorporate skill and content learned in Learning Sequence Activities as they are applied to Classroom Activities. For example, in the elementary general program this could include creating appropriate chanted introductions and codas for familiar songs or chants or composing a song in a given form (e.g., ABA). In the secondary program, this may include improvising an appropriate solo on the student's primary instrument within a larger ensemble work or composing a harmony part in a small vocal ensemble.

*Life Skills.* This subsection focuses on music-related skills. Objectives such as appropriate audience behavior and concert etiquette might be included in this subsection.

## Concepts

This portion of the curriculum includes formal music concepts that may be taught using any of the skills previously mentioned or another appropriate technique. Expressive elements would include such concepts as dynamic markings (e.g., *piano, forte, sfz*), phrasing, and appropriate songs for given occasions (e.g., patriotic occasions, celebratory events). Tone color would include recognizing instruments, voicings, and other sound sources by listening. Form would address the formal organization of musical works, such as ABA, rondo, call and response, and sonata form.

## Ordering Sequential Objectives

When music educators begin to use Music Learning Theory, one of the issues they must come to terms with is the *musical age* versus *chronological age*. Musical age refers to the stage of audiation that a person has reached, whereas chronological age refers to how many years a person has lived. It is entirely possible to have a teenager who is still in the "babble" stage of their musical development; his or her musical age is not the same as the chronological age. This becomes an issue for music educators because schools are set up to teach according to chronological age using grade levels. For this reason, a system needs to be developed to address students' musical progress (musical age) without using grade levels (chronological age) as the two are not always related.

When teachers first start using Music Learning Theory, they should start all grade levels with informal instruction. Often, the younger students advance more rapidly through the stages of audiation than the older students. That is to say that their *musical age* is more advanced than those students who are older *chronologically*.

This presents a problem when writing a curriculum. It is difficult to rank objectives by grade level when the musical and chronological age do not parallel one another. For this reason, objectives should be sequenced continuously, using a numbering or lettering system that does not relate to grade level. When speaking to student progress in music, teachers should refer to the number/letter of the objectives achieved. For example, consider the following partial hierarchy for singing skills in Figure 2 (Taggart, 1995).

1. SINGING/TONAL
   a. Correctly uses singing voice
   b. Sings resting tone/tonic ostinato
   c. Sings pattern
   d. Sings phrases or an entire song

*Figure 2.* Example of singing skill hierarchy

Rather than designating a grade level, the music teacher could refer to the number of the objective to discuss student progress in relation to the curriculum. For example, if students are able to sing a tonic ostinato using a singing voice in solo, the teacher could say the child has reached level 1b.

When referring to Learning Sequence Activities, educators should use the system outlined in the Reference Handbook (Gordon & Woods, 1992a). For example, when referring to rhythm skills, the teacher should say the student is in Unit 2, at the verbal association level, using macrobeats and microbeats in Usual Duple and Usual Triple meter (Gordon & Woods, 1992a, p. 21).

Using this system, there would be little ambiguity about what skills a student had attained in the music program. This could be useful for report cards, program evaluation, student achievement in relation to aptitude, and communication among faculty members about what students know and are able to do in music.

## Conclusion

In order for music to be viewed as an essential part of each student's education, music educators need to explain exactly what they teach and why. Every music program should have a written music curriculum that follows a research-based and appropriate method. Music Learning Theory makes such a method possible and encourages an appropriately sequenced curriculum. While it may seem a daunting task, writing a curriculum using Music Learning Theory will benefit the music faculty, the school district, and, most important, the students in school music programs.

## References

Brandt, R. S., & Tyler, R. W. (1983). *Goals and objectives.* In F. W. English (Ed.), *Fundamental Curriculum Decisions.* Alexandria, VA: Association for Supervision and Curriculum Development.

Doll, W. E. (1993). *A post-modern perspective on curriculum.* New York: Teachers College Press.

Elliot, D. J. (1995). *Music matters: A new philosophy of music education.* New York: Oxford University Press.

Gordon, E. E. (2003). *Learning sequences in music: Skill, content, and patterns.* Chicago: GIA Publications.

Gordon, E. E., & Woods, D. G. (1992a). *Jump right in: The music curriculum, Reference handbook for using Learning Sequence Activities* (2nd ed.). Chicago: GIA Publications.

———. (1992b). *Jump right in: The music curriculum, Rhythm register book one* (2nd ed.). Chicago: GIA Publications.

———. (1992c). *Jump right in: The music curriculum, Tonal register book one* (2nd ed.). Chicago: GIA Publications.

*National standards for arts education: What every young American should know and be able to do in the arts.* (1994). Reston, VA: Music Educators National Conference.

Reimer, B. (1989). *A philosophy of music education* (2nd ed.). Englewood Cliffs, NJ: Prentice Hall.

Sidnell, R. G. (1973). *Building instructional programs in music education.* Englewood Cliffs, NJ: Prentice-Hall.

Steller, A. W. (1983). *Curriculum planning.* In F. W. English (Ed.), *Fundamental curriculum decisions.* Alexandria, VA: Association for Supervision and Curriculum Development.

Taggart, C. C. (1995). *Community music school curriculum: Musicianship program.* Unpublished manuscript, Michigan State University, Community Music School.

Walker, D. F., & Soltis, J. F. (1992). *Curriculum and aims.* New York: Teachers College.

*Suzanne L. Burton*
••••••••••••••
UNIVERSITY OF DELAWARE

# Implementing Music Learning Theory

## Introduction

Implementing Music Learning Theory as a new curricular strategy can be a rewarding process. Through the implementation process, the music educator's understanding of the developmental and sequential nature of music learning grows. In addition, a foundation for making more informed curricular decisions regarding the scope and sequence of the content to be taught and the instructional strategies to be used is formed. As these decisions are put into practice and the curriculum unfolds, the benefits of the implementation process are realized through students who will audiate and perform music with increased musical comprehension and musicianship.

Fullan (1999), an authority on educational change, defines implementation as the process of putting an idea, belief, or practice in place. Change is an inevitable part of program implementation and may prove to be challenging for the music educator (Burton, 1998). Curricular "change can be very deep, striking at the core of learned skills, beliefs and conceptions of education, and creating doubts about [educational] purposes, sense of competence and self concept" (Fullan, 1999, p. 45). For the music educator, changing to a new curricular strategy may mean learning new content and methodology, as well subsequent teaching techniques. For students, a period of time may be needed to adjust to the curricular changes that are taking place. This is a learning experience for teachers and students alike, which often causes a state of curricular disequilibrium, an indication that change is taking place (Fullan, 1999).

Often, the isolated nature of teaching does not allow for receptivity to change (Ornstein & Hunkus, 2004). Furthermore, curricular change in music education may challenge deeply held values and traditions regarding music teaching and learning. Fortunately, through the development of strategies that facilitate the process of curricular change, the likelihood of successfully implementing a Music Learning Theory-based curriculum will increase. Therefore, the purpose of this chapter is to assist music educators with the successful implementation of Music Learning Theory by presenting issues teachers should consider before and throughout the implementation process.

## Before Implementation

Music Learning Theory provides a solid foundation for building a music curriculum. Many practitioners are drawn to Music Learning Theory because of its logical and sequential presentation of content and associated pedagogical techniques (Burton, 1999). To successfully implement a Music Learning Theory-based curriculum, however, the music educator must acquire a thorough understanding of the sequential progression of music learning and develop skills in the delivery of content. A music educator's preparation and skills in using Music Learning Theory will have an effect on the success with which Music Learning Theory is implemented in the educational setting (Burton, 1998, 1999).

### *Preparation*

In seeking information regarding the curricular implementation of Music Learning Theory, Burton (1999) surveyed Music Learning Theory practitioners who were members of the Gordon Institute for Music Learning (N=216, 49% return). In the twenty-one-item, open-ended response questionnaire, respondents were asked to provide information regarding the areas in which they taught music, their educational background, length of time teaching music and using Music Learning Theory, their use of music aptitude testing, and whether they felt prepared to use Music Learning Theory. In the study, two themes emerged regarding implementation. Some respondents commented that they felt that a curriculum based on Music Learning Theory would be worthwhile, yet they were concerned about using Music Learning Theory in the classroom with little preparation, and did not use it as a result. However, other respondents remarked how their preparation has helped with using Music Learning Theory. The following response summarizes the sentiments of those practitioners who are comfortable using Music Learning Theory. "Because of my education I can use Music Learning Theory with confidence." Not having proper guidance or knowing enough about how to use Music Learning Theory is a perceived barrier toward implementation. Preparation to put Music Learning Theory into practice is a key component of the implementation process.

*Content Mastery*

In the same study, Burton (1999) asked experienced Music Learning Theory practitioners to advise those music educators who were beginning to use Music Learning Theory. Having an education grounded in Music Learning Theory was a theme that emerged. "Internalize the structure and sequences before you dive [in] feet first," remarked one respondent. Participants in the study felt that understanding Music Learning Theory and the content and skill sequences before embarking on implementation is extremely important. For successful implementation to occur, music educators should have a solid knowledge base of Music Learning Theory content, sequence, and pedagogy. This knowledge base includes the following:[1]

1. An understanding of audiation, music aptitude, the application of music aptitude testing, and the sequential progression of musical development.
2. An understanding of the role of singing, chanting, moving, performing, improvising, and creating in the development of audiational skill and musicianship.
3. An understanding of the unique teaching strategies associated with Music Learning Theory.
4. An understanding of the measurement and evaluation of student learning at different skill levels.
5. An understanding of how to apply Music Learning Theory in a variety of contexts, such as early childhood music, general music, instrumental music, piano instruction, choral music, and higher education.

A thorough understanding of Music Learning Theory content, sequence, and pedagogy is key to successful implementation. Because the mastery of Music Learning Theory content and associated teaching techniques work in tandem with the practitioner's continuous development of personal musicianship, another area that should be considered before beginning to implement a Music Learning Theory curriculum is the level of musicianship of the music educator.

*Personal Musicianship*

Success in implementing Music Learning Theory is influenced by the level of a music educator's personal musicianship. Therefore, music

---

[1] For more in-depth information, see *Learning Sequences in Music* (Gordon, 2003).

educators must possess certain music-learning related skills (see Figure 1). Music Learning Theory practitioners have found that these skills aid in the development of personal musicianship and audiational ability and are essential to the success of a Music Learning Theory-based curriculum (Burton, 1998, 1999).

---

**Musicianship Skills for Practitioners**

1. Sing in a variety of tonalities and meters.
2. Chant in a variety of meters.
3. Engage in Laban-based movement.
4. Use rhythm and tonal syllables.
5. Create and improvise music.
6. Develop readiness and skills for musical literacy.

---

*Figure 1.* Musicianship skills for practitioners

When personal musicianship skills are developed, content delivery functions best. Through a knowledge base of Music Learning Theory content, sequence, and associated teaching techniques, along with the development of personal musicianship skills, the music educator will have a solid foundation upon which to build a Music Learning Theory-based curriculum.

**Building Support for Implementation**

Educational contexts should frame how a music educator will make known that the foundation of the curriculum will be changed. Burton (1999) found that some Music Learning Theory practitioners, viewing Music Learning Theory to be vital to their music programs, were cautious in their implementation and use of Music Learning Theory due to opposition, a lack of understanding, or a lack of support by colleagues or administrators. Fullan (1999) explains that change will rarely occur without opposition and that most concerns, questions, and doubts will be raised during the implementation process. Therefore, garnering the support of colleagues is the key to successful curriculum implementation and is a critical point for leaders of curricular change to understand (Ornstein & Hunkus, 2004). Ongoing communication will typically allay the reservations and uncertainties that skeptics have toward the implementation of a new curricular strategy

(Ornstein & Hunkus, 2004). Because music educators are often isolated from the academic community in which they teach, they should keep administrators, colleagues, parents, students, and the public informed about the curriculum upon which their music program is based (Taggart, 1991). Informing people of the modifications being made throughout the implementation process will lead to the empowerment of the music educator as change agent and support for the overall program. This crucial point is frequently overlooked (Toohey, 1999).

Progress in the implementation process occurs as steps are taken to increase the number of people who are impacted (Fullan, 1999). For many of the people in the midst of the implementation process, success will be determined by the degree and quality of change as evidenced through actual practice. One way a music educator can demonstrate the success of the curriculum, as well as involve and inform the public, is through an "informance." Informances are performance-based programs presented by students with a focus on demonstrating what students have learned through a curriculum based upon Music Learning Theory (Burton, 2004; Taggart, 1991). Informances may be presented as part of an instrumental or choral concert, elementary school program, or in an early childhood setting involving parents and caregivers (Burton, 2004; Grunow, 1998; Taggart, 1991).

Additional opportunities also exist for music educators to share the benefits of a Music Learning Theory-based curriculum. Holding parent-teacher conferences, being present at school open houses or functions with a video that shows actual music classes with students engaged in music learning, using report cards that reflect students' musical progress as measured by Learning Sequence Activities or other Music Learning Theory outcomes, and departmental newsletters that highlight and explain the music curriculum are also ways that a music educator can make known the goals and results of the curriculum. A shared vision of the merits of using Music Learning Theory among colleagues, administrators, parents, and students will be invaluable support to the music educator as the curriculum is implemented (Burton, 2004).

## Professional Development and Personal Support

Ongoing professional development is necessary to sustain the implementation process and to keep the music educator abreast of how Music Learning Theory is being used in various educational settings. There are many forms of Music Learning Theory-based education available to music educators. The Gordon Institute for Music Learning (GIML) offers

Mastership certification courses in Early Childhood Music, General Music, and Instrumental Music. In addition, Music Learning Theory-based workshops are presented regularly at state and national conferences and are often sponsored by state GIML chapters. Several colleges and universities in the USA and abroad offer music education courses based on Music Learning Theory, and many resources are available through GIA Publications.

Often an outgrowth of attending an inservice is the development of a network or support system of other music educators using Music Learning Theory (Burton, 1998, 1999). Questions regarding aspects of implementation may be answered through such a network, and practical advice may be provided by those who are involved in or have been through the implementation process. An experienced Music Learning Theory colleague who can be confided in and who will act as a mentor may give additional support. Acting as a guide or coach (Senge, et al., 1999), the mentor's duties may range from scheduled weekly conversations with the music educator regarding implementation issues to providing demonstration classes, observations, or formative program evaluation of the implementation process (Little, 2000). Networking or the development of a mentoring relationship will provide the music educator with a personal support system to help sustain the implementation process (Senge, et al., 1999) (see Figure 2).

## Developing a Plan

With content mastery and the development of personal musicianship skills, a plan for implementation may be devised. Developing a plan of action will set the stage for student engagement and for success for the music educator. As the music educator contemplates each step of implementation, the overall plan should develop into a coherent whole.

To guide the planning of a new curricular strategy, such as one based upon Music Learning Theory, certain criteria should be addressed. The music educator's knowledge of the sequential process for the presentation of Music Learning Theory content will simplify this organizational process (Gordon, 2003). The following is a framework to assist the design process of the curriculum at any level of music education (Lowman, 1990; Toohey, 1999):

1. *To whom is the instruction geared?* In answering this question, the backgrounds and needs of the learners must be taken into account. Aspects such as why the students are in music class, the ages of the students, and the gender and ethnic distribution of the class, as well as the socio-economic conditions in which the students live are all

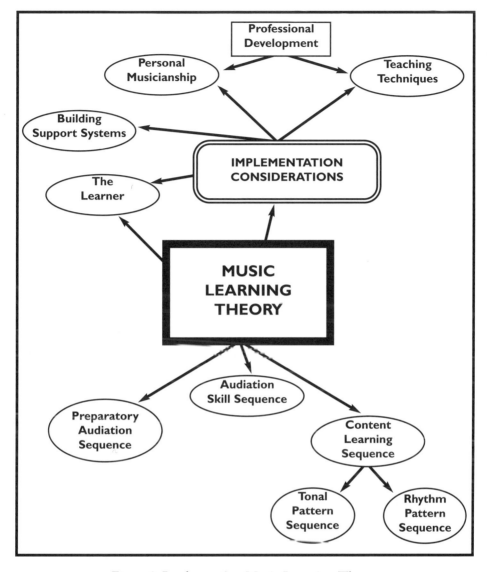

*Figure 2.* Implementing Music Learning Theory

considerations that will help in planning musically relevant learning experiences.

2. *What are the musical backgrounds of the students?* Knowing the musical background of the students and whether they have had prior music learning experiences, as well as determining the music aptitudes and the musically developmental stages of individual students, will provide a starting point from which to sequence a Music Learning Theory-based curriculum.

3. *How will the curriculum be structured for the entire music program?* A curriculum based upon Music Learning Theory will have the development of audiation at its foundation. Unless students are in informal guidance[2] the content, concepts, and skills presented in Learning Sequence Activities (Gordon, 2001) should form the curricular framework and delineate the overarching learning goals. Once the learning goals have been identified, units of study should be planned. Repertoire that is used to reinforce content, concepts, and skills taught through Learning Sequence Activities may be used to structure units of study. In addition, units may embrace the development of proficiency in the primary ways that music is learned (such as singing, chanting, playing instruments, moving, creating, improvising, listening, reading, and writing). Themes, such as music from another culture or within a specific genre, can also be used to outline a unit of study. When the overarching learning goals and units of study have been designed, specific learning objectives can then be created. Learning objectives set the course for each class period and relate directly to the units of study and overarching learning goals. Objectives are put into action in the music class, and, as the practitioner reflects upon the teaching and learning process and the subsequent measurement and evaluation of related student progress, they are likely to undergo revision.

4. *What musical content will be presented in addition to the content found in Learning Sequence Activities?* Learning Sequence Activities will be used to introduce concepts and skills, primarily in Major and Minor tonalities and in Duple and Triple meters. The type of music class, whether it be general music, choir, or instrumental ensemble, must also be taken into account when determining the content to be presented as it will vary from one music learning setting to another. For all settings, the use of a variety of tonalities and meters is recommended (Gordon, 2003b).

5. *What teaching strategies or techniques will be used?* Active, participatory, hands-on, student-centered music learning strategies that will engage students in audiation and develop musicianship form the foundations for teaching strategies. Teaching strategies should include activities such as singing, chanting, moving, performing, improvising and creating music. When appropriate, students should also be engaged in reading and writing music. Individualized instruction and evaluation is

---

[2] For more information on Informal Guidance, see *A Music Learning Theory for Newborn and Young Children* (Gordon, 2003a).

important in gauging how well students are learning what is being taught and for the purposes of curricular evaluation.

6. *How will class periods be structured?* The structure of a class period will vary according to the music learning context. Care should be taken to structure each class period for the inclusion of Learning Sequence Activities and a variety of ways to engage students in the development of personal musicianship. The prioritization of learning objectives will set the direction for each class period. When structuring a class period, the length of time it will take students to complete an activity, as well as allowances for flexibility in the teaching and learning process, should be taken into account.

7. *How will student learning be measured and evaluated?* Learning Sequence Activities provide an optimal means for measuring and evaluating student learning. Students may be evaluated in relation to their peers or in relation to their music aptitudes. Additional means of measurement and evaluation should be designed in association with the learning objectives. Such forms of measurement can include performance-based measurement and evaluation, observation, rating scales, and checklists. Music educators should contemplate the value of providing parents or caregivers with a report card designed to clearly represent evaluation in all of the areas of music learning.

8. *What resources are needed?* Resources that are needed for teaching toward objectives and learning goals will depend on the music learning context. Thinking through the best ways to engage students in developing their musicianship and how to structure learning sequentially and developmentally will serve as a foundation in determining what resources are needed.

Careful contemplation of the above questions and subsequent thorough planning will prepare the music educator to begin implementing a Music Learning Theory-based curriculum.

## Starting the Process

Early success and progress will be important in order to keep the momentum of implementation going (Fullan, 1999). Due to the developmental and sequential nature of music learning, the most successful and practical way to begin using Music Learning Theory is by starting students at a beginning level or with a small population of the school (McCrystal, 1989). For example, implementation might begin with kindergarten at the elementary level, beginning band or orchestra in instrumental music, ninth

501

grade vocal or instrumental music at the high school level, and with freshmen at the collegiate level (Burton, 1998, 1999). Experienced Music Learning Theory practitioners advise those starting to use Music Learning Theory to begin slowly and be persistent with the implementation process (Burton, 1999). By moving slowly and taking time to move through content, teachers will gain confidence in their teaching as well as in developing and using the skills needed for implementation.

**During the Process**

The biggest risk in implementing a new curricular strategy is that long-term implementation will not occur and that little will change (Fullan, 1999; Senge, et al., 1999; Toohey, 1999). Carrying out the implementation of a new curricular strategy involves the development of the curriculum through practice over time. Curricular change occurs as teachers learn through doing. During the implementation of Music Learning Theory, teaching techniques will be explored as the music educator strives for the best fit of content delivery between teacher and student. Goals and objectives may need to be modified to reflect the reality of the variables that are associated with the school day, such as block scheduling, missed classes due to assemblies or other activities, class size, the amount of class time the students receive per week, and the length of the class period (Fullan, 1999; Lowman, 1990; Toohey, 1999). Also, in some instances, the curriculum may need to be redesigned during the implementation process due to over-ambitious or inadequate lesson planning (Burton, 1998).

In addition to sifting through the curricular chaos, the music educator may be personally affected by the change of curricular strategies. A sense of ambiguity, a shift in identity as a music educator, and a redefinition of the teaching role are commonly experienced by teachers involved in curricular change (Toohey, 1999). In fact, taking on the task of curricular change may seem daunting. Music Learning Theory practitioners reported that the benefits of using Music Learning Theory are not always immediate, but the more they used Music Learning Theory and experienced success, the easier it became (Burton, 1999). Persistence is the most important quality needed of the music educator who is involved in curricular change (Burton, 1999; Fullan, 1999). Success in firmly establishing a Music Learning Theory-based curriculum takes time and patience.

**Evaluating the Process**

As the implementation process unfolds, the music educator should examine critically the curriculum and the process of change, keeping in mind that curricular implementation is never a finished process (Ornstein & Hunkus, 2004). Achieving success with the implementation of a Music Learning Theory-based curriculum is highly dependent on the regular evaluation of curricular progress, combined with consistent fine tuning (Toohey, 1999). Accountability and effectiveness become products of evaluation through the music educator's questioning and careful observation of Music Learning Theory in action. While a reflective music educator may monitor the level of implementation in the classroom on a day to day basis, it is also important to develop a regular evaluation plan for the overall implementation process.

When creating a plan for evaluation, the music educator should determine the primary aspects of the implementation process to monitor and evaluate. This evaluation may take the form of addressing specific cause-and-effect questions (see Figure 3). Detailed documentation of whether there has been any change after trying something new will provide relevant evaluative information. Continual communication with all involved in the implementation process will give an ongoing view on the status of change (Ornstein & Hunkus, 2004; Fullan, 1999; Toohey, 1999). Regularly scheduled meetings with the music faculty and the administration will help pinpoint problem areas and identify strengths (Fullan, 1999; Toohey, 1999). Student feedback and progress toward learning goals may also yield meaningful information (Toohey, 1999). By gathering information from a variety of perspectives, the music educator will have formed a comprehensive view of the status of the implementation process of Music Learning Theory into the music curriculum. This will provide essential information on areas that are functioning well or that may need modification.

**Conclusion**

The process of implementing Music Learning Theory as a new curricular strategy takes time and perseverance on the part of the music educator. However, for the music educator and students, the benefits of implementing Music Learning Theory as a curricular strategy are well worth the effort. Through careful preparation, a solid support system, clear goals, continual professional development, and constant evaluation, a high-quality Music Learning Theory-based music curriculum can be successfully established.

**Questions for Evaluation**

1. *Communication with the people involved:*
   - How are other music educators managing the change in curriculum?
   - How does the administration view the curricular change?
   - What is the prevailing attitude of the students toward the change in curriculum?
   - What insights and input can students bring to the evaluation process?
   - How do parents perceive the change in curriculum?

2. *Reviews of the curriculum and student progress:*
   - How are students functioning with the new curriculum?
   - Are learning goals being reached?
   - Are students frustrated? Bored? Challenged?
   - Do the learning goals and objectives need modification?
   - How are teaching strategies working?

3. *Personal reflection of teaching skill and content knowledge:*
   - What can be learned through practitioner reflection and journaling?
   - How might teaching skills be improved with self-observation through videotape or peer observation?
   - What areas need attention? Content delivery? Personal musicianship? Content knowledge?

*Figure 3.* Questions for evaluation

## References

Burton, S. (1998). *A description of the integration of Gordon's Music Learning Theory into a ninth-grade band class.* Unpublished manuscript.

——. (1999). *A survey of practitioners using Gordon's Music Learning Theory.* Unpublished data.

——. (2004). Educate our advocates. *Music Educator's Journal 90* (5), 17-21.

Fullan, M. (1999). *The new meaning of educational change.* New York: Teacher's College Press.

Gordon, E. E. (2001). *Reference handbook for using Learning Sequence Activities.* Chicago: GIA Publications.

———. (2003a). *A Music Learning Theory for newborn and young children.* Chicago: GIA Publications.

———. (2003b). *Learning sequences in music: Skill, content, and patterns.* Chicago: GIA Publications.

Gordon, E. E., Grunow, R., & Taggart, C. C. (1998). *Seminar in Music Learning Theory.* Michigan State University, E. Lansing, MI.

Gordon, E. E., & Taggart, C. C. (1997). *Seminar in Music Learning Theory.* Michigan State University, E. Lansing, MI.

———. (2000). *Seminar in Music Learning Theory.* Michigan State University, E. Lansing, MI.

Little, J. W. (2000). Assessing the prospects for teacher leadership. In *The Jossey-Bass reader on educational leadership.* (pp. 390-418). San Francisco: Jossey-Bass.

Lowman, J. (1990). *Mastering the techniques of teaching.* San Francisco: Jossey Bass.

McCrystal, R. (1989). Facilitating the process of change to a school music curriculum based upon music learning theory. In D. Walters & C. Taggart (Eds.), *Readings in Music Learning Theory.* (pp. 373-380). Chicago: GIA Publications.

Ornstein, A. C., & Hunkus, F. P. (2004). *Curriculum—foundations, principles, and issues.* (4th Ed.). Boston: Pearson Education, Inc.

Senge, P., Kleiner, A., Roberts, C., Ross, R., Roth, R., & Smith, B. (1999a). IV: No help (coaching and support). In: *The dance of change: The challenges of sustaining momentum in learning organizations.* (pp. 103-152). New York: Doubleday.

———. (1999b). VIII: Assessment and measurement. In: *The dance of change: The challenges of sustaining momentum in learning organizations.* (pp. 281-313). New York: Doubleday.

Taggart, C. C. (1991). Our role in educating the educational community. *General Music Today*, 14-17.

Toohey, S. (1999). *Designing courses for higher education.* Philadelphia: Open University Press.

# About the Editors

**Maria Runfola** is Department Chair and Associate Professor for the Graduate School of Education at the State University of New York at Buffalo. She earned her PhD in Music Education from the University at Buffalo. Her professional and research interests include measurement and evaluation in music, music aptitude, assessment in the arts, and early childhood arts education.

Runfola was appointed Chair of the New York State Taskforce for Music Assessment by the Executive Council of the New York State School Music Association. The taskforce's charge was to research and develop a Standards-based Commencement General Education Level (CGEL) exam in Music.

**Cynthia Crump Taggart** is an Associate Professor of Music Education at Michigan State University School of Music where she also directs and teaches in the Early Childhood Music and Young Musicians Program of the MSU Community Music School. Prior to coming to Michigan State, she taught at Case Western Reserve University and the Cleveland Institute of Music. She holds a bachelor of music and master of music from the University of Michigan and a PhD from Temple University. While at Michigan State University,

Taggart received the prestigious Teacher/Scholar Award and was chosen as a CIC Academic Leadership Fellow. At Case Western Reserve University she received the Excellence in Teaching Award for the Arts, Humanities, and Social Sciences. Cynthia also brings substantial teaching experience to her work, as she taught elementary general music and instrumental music in Kenosha, Wisconsin, and Ann Arbor, Michigan. As co-author of *Music Play: The Early Childhood Music Curriculum* and *Jump Right In: The Music Curriculum* (both GIA), Cynthia has presented numerous workshops throughout North America on elementary general music and early childhood music education.

# Index

509

510

511